The Future of Post-Human Law

The Future of Post-Human Law

A Preface to a New Theory of Necessity, Contingency, and Justice

By

Peter Baofu

CAMBRIDGE SCHOLARS PUBLISHING

The Future of Post-Human Law: A Preface to a New Theory of Necessity, Contingency and Justice, by Peter Baofu

This book first published 2010

Cambridge Scholars Publishing

12 Back Chapman Street, Newcastle upon Tyne, NE6 2XX, UK

British Library Cataloguing in Publication Data
A catalogue record for this book is available from the British Library

ISBN (10): 1-4438-1949-2, ISBN (13): 978-1-4438-1949-7

To Those in the Future World Beyond Justice

BOOKS ALSO BY PETER BAOFU

Category I: Social Sciences and Related Fields

- 27. *The Future of Post-Human Organization* (2009)
- 26. *The Future of Post-Human Mass Media* (2009)
- 25. *The Rise of Authoritarian Liberal Democracy* (2007)
- 24. *Beyond the World of Titans, and the Remaking of World Order* (2007)
- 23. *Beyond Capitalism to Post-Capitalism* (2005)
- 22. Volume 1: *Beyond Democracy to Post-Democracy* (2004)
- 21. Volume 2: *Beyond Democracy to Post-Democracy* (2004)
- 20. *The Future of Capitalism and Democracy* (2002)

Category II: Natural Sciences and Related Fields

- 19. *The Future of Post-Human Sexuality* (2010)
- 18. *The Future of Post-Human Urban Planning* (2009)
- 17. *The Future of Post-Human Engineering* (2009)
- 16. *The Future of Post-Human Unconsciousness* (2008)
- 15. *The Future of Complexity* (2007)
- 14. *Beyond Nature and Nurture* (2006)
- 13. *The Future of Post-Human Space-Time* (2006)
- 12. *The Future of Post-Human Consciousness* (2004)

Category III: Formal Sciences and Related Fields

- 11. *The Future of Post-Human Language* (2009)
- 10. *The Future of Post-Human Geometry* (2009)
- 9. *The Future of Post-Human Mathematical Logic* (2008)
- 8. *The Future of Information Architecture* (2008)

Category IV: The Humanities and Related Fields

- 7. *The Future of Post-Human Martial Arts* (2009)
- 6. *The Future of Post-Human Creative Thinking* (2009)
- 5. *The Future of Post-Human Knowledge* (2008)
- 4. *The Future of Aesthetic Experience* (2007)
- 3. *Beyond Civilization to Post-Civilization* (2006)
- 2. Volume 1: *The Future of Human Civilization* (2000)
- 1. Volume 2: *The Future of Human Civilization* (2000)

CONTENTS

List of Tables .... *xi*
Foreword .... *xvii*
Acknowledgments .... *xix*
List of Abbreviations .... *xxi*

Part One: Introduction

Chapter One. Introduction—The Rule of Law 3
The Convenience of a Conventional Wisdom 3
Private Law and Public Law 4
Law and Jurisprudence 10
The Theoretical Debate 12
The Reconstruction Theory of Law 19
Theory and Meta-Theory 20
The Logic of Existential Dialectics 20
Sophisticated Methodological Holism 47
Chapter Outline 55
Some Clarifications 56

Part Two: Necessity

Chapter Two. Necessity and Its Dispensability 115
The Categoricalness of Necessity 115
Necessity and the Mind 115
Necessity and Nature 132
Necessity and Society 145
Necessity and Culture 163
The Hypotheticalness of Necessity 182

Part Three: Contingency

Chapter Three. Contingency and Its Mortality ... 193
The Expediency of Contingency ... 193
Contingency and the Mind ... 194
Contingency and Nature ... 208
Contingency and Society ... 217
Contingency and Culture ... 237
The Temporality of Contingency ... 259

Part Four: Conclusion

Chapter Four. Conclusion—The Future of Law ... 269
The Rethinking of Law ... 269
1st Thesis: The Absoluteness-Relativeness Principle ... 278
2nd Thesis: The Predictability-Unpredictability Principle ... 281
3rd Thesis: The Explicability-Inexplicability Principle ... 283
4th Thesis: The Preciseness-Vagueness Principle ... 286
5th Thesis: The Simpleness-Complicatedness Principle ... 288
6th Thesis: The Openness-Hiddenness Principle ... 290
7th Thesis: The Evolution-Transformation Principle ... 292
8th Thesis: The Symmetry-Asymmetry Principle ... 294
9th Thesis: The Regression-Progression Principle ... 297
10th Thesis: The Same-Difference Principle ... 299
11th Thesis: The Post-Human Reconstruction ... 301
Beyond Justice ... 303

Bibliography ... *399*
Index ... *415*

TABLES

Category I. The Theoretical Debate on Law
Table 1.1. The Classification of Law 61
Table 1.2. The Classification of Jurisprudence 62
Table 2.1. Necessity and Its Dispensability 183
Table 2.2. Main Characteristics of International Law 184
Table 2.3. The Varieties of Principles Behind the Law 185
Table 2.4. The Debate on Divine Law: The Case about the Mosaic Law 187
Table 2.5. Main Characteristics of the Common Law Tradition 189
Table 3.1. Contingency and Its Mortality 261
Table 3.2. Different Versions of the Will to Power in Nature 262
Table 3.3. Main Characteristics of Property Law 263
Table 3.4. Main Characteristics of Contract Law 264
Table 3.5. Main Characteristics of Administrative Law 265

Category II: Visions on Nature
Table 1.3. The Theoretical Debate on Space-Time 63
Table 1.4. Main Reasons for Altering Space-Time 65
Table 1.5. The Technological Frontiers of the Micro-World 66
Table 1.6. Finity, Transfinity, and Infinity 67
Table 1.7. Theoretical Speculations of Multiverses 69
Table 1.8. The Confusion Between "Many Worlds" and "Multiverse" 70
Table 1.9. Hyperspace and Its Challenge 72
Table 1.10. The Problems of Time Travel into the Future 74
Table 1.11. The Problems of Time Travel into the Past 76

Category III: Visions on the Mind

Table 1.12. The Conceptual Dimensions of Consciousness (and Other Mental States) 79
Table 1.13. The Theoretical Levels of Consciousness (and Other Mental States) 80
Table 1.14. The Thematic Issues of Consciousness (and Other Mental States) 83
Table 1.15. Having, Belonging, and Being in Consciousness (and Other Mental States) 84
Table 1.16. The Having-Ness of Consciousness (and Other Mental States) 85
Table 1.17. The Belonging-Ness of Consciousness (and Other Mental States) 86
Table 1.18. The Being-Ness of Consciousness (and Other Mental States) 87
Table 1.19. Cognitive Partiality in Different Mental States 89
Table 1.20. Emotional Non-Neutrality and Behavioral Alteration in Different Mental States 90
Table 1.21. The Limits of Intuition in Unconsciousness 91
Table 1.22. The Wealth/Poverty Dialectics in Different Mental States: The Case of Cognition 92
Table 1.23. The Wealth/Poverty Dialectics in Different Mental States: The Case of Emotion and Behavior 93
Table 1.24. The Theoretical Debate on Nature and Nurture 94
Table 1.25. Physical Challenges to Hyper-Spatial Consciousness 96
Table 1.26. The Theory of Floating Consciousness 97
Table 1.27. The Potential of Unfolding Unconsciousness 99
Table 1.28. The Future Exploration of Unfolding Unconsciousness 100
Table 1.29. Creative Techniques and Traits 101
Table 1.30. The Desirability of Creativity, and Its Dark Sides 102
Table 1.31. Posthuman-Ism, Post-Humanism, and Trans-Humanism 104
Table 1.32. Three Great Future Transformations of the Martial Body 105
Table 1.33. Three Great Future Transformations of the Sexual Body 107

Category IV: Visions on History

Table 1.34. The Trinity of Pre-Modernity 108
Table 1.35. The Trinity of Modernity 109
Table 1.36. The Trinity of Post-Modernity 111
Table 1.37. The Trinity of After-Postmodernity 112

Category V: Visions on Methodology
Table 4.1. Sophisticated Methodological Holism. 304
Table 4.2. On Reductionism and Reverse-Reductionism. 308

Category VI: Visions on Ontology
Table 4.3. The Conception of Existential Dialectics. 311
Table 4.4. The Syntax of Existential Dialectics I: The Principles. 314
Table 4.5. The Syntax of Existential Dialectics II: The Principles as Short Cuts. 327
Table 4.6. The Syntax of Existential Dialectics III: The Principles as Family Resemblances. 329
Table 4.7. The Syntax of Existential Dialectics IV: The Dialectic Constraints Imposed by the Principles. 330
Table 4.8. The Syntax of Existential Dialectics V: Further Clarifications. 333
Table 4.9. The Syntax of Existential Dialectics VI: The Dilemma of Specific vs. General Ontology. 335
Table 4.10. The Semantics of Existential Dialectics. 337
Table 4.11. The Pragmatics of Existential Dialectics. 338
Table 4.12. The Freedom/Unfreedom Dialectics 340
Table 4.13. The Equality/Inequality Dialectics 343
Table 4.14. The Duality of Oppression in Existential Dialectics: Oppression and Self-Oppression 345
Table 4.15. The Structure of Existential Dialectics I: The Freedom/Unfreedom and Equality/Inequality Dialectics 347
Table 4.16. The Structure of Existential Dialectics II: The Wealth/Poverty Dialectics 348
Table 4.17. The Structure of Existential Dialectics III: The Civilization/Barbarity Dialectics 349

Category VII. Visions on Society (Socio-Political)

Table 4.18. The Double Sides of Virtual Organizations 350
Table 4.19. Beyond the World of Titans, and the Remaking of World Order 352
Table 4.20. The Origins of Authoritarian Liberal Democracy 353
Table 4.21. The Theory of Post-Democracy I: The Priority of Freedom over Equality 354
Table 4.22. The Theory of Post-Democracy II: The Priority of Equality over Freedom 356
Table 4.23. The Theory of Post-Democracy III: The Transcendence of Freedom and Equality 357
Table 4.24. Democracy, Non-Democracy, and Post-Democracy....359
Table 4.25. Multiple Causes of the Emergence of Post-Democracy 362
Table 4.26. Some Clarifications on Post-Capitalism and Post-Democracy 364

Category VIII. Visions on Society (Socio-Economic)

Table 4.27. The Theory of Post-Capitalism I.1: By Group—Ex: Spiritual/Communal in the Trans-Feminine Calling....368
Table 4.28. The Theory of Post-Capitalism I.2: By Nation-State—Ex: Spiritual/Communal in the Trans-Sinitic Calling 369
Table 4.29. The Theory of Post-Capitalism I.3: By Region—Ex: Spiritual/Communal in the Trans-Islamic Calling....370
Table 4.30. The Theory of Post-Capitalism I.4: By Universe—Ex: Spiritual/Communal in the Trans-Outerspace Calling 371
Table 4.31. The Theory of Post-Capitalism II: Spiritual/Individualistic in the Post-Human Elitist Calling 372
Table 4.32. Capitalism, Non-Capitalism, and Post-Capitalism 374
Table 4.33. Multiple Causes of the Emergence of Post-Capitalism....377

Category IX: Visions on Culture

Table 4.34. The Theoretical Debate on Civilization 379
Table 4.35. No Freedom Without Unfreedom in the Civilizing Processes 380
Table 4.36. No Equality Without Inequality in the Civilizing Processes 382
Table 4.37. Five Theses on Post-Civilization 384
Table 4.38. Barbarity, Civilization, and Post-Civilization 385
Table 4.39. Types of Super Civilization in the Cosmos 386
Table 4.40. The Civilizational Project from Pre-Modernity to After-Postmodernity 388
Table 4.41. Civilizational Holism 390
Table 4.42. Theories on Civilizational Holism 393

FOREWORD

Dr. Peter Baofu's continuing quest to investigate the status of thinking and future outcomes of human institutions has brought him to examine the Rule of Law. It comes at an appropriate time, when there are serious intellectual disagreements in the literature on the Rule of Law.

Dr. Baofu traces the development of the Rule of Law with the major thinkers who brought it to its current place. However, he also acknowledges the shortcomings that beset its theoretical construction and practical application, and posits a provocative yet original line of thinking, as an incentive for other researchers to consider.

The glove has been thrown down in this volume. Who is ready to accept the challenge?

Sylvan Von Burg
School of Business
George Washington University

ACKNOWLEDGMENTS

As is true for my numerous previous books, this one is written to challenge politically incorrect views, this time about law here, and to offer a new theory to understand its future.

Because of this political incorrectness, this book receives no external funding nor help from any formal organization or institution, as this is something that I often stressed in my previous books.

My only reward is that joyful feeling to work through some ideas which have not been thought of before in history.

Lest I forget, I greatly appreciate the foreword by Sylvan von Burg at George Washington University School of Business.

In any event, and as always, I bear the sole responsibility for the ideas presented in this book.

Abbreviations

ALD = Peter Baofu. 2007. *The Rise of Authoritarian Liberal Democracy: A Preface to a New Theory of Comparative Political Systems.* Cambridge, England: Cambridge Scholars Publishing, Ltd.

BCIV = Peter Baofu. 2006. *Beyond Civilization to Post-Civilization: Conceiving a Better Model of Life Settlement to Supersede Civilization.* NY: Peter Lang Publishing, Inc.

BCPC = Peter Baofu. 2005. *Beyond Capitalism to Post-Capitalism: Conceiving a Better Model of Wealth Acquisition to Supersede Capitalism.* NY: The Edwin Mellen Press.

BDPD1 = Peter Baofu. 2004. Volume 1. *Beyond Democracy to Post-Democracy: Conceiving a Better Model of Governance to Supersede Democracy.* NY: The Edwin Mellen Press.

BDPD2 = Peter Baofu. 2004. Volume 2. *Beyond Democracy to Post-Democracy: Conceiving a Better Model of Governance to Supersede Democracy.* NY: The Edwin Mellen Press.

BNN = Peter Baofu. 2006. *Beyond Nature and Nurture: Conceivng a Better Way to Understand Genes and Memes.* Cambridge, England: Cambridge Scholars Publishing, Ltd.

BWT = Peter Baofu. 2007. *Beyond the World of Titans, and the Renaking of World Order: A Preface to a New Logic of Empire-Building.* Cambridge, England: Cambridge Scholars Publishing, Ltd.

FAE = Peter Baofu. 2007. *The Future of Aesthetic Experience: Conceiving a Better Way to Understand Beauty, Ugliness and the Rest.* Cambridge, England: Cambridge Scholars Publishing, Ltd.

FC = Peter Baofu. 2007. *The Future of Complexity: Conceiving a Better Way to Understand Order and Chaos.* London, United Kingdom: World Scientific Publishing Co.

FCD = Peter Baofu. 2002. *The Future of Capitalism and Democracy.* MD: The University Press of America.

FHC1 = Peter Baofu. 2000. Volume 1. *The Future of Human Civilization.* NY: The Edwin Mellen Press.

FHC2 = Peter Baofu. 2000. Volume 2. *The Future of Human Civilization.* NY: The Edwin Mellen Press.

FIA = Peter Baofu. 2008. *The Future of Information Architecture: Conceiving a Better Way to Understand Taxonomy, Network, and Intelligence.* Oxford, England: Chandos Publishing (Oxford) Limited.

FPHC = Peter Baofu. 2004. *The Future of Post-Human Consciousness.* NY: The Edwin Mellen Press.

FPHCT = Peter Baofu. 2009. *The Future of Post-Human Creative Thinking: A Preface to a New Theory of Invention and Innovation.* Cambridge, England: Cambridge Scholars Publishing, Ltd.

FPHE = Peter Baofu. 2009. *The Future of Post-Human Engineering: A Preface to a New Theory of Technology.* Cambridge, England: Cambridge Scholars Publishing, Ltd.

FPHG = Peter Baofu. 2009. *The Future of Post-Human Geometry: A Preface to a New Theory of Infinity, Symmetry, and Dimensionality.* Cambridge, England: Cambridge Scholars Publishing, Ltd.

FPHK = Peter Baofu. 2008. *The Future of Post-Human Knowledge: A Preface to a New Theory of Methodology and Ontology.* Oxford, England: Chandos Publishing (Oxford) Limited.

FPHL = Peter Baofu. 2009. *The Future of Post-Human Language: A Preface to a New Theory of Structure, Context, and Learning.* Cambridge, England: Cambridge Scholars Publishing, Ltd.

FPHLAW = Peter Baofu. 2010. *The Future of Post-Human Law: A Preface to a New Theory of Necessity, Contingency, and Justice.* Cambridge, England: Cambridge Scholars Publishing, Ltd.

FPHMA = Peter Baofu. 2009. *The Future of Post-Human Martial Arts: A Preface to a New Theory of the Body and Spirit of Warriors.* Cambridge, England: Cambridge Scholars Publishing, Ltd.

FPHML = Peter Baofu. 2008. *The Future of Post-Human Mathematical Logic: A Preface to a New Theory of Rationality.* Cambridge, England: Cambridge Scholars Publishing, Ltd.

FPHMM = Peter Baofu. 2009. *The Future of Post-Human Mass Media: A Preface to a New Theory of Technology.* Cambridge, England: Cambridge Scholars Publishing, Ltd.

FPHO = Peter Baofu. 2009. *The Future of Post-Human Organization: A Preface to a New Theory of Communication, Decision-Making, and Leadership.*.Cambridge, England: Cambridge Scholars Publishing, Ltd.

FPHS = Peter Baofu. 2010. *The Future of Post-Human Sexuality: A Preface to a New Theory of the Body and Spirit of Love-Makers.* Cambridge, England: Cambridge Scholars Publishing, Ltd.

FPHST = Peter Baofu. 2006. *The Future of Post-Human Space-Time: Conceivng a Better Way to Understand Space and Time.* New York: Peter Lang Publishing, Inc.

FPHU = Peter Baofu. 2008. *The Future of Post-Human Unconsciousness: A Preface to a New Theory of Anomalous Experience.* Cambridge, England: Cambridge Scholars Publishing, Ltd.

FPHUP = Peter Baofu. 2009. *The Future of Post-Human Urban Planning: A Preface to a New Theory of Density, Void, and Sustainability.* Cambridge, England: Cambridge Scholars Publishing, Ltd.

• PART ONE •

Introduction

CHAPTER 1
INTRODUCTION—THE RULE OF LAW

> The rule of law is better than the rule of any individual.
> —Aristotle (WK 2009)

The Convenience of a Conventional Wisdom

What makes the rule of law so special that it is to conscientiously punish the "bad" doers and reward the "good" ones—such that, where there is the rule of law, peace and order (for justice) are to be expected, so that "the rule of law is better than the rule of any individual"?

Take the case of international law, as an illustration. While different international courts have been busy going after a small number of the killers of innocent victims in Rwanda and Liberia, they have turned a blind eye to the major powers which have killed—on a much larger and more brutal scale, by comparison—innocent civilians in Iraq and Afghanistan, just to cite two current examples.

The case of Iraq is most illustrative, as Tom Engelhardt (2009) thus reminded us: "Iraq…has been devastated. The American invasion and the occupation that followed acted like whirlwinds of destruction, unraveling a land already bursting with problems and potential animosities."

The reason is that, since the American invasion, "possibly a million or more Iraqis have died….Saddam's killing fields have been dwarfed by a fierce set of destructive American military operations as well as insurgencies…; major cities have been largely or partially destroyed, or ethnically cleansed; millions of Iraqis have been forced from their homes, becoming internal refugees or going into exile; untold numbers of Iraqis have been imprisoned, assassinated, tortured or abused; and the country's cultural heritage has been ransacked. Basic services—electricity, water, food—were terribly impaired and the economy, in the process of being privatized by the neocon overseers of the occupation, was simply wrecked.

Health services were crippled...," and the list can go on. (T. Engelhardt 2009)

In other words, the American invasion and occupation of Iraq has simply devastated the country and its people on an enormous scale, and yet the international courts have turned a blined eye to this most heartbreaking inhumanity. International law thus leads to the travesty of justice.

Contrary to the conventional wisdom conveniently held by many in human history, the rule of law has its other side which has not yet been systematically understood, such that the rule of law is neither possible nor desirable to the extent that the defenders of legal institutions in human history would like us to believe.

Lest any misunderstanding hastily occurs, this is not to imply that the rule of law is absolutely useless, or that the literature in jurisprudence (and other related fields like political philosophy, ethics, law and economics, and the sociology of law) should be dismissed because of their scholarly irrelevance. Of course, neither of these two extreme views is reasonable either.

Instead, this book is to provide an alternative (better) way to understand the nature of law, in relation to its necessity and contingency in the context of justice—while learning from different approaches in the literature but without favoring any one of them (nor integrating them, since they are not necessarily compatible with each other).

In the process, this book offers a new theory to transcend the existing approaches in the literature in a new direction—in that, in the end, there is no justice without injustice and that it will be transcended too.

This seminal project, if successful, will fundamentally change the way that we think about the nature of law, from the combined perspectives of the mind, nature, society, and culture, with enormous implications for the human future and what I originally called its "post-human" fate.

Public Law and Private Law

To start, the term "law" is from "Old English *lagu*, of Scandinavian origin," "akin to Old Norse *lǫg*," and "Old English *licgan*"—and means "to lie," "to stay at rest," or "something laid down or fixed," as the adjective "legal" derives "from Latin *legalis*, from *lex*" (meaning: "statute"). (MWD 2009 & 2009a; WK 2009)

Over time, the term "law" has come to mean "a binding custom or practice of a community," "a rule of conduct or action prescribed or formally recognized as binding or enforced by a controlling authority," or simply "a system of rules, usually enforced through a set of institutions." (MWD 2009; WK 2009)

This set of legal institutions often consists of the "legislature," the "executive," and the "judiciary" in a society, together with the "military," the "police," the "bureaucracy," the "legal profession," and even the "civil society." (WK 2009)

In the literature of legal studies, law can be classified in terms of two major categories, namely, (a) "public law" and (b) "private law"—to be summarized hereafter (in the next two sub-sections), respectively (and also in *Table 1.1*).

Lest any confusion occurs, there are two clarifications here about this classification of law into public law and private law.

Firstly, the classification of law into public law and private law is important not only at the national level but also at the international level. For instance, nowadays, there is international law, which can be likewise classified into "public international law" and "private interntional law."

On the one hand, "public international law" has to do with the legal relationships "between sovereign nations" based on "custom, practice and treaties between sovereign nations, such as the Geneva Conventions. Public international law can be formed by international organisations, such as the United Nations..., the International Labour Organisation, the World Trade Organisation, or the International Monetary Fund." (WK 2009)

On the other hand, "private international law" (also known as "conflict of laws...in civil law countries") concerns "which jurisdiction a legal dispute between private parties should be heard in and which jurisdiction's law should be applied. Today, businesses are increasingly capable of shifting capital and labour supply chains across borders, as well as trading with overseas businesses. Increasing numbers of businesses opt for commercial arbitration under the New York Convention of 1958." (WK 2009; A. Redfem 2004)

And secondly, the distinction between public law and private law still holds, even though "many scholars argue that 'the boundaries between public and private law are becoming blurred,' and that this distinction has become mere 'folklore'"—as will be clear shortly. (L. Bergkamp 2001)

Public Law

With these two clarifications in mind—in "public law," the concern here is about the kind of laws which are "related closely to the state," or about "the relationship between individuals (citizens, companies) and the state," and good examples are "constitutional law," "administrative law," and "criminal law." (WK 2009 & 2009a)

This distinction holds, even though there is a conceptual dispute concerning whether or not different examples of public law (afore-cited) can overlap. For instance, for some scholars, "all law" is "to be specifically enabled, and thereby sub-divisions, of a Constitution"—and therefore "administrative law" and "criminal law" are parts of the Constitution (or the "constitutional law"). (WK 2009a)

Constitutional Law

This conceptual dispute aside—the first example of public law is "constitutional law," which "deals with the relationship between the state and individual, and the relationships between different branches of the state, such as the executive, the legislative and the judiciary." (WK 2009a)

Different countries have different traditions about their own constitutions. For example, in the United States, there is the "written constitutional document" for its own constitution, that is, "the U.S. Constitution." (WK 2009a)

But this is not true in other countries; for instance, "in the United Kingdom of Great Britain and Northern Ireland (U.K.), due to historical and political reasons there does not exist one supreme, entrenched written document. The U.K. has an unwritten constitution—the constitution of this state is usually found in statutes, such as the Magna Carta, the Petition of Right, the Bill of Rights, the Act of Settlement 1700, the Parliament Act 1911, and the Parliament Act 1949." (WK 2009a)

Yet, "in reality, much of the constitution [or the constitutional dispute] is a political phenomenon, rather than a legal one." (WK 2009a)

Administrative Law

The second example of public law concerns "administrative law," which "refers to the body of law which regulates bureaucratic managerial procedures and defines the powers of administrative agencies." (WK 2009a)

Administrative law is often "enforced by the executive branch of a government rather than the judicial or legislative branches (if they are different in that particular jurisdiction)." (WK 2009a)

And "this body of law regulates international trade, manufacturing, pollution, taxation, and the like. This is sometimes seen as a subcategory of Civil law and sometimes seen as public law as it deals with regulation and public institutions." (WK 2009a)

Criminal Law

And the last example of public law is "criminal law" (also known as "penal law"), which "involves the state imposing sanctions for crimes committed by individuals so that society can achieve justice and a peaceable social order." (WK 2009a)

In many cases, the "common characteristic" of criminal law "is the potential for unique and often severe impositions as punishment for failure to comply. Criminal punishment, depending on the offense and jurisdiction, may include execution, loss of liberty, government supervision (parole or probation), or fines." (WK 2009b)

In this sense, "criminal law" differs from those laws in the division of "private law" which have to do with "civil law," because "civil actions are disputes between two parties that are not of significant public concern." (WK 2009a)

Private Law

In "private law," on the other hand, the concern here is more about the kind of laws which are related to civil society, or about "the area of law in a society that affects the relationships between individuals or groups without the intervention of the state or government," and good examples include "property law," "trust law," "contract law," and "tort law." (WK 2009 & 2009a)

But this view of private law "is confounded by laws that regulate private relations while having been passed by legislative enactment. In some cases these public statutes are known as laws of public order, as private individuals do not have the right to break them and any attempt to circumvent such laws is void as against public policy." (WK 2009a)

Property Law

This conceptual problem aside—the first example of private law concerns "property law," which "governs the various forms of ownership in real property (land as distinct from personal or movable possessions) and in personal property, within the common law legal system." (WK 2009c)

However, "in the civil law system, there is a division between movable and immovable property. Movable property roughly corresponds to personal property, while immovable property corresponds to real estate or real property, and the associated rights and obligations thereon." (WK 2009c)

Historically, in many countries, "all property was owned by the monarch" (or the equivalent top authority that was), and "it devolved through feudal land tenure or other feudal systems of loyalty and fealty." (WK 2009c)

In Western Europe, it is "the Napoleonic code," which " was among the first government acts of modern times to introduce the notion of absolute ownership into statute"; but in the Islamic world, "protection of personal property rights was present in medieval Islamic law and jurisprudence," (WK 2009c; J. Makdisi 2005)

Trust Law

The second example of private law is "trust law," which concerns "an arrangement whereby property (including real, tangible and intangible) is managed by one person (or persons, or organizations) for the benefit of another." (WK 2009d)

In this sense, "a trust is created by a settlor (or *feoffor to uses*), who entrusts some or all of his property to people of his choice (the trustees or *feoffee to uses*). The trustees hold legal title to the trust property (or *trust corpus*), but they are obliged to hold the property for the benefit of one or more individuals or organizations (the beneficiary or *cestui que use* or *cestui que trust*), usually specified by the settlor, who hold equitable title. The trustees owe a fiduciary duty to the beneficiaries, who are the 'beneficial' owners of the trust property." (WK 2009d)

In some countries like "the United States, the settlor is also called the trustor, grantor, donor, or creator." (WK 2009d) And "trusts can be created during a person's life (usually by a trust instrument) or after death in a will." (WK 2009d)

Contract Law

The third example of private law concerns "contract law," which is about any "exchange of promises for the breach of which the law will provide a remedy." (WK 2009e; A. Sullivan 2003)

In a contract, "[t]he parties must have the necessary capacity to contract and the contract must not be either trifling, indeterminate, impossible or illegal. Contract law is based on the principle expressed in the Latin phrase *pacta sunt servanda* (usually translated 'pacts must be kept,' but more literally 'agreements are to be kept'). Breach of contract is recognized by the law and remedies can be provided." (WK 2009e; H. Wehberg 1959)

A contract can be both written and oral. For instance, "[i]n daily life, most contracts can be and are made orally, such as purchasing a book or a sandwich. Sometimes written contracts are required by either the parties, or by statutory law within various jurisdiction for certain types of agreement," like "buying a house or land." (WK 2009e)

A contract also requires mutual consent, since "contract relies on the notion of consensual exchange and has been extensively discussed in broader economic, sociological and anthropological terms." (WK 2009e)

In fact, "contract is a form of economic ordering common throughout the world, and different rules apply in jurisdictions applying civil law (derived from Roman law principles), Islamic law, socialist legal systems, and customary or local law." (WK 2009e)

Tort Law

And the fourth example of private law has to do with "tort law," which is "a body of law that addresses, and provides remedies for, civil wrongs not arising out of contractual obligations." (WK 2009f)

Four main features of tort law can be described here.

Firstly, tort law concerns both intentional and unintentional acts. In other words, "torts cover intentional acts and accidents (negligent acts)." (WK 2009f)

Secondly, tort law differs from "criminal law," because, in the latter, "the offense is against the State and the State is the plaintiff," but, "in tort law, the offense is against a person and that person is the plaintiff." (WK 2009f)

Thirdly, tort law relies on the notion of "the standard of care—a legal phrase that means distinguishing between when conduct is or is not tortious. Put another way, the big issue is whether a person suffers the loss from his own injury, or whether it gets transferred to someone else." (WK 2009f)

In the West, for example, "the touchstone of tort liability is negligence. If the injured party cannot prove that the person believed to have caused the injury acted with negligence, at the very least, tort law will not compensate them. Tort law also recognizes intentional torts and strict liability, which apply to defendants who engage in certain actions." (WK 2009f)

And fourthly, "in tort law, injury is defined broadly. Injury does not just mean a physical injury"; for example, injuries can include "any invasion of any number of individual interests" like "property rights," "prospective economic advantages from contracts," "freedom from emotional distress," "privacy interests," "reputation," and "freedom of movement." (WK 2009f)

Law and Jurisprudence

Of course, there are other examples of both private law and public law (besides the ones as cited in the previous section).

For example, there are other categories of laws like "company law" (mostly from "trust law"), "commercial law" (mostly from "contract law" and "property law"), "intellectual property law" (mostly from "property law" and "contract law"), "immigration law" (mostly from "constitutional law," "administrative law," and "criminal law"), and others. (WK 2009)

Yet, there are two good reasons for not listing all possible examples of private law and public law here.

Firstly, many of these other laws are derived from the most fundamental laws as cited in the examples of private law and public law (in the previous section).

And secondly, the examples of private law and public law (in the previous section) are supposed to be illustrative (not exhaustive), for the introductory purpose at hand.

With this clarification in mind—the next step to study the nature of law requires a good understanding of the main assumptions and principles behind the creation of law over time.

This deeper analysis of the nature of law then leads us to the sub-field of "jurisprudence," which is about "the theory and philosophy of law." (WK 2009g)

These specialized scholars on the deeper nature of law are known as "scholars of jurisprudence" or "legal philosophers," who "hope to obtain a deeper understanding of the nature of law, of legal reasoning, legal systems and of legal institutions." (WK 2009g)

Those who are lawyers by profession often do not specialize in jurisprudence but in the technical aspects of law for practical uses (for example, for their clients in court); jurisprudence remains a domain of interest primarily for philosophers, or more precisely, legal philosophers. In other words, there is a division of expertise here, in that lawyers often do not know well the philosophical foundation of law in theory, whereas legal philosophers often are not very well informed about the technical aspects of law in practice.

This qualification aside—there are two main types of jurisprudence to be introduced hereafter, namely, (a) "analytic jurisprudence" and (b) "normative jurisprudence"—to be shown below (and summarized in *Table 1.2*). (WK 2009g)

Analytical Jurisprudence

In "analytic jurisprudence," the concern here is about some most fundamental questions in legal philosophy like "What is law?" "What are the criteria for legal validity?" "What is the relationship between law and morality?" "What is the relationship between law and power/sociology?" and so on. (WK 2009g & 2009h)

Thus, the word "analytic" here (in "analytic jurisprudence") refers to the task of "clarifying" in its close relationship with "modern analytical philosophy," because it tries to clarify and "understand the nature of law. Since the boundaries of analytical philosophy are somewhat vague, it is difficult to say how far it extends. H. L. A. Hart was probably the most influential writer in the modern school of analytical jurisprudence, though its history goes back at least to Jeremy Bentham." (WK 2009h)

However, one should not confuse "analytical jurisprudence" in the current context with "legal formalism," since the latter is about "the idea that legal reasoning is or can be modelled as a mechanical, algorithmic process….Indeed, it was the analytical jurists who first pointed out that legal formalism is fundamentally mistaken as a theory of law." (WK 2009h)

For instance, "analytic, or 'clarificatory' jurisprudence uses a neutral point of view and descriptive language when referring to the aspects of legal systems. This was a philosophical development that rejected natural law's fusing of what law is and what it ought to be. David Hume famously argued in *A Treatise of Human Nature* that people invariably slip between describing that the world is a certain way to saying therefore we ought to conclude on a particular course of action. But as a matter of pure logic, one cannot conclude that we ought to do something merely because something is the case." (WK 2009h)

So, for analytic legal philosophers, "analysing and clarifying the way the world is must be treated as a strictly separate question to normative and evaluative ought questions." (WK 2009h)

Normative Jurisprudence

In "normative jurisprudence," by contrast, the conern here is more about "what law ought to be." (WK 2009g)

Thus, normative legal philosophers are more concerned with "normative, or 'evaluative' theories of law. What is the goal or purpose of law? What moral or political theories provide a foundation for the law? What is the proper function of law? What sorts of acts should be subject to punishment, and what sorts of punishment should be permitted? What is justice? What rights do we have? Is there a duty to obey the law? What value has the rule of law?" (WK 2009i)

For instance, some normative legal philosohers in the tradition of "virtue jurisprudence" focus on "the role of character in morality. Virtue jurisprudence is the view that the laws should promote the development of virtuous characters by citizens. Historically, this approach is associated mainly with Aristotle or Thomas Aquinas later. Contemporary virtue jurisprudence is inspired by philosophical work on virtue ethics." (WK 2009i)

Of course, there are many other traditions in normative jurisprudence (other than the one of virtue jurisprudence), and good examples include "critical legal studies," "libertarian theories of law," and the like. (WK 2009i)

The Theoretical Debate

So, which type of jurisprudence should we accept? Analytic jurisprudence? Normative jurisprudence? Or something else?

This hotly contested question then leads us to the theoretical debate on the nature of law in jurisprudence (and other related ones like political philosophy, ethics, law and economics, and the sociology of law, just to cite a few examples).

Three main categories of theoretical approaches in the literature of jurisprudence can be summarized hereafter, with the third to be my original contribution to the literature.

These three categories of theoretical approaches can be called, in the absence of better words, namely, (a) the *necessity* argument, (b) the *contingency* argument, and (c) the *reconstruction* argument—to be summarized hereafter, respectively (and to be further elaborated in the rest of the book, with Chapter Two on necessity, Chapter Three on contingency, and Chapter Four on reconstruction).

At this juncture, two clarifications are needed, in order to avoid any hasty misunderstanding.

Firstly, needless to say, there can be other arguments (and theories within each) besides these three categories. My purpose to select these three here is to be solely illustrative (not exhaustive), which is deemed sufficient for the purpose at hand in this introductory section.

And secondly, the three categories are also not necessarily mutually exclusive. For instance, those who advocate the "necessity" argument can also accept the "contingency" argument, but the important point to remember here is that they do not focus on the latter. And the reverse can be said about those who advocate the "contingency" argument. Thus, their disagreement is one in degree, not in kind.

The Necessity Argument

With these two clarifications in mind—the first major theoretical category can be called, in the absence of better words, the *necessity* argument, which justifies the validity of a law on the basis of some universality, relatively speaking of course, and can be classified in terms of three different versions, namely, (a1) the moral, (a2) the religious, and (a3) the natural—to be summarized hereafter, in that order.

In this sense, the word "necessity" in the argument is revealing, because of its meaning for something which can be universal, relatively speaking again.

The Moral

The moral version of the necessity argument is to focus more on the role of morality to provide a solid foundation for the law.

For instance, Immanuel Kant (1724–1804), in *Groundwork of the Metaphysics of Morals* (1953), "believed a moral imperative requires laws 'be chosen as though they should hold as universal laws,'" on the basis of reason. (WK 2009)

Kant's moral imperative, however, should not be confused with the conventional understanding of "the Golden Rule," which merely "demands that one's actions conform to one's own standard." (WK 2009j)

By contrast, "Kant's moral imperative places the standard for moral good in reason," to the extent that "people should always be treated with respect to their personhood and dignity, and always as ends in themselves"; and although "they can be treated as a means and an end at the same time," they should never be treated "only as a means." (WK 2009j)

In this sense, a law cannot be created as a means to promote "power," "wealth," "honour," "health," and other mundane desires. (WK 2009j) Instead, a law must pass the test that "people should always be treated with respect to their personhood and dignity, and always as ends in themselves." (WK 2009j)

But the critics are not convinced by Kant's argument. Consider two classic criticisms below.

Firstly, for David Hume (1711–1776), reason by itself "could not be a ground for moral choices," because, as he thus wrote: "Reason is, and ought only to be the slave of the passions, and can never pretend to any other office than to serve and obey them." (WK 2009k; D. Hume 2003)

And secondly, for Arthur Schopenhauer (1788–1860) in *On the Basis of Morality* (1965), "actions are not moral when they are performed solely from duty"; any law which is based on this kind of moral duty is "cold and egoistic." (WK 2009j)

The Religious

Another version of the necessity argument has to do with religion, and a good illustration here involves the Islamic philosopher, "Abū 'l-Walīd Muḥammad ibn Aḥmad ibn Rushd (Arabic: أبو الوليد محمد بن احمد بن رشد), better known just as Ibn Rushd (Arabic: ابن رشد), and in European literature as Averroes," who lived in 1126–1198. (WK 2009l)

For Averroes, religion can provide a solid foundation for the law, because "there is no conflict between religion and philosophy, rather that they are different ways of reaching the same truth." (WK 2009l)

This then means that there are "two kinds of Knowledge of Truth. The first being…[the] knowledge of truth of religion being based in faith and thus could not be tested, nor did it require training to understand. The second knowledge of truth is philosophy, which was reserved for an elite few who had the intellectual capacity to undertake this study." (WK 2009l)

Thus, faith can provide the guidance for a solid foundation for the law. In the Islamic tradition, the faith in question refers to its sources in the *Qur'an* ("the holy scripture of Islam"), *Sunnah* ("the religious actions and quotations of the Islamic Prophet Muhammad and narrated through his Companions and Shia Imams"), *consensus*, and *'aql* (intellect)—especially in relation to "*Fiqh* (Islamic jurisprudence), *Sharia* (Islamic law), and *Kalam* (Islamic theology)." (WK 2009m & 2009n)

For instance, Averroes appealed to the authority of the Prophet Muhammad in his argument against usury, as he "reported that Ibn 'Abbas, a sahaba (companion) of Muhammad, did not accept *Riba al-Fadl* (interest in excess) because, according to him, the Prophet Muhammad had clarified that there was no Riba except in credit." (WK 2009l; K. Zaheer 2004)

And Averroes also "discussed the role of Islamic criminal jurisprudence in the Islamic dietary laws in regard to the consumption of alcohol. He stated that physical punishment for alcoholic consumption was not originally established as part of the Sharia in Muhammad's time but was later decided by the Shura (consultive council) of the Rashidun Caliphate." (WK 2009l)

For the critics, however, the appeal to religion for the foundation for the law makes sense only for the believers. But for those who do not accept the faith in question, the law loses its appeal and is thus not necessary.

The Natural

And the third version of the necessity argument concerns the role of nature on the foundation for the law.

An excellent illustration here is the idea of "the will to power" by Friedrich Nietzsche, "who rejected the principle of equality" in morality and instead "believed that law emanates from the will to power, and cannot be labelled as 'moral' or 'immoral.'" (WK 2009; N. Kazantzakis 1909; J. Linarelli 2004)

In *The Gay Science* (1974: §301), Nietzsche thus wrote about nature: "Whatever has value in our world now does not have value in itself, according to its nature—nature is always value-less, but has been *given* value at some time, as a present—and it was *we* who gave and bestowed it. Only we have created the world *that concerns man*!" (J. Linarelli 2004)

For Nietzsche, "natural law fits nicely within [his] conception of 'slave morality.' Natural law is the belief system of the 'last man.' It is 'human all too human'....Nietzsche takes the opposite view; to be reasonable is human all too human. The reasonable person is the last man, someone satisfied with happiness." (J. Linarelli 2004)

Instead, Nietzsche proposed an alternative version of natural law, in the form of "the will to power," which "is the struggle of humans over time to learn and develop norms of behavior through species preserving error. It is both creative and destructive. It creates because humans use will to power to produce values and to make sense of existence. It destroys because it must overcome old values that no longer serve us." (J. Linarelli 2004: 15)

In this way, "Nietzschean will to power differs fundamentally from natural law philosophy [traditionally understood] because the world is chaotic and we cannot understand it through reason. There is no right reason or moral reality that we must ultimately discover if we think or try hard enough. Will to power is the fundamental human ability to struggle through the incomprehensible accident of the world to make life sensible and practical." (J. Linarelli 2004: 15)

Thus, the will to power is not for "self preservation" but for the "enhancement of life. Nietzsche was not a moral skeptic. Humans must overcome; the goal is becoming overman, not to model one after a saint or God." (J. Linarelli 2004: 16)

In the end, laws should be constructed to allow superior individuals to pursue this overcoming for the "enhancement of life," not resenting them (as in slave morality).

But, for the critics, the Nietzschean call for the will to power has its dark side unsaid, as Jacques Derrida (1984:24) once thus wrote: "One may wonder why the only teaching institution or the only beginning of a teaching institution that ever succeeded in taking as its model the teaching of Nietzsche on teaching will have been a Nazi one."

The Contingency Argument

Unlike the necessity argument—there is an opposite viewpoint, which can be called, in the absence of better words, the *contingency* argument, as it pays more attention, relatively speaking again, on (b1) the societal and (b2) the cultural factors, both of which shape over time how a law becomes accepted and established, not because it is necessary but because it is contngent on the circumstantial forces of history.

In this sense, the word "contingency" in the argument is suggestive, because of its meaning for something which is not necessary but contingent, in relation to societal and cultural causes.

Hereafer is the summary of the societal causes in (b1) and the cultural causes in (b2), in accordance to the contingency argument—in that order.

The Societal

The societal version of the contingency argument is to pay more attention to societal causes in shaping the outcome of a law.

A good example involves law and economics by the 1991 Nobel Prize winner Ronald Coase, who, in "The Problem of Social Cost" (1960), made the essential point that "if we lived in a world without transaction costs, people would bargain with one another to create the same allocation of resources, regardless of the way a court might rule in property disputes." (WK 2009)

More specifically, "Coase used the example of a nuisance case named Sturges v Bridgman, where a noisy sweetmaker and a quiet doctor were neighbours and went to court to see who should have to move. Coase said that regardless of whether the judge ruled that the sweetmaker had to stop using his machinery, or that the doctor had to put up with it, they could strike a mutually beneficial bargain about who moves house that reaches the same outcome of resource distribution. Only the existence of transaction costs may prevent this." (WK 2009 & 2009o)

So, Coase's claim here is that "the law ought to pre-empt what would happen, and be guided by the most efficient solution. The idea is that law and regulation are not as important or effective at helping people as lawyers and government planners believe. Coase and others like him wanted a change of approach, to put the burden of proof for positive effects on a government that was intervening in the market, by analysing the costs of action." (WK 2009)

For the critics, however, Coase's argument represents the recurrent conservative ideology of free market, which has been advocated by "economists and lawyers including Milton Friedman and Gary Becker," in their vocal call for "deregulation and privatisation," against "state regulation or what they see as restrictions on the operation of free market." (WK 2009; S. Jakoby 2005)

Yet, does the free market solution really work, as much as the free-marketers would like us to believe? The critic like Steve Kangas (2008), for instance, questioned the fundamental assumptions in Coase's work, in relation to (i) property rights, (ii) efficient and identical use of resources, (iii) transaction costs in bargaining, (iv) perfect competition and information, and (v) wealth and income effects.

In the process, Kangas (2008) showed that Coase's work does not even guarantee in principle that "transaction costs can be reduced in free market." So, the critical implication here is, Why should the court be guided by the economic idea of efficiency for the unrestricted operation of free market, as the free-marketers like Coase would want us to believe?

The Cultural

Unlike the societal version of the contingency argument—the cultural version is more concerned with the influence of culture on the formulation of a law over time.

An excellent example here concerns "the German Historical School of Law," which is "a 19th century intellectual movement in the study of German law. With Romanticism as its background, it emphasized the historical limitations of the law." (WK 2009p)

With the writings of Gustav Hugo and Friedrich Carl von Savigny (1831) in mind, "the basis premise of the German Historical School is that law is not to be regarded as an arbitrary grouping of regulations laid down by some authority. Rather, those regulations are to be seen as the expression of the convictions of the people, in the same manner as language, customs and practices are expressions of the people. The law is grounded in a form of popular consciousness called the Volksgeist." (WK 2009p)

In this sense, although "laws can stem from regulations by the authorities,…more commonly they evolve in an organic manner over time without interference from the authorities. The ever-changing practical needs of the people play a very important role in this continual organic development." (WK 2009p)

So, lawyers and judges, for instance, should "base their…work on law on ascertaining the will of the people. In this way,…[they] embody the popular will." (WK 2009p)

But, for the critics, the German historicists are rather too one-sided, in ignoring other factors which can determine the development of law over time. For instance, some argue for "Vernunftsrecht (Natural Law)," in that "law could be discovered only by rational deduction from the nature of man"—not that it should embody "the popular will." (WK 2009p)

The Reconstruction Argument

And the third argument is different from both the necessity argument and the contingency argument and can be called, in the absence of better words again, the *reconstruction* argument, which learns from all other theoretical approaches (including the two previous arguments and also other ones as will be introduced in the rest of this book), without, however, heavily favoring any of them, nor trying to integrate them (as they are not necessarily compatible with each other).

In fact, in the two volumes of *The Future of Human Civilization* (or *FHC* in 2000), I already went to great lengths to explain, among many other issues, why the theoretical debate in the literature on necessity vs. contingency end up impoverishing our understanding of reality within this narrow dichotomy. For instance, neither those for natural law nor the critics in postmodernism are exclusively right over the others. In the end, I originally proposed that there is no justice without injustice.

Without repeating what was already analyzed in *FHC*, my reconstruction argument here goes a step further, this time, in the context of jurisprudence, that is, to transcend the different arguments in the debate into a new direction not proposed before.

The Reconstruction Theory of Law

My *reconstruction* argument can be more precisely called *the reconstruction theory of law*, since it is to propose a new theory of justice.

The reconstruction theory of law has three distinctive features to remember.

Firstly, it makes good use of all theoretical approaches in the literature on law (like the necessity argument and the contingency argument)—especially from the most comprehensive combined perspectives of the mind, nature, society, and culture.

Secondly, as it is the case for many other theories of mine in my previous books, my theory here does not heavily favor any specific theory over others in the literature, nor trying to integrate them (as they are not necessarily compatible with each other).

And thirdly, it contains eleven major theses, namely, (a) the first thesis: the absoluteness-relativeness principle, (b) the second thesis: the predictability-unpredictability principle, (c) the third thesis: the explicability-inexplicability principle, (d) the fourth thesis: the preciseness-vagueness principle, (e) the fifth thesis: the simpleness-complicatedness principle, (f) the sixth thesis: the openness-hiddenness principle, (g) the seventh thesis: the evolution-transformation principle, (h) the eighth thesis: the symmetry-asymmetry principle, (i) the nineth thesis: the regression-progression principle, (j) the tenth thesis: the same-difference principle, and (k) the eleventh thesis: the post-human reconstruction—to be elaborated in the rest of the book, with a summary in the concluding chapter.

In the end, there is no justice without injustice (as first proposed in *FHC*), in accordance to existential dialectics—and it will be transcended too.

Of course, as this is something that I often stress in my previous books, other principles (besides the ten as cited above) are also relevant, but these ten are the most relevant in the current case study (as will be explained further in Chapter Four, the concluding chapter), although different case studies will, of course, reveal different degrees of relevance of the principles.

This seminal project, if successful, will fundamentally change the way that we think about the nature of law, from the combined perspectives of the mind, nature, society, and culture, with enormous implications for the human future and what I originally called its "post-human" fate.

Theory and Meta-Theory

The reconstruction argument, or the reconstruction theory of law, presupposes some kind of meta-theory, in special relation to methodology and ontology—just as all theories, either explicitly or implicitly, require their own versions of meta-theory.

In my case, as this is something that I regularly explained in my previous books, I already proposed my distinctive approach to methodology (known as "sophisticated methodological holism") and ontology (known as "existential dialectics").

The next two sections are to introduce my meta-theory, or existential dialectics and sophisticated methodological holism, respectively.

A Unified Theory of Everything

In the end, my distinctive approach to meta-theory serves as a foundation to unify all domains of knowledge for an overarching understanding of all forms of reality (by way of some ontological principles and the comprehensive perspectives of the mind, nature, society, and culture—as will be explained in the next two sections).

This is so, without commiting the sins of reductionism and reverse-reductionism (as often seen in many holistic approaches, with the fad of sysems approach as a most recent notorious example), since my distinctive approach makes good use of different schools of thought without favoring any of them nor trying to integrate them (as they are not necessarily compatible with each other), so as to adjust for subjectivity, diversity, conflict, and complexity, for example.

In this sense, the word "unified" does not have to mean integrative approach, in a narrow sense, nor systems approach, in a broad one, both of which I reject while learning from them.

This overarching project (consisting of numerous theories of mine, as will be summarized in the next section), thus, constitutes my grand unifed theory of everything in the world and beyond.

The Logic of Existential Dialectics

To start, the ontology of existential dialectics can be summarized in this section—to be repeated, *often verbatim* (with only a few updated revisions), from my previous works—as this is something that I often do in each book of mine as an introduction to some background information for the convenience of the readers.

After all, this book, like all others of mine, is in conversation with all previous ones of mine, for the final aim to converge all of them into a larger grand project on the future of intelligent life, both here on earth and there in deep space unto multiverses.

The summary can be organized in relation to (a) the conception of existential dialectics (or its ontics), (b) the syntax of existential dialectics (or its ontomethodology and ontologic), (c) the semantics of existential dialectics (or its ontosemantics), and (d) the pragmatics of existential dialectics (or its ontopragmatics), respectively hereafter—again *often verbatim*.

This means that, for those readers who had read some of my previous books, the summary below is really nothing new (*almost verbatim*, with only some minor revisions) and can be skipped.

But for those who have never read my previous books, it is a good review of them.

The Conception of Existential Dialectics (or Its Ontics)

This ontology was originally designated as "existential dialectics" in *Beyond Capitalism to Post-Capitalism* (herein abbreviated as *BCPC*), although it was already analyzed in other books of mine like the 2 volumes of *The Future of Human Civilization* (*FHC*), *The Future of Capitalism and Democracy* (*FCD*), *The Future of Post-Human Consciousness* (*FPHC*), and the 2 volumes of *Beyond Democracy to Post-Democracy* (*BDPD*).

Lest any confusion occurs, it is important to stress at the outset that the word 'existential' in "existential dialectics" has nothing to do with Existentialism, which I rebuked in *FHC*, *FCD*, and also *FPHC*. Instead, the word here merely refers to the existence of intelligent life (both primitive and advanced) in a broad sense.

Some Basic Concepts

The conception of existential dialectics (or its ontics) makes use of different concepts (like "sets," "elements," "relations," "operations," "functions," "truth values," "axioms," "postulates," and "principles"—as shown in *Table 4.3*), which are important for the understanding of any logic of ontology.

That clarified—existential dialectics, as a language of ontology, can be analyzed in different ways that a language, as an analogy, is often analyzed, namely, in relation to phonology ("the study of patterns of a language's sounds"), phonetics ("the study of the physical aspects of sounds of human language"), morphonology ("the study of the internal structure of words"), syntax ("the study of how words combine to form grammatical sentences"), semantics ("the study of the meaning of words [lexical semantics] and fixed word combinations [phraseology]"), and pragmatics ("the study of how utterances are used…literally, figuratively, or otherwise…in communicative acts"). (WK 2007)

But since my theory of existential dialectics makes use of the English language for communication here, it does not propose a new way to make the patterns of a language's sounds (as in phonology), to study the physical aspects of sounds (as in phonetics), or even to strive for a new organization of the internal structure of words for the English language (as in morphonology).

For this reason, the language of existential dialectics to be analyzed hereafter is not concerned with the phonological, phonetic, and morphonological aspects of the English language. Instead, the analysis will explore the syntax, semantics, and pragmatics of existential dialectics as a language of ontology to improve our understanding of reality.

The Ontic Dispute

But first, there is an ontic dispute to be addressed, which is related to what I called "the dilemma of ontology" as introduced earlier in *Sec. 1.4* of *The Future of Post-Human Knowledge* (*FPHK*).

A good point of departure concerns what I want to call *the ontic dispute*, on how to understand the very nature of ontology.

Traditionally, scholars in the field used to study the conception of ontology in terms of its entities (e.g., material objects, abstract numbers), properties (e.g., duration, plurality), and relationships (e.g., causation).

This is a good starting point, but it suffers from different problems. Consider three examples of bias below, which are quite common in the literature, and the recent version (of treating concepts and principles in ontology on the basis of "plurality," "dynamism," "duration," "interaction," "life," "consciousness," and "volition") by Reginald Firehammer (2005) only constitutes a latest addition to this old (impoverishing) tradition.

Firstly, the classification of entities, properties, and relationships is too material-centric, in often focusing more on the existence of material entities than on non-material ones.

Secondly, the classification is too anthropo-centric, in often favoring the factor of human agency in depicting reality.

And lastly, the classification is too confused among the three categories relating to each other, in often lumping them together without due consideration of their intricated interrelationships (both in relation to each and in relation to all).

A good alternative is precisely what I want to offer in this debate, that is, a new classification of ontological entities, properties, and their relationships in terms of *method*, *structure*, *process*, *agency*, and *outcome* instead.

In relation to method, it concerns how ontology is to be studied. In this sense, the word 'method' here should not be confused with the different usage of the same term 'method' as a technique of investigation in the context of methodology (as already introduced in *Sec. 1.2* of *FPHK*).

In relation to structure, it concerns what the general patterns of entities, properties, and relationships are.

In relation to process, it concerns how these general patterns change over time.

In relation to agency, it concerns how agency affects any change of these general patterns over time (without putting, however, too much emphasis on the role of human agency).

And in relation to outcome, it concerns what the outputs of this change over time are.

The Syntax of Existential Dialectics (or Its Ontomethodology and Ontologic)

The syntax of existential dialectics, analogously speaking, refers here to the structure of an ontology which can be studied by way of combining ideas into complex relationships like ontological principles to depict reality in the world—and can be analyzed in seven sub-sections, namely, (a) the selection criteria, (b) further clarifications on classification, (c) ontomethodology, (d) ontologic, (e) the principles as short cuts, (f) the principles as family resemblances, and (g) the dialectic constraints imposed by the principles, respectively hereafter.

The Selection Criteria

To start, not any pair of relationship can be chosen as an ontological principle in existential dialectics; otherwise, there could be billions of them under the sky.

Four illustrations below suffice to clarify this point.

(a) Firstly, an ontological principle cannot *overlap* with other principles, in that it is too closely related with other ones.

Of course, one cannot totally rule out any relationship between two entities, especially in a complex world of everything being linked to everything else—but the comparison here is relative, not absolute.

In this sense, the flexibility-inflexibility pair cannot be an ontological principle, since it has something closely in common with other ones (like the simpleness-complicatedness principle, for instance).

As an illustration, something which is flexible in interpretation is more likely to allow multiple viewpoints and thus makes the overall picture more complicated than otherwise (simple).

(b) Secondly, an ontological principle cannot be *redundant* in relation to other principles, in that it somehow duplicates other principles.

In this sense, for instance, the directness-indirectness pair cannot be an ontological principle, because it somehow duplicates other ontological principles (like the preciseness-vagueness principle, for instance).

As an illustration, something which is direct means to be right to the point and does not need to go to an unnecessarily long loop—so it is less vague, in being clearer about the thing in question.

(c) Thirdly, an ontological principle cannot be *derived* from other ones—as if it is a child-parent relationship.

In this sense, the convenience-inconvenience pair cannot be an ontological principle, because it can be derived from other ones (like the slowness-quickness principle, for instance).

For instance, something which is convenient already implies that it can be obtained quickly (rather than slowly)—all things considered.

(d) Fourthly, an ontological principle cannot be *trivial* (or *parochial*)—as if it is only one component competing with other ones for inclusion in a set.

In this sense, the consistency-inconsistency pair cannot be an ontological principle, because its validity is limited (or parochial), as it can be easily challenged and replaced by opposing major (not minor) theories (e.g., the correspondence theory of truth, the pragmatic theory of truth, the semantic theory of truth, and whatnot), not just in accordance to the consistency theory of truth (for consistency).

In this sense, the consistency argument is only one among different opposing arguments in relation to the logic of what constitutes "truth."

Although these examples are not exhaustive, they illustrative the selectiveness of any ontological principle to be existentially dialectic.

Further Clarifications on Classification

Lest any misunderstanding carelessly occurs, some further clarifications on classification should be made here (and summarized in *Table 4.8*).

(a) Firstly, the total number of ontological principles is unknown, to be discovered later, as our knowledge of the world becomes more advanced.

Consequently, the principles as introduced in my books are not exhaustive, with new ones being added, whenever more of them are discovered in later research.

At least, future generations can pick up where I leave off and continue the discovery.

In this sense, my work should be treated as a pioneering effort for the development of a systematic, comprehensive analysis of a new general ontology for the future of knowledge.

(b) Secondly, the principles are not rigidly classified, as they can be reclassified in a different way.

For instance, the preciseness-vagueness principle is classified under the category of "structure" but can be reclassified under the category of "method," although in so doing, it has a different meaning in the context of method.

The same logic applies to the same-difference principle under the category of "outcome," which can be reclassified under the category of "structure," although in so doing, once more, it has a different meaning in the context of structure.

(c) Thirdly, the principles are to be understood together, not that each prinicple is to be treated independently of others. After all, the principles are mutually constraining, in that they work together as a whole.

(d) Fourthly, the principles are relevant to all subject matters, but some principles are more useful to some subject matters than others—as implied in the symmetry-asymmetry principle.

And (e) fifthly, the principles constitute only two levels of analysis, this time, at the ontological and methodological levels—while other levels of analysis (from the perspectives of the mind, nature, society, and culture) are also needed, in order to understand reality in its totality (as explained in the section on "sophisticated methodological holism," so as to avoid the dual dangers of reductionism and reverse-reductionism).

Ontomethodology

With these selection criteria and clarifications in mind—the syntax of existential dialectics can be divided into two main smaller sections for analysis, since they are related to each other in the context of some fundamental principles, that is, (a) ontomethodology and (b) ontologic, to be addressed hereafter, respectively.

In the context of ontomethodology, some ontological principles are proposed here in relation to the nature of methodology, which however is tied up with the general issue of ontology in the context of knowledge.

In this sense, ontomethodology (in the context of these ontological principles in the category of method) are related with ontologic in general (in the context of ontological principles in general).

Some good instances of ontological principles involving ontomethodology include the formalness-informalness principle, the predictability-unpredictability principle, the explicability-inexplicability principle, the partiality-totality principle, and the absoluteness-relativeness principle, which will be introduced in conjunction with ontological principles in the ontologic of existential dialectics in general hereafter.

Ontologic

With this clarification of the relationship between ontomethodology and ontologic in mind (which is comparable to the relationship between methodology and ontology as described in *Sec. 1.3* of *FPHK*)—the first three principles in the ontological logic of existential dialectics were introduced in *BCPC*. And more principles were later added to the logic in my subsequent books (like *FC*, *FAE*, and others).

More specifically, in *BCPC*, I proposed three principles (based on previous works of mine, not just something out of the blue) for the ontological logic, namely, (a) the regression-progression principle on the direction of history, (b) the symmetry-asymmetry principle on the relationships among existents, and (c) the change-constancy principle on the alteration of things—or in a more elegant term, the dynamics of space-time (in *FC*).

In *The Future of Complexity* (*FC*), I added three more principles, on top of the three aforementioned, namely, (d) the partiality-totality principle on the relationships between the parts and the whole, (e) the order-chaos principle on the pattern of things, and (f) the predictability-unpredictability principle on the occurrence of things—as part of the ontological logic of existential dialectics.

In *The Future of Aesthetic Experience* (or simply *FAE*), another principle is added, namely, (g) the evolution-transformation principle (on the multiple kinds of agency).

Also in *FAE*, I then reclassified the seven principles into four categories, namely, (i) in relation to method, for the partiality-totality principle and the predictability-unpredictability principle, (ii) in relation to process, for the change-constancy principle and the order-chaos principle, (iii) in relation to agency, for the symmetry-asymmetry principle and the evolution-transformation principle, and (iv) in relation to outcome, for the regression-progression principle.

In *The Rise of Authoritarian Liberal Democracy* (*ALD*), I added two more principles, namely, (h) the softness-hardness principle on the force of agency (which is to be classified under the category about agency) and (i) the same-difference principle on the metamorphosis of change (which is to be classified under the category about outcome).

In *The Future of Information Architecture* (*FIA*), I introduce three additional principles, that is, (j) the simpleness-complicadness principle on the interconnection among things, (k) the preciseness-vagueness principle on the refinement of things, and (l) the slowness-quickness principle on the speed of change—with the first two in relation to structure and the third in relation to process.

In *The Future of Post-Human Unconsciousness* (*FPHU*), I added three more principles, that is, (m) the openness-hidden principle on the detection of things, in relation to structure, (n) the explicability-inexplicability principle on the underlying mechanisms of things, in relation to method, and (o) the expansion-contraction principle on the growth of things, in relation to process.

In *The Future of Post-Human Knowledge* (*FPHK*), I added one more principle, that is, (p) the absoluteness-relativeness principle on the multiplicity of entities, in relation to method.

In *The Future of Post-Human Mathematical Logic* (*FPHML*), I added one more principle, that is, (q) the formalness-informalness principle on the formal requirements of systems, in relation to method.

In *The Future of Post-Human Engineering* (*FPHE*), I added one more principle, that is, (r) the theory-praxis principle on the duality of knowledge, in relation to agency.

In *The Future of Post-Human Creative Thinking* (*FPHCT*), I added one more principle, that is, (s) the convention-novelty principle on the nature of creative thinking, in relation to agency.

In *The Future of Post-Human Geometry* (*FPHG*) here, I added one more principle, that is, (t) the finiteness-transfiniteness principle on the nature of numbers, in relation to structure.

And in *The Future of Post-Human Urban Planning* (*FPHUP*), I added one more principle, that is, (u) the denseness-emptiness principle on the distribution of entities in space, in relation to structure.

With this update, there are twenty-one principles so far in existential dialectics, that is, five principles for the category in relation to method (viz., the formalness-informalness principle, the partiality-totality principle, the predictability-unpredictability principle, the explicability-inexplicability principle, and the absoluteness-relativeness principle), five principles for the category in relation to structure (viz., the finiteness-transfiniteness principle, the simpleness-complicatedness principle, the preciseness-vagueness principle, the openness-hiddenness principle, and the denseness-emptiness principle), four principles for the category in relation to process (viz., the change-constancy principle, the slowness-quickness principle, the order-chaos principle, and the expansion-contraction principle), five principles for the category in relation to agency (viz., the theory-praxis principle, the convention-novelty principle, the symmetry-asymmetry principle, the evolution-transformation principle, and the softness-hardness principle), and two principles for the category in relation to outcome (viz., the regression-progression principle and the sameness-difference principle).

There are thus twenty-one principles in existential dialectics—so far (as summarized in *Table 4.4*).

The Principles as Short Cuts

Yet, these principles should be treated with caution, lest misunderstanding occurs, since they do not constitute rigid dualities (or dichotomies).

The reason is that each pair in an ontological principle consists of two opposites, which are, however, merely short cuts both for multiple variations and degrees, as well as for different interactions with multiple other entities unlike them.

In this light, each pair can end up having hundred (or even thousand, if not more) different versions, which interact with hundred (or even thousand, if not more) other entities—as summarized in *Table 4.5*.

There are two clarifications here.

Firstly, this conception of shortcuts is not mutually exclusive nor absolute, in that the opposites can come in all shapes and sizes, with different degrees. For instance, by analogy, just as there are different degrees of the two colors "white" and "black"—there are likewise different degrees of the opposites in each ontological pair, to the extent that there can be multiple entities (not only two) interacting with each other in each pair.

And secondly, this conception of shortcuts do not ignore other possible entities in interacting with the two opposites (with their different versions) in each pair. For instance, by analogy, there are not only the two colors "white" and "black" as opposites, since there are other colors too besides them like "yellow," "green," "purple," or else. The same logic can be applied to each ontological pair, in that they also interact with other entities, not with only two of them (with their different versions).

Therefore, with these two clarifications in mind—each pair in an ontological principle serves only as an abbreviation for something more complicated and, therefore, although it contains two opposites, it should not be confused as a duality (dualism).

Existential dialectics rejects any dualism (or dichotomy) as too rigid and instead allows the multiplicity of entities, to the extent that between the two opposites in each pair exist many other alternatives to choose from. They are named in that short form for aesthetic elegance, instead of listing all possible entities between the two opposites in the title.

To be dialectic is to go beyond any rigid dichotomy and transcend into something different altogether in the long haul. One may be tempted to call the dialectic logic here with a different name like existential "multilectics" (instead of "dialectics"), but this naming is incorrect (or even misleading), for the two reasons aforestated.

After all, each ontological pair come in all shapes and sizes (with different degrees) and do not exist by themselves but also interact with other entities unlike them. The virtue of revealing an ontological pair is to show how they relate within themselves (in multiple versions) and also interact with others unlike them (also in multiple versions).

This will be clear in a later sub-section titled "the dialectic constraints imposed by the principles."

The Principles as Family Resemblances

In addition, each ontological principle is generic, with some other comparable ontological pairs to be put in the same family (like a *family resemblance*)—as summarized in *Table 4.6*.

Ludwig Wittgenstein (1953) once suggested the idea of "family resemblance" in explaining different games classified under the same family called *games*.

Why should, for instance, playing football and chess as playing "games," when it is well understood that football is not the same as chess? The answer is that, although each game is different and has different rules, many of them (though not all) share, more or less, some commonalites (e.g., scoring as necessary for winning).

And this is so, even though some games share more than some others in any given selection of critieria, and no two games are exactly identical. So, Wittgenstein's point here is that there is no essential core which is common to all games, and the best that one can look for is some characteristics which are common to many (but not all) games. (A. Biletzki 2006)

By the same logic—in the previous section on selection criteria, the flexibility-inflexibility pair can be put in the family resemblance of the simpleness-complicatedness principle, although the two pairs are not exactly identical. Likewise, the directness-indirectness pair can be put in the family resemblance of the preciseness-vagueness principle, although, again, the two pairs are not exactly identical.

In this sense, which specific pair in a family should be used to designate the name of the family can be at times a bit arbitrary, but with good reason.

For illustration, in the context of method, the partiality-totality principle can take the different form like individualisticness-holisticness, just as the explicability-inexplicability principle can take the different form like underlyingness-regularness—although each two pairs are not exactly identical and have slightly different meanings and usages.

A more comprehensive listing of this family resemblance for all other principles is shown in *Table 4.6* on the syntax of existential dialectics.

In fact, this section on family resemblances overlaps with the semantics of existential dialectics, which will be introduced later in the next section (and summarized in *Table 4.10*).

The Dialectic Constraints Imposed by the Principles

The principles, as they constitute the syntax of existential dialectics, are dialectic in character, such that, when they are applied, they impose dialectic constraints on how reality is to be understood.

Consider, say, the symmetry-asymmetry principle as an illustration here, in order to summarize two main characters of the dialectic constraints in question (as summarized in *Table 4.7*).

Firstly, to be dialectic here is to go beyond the narrow dichotomies (and, for that matter, any rigid multi-dimensional classificatory scheme), be they about "self" vs. "world," "freedom" vs. "unfreedom," "barbarity" vs. "civilization," "individuality" vs. "communality," and so on.

One way to do so (to go beyond) is to consider them all in terms of co-existence (without favoring one over the rest). For instance, my theory of "post-civilization" (to be summarized later in the section on the pragmatics of existential dialectics) is to go beyond barbarity and civilization in terms of understanding barbarity and civilization as being co-existent.

Similarly, the same logic can be said in relation to my theories of "post-democracy," "post-capitalsm," and others (also to be introduced later in the section on the pragmatics of existential dialectics), in regard to freedom vs. unfreedom, equality vs. inequality, communality vs. individuality, spirituality vs. materiality, and so on.

But to consider them all (in the dichotomies—and, for that matter, in any rigid multi-dimensional classifactory scheme) as co-existent is not the same as to imply that the opposing categories in any classificatory scheme are all equal, since, in accordance to the symmetry-asymmetry principle (as an illustration here), if they are equal in terms of being considered as co-existent, they are asymmetric in terms of being unequal in dialectic interaction (e.g., X can be more dominant than Y in case A, or Y is more dominant than X in case B), although in some special cases, they can be relatively equal.

For this reason, there are different versions of "post-democracy" and "post-capitalism" in my theories. As an illustration, in version I of the theory of post-democracy, freedom is more dominant than equality, whereas in version II of the theory of post-democracy, equality is more so than freedom.

But this "X more than Y" has to be understood in the context of dialectic logic (not in symbolic logic, as conventionally understood), in that both "X" and "Y" are important in post-democracy (in the context of dialectic logic), but in an asymmetry way.

By contrast, in symbolic logic, it often favors one over the other—be it in regard to privileging freedom over equality in Fascism, favoring freedom relatively more than equality in Liberal Democracy, or favoring equality relatively more than freedom in Socialist Democracy. In regard to the latter two cases (about Liberal Democracy and Socialist Democracy), the difference between dialectic logic and symbolic logic can be one in degree, not in kind—in this sense, albeit not in other senses.

The same reasoning can be said about the relatonships between individuality and communality, between spirituality and materiality, and between formal legalism and informal legalism in the different versions of my theory of "post-capitalism."

Secondly, to be dialectic is to go beyond the narrow dichotomies (and, for that matter, any rigid multi-dimensional classificatory scheme) in another way, this time, in a transcendent way, that is, in exploring other possibilities or even other issues not considered within the narrow confines of narrow dichotomies (and, for that matter, any rigid multi-dimensional classificatory scheme).

As an analogy, in this second meaning, to go beyond the narrow dichotomy of "black" vs. "white" is not just to choose both "black" and "white" (as in the first meaning) but also to explore other options (e.g., "green," "purple," "blue," etc.—and, alternatively, "shade," "line," "curve," etc.).

By the same reasoning, to go beyond "democracy" is to transcend democracy (as in version III of my theory of "post-democracy") and to explore other possibilties of lifeforms (e.g., "floating consciousness," "hyper-spatial consciousness," etc., to live beyond the narrow obsession with freedom and equality).

This dialectic character of the principles in existential dialectics has important implications for the pragmatics of existential dialectics (as will be clear shortly, in the section on the pragmatics of existential dialectics).

The Semantics of Existential Dialectics (or Its Ontosemantics)

The syntax of existential dialectics so understood in terms of ontological principles only gives us the structure of ontology in the world, in an abstract (general) sense. These principles by themselves do not tell us the specific meanings in a given context.

In order to grasp the specific meanings of the principles in a given context, it is necessary to study the semantics of existential dialectics (as summarized in *Table 4.10*).

And the analysis of the ontological principles as family resemblances in the previous section on syntax is only a starting point (and thus overlaps a bit with the semantics of existential dialectics here).

For this reason, I have often gone to great lengths in my previous books on different subjects to explain the specific meanings of the principles when applied in different contexts.

Consider two examples below for illustration, which are not exhaustive.

In *FPHST*, for instance, I used the first three principles (i.e., the change-constancy principle, the regression-progression principle, and the symmetry-asymmetry principle) to propose "the perspectival theory of space-time," for a better way to understand space and time—especially, though not exclusively, in relation to future post-human history (as summarized in *Table 1.3*, *Table 1.4*, *Table 1.5*, and *Table 1.7*).

In so doing, I had to introduce concepts and theories specific to the field of physics and other related fields (e.g., "absolute space" and "absolute time" in "classical mechanics" and "relative space-time" in "the theory of relativity").

And in *BNN*, I also exploited the three principles to propose the "transcendent" approach to the study of genes and memes as a new way to understand the interaction between nature and nurture.

In so doing, I had to explore concepts and theories in the world of evolutionary biology (e.g., "mutation," "variation," "adaptation," "selection," and "inheritance" in classical evolutionary theory) and neural biology (e.g., "chromosome," "gene," "DNA," "RNA," "protein," "neuron," "neural network," and "behavior").

Other examples, besdies these two here, are given in other books of mine on different topics.

Therefore, this semantic dimension of existential dialectics is important, since, in each of my books when the ontological principles are used, each principle becomes relevant in a different meaning when contextualized within a given case study in question.

In this book, for instance, the principles are relevant in relation to the subject matter of law (as summarized in the concluding chapter), and they can be shown in all shapes and sizes (since they are also to be treated as "short cuts," as indicated before), without, however, being reduced to "specific ontology" (as opposed to "general ontology"), as explained in *Table 4.9*.

The Pragmatics of Existential Dialectics (or Its Ontopragmatics)

Even the semantics of existential dialectics is not enough to understand reality, since semantics by itself does not tell us the nature of intentionality and interests in relation to the matrix of power formations and conflicting interests when existential dialectics as an ontology is applied.

Surely, one cannot completely separate the pragmatics of existential dialectics from its semantics or syntax, but the point here is to give each a more elaborated analysis.

For this reason, the pragmatics of existential dialectics needs to be studied too, in special relation to the inclusion of power formation and conflicting interests in the application of the principles of existential dialectics (as summarized in *Table 4.11*).

It is thus no wonder that all my previous books have shown in different ways how and why these ontological principles and their theoretical applications can reveal the future world to come in a way that humans have never known, in a totally different battleground for competing human (and later post-human) interests by myriad groups fighting for their own versions of hegemony.

Perhaps a summary of my previous works in relation to existential dialectics and their contributions to my new theories as proposed over the years is deemed revealing here, for the further understanding of the pragmatics of existential dialectics (in close relation to the semantics of existential dialectics too).

That stressed—the following summary in four sub-sections is something that I often do in my previous books too, as a way to introduce the intellectual background of my ideas.

So, for those readers who had read my previous works, the following sub-sections serve as a reminder, as they are repeated hereafter *often verbatim* (with only some minor changes, with the rest kept intact).

These sub-sections are, namely, (a) the two-way street connecting theory with meta-theory, (b) the theoretical application of existential dialectics, (c) direct and indirect applications of existential dialectics, and (d) multiple applications of existential dialectics—to be summaried herefafter, respectively.

The Two-Way Street Connecting Theory and Meta-Theory

However, lest any misunderstanding occurs, it is important to remember that the pragmatics of existential dialectics is not a one-way street (that is, using the ontological principles for theoretical insights in praxis) but a two-way one, namely, (a) from meta-theory to theory, and (b) from theory to meta-theory.

(a) On one side of the street, the ontological principles can inspire some theoretical insights in praxis, that is, in relation to some specific fields.

(b) On the other (opposing) side of the street, however, the study of a subject matter in the specific fields in turn reveals some more hitherto unknown ontological principles to be discovered and identified.

For this reason, three new principles were added in *FC*, one in *FAE*, two in *ALD*, and three in *FIA*, on top of the original three in *BCPC*, for example (as there are more)—after some research on the specific subject matters.

Both theory and meta-theory enrich each other in all my works over the years.

The Theoretical Application of Existential Dialectics

This two-way street connecting theory and meta-theory has contributed to my original construction of 39 specific theories in 28 books (so far, up to now) on numerous fields in all domains of knowledge, which can be classified in terms of specific "meta-theories" (about epistemology, methodology, logic, ontology, etc.) and specific "theories" (about the mind, nature, culture, society, and the rest—as will be further explained later in the sub-section on "the holistic organization of an inquiry" in the section about "sophisticated methodological holism").

The final aim of my numerous new specific theories (on both theory and meta-theory) is to converge all of them (as proposed in my numerous books) into a unified theory of everything about the future of intelligent life, both here on earth and in deep space.

In fact, all these theories of mine serve as a foundation to unify all domains of knowledge for an overarching understanding of all forms of reality (by way of some ontological principles and the comprehensive perspectives of the mind, nature, society, and culture). This overarching project (consisting of numerous theories at both the theoretical and meta-theoretical levels), thus, constitutes a unifed theory of everything.

With this grand project in mind—the summary of my specific theories on meta-theory are given in this section (on "existential dialectics") and the next (on "sophisticated methodological holism"), whereas the specific theories on theory will be summarized in the following categories of (a) society, (b) culture, (c) the mind, (d) nature, and (e) the rest, as shown below, in that order.

(a) Society

The category of "society" here can be divided into four sub-categories, i.e., (a1) social organizations, (a2) social institutions, (a3) social structure, and (a4) social systems.

(a1) Social Organizations

In relation to social organizations, I proposed a new thesis on the ambivalent nature of virtual organizations in the future, known as "the theory of e-civic alienation" in *FCD* (and summarized in *Table 4.18*).

And in *FPHO*, another theory called "the combinational theory of organization" is worked out, although it was first proposed in Ch.6 of *ALD*.

(a2) Social Institutions

There are different social institutions, be they about (a2.1) politics, (a2.2) economics, (a2.3) military affairs, (a2.4) mass media, and (a2.5) law, for instance.

(a2.1) In relation to politics, I offered different visions on (a2.1.1) political theory, (a2.1.2) comparative politics, and (a2.1.3) international relations, to cite three main ones.

(a2.1.1) In the context of political theory, my vision of a path-breaking political system in future times concerns the different forms of "post-democracy" to supersede democracy unto the post-human age.

My vision of post-democracy was called "the theory of post-democracy" (as summarized in *Table 4.21*, *Table 4.22*, and *Table 4.23*), whereas *Table 4.24* explains the distinctions among democracy, non-democracy, and post-democracy.

And *Table 4.25* stresses the multiple causes of the emergence of post-democracy, while *Table 4.26* clarifies some possible misunderstandings in regard to post-capitalism and post-democracy.

(a2.1.2) In the context of comparative politics, I also showed, in *ALD*, how and why authoritarianism can be an advanced form of liberal democracy (just as it has its own counterpart in non-liberal democracy), or what I originally called "authoritarian liberal democracy" (as summarized in *Table 4.20*), before it is to be superceded by "post-democracy."

(a2.1.3) In the context of international relations (both at the institutional and structural levels), I provided, in *BWT*, "the theory of cyclical progression of empire-building," for a better way to understand the logic of empire-building on earth and beyond—with the rise of what I originally envisioned as "hyper-empires" (like "the Chinese Union" and "the Indian Union"), "meso-empires" (like "the European Union" and "the North American Union") and "micro-empires" (like "the Middle Eastern Union" and "the Latin American Union") in the coming "post-post-Cold War era" as a visionary illustration, as summarized in *Table 4.19*.

(a2.2) In relation to economics, I also offered another vision, this time to understand the future forms of economic systems, that is, the different forms of "post-capitalism" to supersede capitalism unto the post-human age.

My vision of post-capitalism was referred to (in *FCD*, *BDPD* and *BCPC*) as "the theory of post-capitalism" (as summarized in *Table 4.27*, *Table 4.28*, *Table 4.29*, *Table 4.30*, and *Table 4.31*). And *Table 4.32* clarifies the differences among capitalism, non-capitalism, and post-capitalism, whereas *Table 4.33* shows multiple causes of the emergence of post-capitalism.

This vision on "post-capitalism" constitutes the third theoretical application of existential dialectics, this time, in that there is no wealth without poverty (or the wealth/poverty dialectics).

(a2.3) In relation to military affairs, I also proposed "the multifaceted theory of war and peace" (in *FCD*, although it was first so labeled in *FPHK*) for a new way to understand the causes of war—and, for that matter, the rise and fall of different forms of warfare over time.

(a2.4) In relation to mass media, I also proposed a new theory of communication, that is, "the totalistic theory of communication," in *The Future of Post-Human Mass Media* (or in short, *FPHMM*). This issue about mass media was also addressed in detail in *FHC*.

(a2.5) And in relation to law, I propose a new theory of law (known as "the reconstruction theory of law") in *The Future of Post-Human Law* (or in short, *FPHLAW*).

(a3) Social Structure

In relation to social structure, I proposed two additional theories, that is, "the theory of the cyclical progression of hegemony" in *FCD* (and also in *FPHC* and *BDPD*), and "the theory of the cyclical progression of empire-building" (in *BWT*, as already indicated above)—with important implications for the symmetry-asymmetry princple in existential dialectics, just to cite one example.

(a4) Social Systems

In relation to social systems, there are several sub-categories for illustration, which can be about (a4.1) urbanization, (a4.2) technology, (a4.3) demography, (a4.4) the environment, and (a4.5) social trends as a whole.

(a4.1) In relation to urbanization, I proposed "the contingent theory of urban planning" in *FPHUP* for a new way to understand density and void.

(a4.2) In relation to technology, I worked out "the ambivalent theory of technology" in *FPHE* for a new way to understand the nature of technology.

Some other books (like *FPHMM*, *FAE*, *FCD*, and *FHC*) also deal with technology, and a good example concerns "the synthetic theory of information architecture" in *FIA* on taxonomy, network, and intelligence, in conjunction with the rise of technology.

(a4.3) In relation to demography, I proposed, first in *FHC* (and later in other books like *FCD*, *FPHC*, *FPHU*, etc.), the theory of "post-humanity," in relation to the "post-human" age at some distant point of "after-postmodernity," long after human extinction, to be eventually superseded by "post-humans" of various forms.

Some good candidates of the post-human lifeforms include, for instance, "thinking robots," "thinking machines," "cyborgs," "genetically altered superior beings," "floating consciousness," "hyper-spatial consciousness," and "unfolding unconsciousness." This post-human vision of mine was first originally worked out in *FHC* and further elaborated in both *FCD*, *FPHC*, and *FPHU*, for instance.

Additional post-human life-forms were later proposed in some other subsequent books of mine (as will be shown shortly).

Lest any confusion occurs, I need to emphasize two clarifications here about the term "post-human" as a neologism in my works.

Firstly, the word "post-human" here should *not* be confused with another term which looks similar but has a totally different meaning in the literature of postmodernism, namely, "post-humanism"—which constitutes a critique of "humanism" as tradionally understood (especially, though not exclusively, in relation to the idea of progress in science and reason in the Enlightenment project). (WK 2008)

And secondly, the word "post-human" here should also *not* be confused with a similar term which is used to champion the ideology of technology for the future co-existence between humans and cyborgs in "trans-humanism." (WK 2008a)

Instead, my term "post-human" in relation to "posthuman-ism" also rejects "transhumanism" (especially, though not exclusively, in relation to the promises of technology) and refers to something else altogether, that is, the future extinction of humans and its post-human successors in deep space and beyond unto multiverses.

With these two clarifications in mind (as summarized in *Table 1.31*)—in the end, a most fundamental question about intelligent life now has an answer, in that, if asked, "What is the future of human civilization?"—my answer in *FCD* (89) is thus: "As addressed in Ch.7 of *FHC*, a later epoch of the age of after-postmodernity (that is, at some point further away from after-postmodernity) will begin, as what I called the 'post-human' history (with the term 'post-human' originally used in my doctoral dissertation at M.I.T., which was finished in November 1995, under the title *After Postmodernity*, still available at M.I.T. library, and was later revised and published as *FHC*). The post-human history will be such that humans are nothing in the end, other than what culture, society, and nature (with some luck) have shaped them into, to be eventually superseded by post-humans (e.g., cyborgs, thinking machines, genetically altered superior beings, and others), if humans are not destroyed long before then."

(a4.4) In relation to the environment, I also addressed the issue of sustainability, especially in *FHC*, *FCD*, and *FPHUP*. For instance, in *FPHUP*, I specifically proposed a new theory on the need to go beyond the contemporoary obsession with sustainability, in the context of not only the environment but also other issues.

(a4.5) In relation to social trends as a whole, I proposed in Ch.9 of *FCD* (367-8), that "civilizational history will continue into the following cyclical progression of expansion, before it is to be superseded (solely as a high probability, since humans might be destroyed sooner either by themselves or in a gigantic natural calamity) by posthumans at some distant point in after-postmodernity (which I already discussed in *FHC*)" unto multiverses (different constellations of universes):

Local → Regional → Global →Solar →
Galactic → Clustery…→ Multiversal

In *BDPD*, this thesis of mine was referred to as "the theory of the cyclical progression of system integration and fragmentation," at the systemic level—in close relation to another thesis analyzed in Ch.9 of *FCD*, which was called, in the absence of better words, "the multifaceted theory of war and peace" in *FPHK* (as already indicated above).

In *FC*, I also proposed "the dialectic theory of complexity" to account for the factor of uncertainty, which can have a major role to play in the world.

(b) Culture

The category of "culture" here can also be divided into different sub-categories like (b1) aesthetics, (b2) religion, (b3) popular (mass) culture, (b4), logic, (b5) civilization as a whole, (b6) epistemology (methodology), (b7) metaphysics (ontology), (b8) ethics, and (b9) ideology, for instance.

However, epistemology (methodology) in (b6), metaphysics (ontology) in (b7), ethics in (b8), and ideology in (b9) are already discussed elsewhere, be they about "meta-theory" (e.g., methodology and ontology under the categories of "existential dialectics" here and "sophisticated methodological holism" in the next section) or "theory" (e.g., ideology and ethics under the categories of "social institutions," as described earlier, and also "civilization as a whole," as will be addressed shortly).

The rest, that is, aesthetics in (b1), religion in (b2), popular (mass culture) in (b3), logic in (b4), and civilization as a whole in (b5) will be addressed hereafter, in that order.

(b1) Aesthetics

In relation to aesthetics, I proposed "the transformative theory of aesthetic experience" in *FAE* about some great transformations of aesthetic experience in future history.

(b2) Religion

In relation to religion, I proposed "the comparative theory of religion" in *FHC* (and also in *FCD*, although it was first so labeled in *FPHK*).

(b3) Popular (Mass) Culture

In relation to popular culture, I proposed, in *FHC*, a new way to understand mass culture in terms of some fundamental dilemmas, which is called, in the absence of better words, "the dualistic theory of mass culture" in *FPHO*. This is also related to another new theory (of mine) on communication in *FPHMM* (as mentioned before).

(b4) Logic

In relation to logic, I also worked out, in *FPHML*, "the contrastive theory of rationality" for a new way to understand rationality and knowledge (in the context of mathematical logic).

(b5) Civilization as a Whole

In relation to civilization as a whole, I also argued, in *FHC*, no freedom without unfreedom (as shown in *Table 4.12*) and no equality without inequality (as shown in *Table 4.13*), especially in relation to the seven dimensions of life existence first worked out in *FHC* (i.e., the technological, the everyday, the true, the holy, the sublime/beautiful, the good, and the just).

Even more interestingly, in *BDPD* and later in *BCIV*, I further revealed a theoretical refinement of existential dialectics, this time, in arguing that there is no civilization without barbarity, with human civilization to be eventually superseded by what I originally analyzed as "post-human post-civilization" (which should not be confused with "post-human civilization"), in the context of the freedom/unfreedom and equality/inequality dialectics.

In the final analysis, civilization cannot live without barbarity and has to learn to co-exist with it in ever new ways. Preposteorus as this may seem to many contemporaries—it is no more imperative to preserve civilization than necessary to destroy barbarity, and the ideal of civilization is essentially bankrupt, to be eventually superseded by "post-civilization" (as summarized in *Tables 4.34-4.42*).

This freedom/unfreedom and equality/inequality dialectics holds in pre-moderny, modernity, postmodernity, and what I orignally called "after-postmodernity" in *FHC* and *FCD*—especially, though not exclusively, in the context of the emergence of "post-humans."

There are two specific theories about "after-postmodernity" here. The first theory about "after-postmodernity" is about the trinity of pre-modernity, modernity, postmodernity, and after-postmodernity at the cultural level—and was called, in *BDPD*, "the theory of the trinity of modernity to its after-postmodern counterpart," although it was first analyzed in *FHC* and later in *FCD* and also *BCIV* (as summarized in *Table 1.34*, *Table 1.35*, *Table 1.36*, and *Table 1.37* and will be elaborated further in the later sub-section on "the rest" about future history).

The second theory about "after-postmodernity" is about pre-modernity, modernity, postmodernity, and after-postmodernity at the historical level. For instance, a conclusion in *FHC*, which is shocking indeed for many contemporaries, is none other than that "[t]he post-human history will therefore mark the end of human history as we know it and, for that matter, the end of human dominance and, practically speaking, the end of humans as well. The entire history of human civilization, from its beginning to the end, can be summarized by four words, linked by three arrows (as already discussed in *FHC*)":

Pre-Modernity → Modernity →
Post-Modernity → After-Postmodernity

In *BDPD*, this thesis of mine was specifically called "the theory of the evolution from pre-modernity to after-postmodernity," at the historical level—as shown in *Table 1.34*, *Table 1.35*, *Table 1.36*, and *Table 1.37* (and will be elaborated further in the later sub-section on "the rest" about future history).

Therefore, "[t]he end of humanity in the coming human extinction is the beginning of post-humanity. To say an untimely farewell to humanity is to foretell the future welcome of post-humanity." (P. Baofu 2002: 89) This thesis of mine was known in *BDPD* as "the theory of post-humanity," at the systemic level—as already indicated in (a4.3) above.

(c) The Mind

This theory about "post-humans" brings us to the category of "the mind" here, which, as is often understood in everyday's usage, refers to the "brain" and the "body" (together with their interactions) and has different levels of consciousness which can be both "spiritual" and non-spiritual.

Therefore, the "mind" already presupposes the "brain," "body," and "spirit" (or "soul"), so that one does not fall into the intellectual trap of the "mind-body dualism" as debunked in modern (and especially, postmodern) philosophy (which I already went to great lengths to explain in *The Future of Human Civilization*).

That said—the category of "the mind" can be divided into two sub-categories, namely, in relation to (c1) biology and (c2) psychology.

(c1) Biology

In relation to biology, there are two concerns here, namely, (c1.1) genes and intelligence and (c2.2) the human body.

(c1.1) In relation to genes and intelligence, I worked out "the theory of contrastive advantages" (which was originally proposed in *FCD* and further worked out in *BNN*, as summarized in *Table 1.24*), to show the nature-nurture interactions of multiple levels in action (e.g., the biological, the psychological, the structural, the systemic, the cultural, and others) for humans and post-humans on earth and beyond, to the extent that different groups, be they on the basis of race, gender, ethnicity, class, age, or else, are not equal, on average, and have never been, nor will they be, even if there can be exceptions.

(c2.5) In relation to the human body, for instance, in *FPHMA*, I suggested "the expansive-contractive theory of martial arts," in which two great future transformations of the martial body were envisioned, that is, both "with the hyper-martial body" and "without the body" (as summarized in *Table 1.32*)—although this issue can also be classified under the category of "culture."

And in *FPHS*, I proposed "the theory of virtual sexuality," in which three great future transformations of the sexual body were envisioned, that is, "virtual pleasure," "the hyper-sexual body," and "the post-sexual floating mind" (as summarized in *Table 3.4*).

(c2) Psychology

In relation to psypchology (which also overlaps with biology too, however), I also proposed some greater transformations of the mind to come in the future, especially though not exclusively in the post-human age.

These greater transformations of the mind in psychology can be further sub-divided into different categories, namely, (c2.1) consciousness, (c2.2) unconsciousness, (c2.3) creativity, and (c2.4) learning.

(c2.1) In relation to consciousness, I analyzed, in *FPHC*, the nature of consciousness in relation to the conceptual dimensions of consciousness (as shown in *Table 1.12*), the theoretical levels of consciousness (as shown in *Table 1.13*), the thematic issues of consciousness (as shown in *Table 1.14*), the different dimensions of human existence (viz., having-ness, belonging-ness, and being-ness) in relation to consciousness (as shown in *Table 1.15*, *Table 1.16*, *Table 1.17*, and *Table 1.18*).

In *BCPC*, the nature of consciousness was further explored in relation to cognition, emotion, and behavior, which can be in consciousness and other mental states (e.g., subconsciousness and unconsciousness), in the context of existential dialectics, as shown in *Table 1.19*, *Table 1.20*, *Table 1.21*, *Table 1.22,* and *Table 1.23*.

In fact, in *FCD*, I already proposed three different theories in relation to the limits of cognition, emotion, and behavior, namely, "the theory of cognitive partiality," "the theory of emotional non-neutrality," and "the theory of behavioral alteration."

Then, I argued that the existence of human consciousness will be superseded one day with "floating consciousness" (as first proposed in *FCD*) and "hyper-spatial consciousness" (as first proposed in *FPHC*) as a climax of evolution in consciousness, after the future extinction of human consciousness (as shown below):

Primordial consciousness → Human consciousness →
Post-human consciousness (with floating consciousness and hyper-spatial consciousness as a climax in the evolution of consciousness)

In *BDPD*, these latest theses of mine were called "the theory of floating consciousness" and "the theory of hyper-spatial consciousness," both at the cosmological and psychological levels (as summarized in *Table 1.26* and *Table 1.25*).

(c2.2) In relation to unconsciousness, for instance, in *FPHU*, the unconsious mind will undergo tremendous change, to the rise of what I originally called "unfolding unconsciousess" in relation to anomalous experience, as a climax of evolution in unconsciousness, in conjunction with the conscious mind (both human now and post-human later), especially at the psychological level, as shown below:

Primordial unconsciousness → Human unconsciousness →
Post-human unconsciousness (with unfolding unconsciousness as a climax in the evolution of unconsciousness)

In *FPHU*, this thesis of mine is called "the theory of unfolding unconsciousness" in a small sense, or "the unfolding theory of anomalous experience," in a larger one, as shown in *Table 1.27* and *Table 1.28*.

(c2.3) In relation to creativity, for instance, in *FPHCT*, I also proposed "the comprehensive theory of creative thinking" to explore the role of creative thinking, in relation to technology and other factors, together with my original proposal of important creative techniques and traits (as shown in *Table 1.29*) and its double nature of desirability and undesirability (as shown in *Table 1.30*).

(c2.4) In relation to learning, for instance, in *FPHL*, I worked out "the multilogical theory of learning" for a new way to understand the nature of structure and context in language, in relation to learning and its future development in the context of the mind.

(d) Nature

The category of "nature" here refers to the state of nature, which can be divided into some sub-categories like (d1) physics, (d2) cosmology, (d3) biology, and (d4) geography.

But since biology in (d3) overlaps with biology in (c1)—only phyiscs, cosmology, and geography are addressed here.

(d1) Physics

In relation to physics, I also proposed "the perspectival theory of space-time" in *FPHST* (based on *FPHC*) for a new way to understand space and time, as shown in *Table 1.3*, *Table 1.4*, and *Table 1.5*.

In *FPHG* (based on *FPHC* and *FPHST*), I proposed "the selective theory of geometry" for a new way to understand geometry, with implications for the understanding of space-time in the context of infinity, symmetry, and dimensionality for future lifeforms that our world has never known (as shown in *Table 1.6*, *Table 1.7*, *Table 1.8; Table 1.9*, *Table 1.10,* and *Table 1.11*).

And in *FC*, I proposed "the dialectic theory of complexity" for a new way to understand order and chaos in the state of nature and beyond.

(d2) Cosmology

In relation to cosmology, my theories on physics (as indicated above) already have important implications for understanding the nature and the future of the universe.

In addition, I also proposed "the theory of hyper-spatial consciousness" in *FPHC* (and also in *FPHG*) for a new way to understand the future evolution of the mind to enter into different dimensions of space-time that our current world has never known.

(d4) Geography

In relation to geography, I also proposed "the theory of the geopower of nature" in *ALD* for a different way to understand the relationships between geography and other entities (like the mind, culture, and society).

(e) The Rest

The category of "the rest" here refers to what cannot be strictly classified in any of the previous categories (i.e., society, culture, the mind, and nature). A good illustration of "the rest" refers to that which is, namely, (e1) historical.

(e1) Historical

Precisely here, I proposed "the theory of the evolution from pre-modernity to after-postmodernity" (as first worked out in *FHC* and later in *FCD* and *FPHC*), which overlaps—as a reminder from (b5)—with the issue concerning "civilization as a whole" in (b5).

For instance, in both *FCD* and *FPHC*, I worked out the structure of "post-human civilization" in terms of the trinity of after-postmodernity (i.e., "free-spirited after-postmodernity," "post-capitalist after-postmodernity," and "hegemonic after-postmodernity").

Both conceptually and theoretically, the trinity of after-postmodernity is a sequential extension to the trinity of modernity (i.e., "free-spirited modernity," "capitalist modernity,"and "hegemonic modernity") and the trinity of postmodernity (i.e., "free-spirited postmodernity," "capitalist postmodernity," and "hegemonic postmodernity") as first proposed in *FHC*.

And the trinity of pre-modernity (i.e., "pre-free-spirited pre-modernity," "pre-capitalist pre-modernity" and "hegemonic pre-modernity") was later conceived in *BCIV* to complete the historical set from pre-modernity to after-postmodernity.

In *BDPD*, this thesis about the trinity of pre-modernity, modernity, postmodernity, and after-postmodernity was collectively known as "the theory of the trinity of modernity to its after-postmodern counterpart," at the cultural level—as already so mentioned in (b5) earlier, and summarized in *Table 1.34*, *Table 1.35*, *Table 1.36*, and *Table 1.37*.

At the structural level, all these trinities are subject to the existential constraints (e.g., the freedom/unfreedom and equality/inequality dialectics in the context of "the cyclical progression of hegemony"), be the historical epoch in pre-modernity, modernity, postmodernity, or after-postmodernity in future times. Each of the historical epochs has its ever new ways of coming to terms with the ever new (different) mixtures of freedom/unfreedom and equality/inequality.

This is importantly so, not because, as is falsely assumed in conventional wisdom, one certain way is superior (or better) than another in terms of achieving more freedom and less unfreedom, or more equality with less inequality.

On the contrary, indeed, in each of the historical epochs, each increase of unfreedom greets each freedom achieved, just as each increase of inequality welcomes each equality achieved, albeit in ever new (different) ways. In *BDPD*, this thesis of mine was labeled as "the theory of the cyclical progression of hegemony," at the structural level, though it was first analyzed in *FCD*.

In *BDPD*, more theoretical applications of existential dialectics were further examined, in relation to five main features, in the context of the duality of oppression, namely, (a) that each freedom/equality achieved is also each unfreedom/inequality created, (b) that the subsequent oppressiveness is dualistic, both by the Same against the Others and itself and by the Others against the Same and themselves, (c) that both oppression and self-oppression can be achieved by way of downgrading differences (between the Same and the Others) and of accentuating them, (d) that the relationships are relatively asymmetric among them but relatively symmetric within them, even when the Same can be relatively asymmetric towards itself in self-oppression, and the Others can be likewise towards themselves, and (e) that symmetry and asymmetry change over time, with ever new players, new causes, and new forms, be the locality here on Earth or in deep space unto multiverses—as summarized in *Table.4.12*, *Table 4.13*, *Table 4.14*, and *Table 4.15*.

The same logic also holds both in relation to wealth and poverty (as addressed in *BCPC* and summarized in *Table 4.16* on the wealth/poverty dialectics) and in relation to civilization and barbarity (as addressed in *BCIV* and summarized in *Table 4.17* on the civilization/barbarity dialectics).

In *BDPD*, this thesis on existential dialectics was labeled as "the theory of existential dialectics."

Direct and Indirect Applications of Existential Dialectics

A different way to appreciate the usefulness of existential dialectics is by way of the analysis of its (a) direct and (b) indirect applications.

(a) In direct applications, on the one hand, the logic of existential dialectics can shed some theoretical insights on diverse phenomena in the world, and good instances are the usage of the principles of existential dialectics for the theoretical insights on the freedom/unfreedom dialectics, the equality/inequality dialectics, and the wealth/poverty dialectics—as introduced earlier in (b5) and (e) in the previous sub-section.

For instance, my books like *FPHST*, *BNN*, *FAE*, *FC*, *FIA*, *FPHU*, *FPHK*, *FPHML*, *FPHE*, *FPHMM*, *FPHCT*, *FPHG*, *FPHUP*, *FPHL*, *FPHO*, *FPHMA, FPHS*, and *FPHLAW* use the principles to reveal some theoretical insights on the perspectives of space and time (as in *FPHST*), of nature and nurture (as in *BNN*), of beauty and ugliness (as in *FAE*), of order and chaos (as in *FC*), of taxonomy and network (as in *FIA*), of the unconscious mind (as in *FPHU*), of the nature of knowledge (as in

FPHK), of mathematical logic (as in *FPHML*), of engineering (as in *FPHE*), of mass media (as in *FPHMM*), of creative thinking (as in *FPHCT*), of geometry (as in *FPHG*), of urban planning (as in *FPHUP*), of language (as in *FPHL*), of organization (as in *FPHO*), of martial arts (as in *FPHMA*), of sexuality (as in *FPHS*); and of law (as in *FPHLAW*).

(b) In indirect applications, on the other hand, the theoretical insights can further be used to reveal other phenomena directly from them (viz., the theoretical insights) and therefore indirectly from the principles themselves.

A good illustration is of course the use of the theoretical insights on the freedom/unfreedom and equality/inequality dialectics for the understanding of the civilization/barbarity dialectics.

This distinction between direct and indirect applications may sound a bit academic, since even in indirect applications, the phenomena under study can still be directly related back to the principles themselves.

In the previous example, as an illustration, the civilization/barbarity dialectics can be directly related to the principles of existential dialectics without the intermediate role of the freedom/unfreedom and equality/inequality dialectics.

Multiple Levels of Application

There is another issue to be clarified, however. In other words, the theoretical insights can be applied to multiple levels of analysis—even though, in a given example, it may refer to one level or a few only.

For instance, in the example concerning the freedom/unfreedom dialectics, it can be used at the structural level (e.g., in relation to the theory of the cyclical progression of hegemony), but it can also be exploited for other levels (e.g., the theory of post-capitalism at the institutional level).

All these levels of application should not be misleadingly construed, as I stress this before, as a one-way street (that is, to use the ontological principles for theoretical application at multiple levels of specific analysis) but a two-way one, in which theoretical insights in praxis, when studied in more specific contexts, can in turn refine the nature of existential dialectics (for example, with the addition of new principles).

Sophisticated Methodological Holism

The summary of my original meta-theory on methodology is provided below, again, to be repeated *often verbatim* from my previous works—as this is something I regularly do in each new book to introduce my past works, which are in conversation with this current one.

This means that, for those readers who had read some of my previous books, the summary below is really nothing new (*almost verbatim*, with only some minor revisions) and can be skipped.

That clarified—this original contribution of mine to the study of methodology takes the form of an approach known as "the theory of methodological holism" or "methodological holism" in short, as already worked out in *FPHC* (2004).

I have made good use of this methodological approach of mine for all of my previous works.

The Confusion of Holism with Systems Approach

Yet, it is imperative to stress at the outset, as I often emphasized this in all my previous books, that my approach of "methodological holism" does not oppose or exclude "methodological individualism" (as some readers may be tempted to assume, as is conventionally understood) but actually includes it.

The confusion here has to do with equating holism with systems approach in general (be it about systems theory, chaos theory, complexity theory, or else), which I debunked, while learning something from it, as already elaborated in *The Future of Complexity* (2007).

In other words, my meta-theory of holism, or sophisticated methodological holism in short, makes a distinction between doing holistic work and doing systems work, for two reasons.

The first reason is that holism, in my theory, does not imply systems approach, since it rejects systems approach because of the myriad problems that the literature on systems approach has been unable to resolve, while learning something from it.

And the second reason is that my theory is related to the other theory of mine, that is, existential dialectics, which does not exclude methodological individualism (but includes it, because it simply goes beyond both reductionism and reverse-reductionism in a dialectic way).

For these reasons (and others too, as summarized in *Table 4.1*), my version of methodological holism is *sophisticated*—not *vulgar* as sometimes used by inapt scholars employing the same term.

The Ontological Constraints

With this caveat about the confusion of holism with systems approach in mind—sophisticated methodological holism is subject to some ontological constraints, and five good examples include "the partiality-totality principle," "the predictability-unpredictability principle," "the explicability-inexplicability principle," "the absoluteness-relativeness principle," and "the formalness-informalness principle" in existential dialectics.

Of course, there can be more than five ontological principles in relation to method, but the five examples here are sufficient to illustrate the point in question.

With this caveat in mind—the first two were already analyzed in previous books of mine like *FC* and *FAE*, whereas the third one was addressed in *FPHU*, and the last two were accounted for in *FPHK* and *FPHML*, respectively.

For now, it suffices to show that sophisticted methodological holism, because of these ontological constraints on methodology, targets two major sins of methodology, namely, what I call, in the absence of better words, (a) *reductionism* and (b) *reverse-reductionism*—both of which come in all shapes and sizes, to be summarized below (and also shown in *Table 4.2*).

Against the Varieties of Reductionism

There are four versions of reductionism to be summarized here, which sophisticated methodological holism rejects, namely, (a1) conceptual, (a2) theoretical, (a3) methodological, and (a4) ontological forms of reductionism.

(a1) In conceptual reductionism, a good case in point concerns myriad dualities like mind vs. body, self vs. world, democracy vs non-democracy, and the like (as already addressed in *FHC*, *FPHC*, and *BDPD*, for instance).

(a2) In theoretical reductionism, an illuminating case study is best exemplified by what I originally called "the foundation fallacy" in *FPHST*, in any attempt to naively understand space-time from the physical perspective as the foundation and, consequently, to dangerously dismiss (or belittle) other perspectives.

In *FAE*, I elaborated further these versions of reductionism in the literature on aesthetics (e.g., form vs. content, representation vs. expression, critics vs. artists, and externalism vs. internalism).

In *FIA*, I revealed other forms of reductionism in the literature on information architecture (e.g., the constructivist argument and the representational argument).

In *FPHU*, I showed the persistent legacy of reductionism, this time, in the literature on anomalous experience (e.g., the obsession with physics, chemistry, and biology for explaining anomalous experience).

In *FPHE*, I examined another case of reductionism in action, in the context of engineering (e.g., technical constraints vs. normative constraints).

In *FPHMM*, I elaborated one more version of reductionism, in relation to the three domains of communication (e.g., the competing views on sending, connecting, and receiving).

In *FPHCT*, I explored another version of reductionism, in relation to invention and innovation (e.g., the bio-psychological argument vs. the socio-cultural arguments).

In *FPHG*, I identified another version of reductionism, in relation to infinity, symmetry, and dimensionality (e.g., the Euclidean argument vs. the non-Euclidean arguments).

In *FPHUP*, I analyzed another version of reductionism, in relation to density and void (e.g., the engineering argument and the ecology argument).

In *PFHL*, I examined another version of reductionism, in relation to structure and context (e.g., the structuralist argument and the contextualist argument).

In *PFHO*, I explored another version of reductionism, in relation to communcation, decision-making, and leadership (e.g., the rational-system argument vs. the natural-system argument vs. the open-system argument).

In *PFHMA*, I revealed another version of reductionism, in relation to the martial body and spirit (e.g., the spiritual argument vs. the materialist argument vs. the defensive argument).

In *PFHS*, I analyzed another version of reductionism, in relation to the sexual body and spirit (e.g., the naturalist argument vs. the constructivist argument).

And in *PFHLAW*, I analyze another version of reductionism, in relation to law (e.g., the necessity argument vs. the contengency argument).

(a3) In methodological reductionism, a good illustration can be the debate between different versions of qualitative and quantitative methods (as already analyzed in *FC* and also *FHC*).

In *FPHML*, I examined similar reductionism, this time, in the literature on mathematical logic (e.g., the obsession with consistency, soundness, and completeness).

(a4) In ontological reductionism, an excellent instance involves another debate, this time between emergentism and reductionism in complexity theory (as addressed in *FC*) and also in psychology (as elaborated in *FPHC*, in the context of Being and Belonging).

But to target against the varieties of reductionism constitutes only a side of the same coin, and the other side concerns the varieties of reverse-reductionism.

Against the Varieties of Reverse-Reductionism

The other side of the same coin is the reverse version of reductionism, which is what I want to call, in the absence of better words, *reverse-reductionism.*

My sophisticated version of methodological holism targets against the varieties of reverse-reductionism (just as it also rejects the ones of reductionism).

Perhaps nothing expresses better the popularity of reverse-reductionim than the "anything-goes" mentality in postmodernism of our time, as shown in the following four versions.

(b1) In conceptual reverse-reductionism, any concept of "art" (e.g., fine art, applied art, outsider art, junk art) is welcome in postmodernism (as already analyzed in Ch.4 of *FHC*—and also in *FAE*).

(b2) In theoretical reverse-reductionism, a variety of art and literary theories co-exist. Take the case of literature, as there are now Literary Structuralism, Marxist Literary Criticism, New Criticism, Phenomenology, Hermeneutics, Language-Game Literary Criticism, Feminist Literary Criticism, Reception Theory, Reader Response Criticism, Poststructuralism, Semiotics, Pyschoanalytic Literary Criticism, just to cite some well-known ones, with no one being said to be better than any others (as detailedly analyzed in Ch.4 of *FHC*). (S. Raman 1997)

In *BNN*, I even introduced "the compromise fallacy" as another good illustration of theoretical reverse-reductionism, in misleadingly treating both genetic and environmental approaches as equally valid.

(b3) In methodological reverse-reductionism, multiple methodologies are deemed as acceptable in postmodernism (e.g., doing art without praxis, doing art with praxis, and doing art by sublation), as analyzed in Ch.4 of *FHC*.

(b4) In ontological reverse-reductionism, no privileged ontology is allowed, and the door is open practically for anything in postmodernism (e.g., the equal status of the ontology of Being vs. that of Becoming, as already addressed in Ch.4 of *FHC*—and also in *FPHC*).

In *FAE*, I also introduced another version of reverse-reductionism, that is, "the pluralist fallacy," in the context of understanding aesthetic experience, for instance—although this fallacy has been committed not exclusively in relation to the ontological level (but also at the conceptual, theoretical, and methodological ones).

These dual dangers against reverse-reductionism (in this sub-section) and reductionism (in the previous sub-section) are something that sophisticated methodological holism rejects.

This point is important enough, since many scholars often favor one against the other, but it is vital to target both.

The Holistic Organization of an Inquiry

With these dual dangers against reductionism and reverse-reductionism in mind—sophisticated methodological holism suggests that an inquiry of any given phenomenon is more complete, if treated in the context of a comprehensive analysis at all relevant levels, which challengingly encompass all the fields of human knowledge, ranging from the natural sciences and formal sciences through the social sciences to the humanities, so as to adjust for subjectivity, diversity, conflict, and complexity, for instance.

As a reminder (from an earlier sub-section), one should guard against equating holism with systems approach in general (be it about systems theory, chaos theory, complexity theory, or else), which I debunked, while learning something from it, as already elaborated in *The Future of Complexity* (2007)—for two reasons.

The first reason is that my meta-theory of holism, or sophisticated methodological holism in short, does not imply systems approach, since it rejects systems approach because of the myriad problems that the literature on systems approach has been unable to resolve, while learning something from it.

And the second reason is that my theory is related to the other theory of mine, that is, existential dialectics, which does not exclude methodological individualism (but includes it, because it simply goes beyond both reductionism and reverse-reductionism in a dialectic way).

For these reasons (and others too, as summarized in *Table 4.1*), my version of methodological holism is *sophisticated*—not *vulgar* as sometimes used by inapt scholars employing the same term.

With this reminder in mind—this section is also something that I had already stressed in all my previous books and repeat (*often verbatim*) hereafter. But, for those readers who had read my previous books, this serves as a reminder.

This reminder aside—there are multiple ways to engage in a holistic inquiry with all relevent levels of analysis. Over the years, I have proposed different ways to fulfill this holistic methodological requirement, as repeated in my previous books.

Hereafter is a summary of four major ways, namely, (a) by discipline, (b) by domain, (c) by subject, and (d) by meta-analysis—all of which fulfill the holistic requirement of sophisticated methodological holism on a given issue (without, however, rejecting methodological individualism).

(a) In a holistic organization by discipline, a good illustration is the multiple levels of analysis, namely, (a1) the micro-physical, (a2) the chemical, (a3) the biological, (a4) the psychological, (a5) the organizational, (a6) the institutional, (a7) the structural, (a8) the systemic, (a9) the cultural, (a10) the macro-physical (cosmological), and (a11) other relevant levels, which are either a combination of all these levels or the practical applications with a combination of them.

This holistic organization by discipline is used in *FCD* and *BCPC*, for instance.

(b) In a holistic organization by domain, some good candidates include the classification of different perspectives of analysis in relation to (b1) nature, (b2) the mind, (b3) society, and (b4) culture, as already worked out in *BCIV*, *FPHST*, *FC*, *FAE*, *FPHU*, *FPHK*, and *FPHE*.

Culture in (b4), in this re-classification, is the same as culture in (a9) and can be further divided into different sub-categories, with good examples like (a9i) epistemology (methodology), (a9ii) aesthetics, (a9iii) ethics, (a9iv) metaphysics (ontology), and (a9v) religion. For clarification, epistemology (methodology) in (a9i) and metaphysics (ontology) in (a9iv) overlap with the category of "meta-theory."

Society in (b3) includes the organizational in (a5), the institutional in (a6), the structural in (a7), and the systemic in (a8).

The mind (b2) has more to do with the chemical in (a2), the biological in (a3), and the psychological in (a4), although it can overlap with (a1), (b3) and (b4), for instance.

It should be stressed that the "mind" here also includes the categories like the "brain," "body," and the "spirit" (or the "soul")—whenever needed in a given context, so that one does not fall into the intellectual trap of the "mind-body dualism" in the history of modern (and especially, postmodern) philosophy, which I already went to great lengths to explain in *The Future of Human Civilization*. After all, in everyday's usage, the "mind" already implies the "brain" and the "body" (together with their interactions) and has different levels of consciousness which can be both spiritual and non-spiritual.

And nature in (b1) refers to the micro-physical in (a1) and the macro-physical (cosmological) in (a10), although it can also overlap with (a2), (a3) and (a4).

(c) In a holistic organization by subject, some excellent examples concern the analysis of consciousness in *FPHC* (i.e., on Having, Belonging, and Being); of civilization in *FHC* (i.e., the True, the Holy, the Everyday, the Technological, the Beautiful/Sublime, the Good, and the Just); of international politics in *BWT* (i.e., Hyper-Empires, Meso-Empires, and Micro-Empires); of nature and nurture in *BNN* (i.e., genes and memes); of information architecture in *FIA* (i.e., taxonomy and network); of mathematical logic in *FPHML* (i.e., consistency, soundness, and completeness); of communication in *FPHMM* (i.e., sending, connecting, and receiving); of creative thinking in *FPHCT* (i.e., invention and innovation); of geometry in *FPHG* (i.e., infinity, symmetry, and dimensionality); of urban planning in *FPHUP* (i.e., density and void), of language in *FPHL* (i.e., structure and context), and of organization in *FPHO* (i.e., communication, decision-making, and leadership), in *FPHMA* (i.e., the martial body and the martial spirit), in *FPHS* (i.e., the sexual body and the sexual spirit), and in *FPHLAW* (i.e., necessity and contingency)—by incorporating all the relevent levels of analysis as cited above in each.

(d) And in a holistic organization by meta-analysis, two good cases in point involve the works on post-capitalism in *BCPC* and on authoritarian liberal democracy in *ALD*, with the classification of analysis in theory and meta-theory.

The essential point to remember here, as I thus stress in all my previous books, is that the multiple levels of analysis can be reorganized in many different ways, insofar as none of the levels (if relevant to an inquiry in question) is ignored or dismissed, to avoid the danger of reductionism (and for that matter, the one of reverse-reductionism, in the opposite direction).

Three Clarifications

Three clarifications are needed here, however, to avoid any hasty misunderstanding.

Firstly, the entities in each classification are not mutually exclusive. For instance, in the holisitc organization by domain, nature in (b1) can also be linked to the chemical in (a2), the biological in (a3), and the systemic in (a8). And the mind (b3) can alternatively be related to the micro-physical in (a1) and the chemical in (a2), for example.

Secondly, there is also the important factor of luck (or uncertainty in conventional usage), but it is already implied or allowed in each of the organizations of an inquiry—especially in relation to the predictability-unpredictability principle in existential dialectics. This topic about uncertainty was already addressed in *FHC*—and more extensively, in *FC*, in the context of order and chaos.

And lastly, the comparison in a classification is not absolute, but relative, as there are often some shades of gray, not exactly black or white (figuratively speaking).

Some further clarifications and qualifications of sophisticated methodological holism are shown in *Table 4.1*.

Some Distinctive Usefulness

In the end, sophisticated methodological holism—when applied, especially though not exclusively, as illustrated in my numerous works—can enrich the understanding of reality in some distinctive ways. Here are three examples (as revealed in each of my books).

Firstly, it provides a comprehensive analysis of a subject matter, from which much can be learned about reality, both in relation to the perspectives of the mind, nature, society, and culture and also in relation to a new classification of the subject matter.

Secondly, it suggests some visions of the future in relation to the subject matter in question.

And thirdly, it proposes some insights on meta-theory (e.g., methodology and ontology) in general—with the clear understanding, however, of the dilemma of specific vs. general ontology (as shown in *Table 4.9* on the syntax of existential dialectics in the context of the dilemma of ontology).

For this very reason, all of these ways are important, without reducing one into the analysis of another. (*FPHCT*)

Chapter Outline

With this summary of my two original meta-theories (on methodology and ontology, *almost verbatim* from my previous works) in mind—this book is organized in four main parts, namely, (a) Part I on the introduction to this book, (b) Part II on necessity, (c) Part III on contingency, and (d) Part IV on the conclusion of the book—and thus has four chapters.

The introductory chapter here, that is, Chapter One titled "Introduction—The Rule of Law," begins by questioning the convenience of the conventional wisdom about the rule of law and then summarizes the distinction between public law and private law, and the relationship between law and jurisprudence—together with the theoretical debate in the literature, my reconstruction theory of law, the relationship between theory and meta-theory, existential dialectics, sophisticated methodological holism, and some further clarifications.

Chapter Two titled "Necessity and Its Dispensability" examines the nature of necessity in the context of law from the perspectives of culture, society, nature, and the mind, with a constructive evaluation of each.

Chapter Three titled "Contingency and Its Mortality" then analyzes the nature of contingency in the context of law from the perspectives of culture, society, nature, and the mind, with a critical assessment of the strengths and weaknesses of each.

The last chapter titled "Conclusion—The Future of Law" summarizes the analysis in the book with eleven major theses, namely, (a) the first thesis: the absoluteness-relativeness principle, (b) the second thesis: the predictability-unpredictability principle, (c) the third thesis: the explicability-inexplicability principle, (d) the fourth thesis: the preciseness-vagueness principle, (e) the fifth thesis: the simpleness-complicatedness principle, (f) the sixth thesis: the openness-hiddenness principle, (g) the seventh thesis: the evolution-transformation principle, (h) the eighth thesis: the symmetry-asymmetry principle, (i) the nineth thesis: the regression-progression principle, (j) the tenth thesis: the same-difference principle, and (k) the eleventh thesis: the post-human reconstruction—to be elaborated in the rest of the book, with a summary in the concluding chapter. In the end, there is no justice without injustice—and it will be transcended too.

This seminal project, if successful, will fundamentally change the way that we think about the nature of law, from the combined perspectives of the mind, nature, society, and culture, with enormous implications for the human future and what I originally called its "post-human" fate.

Some Clarifications

But some additional clarifications are needed, before a formal analysis of the necessity of law is to begin in Chapter Two.

These clarifications, lest any potential misunderstanding by the readers occurs, refer to (a) the conversation with my previous books, (b) the illustrative selection of case studies and examples, (c) detailed analysis versus overall synthesis, and (d) the use of neologisms.

These clarifications are something that I also regularly repeat in my previous books too, so these points are repeated hereafter, *often verbatim*—albeit in a different context this time.

In Conversation with My Previous Books

Firstly, my theory of virtual sexuality is constructed on the theoretical foundation of my previous books (i.e., *FHC*, *FCD*, *FPHC*, *BDPD*, *BCPC*, *BCIV*, *FPHST*, *BNN*, *BWT*, *FC*, *FAE*, *ALD*, *FIA*, *FPHU*, *FPHK*, *FPHML*, *FPHE*, *FPHMM*, *FPHCT*, *FPHUP*, *FPHL*, *FPHO*, *FPHMA*, and *FPHS*—as explicated in "The List of Abbreviations").

Just consider the following two illustrations, namely, (a) in relation to other related theoretical debates and (b) in relation to different visions as worked out in my previous books.

(a) The first illustration is that the theoretical debate on the nature of law (in relation to its necessity and contingency) also involves a few other related theoretical issues.

These other related theoretical issues have to do with some deeply contested theoretical debates, which, however, I had already gone to great lengths to analyze in my numerous (previous) books, as summarized below. It should also be stressed, lest misunderstanding occurs, that each of the theoretical debates (as listed below) does not exhaust the issues covered in the books, as each book covers more issues than what is listed below.

- On Morality and Justice
  - –Ex: 2 volumes, *The Future of Human Civilization*
  - –Ex: *The Future of Capitalism and Democracy*
  - –Ex: *Beyond Democracy to Post-Democracy*
  - –Ex: *Beyond the World of Titans, and the Remaking of World Order*
  - –Ex: *The Rise of Authoritarian Liberal Democracy*
- On Conflict Resolution
  - –Ex: *The Future of Capitalism and Democracy*
- On Being and Belonging
  - –Ex: *The Future of Post-Human Consciousness*
  - –Ex: 2 volumes, *The Future of Human Civilization*
- On Nature and Nurture
  - –Ex: *Beyond Nature and Nurture*
- On Greed and Excess
  - –Ex: 2 volumes, *The Future of Human Civilization*
  - –Ex: *The Future of Capitalism and Democracy*

–Ex: *Beyond Capitalism to Post-Capitalism*
- On Freedom and Unfreedom
  –Ex: 2 volumes, *The Future of Human Civilization*
  –Ex: *The Future of Capitalism and Democracy*
  –Ex: *Beyond Capitalism to Post-Capitalism*
  –Ex: *Beyond Democracy to Post-Democracy*
  –Ex: *Beyond Civilization to Post-Civilization*
- On Cognition
  –Ex: *The Future of Post-Human Unconsciousness*
  –Ex: *The Future of Post-Human Consciousness*
  –Ex: *The Future of Capitalism and Democracy*
  –Ex: *The Future of Post-Human Creative Thinking*
- On Intuition
  –Ex: *The Future of Post-Human Unconsciousness*
  –Ex: *The Future of Post-Human Consciousness*
  –Ex: *Beyond Capitalism to Post-Capitalism*
  –Ex: *The Future of Capitalism and Democracy*
- On Emotion
  –Ex: *The Future of Post-Human Unconsciousness*
  –Ex: *The Future of Post-Human Consciousness*
  –Ex: *The Future of Aesthetic Experience*
  –Ex: *Beyond Capitalism to Post-Capitalism*
  –Ex: *The Future of Capitalism and Democracy*
- On Behavior
  –Ex: *The Future of Post-Human Language*
  –Ex: *The Future of Post-Human Unconsciousness*
  –Ex: *The Future of Post-Human Consciousness*
  –Ex: *Beyond Capitalism to Post-Capitalism*
  –Ex: *The Future of Capitalism and Democracy*
- On Different Dimensions of Human Existence
  –Ex: 2 volumes, *The Future of Human Civilization*
- On Modernity, Post-Modernity, and After-Postmodernity
  –Ex: 2 volumes, *The Future of Human Civilization*
  –Ex: *Beyond Civilization to Post-Civilization*
- On Uncertainty
  –Ex: *The Future of Complexity*
  –Ex: 2 volumes, *The Future of Human Civilization*

Therefore, those who are interested in these other theoretical issues (and debates) which are related to the current context can consult these other books of mine for more details.

(b) And the second illustration is that one of the major theses of this book concerns the future of law which is closely linked with the different visions that I had worked out in my previous books, in relation to the mind, nature, society, and culture.

Of course, for the convenience of the readers, a summary of some of these visions will be provided whenever necessary, as shown in the two sections on meta-theory above (*often verbatim*) and in different tables at the end of some chapters.

Yet, I still expect the readers to read my previous books directly for more details—as this book is written in conversation with my previous ones.

Case Studies and Examples

Secondly, the case studies and examples in the chapters are not exhaustive but solely illustrative. Nor are they necessarily mutually exclusive, as they can be reclassified in a different way. And exceptions are allowed.

One is tempted to assume, however, that, since the case studies and their examples are not exhaustive, more case studies and examples are needed. But the problem here is that just adding more of them does not necessarily change the conclusions to be drawn and may even lead to redundancy.

After all, the case studies and examples used in this book are chosen with care and deemed sufficient for the purpose at hand, even though they are solely illustrative.

Detailed Analysis versus Overall Synthesis

Thirdly, there is a distinction between detailed analysis and overall synthesis, in that the former is, especially though not exclusively, more for the specialized viewpoint of a specific discipline, whereas the latter is, especially though not exclusively, more for the broad horizon of an interdisciplinary approach—relatively speaking, of course.

Or, by analogy, there is a distinction between depicting a "tree" (with tiny details) in a "forest" and viewing the entire "forest" itself (with the broader horizon).

This book, like all previous ones of mine, tries to strike a balance between the two forms of understanding, although this does not imply that the two forms should be exactly equally offered, in an exact 50-50 balance.

Instead, the book, more often than not, does not allow the tiny details to obscure the larger picture in a given case study, because the entire book is inter-disciplinary in nature and tries to look at the entire "forest," not being bogged down with the detailed analysis of an individual "tree" in the forest, by analogy.

In this sense, although detailed analysis can be provided whenever needed for a given case study, the important point to remember is the overall horizon with its broadness of scope.

The Use of Neologisms

And fourthly, I use different neologisms in my books, mostly to introduce my original concepts and theories, and good instances include those here or elsewhere in my previous books (e.g., "the reconstruction theory of law," the "hyper-sexual body," "post-democracy," "hyper-spatial consciousness," "post-capitalism," and whatnot). Needless to say, they are used here solely for our current intellectual convenience, as they will be renamed differently in different ways in future history.

As I thus wrote in *FCD* (508-9), "all these terms 'post-capitalism,' 'post-democracy'...and other ones as introduced in...[the] project (e.g.,...'posthuman elitists,' and 'posthuman counter-elitists,' just to cite a few of them) are more for our current intellectual convenience than to the liking of future humans and post-humans, who will surely invent more tasteful neologisms to call their own eras, entities, and everything else, for that matter. But the didactic point here is to use the terms to foretell what the future might be like, not that its eras and entities must be called so exactly and permanently. After all, William Shakespeare (1995: Act II, Scene II, Line 47) well said long ago: 'What is in a name? That which we call a rose by any other name would smell as sweet.'"

As I had also stressed time and again before, each of the neologisms can be re-written as a different "X," only to be re-named differently by the powers that be in different eras of future history.

With these clarifications for thought in mind—I now proceed to Chapter Two on the necessity of law.

Table 1.1. The Classification of Law

• **Public Law**
—Ex: constitutional law
—Ex: administrative law
—Ex: criminal law

• **Private Law**
—Ex: property law
—Ex: trust law
—Ex: contract law
—Ex: tort law

Notes: Four clarifications are needed here.
Firstly, the classification of law into public law and private law is important not only at the national level but also at the international level. For instance, nowadays, there is international law, which can be likewise classified into "public international law" and "private interntional law." (WK 2009)
Secondly, the distinction between public law and private law still holds, even though "many scholars argue that 'the boundaries between public and private law are becoming blurred,' and that this distinction has become mere 'folklore." (L. Bergkamp 2001)
Thirdly, there are other categories of laws which are not listed above, but many of them are derived from the most fundamental laws as cited in the examples of private law and public law. Good examples are "company law" (mostly from "trust law"), "commercial law" (mostly from "contract law" and "property law"), "intellectual property law" (mostly from "property law" and "contract law"), "immigration law" (mostly from "constitutional law," "administrative law," and "criminal law"), and others. (WK 2009)
Fourthly, the examples of private law and public law are supposed to be illustrative (not exhaustive), for the introductory purpose at hand.
Source: A summary of *Sec.1.2* of *FPHLAW*. See text for citations.

Table 1.2. The Classification of Jurisprudence

- **Analytical Jurisprudence**
  —Ex: "What is law?"
  —Ex: "What are the criteria for legal validity?"
  —Ex: "What is the relationship between law and power/sociology?"

- **Normative Jurisprudence**
  —Ex: "What is the goal or purpose of law?"
  —Ex: "What moral or political theories provide a foundation for the law?"
  —Ex: "What sorts of acts should be subject to punishment, and what sorts of punishment should be permitted?"
  —Ex: "What rights do we have?"
  —Ex: "Is there a duty to obey the law?"
  —Ex: "What value has the rule of law?"

Notes: The examples in each category are solely illustrative (not exhaustive), and the comparison is relative (not absolute), nor are they necessarily mutually exclusive. Some can be easily re-classified elsewhere. As generalities, they allow exceptions
Source: A summary of *Sec. 1.3* of *FPHLAW*. See text for citations, especially in relation to WK (2009g), WK (2009h), and WK (2009i).

Table 1.3. The Theoretical Debate on Space-Time (Part I)

- **Isaac Newton's Absolutist (Substantivist) Theory of Space-Time**
  —space and time are independent from each other. The structure of space-time is $E3 \times E1$ (with the structure of space, *P*, as the set of spatial locations in a three-dimensional Euclidean space, *E3*, and the structure of time as the set of temporal moments, *T*, in the one-dimensional real time, *E1*).
  —space and time are also independent from the effects of matter and events. The existence of space and time is possible even in a world absent of matter (and, for that matter, even in a world absent of events), as if they were material objects but with their total unchangingness thorough time.

- **Albert Einstein's Relativist Theory of Space-Time**
  —space and time are interchangeable (not absolute), just as matter and energy are equivalent (not independent) with the famous equation, $E = mc^2$ (as in the special theory of relativity in 1905).
  —space-time and matter-energy are also relative in a grand union (as in the general theory of relativity in 1915). Thus, each pair affects the other pair, as "matter 'tells' spacetime how to curve [in a non-Euclidean geometry] and curved spacetime 'tells' matter how to behave….Space contracts near mass and dilates away from it. Time dilates near mass and contracts away from it. Clocks positioned farther away from the mass of the earth run faster than clocks closer to the earth." (L. Shlain 1991: 328-330)

(continued on next page)

Table 1.3. The Theoretical Debate on Space-Time (Part II)

- **Peter Baofu's Perspectival Theory of Space-Time**
  —space and time can be understood from multiple perspectives, be they in relation to culture, society, nature, and the mind, with each perspective revealing something about the nature of space-time and simultaneously delimiting its view. This is subject to "the regression-progression principle" in existential dialectics.
  —each perspective of space and time exists in society and culture with good reasons, with some being more successful and hegemonic (dominant) than others. This is subject to "the symmetry-asymmetry principle" in existential dialectics.
  —space and time will not last, to be eventually superseded (altered) by post-humans in different forms (e.g.,stretching/shrinking space-time, engineering more dimensions of space-time, and manipulating multiverses), be they here in this universe or in multiverses. Thus, even the physical existence of space-time cannot last forever, with ever more transformations in the process. This is subject to "the change-constancy principle" in existential dialectics.
  —the conventional wisdom (especially by physicists) of treating the physical perspective of space and time as the foundation of all other perspectives (of space and time) and of regarding them as much less important is a form of reductionism,committing what I call *the foundation fallacy*, in misleadingly dismissing the multiple perspectives of space and time in relation to culture, society, nature, and the mind.

Notes: The examples in each category are solely illustrative (not exhaustive), and the comparison is relative (not absolute), nor are they necessarily mutually exclusive. Some can be easily re-classified elsewhere. As generalities, they allow exceptions.
Source: A summary of *Sec.1.1*, *Sec.1.2*, and *Sec.1.3* of *FPHST*—and, for that matter, the rest of *FPHST*

Table 1.4. Main Reasons for Altering Space-Time

- **The Need to Make New Energy-Matter**
  —Ex: manipulating molecular bonds for new materials
  —Ex: creating nanotechnologies on the atomic scale
  —Ex: engineering the atomic nucleus
  —Ex: restructuring most elementary particles
  —Ex: inventing new forms of matter and energy

- **The Need to Create New Space-Time**
  —Ex: creating "warp drive" (as in science fiction) for space travel
  —Ex: creating "pocket universes"

- **The Need to Conquer the Cosmos unto Multiverses**
  —Ex: spreading floating consciousness and hyper-spatial consciousness, besides other forms that humans have never known, in the cosmos and beyond unto multiverses for ultimate conquest

Notes: The examples in each category are solely illustrative (not exhaustive) nor necessarily mutually exclusive, and the comparison is relative (not absolute). As generalities, they allow exceptions. Also, it should be stressed that the three reasons are all related, in that they all contribute to the evolution of intelligent life in the cosmos unto multiverses in the most distant future beyond our current knowledge.
Sources: A summary of *Sec.6.2* of *FPHST*. See also *FHC*, *FCD*, *FPHC*, *FC*, *FPHU*, and *FPHG*, for example.

Table 1.5. The Technological Frontiers of the Micro-World

- **Type I-Minus**
  —Ex: building structures and mining

- **Type II-Minus**
  —Ex: playing with the genetic makeups of living things

- **Type III-Minus**
  —Ex: manipulating molecular bonds for new materials

- **Type IV-Minus**
  —Ex: creating nanotechnologies on the atomic scale

- **Type V-Minus**
  —Ex: engineering the atomic nucleus

- **Type VI-Minus**
  —Ex: restructuring most elementary particles

- **Type Ω-Minus**
  —Ex: altering the structure of space-time

Notes: As already indicated in *Sec.4.4.2.2* of *FPHC*, the problem with this micro-classification (from Barrow's work) is that the civilization types (with the exception of Type Ω-Minus, for example) are not quite distinct, since many of them can be achieved more or less in a civilization, to the extent that Type II-minus and Type III-minus, just to cite two plausible types, can be historically contemporaneous, relatively speaking, unlike the vast historical distance between, say, Type O and Type I (or Type I and Type II) civilizations. In other words, the micro-classification here is not very useful to understand civilization types but is revealing to see the technological frontiers of the micro-world.
Sources: A reconstruction from J.Barrow (1998:133), as originally shown in *Table 4.7* of *FPHC*. See *FPHC* for more info.

Table 1.6. Finity, Transfinity, and Infinity (Part I)

- **Infinity**

—The term "infinity," which is "symbolically represented with ∞," derives from the Latin *infinitas* (or "unboundedness"), to refer to "several distinct concepts—usually linked to the idea of 'without end'—which arise in philosophy, mathematics, and theology." (WK 2008c)

—In the context of mathematics, "infinity" is often "treated as if it were a number (i.e., it counts or measures things: 'an infinite number of terms') but it is a different type of 'number' from the real numbers. Infinity is related to limits,…large cardinals,…projective geometry, extended real numbers and the absolute Infinite," for instance. (WK 2008c)

- **Transfinity**

—To avoid confusion, my usage of the word "transfinite" (as used here in the ontological principle) is not the same as the one which was originally coined by Georg Cantor to refer to "cardinal numbers or ordinal numbers that are larger than all finite numbers, yet not necessarily absolutely infinite" (in the mind of God), as opposed to "relative" infinity (in the mind of Man). (WK 2008d) In other words, for Cantor, there are two kinds of infinity, "absolute" and "relative"—with "relative" infinity or "transfinity" (in the mind of Man) being dependent on "absolute" infinity (in the mind of God) for its existence.

—By contrast, my usage of the word "transfinite" here differs radically from the one used by Cantor (and other mathematicians) and is more limited, in light of the problems confronting any attempt to understand the idea of infinity, be it by intuition, imagination, and conception (as already shown in the prevous three sub-sections).

—With this clarification in mind, I allow numbers which can be many times larger—or smaller, for that matter—than the finite things that we encounter in daily life, but they do not have to be related to the idea of infinity at all (which may not exist).

(continued on next page)

Table 1.6. Finity, Transfinity, and Infinity (Part II)

- **Transfinity *(cont'd)***
  —Of course, there may be some *borderline* cases, in which it is not clear whether the number in question is transfinite (in my usage) or simply a mathematical convenience. A good example of a borderline case is the Planck unit of length for "the smallest space possibly measured in nature," which is "less than billionths of trillionths of trillionths of an inch" (or something like 1.6×10^{-35} meters). (P. Baofu 2006a; N. McAleer 1987: 219; WKV 2008; D. Corbett 2008)
  —The ideas concerning symmetry and dimensions in the examples above were addressed in Chapter Three and Chapter Four of *FPHG*. For now, it suffices to further add that it is mind-boggling to even conceive or imagine extreme numbers like the Planck unit of length (or others). Does it really exist at all? Or is it merely a mathematical convenience to describe a physical situation that the human mind does not understand properly?
  —In any event, "transfinity" (in my usage) can be used as a further extension (of number) to the finite numbers in daily life—albeit with some borderline cases in mind.

- **Finity**
  —It refers to numbers which are bounded (that is, with an end), especially (though not exclusively) in relation to things in everyday life.

Source: From *Sec. 1.4* and *Sec. 2.2.3* of *FPHG*

Table 1.7. Theoretical Speculations of Multiverses

- **"Baby Universes" (Ex: Andre Linde and others)**
  —Ex: In a flat universe theory, "even if our part of it eventually collapses,...some spots in the cosmos would suddenly start inflating on their own, creating brand-new 'baby universes.'" (P. Baofu 2000: 623)

- **"Parallel Universes" (Ex: Stephen Hawking and others)**
  —Ex: In quantum cosmology, there allows the existence of infinite numbers of parallel universes, with tunneling among them. (M. Kaku 1994: 256) Hawking later revised his views on this.

- **"Pocket Universes" (Ex: Alan Guth)**
  —Ex: "As the pocket universes live out their lives and recollapse or dwindle away, new universes are generated to take their place....While life in our pocket universe will presumably die out, life in the universe as a whole will thrive for eternity." (A. Guth 1997: 248; P. Baofu 2002: 482)

- **"Brane Worlds" (Ex: Warren Siegel, Lisa Randall, and others)**
  —Ex: Our universe is stuck on a membrane of space-time embedded in a larger cosmos, with different brane worlds connecting and/or colliding with each other.

Notes: These examples are solely illustrative (not exhaustive), and some of the items can be reclassified somewhere else. Nor are they always mutually exclusive. Since they are generalities, exceptions are expected.
Source: From *Table 4.8* of *FPHC*

Table 1.8. The Confusion between "Many Worlds" and "Multiverse" (Part I)

- **First Problem**
  —The first problem in this second confusion concerns a debate between the "many-worlds" interpretation of quantum mechanics by Hugh Everett (1957) and others, and the Copenhagen interpretation by Niels Bohr and Werner Heisenberg on the effects of quantum states after interacting with an external environment (e.g., by a measuring observer).
  —On the one hand, the Copenhagen interpretation of quantum mechanics is more indeterministic in its concern with the probabilities of the outcomes of a wave function after interacting with an external environment (e.g., by a measuring observer using light to detect, for example, "an electron in a particular region around the nucleus at a particular time." (WK 2008e) Each wave function for the state of a particle refers to "a mathematical representation used to calculate the probability for it to be found in a location, or state of motion." (WK 2008f) And the "wavefunction collapse" means that "the act of measurement causes the calculated set of probabilities to 'collapse' to the value defined by the measurement." (WK 2008f)
  —On the other hand, the Everett's interrpetation is more deterministic, in rejecting "the objective reality of wavefunction collapse" and "instead explaining the subjective appearance of wavefunction collapse with the mechanism of quantum decoherence." (WK 2008g) The words "quantum decoherence" here refers to "the mechanism by which quantum systems interact with their environments to exhibit probabilistically additive behavior," in such a way that "the quantum nature of the system is simply 'leaked' into the environment." (WK 2008g) For example, "[a]s a result of an interaction, the wave functions of the system and the measuring device become entangled with each other. Decoherence happens when different portions of the system's wavefunction become entangled *in different ways* [italic added] with the measuring device...." (WK 2008g) Thus, for Everett, the appearance of "wavefunction collapse" can be explained by "quantum decoherence" for quantum states to branch out in different independent worlds after interacting with an external environment.

(continued on next page)

Table 1.8. The Confusion between "Many Worlds" and "Multiverse" (Part II)

- **First Problem** ***(cont'd)***
  —Yet, a major criticism against Everett's interpretation is that these different independent worlds in Everett's sense "will never be accessible to us," because of the interference by the measuring observer in an external environment. (WK 2008g)
  —For illustration, "once a measurement is done, the measured system becomes entangled with both the physicist who measured it and a huge number of other particles, some of which are photons flying away towards the other end of the universe; in order to prove that the wave function did not collapse one would have to bring all these particles back and measure them again, together with the system that was measured originally. This is completely impractical, but even if one can theoretically do this, it would destroy any evidence that the original measurement took place (including the physicist's memory)." (WK 2008g)
  —But then, the critics ask, If these independent worlds in Everett's sense are inaccessible to us, how do we know much of anything really about them?

- **Second Problem**
  —What is relevant at the quantum mechanical level may not necessarily apply to the world at the physicsl level.
  —In fact, the persistent inability among contemporoary physicists to unifiy the theory of relativity for large objects at the physical level and quantum mechanics for tiny objects at the quantum mechanical level should warn us about the danger of reductionism, by reducing the understanding of different universes ("parallel universes") at the physical level from a generalization of "many worlds" at the quantum mechanical level.

- **Third Problem**
  —There is no empirical evidence to suggest that there are infinite (or extremely many) possible worlds in the cosmos as the many-worlds model by Everett would have us to believe.

Source: From *Sec.4.4.1* of *FPHG*

Table 1.9. Hyperspace and Its Challenge (Part I)

- **First Problem**
  —Hyperspace for intra- and inter-universal travel is assumed to be possible, on the basis of four main assumptions; although there may be others, these are the often cited ones.
  —The first assumption concerns the existence of "entry" and "exit" points in hyperspace, which is easier said than done to enter, go through, and then exit hyperspace.
  —For instance, using hyperspace "requires complex calculations…of single or multiple hyperspace jumps and the control of the jump….Peturbations such as those experienced by ship in space from the gravitional field around an object such as a planet or even a star are exacerbated in hyperspatial travel, since mass in real space distorts hyperspace in an equal measure. 'Jumping' near to a gravitational mass is likely to make resulting exit from hyperspace to be highly uncertain, with the level of improbability *i* increasing with the square of the distance to the nearest gravitional 'well.'" (WK 2008h)
  —Besides, "[o]nly spaceships equipped with a special force field can enter hyperspace, because exposure to hyperspace even for short period of time is hazardous to unprotected humans." (WK 2008h)

- **Second Problem**
  —The second assumption concerns the faster-than-light speed. It is well known that Einstein argued for the speed of light as the ultimate limit, but nowadays phyiscists do allow the violation of this limit under certain conditions (like the hypothetical existence of tachyons, as will be explained further in a later sub-section on time travel).
  —Even then, there is a challenge to explain in science fiction "why ships can travel faster than light in hyperspace," and two good arguments are that "hyperspace may be smaller than real space and therefore a star ship's propulsion seems to be greatly multiplied, or else the speed of light in hyperspace is not a barrier as it is in real space. Whatever the reasoning, the general effect is that ships traveling in hyperspace seem to have broken the speed of light, appearing at their destinations much more quickly and without the shift in time that the Theory of Relativity would suggest." (WK 2008h)

(continued on next page)

Table 1.9. Hyperspace and Its Challenge (Part II)

- **Third Problem**
  —The third assumption concerns the speed of time (to be measured, say, by a clock), but this is elaborated in a different section on the related issue of "time travel" (as shown in a different table on time travel).

- **Fourth Problem**
  —The fourth assumption concerns spatial shortcut, as it is possible, because of the curvature of space, in that "the manifold of ordinary three-dimensional space is curved in four or more 'higher' spacial dimensions (a 'hyperspace' in the geometric sense…). This curvature causes certain widely separated points in three-dimensional space to nonetheless be 'adjacent' to each other four-dimensionally. Creating an aperture in 4D space (a wormhole) between these locations can allow instantaneous transit between the two locations; a common comparison is that of a folded piece of paper, where a hole punched through two folded sections is more direct than a line drawn between them on the sheet. This idea probably arose out of certain popular descriptions of General Relativity and/or Riemannian manifolds, and may be the original form from which later concepts of hyperspace arose." (WK 2008h)
  —But this does not mean that hyperpsace is always safe. In fact, "in some science fiction, the danger of hyperspace travel is due to the chance that the route through hyperspace may take a ship too close to a celestial body with a large gravitational field, such as a star. In such scenarios, if a starship passes too close to a large gravitational field while in hyperspace, the ship is forcibly pulled out of hyperspace and reverts to normal space. Therefore, certain hyperspace 'routes' may be mapped out that are safe, not passing too close to stars or other dangers." (WJ 2008h)

Source: From *Sec.4.4.1* of *FPHG*

Table 1.10. The Problems of Time Travel into the Future (Part I)

- **First Problem**
  - —The first problem concerns "time dilation under the Theory of Special Relativity" (which separates space-time from mass-energy as special cases). Suppose you are on a moving train and an observer outside the train is watching you along the tracks. As your train moves along at the speed of light (or something close to it), "time, as measured by your watch, ticked along at a slower pace than time measured by the observer. Not only that, distance changed, too. For the observer, a one-foot ruler whizzing by on the train would have measured less than a foot." (NO 2000)
  - —In fact, you may not even notice that this slower clicking of the clock; in fact, everything looks normal to you inside the train as it was before: "The weird thing is that, for you on the train, time wouldn't seem to be moving slower and your ruler wouldn't be shorter—all would appear normal." (NO 2008) By contrast, you instead think that "time on the rest of the Earth would appear to be ticking along slower and its rulers would be shorter." (NO 2000) So, both of you insist that the other clock (not his) is clicking more slowly—assuming, of course, an inertial frame of reference.
  - —Now, change the story a bit, in that, this time, instead of an "inertial reference frame," acceleration is allowed, and you are on your way to board a spaceship. As an illustration, suppose "[y]ou board a spaceship and take off for deep space. The ship approaches the speed of light. Time for you seems to pass as it always has. It takes you about five seconds to tie your shoe. But to an observer on Earth (assuming he or she could watch you), you are moving at a snail's pace. It takes hours to tie your shoe." (NO 2000) In any event, "you continue on your journey. You slow down, stop, and accelerate back to Earth. You arrive home. You have aged two years during your flight. Two hundred years have passed on Earth. You have successfully travelled forward through time." (NO 2000) In this case, both the observer (if he is still alive) and you agree that you have aged less.

(continued on next page)

Table 1.10. The Problems of Time Travel into the Future (Part II)

- **First Problem *(cont'd)***
  —In other words, when you are back to Earth, a lot of things have changed since, and you may find rather strange to be in a new environment which you hardly recognize, when compared with what you used to think as your city, or the Earth (two years ago, well, in accordance to your time of measurement). This means that you are in the future (two hundred years later), even though you are still relatively young (only two years older). But, can you go back? Well, no. The reason is that "[a]ccording to relativity, you can only move through time in one direction." (NO 2000)

- **Second Problem**
  —The second problem concerns "time dilation under the Theory of General Relativity" (which unifies space-time with mass-energy in a general theory), the same result of time dilation occurs.
  —For instance, when "one clock is deeper in a gravity well than the other," a result is that "the clock deeper in the well" will "tick…more slowly; this effect must be taken into account when calibrating the clocks on the satellites of the Global Positioning System, and it could lead to significant differences in rates of aging for observers at different distances from a black hole." (WK 2008i)
  —More precisely, by way of another example, "it has been calculated that, under general relativity, a person could travel forward in time at a rate four times that of distant observers by residing inside a spherical shell with a diameter of 5 meters and the mass of Jupiter. For such a person, every one second of their 'personal' time would correspond to four seconds for distant observers. Of course, squeezing the mass of a large planet into such a structure is not expected to be within our technological capabilities in the near future." (WK 2008i; R. Gott 2002)
  —The point here, however, is that time travel into the future, in this sense, is allowed, theoretically speaking, but in a very limited way, from the theory of relativity. But one can also ask, What if the theory of relativity were wrong? Well, in that case, there would be a need to find a better theory to explain time travel into the future.

Source: From *Sec.4.4.2* of *FPHG*

Table 1.11. The Problems of Time Travel into the Past (Part I)

• **First Problem**

—The first problem concerns the faster-than-light-speed, since, in accordance to the theory of special relativity, when an object goes faster than the speed of light, something weird can happen, in that, instead of having the clock clicking more slowly, it is moving backward, in relation to some inertial frame of reference—which then raisies the issue of whether time travel into the past is possible at all.

—But the problem here is about the violation of the law of casuality. In everyday language, an excellent illustration of causality violation is that, suppose you travel back into the past and then kill your parents, this then means that you could not have been born. But this is not true, since you are alive.

—Yet, "in the case of a hypothetical signal moving faster than light, there would always be some frames in which the signal was received before it was sent, so that the signal could be said to have moved backwards in time." The violation of casuality exists in this case.

—The first part of the problem is that, in accordance to the theory of special relativity, "it would take an infinite amount of energy to accelerate a slower-than-light object to the speed of light"—let alone the energy needed to propel an object to go faster than the speed of light. (WK 2008i) Although some suggest the possibility of "negative energy," it remains to be seen to what extent this is true.

—And the second part of the problem is that, "although relativity does not forbid the theoretical possibility of tachyons which move faster than light at all times, when analyzed using quantum field theory it seems that it would not actually be possible to use them to transmit information faster than light and there is no evidence for their existence." (WK 2008i; S. Chase 1993)

(continued on next page)

Table 1.11. The Problems of Time Travel into the Past (Part II)

• **Second Problem**

—The second problem concerns cosmic string and black holes, since it is the theory of general relativity which "extends the special theory to cover gravity, illustrating it in terms of curvature in spacetime caused by mass-energy and the flow of momentum." (WK 2008i)

—On the other hand, "[g]eneral relativity describes the universe under a system of field equations...and there exist solutions to these equations that permit what are called 'closed time-like curves,' and hence time travel into the past....The first of these was proposed by Kurt Gödel, a solution known as the Gödel metric, but his (and many others') example requires the universe to have physical characteristics that it does not appear to have." (WK 2008i; K. Thorne 1994)

—But then, the problem now becomes: "Whether general relativity forbids closed time-like curves for all realistic conditions is unknown." (WK 2008i)

• **Third Problem**

—The third problem concerns wormholes and related ones, and "[w]ormholes are a hypothetical warped spacetime which are also permitted by the Einstein field equations of general relativity, although it would be impossible to travel through a wormhole unless it was what is known as a traversable wormhole." (WK 2008i; M. Visser 1995) In other words, "a wormhole is a hypothetical topological feature of spacetime that is fundamentally a 'shortcut' through space and time. Spacetime can be viewed as a 2D surface, and when 'folded' over, a wormhole bridge can be formed. A wormhole has at least two mouths which are connected to a single throat or tube. If the wormhole is traversable, matter can 'travel' from one mouth to the other by passing through the throat." (WK 2008j)

—But the problem here is three-fold, as shown in what follows.

(continued on next page)

Table 1.11. The Problems of Time Travel into the Past (Part III)

- **Third Problem *(cont'd)***
  —The first part of the problem is that "there is no observational evidence for wormholes." (WK 2008j)
  —The second part of the problem is that it is not clear how exactly wormholes (and black holes, for that matter) could allow time travel into the past at all.
  —And the third part of the problem is that if using wormholes (and black holes, for that matter) to travel into the past requires something to go faster than light too, then this raises another issue concerning the two problems as previously indicated in the sub-section on the faster-than-light-speed.

- **Fourth Problem**
  —The fourth problem is that some physicists have argued that, even should time travel into the past be possible, by way of these three methods, the person still would not return to the same past history that he exactly experienced before, but in a different one. (WK 2008i)
  —In other words, "strictly speaking," time travel into the past is not "really" possible, in light of these criticisms, so there is no need to worry that one could travel into the past and kill one's parent, as a way to violate the law of casuality.

Source: From *Sec.4.4.2* of *FPHG*

Table 1.12. The Conceptual Dimensions of Consciousness (and Other Mental States)

- **On Heredity and Time**
  —Heredity and the Environment
  —The Past and the Present

- **On Layers of Mental States and Abnormality**
  —Consciousness, Unconsciousness, and Preconsciousness
  —Normality and Paranormality

- **On Organicity and Motivation**
  —Mechanicity and Organicity
  —Primary Motivations and Multiple Motivations

- **On Other (Mostly Epistemic) Considerations**
  —Synthesis and Analysis
  —Situation and the Subject
  —Process and Outcome
  —Reasoning and Other Modes of Thinking
  —Meta-Conceptual Nominalism and Realism

Notes:: These examples are solely illustrative (not exhaustive), and some of the items can be reclassified somewhere else. Nor are they always mutually exclusive. Since they are generalities, exceptions are expected.
Sources: From *FPHC*. A re-construction, but with my own contribution, originally from G.Lindzey & C.Hall, *Introduction to Theories of Personality* (NY: John Wiley & Sons, 1985).

Table 1.13. The Theoretical Levels of Consciousness (and Other Mental States) (Part I)

- **At the Micro-Physical Theoretical Level**
  - —Quantum-Mechanics
  - —Electromagnetism

- **At the Chemical Theoretical Level**
  - —Biochemistry

- **At the Biological Theoretical Level**
  - —Evolutionary Biology
  - —Neuroscience
  - —Artificial Intelligence

- **At the Psychological Theoretical Level**
  - —Psychodynamic Psychology
    - Psychoanalytical Psychology
    - Analytical Psychology
    - Socially Oriented Psychology
  - —Experimental (Behavioral) Psychology
    - Operant Reinforcement Theory
    - Stimulus-Response Theory
    - Social Learning Theory
  - —Cognitive (Gestalt) Psychology
    - Humanist Psychology
    - Existential Psychology
    - Field Theory
  - —Psychometric Psychology
    - Idiographics
    - Constitutional Psychology
  - —Social Psychology
    - Symbolic Interactive Theory
    - Social Exchange Theory

(continued on next page)

Table 1.13. The Theoretical Levels of Consciousness (and Other Mental States) (Part II)

- **At the Organizational Theoretical Level**
  - —Managerial-Bureaucratic Theory
  - —Oligarchic Theory
  - —Network Theory

- **At the Institutional Theoretical Level**
  - —Functionalist Theory
  - —Anomic Theory

- **At the Structural Theoretical Level**
  - —Conflict Theory
    - Marxian Theory
    - Critical Theory
    - Weberian Theory
  - —Games Theory (in Formal Theory)
  - —Feminist Theory
    - Feminist Concerns
    - Feminist Hopes

- **At the Systemic Theoretical Level**
  - —Equilibrium Theory
  - —System Theory
  - —Chaos Theory

- **At the Cosmological Theoretical Level**
  - —Superluminal Model
  - —The Theory of Floating Consciousness

(continued on next page)

Table 1.13. The Theoretical Levels of Consciousness (and Other Mental States) (Part III)

- **At the Cultural Theoretical Level**
    - —Substantive Theories
        - Structuralist Theory
        - Post-Structuralist Theory (in Postmodernism)
    - —Meta-Theories
        - Epistemic Objectivism vs. Epistemic Historicism
        - Epistemic Subjectivism vs. Epistemic Non-Subjectivism
            - –Phenomenology
            - –Ethnomethodology
            - –Hermeneutics
        - Epistemic Relativism vs. Epistemic Absolutism
        - Epistemic Reductionism vs. Epistemic Emergencism

- **At Other Levels**
    - —Structuration Theory
    - —Reflexive Socioanalysis

Notes: These examples are solely illustrative (not exhaustive), and some of the items can be reclassified somewhere else. Nor are they always mutually exclusive. Since they are generalities, exceptions are expected.
Source: From many different sources as indicated in *FPHC*

Table 1.14. The Thematic Issues of Consciousness (and Other Mental States)

- **The Factor of History**
  —Pre-Modernity
  —Modernity
  —Postmodernity
  —After-Postmodernity

- **The Importance of Needs**
  —Having (e.g., the everyday, the technological)
  —Belonging (e.g., the just and the good)
  —Being (e.g., the true, the holy, the sublime/beautiful, and the good)

Notes: These examples are solely illustrative (not exhaustive). Nor are they always mutually exclusive. Since they are generalities, exceptions are expected. Also, some categories overlap with others; for instance, the good is also related with being-ness, just as the everyday can be connected with belong-ness.
Sources: From *FPHC*, based on *FHC* and *FCD*

Table 1.15. Having, Belonging, and Being in Consciousness

- **Having (e.g., About the Everyday and Technological)**
  —Ex: Physiological needs (e.g., thirst, hunger, sex)
  —Ex: Safety (e.g., stability, freedom from fear and anxiety)

- **Belonging (e.g., About the Good and Just)**
  —Ex: Social interaction
  —Ex: Friendship, acquaintance
  —Ex: Love, family
  —Ex: Self-respect, respect from others

- **Being (e.g., About the True, Holy, Beautiful/Sublime, and Good)**
  —Ex: Understanding of reality about self and world
  —Ex: Spiritual quest for holiness, beauty, sublimity, and goodness

Notes: These examples are solely illustrative (not exhaustive), and some of the items can be reclassified somewhere else. Nor are they always mutually exclusive. Since they are generalities, exceptions are expected.
Sources: From *FPHC*, based on *FHC* and *FCD*

Table 1.16. The Having-Ness of Consciousness (and Other Mental States)

- **At the Micro-Physical Level**
  —Ex: The finer physics of nutrition

- **At the Chemical Level**
  —Ex: Food guide pyramid

- **At the Bio-Psychological Level**
  —Ex: The hierarchy of needs

- **At the Institutional Level**
  —Ex: The production of commodity fetishism

- **At the Organizational Level**
  —Ex: Mass standardization (and customization); bureaucratic rationality

- **At the Structural Level**
  —Ex: The divide between the haves and the have-nots

- **At the Cultural Level**
  —Ex: The bondage of greater expectations

- **At the Systemic Level**
  —Ex: The technological transformation of poverty with transvaluations

- **At the Cosmological Level**
  —Ex: Floating consciousness in deep space without the human physiological needs

Notes: These examples are solely illustrative (not exhaustive), and some of the items can be reclassified somewhere else. Nor are they always mutually exclusive. Since they are generalities, exceptions are expected.
Sources: From *FPHC*. See also *FCD* and *FHC*.

Table 1.17. The Belonging-Ness of Consciousness (and Other Mental States)

- **At the Micro-Physical Level**
  —Ex: Statistical physics and social networks

- **At the Chemical Level**
  —Ex: Olfaction and social relations

- **At the Bio-Psychological Level**
  —Ex: Dual human nature on relationships

- **At the Institutional Level**
  —Ex: Private property and social cleavage

- **At the Organizational Level**
  —Ex: Legal formalism and iron cage

- **At the Structural Level**
  —Ex: Class conflicts and social alienation

- **At the Cultural Level**
  —Ex: Ruthless society and the culture of law

- **At the Systemic Level**
  —Ex: Human extinction and post-human relations

- **At the Cosmological Level**
  —Ex: The transcendence of equality in the cosmos and beyond

Notes: These examples are solely illustrative (not exhaustive), and some of the items can be reclassified somewhere else. Nor are they always mutually exclusive. Since they are generalities, exceptions are expected.
Sources: From *FPHC*. See also *FCD* and *FHC*.

Table 1.18. The Being-Ness of Consciousness (and Other Mental States) (Part I)

- **At the Micro-Physical Level**
  —Ex: Space-time and matter-energy in classical mechanics, quantum mechanics, and the theory of relativity

- **At the Chemical Level**
  —Ex: Drugs and well being

- **At the Biological Level**
  —Ex: Neuroscience and mystical experiences

- **At the Psychological Level**
  —Ex: Reductionism and emergencism

- **At the Institutional Level**
  —Ex: The proliferation of cults and sects, and the corporate-art industry

- **At the Organizational Level**
  —Ex: The organization of ideas in the scheme of things

- **At the Structural Level**
  —Ex: Disciplinary power and control in the order of things

- **At the Systemic Level**
  —Ex: Mutualism and ecological psychology

- **At the Cultural Level**
  —Ex: The recurrence of competing spirits, and floating consciousness as a climax of evolution

(continued on next page)

Table 1.18. The Being-Ness of Consciousness (and Other Mental States) (Part II)

- **At the Cosmological Level**
  —Ex: The search for elsewherewhen, and the evolution of other consciousnesses (e.g., the hyper-spatial consciousness)

Notes: These examples are solely illustrative (not exhaustive), and some of the items can be reclassified somewhere else. Nor are they always mutually exclusive. Since they are generalities, exceptions are expected.
Sources: From *FPHC*. See also *FCD* and *FHC*.

Table 1.19. Cognitive Partiality in Different Mental States

- **The Conscious**
  - —*Biased*
    - Ex: Self-overratingness
    - Ex: Self-modesty
    - Ex: Self-fulfilling prophesy
  - —*Shallow*
    - Ex: Attribution error
    - Ex: Heuristics
    - Ex: Illusory thinking
  - —*Short-term*
    - Ex: Deindividuation
  - —*Materialistic*
    - Ex: Hierarchy of needs

- **The Subconscious**
  - Ex: mental reconstruction
  - Ex: stereotyping

- **The Unconscious**
  - Ex: automatic processing
  - Ex: cognitive intuition

Notes: These examples are solely illustrative (not exhaustive), and some of the items can be reclassified somewhere else. Nor are they always mutually exclusive. Since they are generalities, exceptions are expected. And the comparison is relative, not absolute.
Source: From *BCPC*

Table 1.20. Emotional Non-Neutrality and Behavioral Alteration in Different Mental States

- **The Emotional**
  —*Conscious*
  Ex: Feelings
  —*Subconscious*
  Ex: Moods
  —*Unconscious*
  Ex: Empathy
  Ex: Instincts

- **The Behavioral**
  —*Conscious*
  Ex: Foot-in-the-door
  Ex: Role playing
  Ex: Saying-is-believing
  —*Subconscious*
  Ex: Discrimination
  —*Unconscious*
  Ex: Non-Verbal Communication

Notes: These examples are solely illustrative (not exhaustive), and some of the items can be reclassified somewhere else. Nor are they always mutually exclusive. Since they are generalities, exceptions are expected. And the comparison is relative, not absolute.
Source: From *BCPC*

Table 1.21. The Limits of Intuition in Unconsciousness

- **Cognitive Intuition (or Intuitive Thinking)**
  - —*Features*
    - Ex: mental schemas
    - Ex: expertise
    - Ex: blindsight
  - —*Problems*
    - Ex: inaccurate
    - Ex: non-explanatory

- **Emotional Intuition**
  - —*Features*
    - Ex: empathy
    - Ex: instincts
  - —*Problems*
    - Ex: over-generalized
    - Ex: non-explanatory

- **Behavioral Intuition**
  - —*Features*
    - Ex: prosemics
    - Ex: kinesics
  - —*Problems*
    - Ex: unreliable
    - Ex: non-explanatory

Notes: These examples are solely illustrative (not exhaustive), and some of the items can be reclassified somewhere else. Nor are they always mutually exclusive. Since they are generalities, exceptions are expected. And the comparison is relative, not absolute.
Source: From *BCPC*

Table 1.22. The Wealth/Poverty Dialectics in Different Mental States: The Case of Cognition

- **The Conscious**
  - —*Biased*
    - Ex: If richer in self-serving bias, then poorer in understanding others
  - —*Shallow*
    - Ex: If richer in heuristic thinking, then poorer in comprehending reality
  - —*Short-term*
    - Ex: If richer in short-term tendency, then poorer in long-term planning
  - —*Materialistic*
    - Ex: If richer in physiological obsession, then poorer in spiritual enlightenment

- **The Subconscious**
  - Ex: If richer in mental reconstruction, then poorer in accuracy of recall
  - Ex: If richer in stereotyping, then poorer in understanding groups

- **The Unconscious**
  - Ex: If richer in automatic processing, then poorer in depth of analysis
  - Ex: If richer in cognitive intuition, then poorer in reliability of judgments

Notes: These examples are solely illustrative (not exhaustive), and some of the items can be reclassified somewhere else. Nor are they always mutually exclusive. Since they are generalities, exceptions are expected. And the comparison is relative, not absolute.
Source: From *BCPC*

Table 1.23. The Wealth/Poverty Dialectics in Different Mental States: The Case of Emotion and Behavior

- **Emotion**
  - —*Conscious*
    - Ex: If richer in relying on familiarity and similarity for social attraction, then poorer in having diverse social relations
  - —*Subconscious*
    - Ex: If richer in moodiness, then poorer in sober thinking
  - —*Unconscious*
    - Ex: If richer in empathy, then poorer in task-oriented efficiency
    - Ex: If richer in instincts, then poorer in critical thinking

- **Behavior**
  - —*Conscious*
    - Ex: If richer in foot-in-the-door technique, then poorer in instant Gratification
    - Ex: If richer in role playing, then poorer in identity stability
  - —*Subconscious*
    - Ex: If richer in discriminating, then poorer in social harmony
  - —*Unconscious*
    - Ex: If richer in kinesics and proxemics, then poorer in verbal skills, relatively speaking.

Notes: These examples are solely illustrative (not exhaustive), and some of the items can be reclassified somewhere else. Nor are they always mutually exclusive. Since they are generalities, exceptions are expected. And the comparison is relative, not absolute.

Source: From *BCPC*

Table 1.24. The Theoretical Debate on Nature vs. Nurture (Part I)

- **The Environmental Approach**
  —*Thesis*: It focuses, relatively speaking, more on the environment (culture and society) in explaining the achievement gap among individuals and for that matter, countries or regions, when contrasted with the natural factors.
  —*Discourse*: Examples include Jose Ortega y Gasset ("Man has no nature; what he has is history"), Ashley Montagu ("Man is man because he has no instincts, because everything he is and has become he has learned from his culture, from the man-made part of the environment, from other human beings"), Stephen Jay Gould ("[The] brain [is] capable of a full range of behaviors and predisposed to none"), and Jesse Jackson (who blames white racism for the failure of blacks to close the achievement gap between whites and blacks in America). The works on dependency theory in international political economy (with a Marxian influence) and on the Protestant work ethic (by Max Weber) also point to this environmental direction.

- **The Genetic Approach**
  —*Thesis*: It focuses instead, relatively speaking again, on hereditory factors (e.g., genes and evolution) in explaining the achievement gap among individuals and for that matter, countries or regions, when contrasted with the envrionmental factors.
  —*Discourse*: Examples are Hans Eysenck and William Sheldon (in constitutional psychology), Konrad Lorenz (in his work on innate aggressive human nature), Gary Marcus (on the complexities of human thought by a tiny number of genes) and Robert Plomin, together with Michael Owen and Peter McGuffin (on the genetic basis of complex human behaviors).

(continued on next page)

Table 1.24. The Theoretical Debate on Nature vs. Nurture (Part II)

- **The Compromise Approach**
  —*Thesis*: It seeks the middle-of-the-road argument in regard to nature and nurture and regards all differences among individuals and groups as the result of the mixture of both nature and nurture, more or less equally.
  —*Discourse*: Examples include C. Murray and R. Herrnstein ("It seems highly likely to us that both genes and environment have something to do with this issue") and Dan Dennett ("Surely 'everyone knows' that the nature-nurture debate was resolved long ago, and neither side wins since everything – is – a – mixture – of – both – and - it's – all – very -complicated…."

- **The Transcendent Approach**
  —*Thesis*: It goes beyond both nature and nurture (without, however, committing the compromise fallacy) in showing their closely intertwined interactions in producing the behavioral differences as often seen in individual human endeavors on the micro scale, and for that matter, in country (or regional) endeavors on the macro one—in the context of my five theses, namely, (a) the compromise fallacy, (b) no oppression without self-oppression, (c) no success without failure, (d) the factor of randomness, and (e) the post-human vision, to be elaborated in Chapter Six.
  —*Discourse*: Peter Baofu proposed this approach on the basis of his "theory of contrastive advantages" (as an original theoretical contribution to the debate, which was first proposed and analyzed in *The Future of Capitalism and Democracy*). In the end, the human genes will not last, to be eventually superseded by post-human life forms, so the debate between genes and memes has obscured something profoundly important about the future that the world has never known. And the debate is also misleading and faulty in its dichotomy.

Source: From *BNN*. See the book for citations and details.

Table 1.25. Physical Challenges to Hyper-Spatial Consciousness

- **The Understanding of a Higher-Dimensional World of Space-Time**
  —Ex: 4 for traditional aspects of space-time (e.g., length, width, breadth and time) plus 6 more new dimensions in theory of hyper-space, with profound implications for practical applications to new forms of consciousness.

- **The Mastering of Dark Matter and Dark Energy**
  —Ex: "ordinary matter" (e.g., atoms, molecules) as a mere 4.4% of the universe, with 23% made of "cold dark matter" and the rest (about 73%) of mysterious "dark energy," with fundamental significance to questions about the limit of the speed of energy (or info), the availability of energy for use, and the nature of space-time, just to cite some examples.

- **The Exploration of Multiverses**
  —Ex: theoretical speculation of other universes (e.g., "baby universes," "gateways" in black holes, "wave function of the universe," "many worlds," "brane worlds"), with potentially seminary discoveries of different physical laws in relation to matter-energy and space-time, and vital differences to the future of post-human conquest of other universes (for the emergence of new forms of consciousness).

Notes: These examples are solely illustrative (not exhaustive), and some of the items can be reclassified somewhere else. Nor are they always mutually exclusive. Since they are generalities, exceptions are expected. The point here is to give a rough picture of the evolution of consciousness to the hyper-spatial consciousness and others totally unknown to current earthlings. As a note of clarification, it makes no difference to my argument as to whether or not the hyper-spatial consciousness may emerge before, during, and after floating consciousness.
Source: From *Table 4.5* of *FPHC*

Table 1.26. The Theory of Floating Consciousness (Part I)

- **At the Micro-Physical Level**
  —Ex: intelligent life without the human physical-chemical system

- **At the Chemical Level**
  —Ex: space radiation and toxins

- **At the Bio-Psychological Level**
  —Ex: exo-biological evolution in deep space
  —Ex: genetic engineering of new beings

- **At the Institutional Level**
  —Ex: post-capitalism
  —Ex: post-democracy

- **At the Organizational Level**
  —Ex: less legal-formalistic routines

- **At the Structural Level**
  —Ex: alien forms of violence

- **At the Cultural Level**
  —Ex: transcending freedom
  —Ex: transcending equality

(continued on next page)

Table 1.26. The Theory of Floating Consciousness (Part II)

- **At the Cosmological Level**
  —Ex: parallel universes
  —Ex: pocket universes

- **At the Systemic Level**
  —Ex: space habitats (in zero-gravity)

Notes: Each example draws from the works of different scholars in the field. For instance, at the cosmological level, the idea of parallel universes is from the theoretical speculation in quantum cosmology by Stephen Hawking and others, while the one of pocket universes comes from the theoretical work of Allan Guth at MIT. And at the institutional level, I proposed post-capitalism and post-democracy in *FCD* (and later, from *BDPD* and *BCPC*). In addition, the examples are solely illustrative (not exhaustive), and some of the items can be reclassified somewhere else. Nor are they always mutually exclusive. Since they are generalities, exceptions are expected.
Sources: From *FPHC*—and, originally, from *FCD*

Table 1.27. The Potential of Unfolding Unconsciousness

- **Superior Senses**
  - —*Through space*
    - Ex: clair-sentience (in feeling)
    - Ex: clair-voyance (in seeing)
    - Ex: clair-audience (in hearing)
    - Ex: clair-austance (in tasting)
    - Ex: clair-alience (in smelling)
    - Ex: clair-cognizance (in knowing)
  - —*Through time*
    - Ex: pre-cognition (in knowing), pre-sentiment (in feeling)
    - Ex: retro-cognition (in knowing), retro-sentiment (in feeling)

- **Superior Contacts**
  - —*With living minds*
    - Ex: telepathy
  - —*With the dead*
    - Ex: mediumship
  - —*With other-living entities*
    - Ex: telekinesis

Notes: The categories and examples are solely illustrative (not exhaustive), and the comparison is relative (not absolute), nor are they necessarily mutually exclusive. And some can be easily re-classified elsewhere. As generalities, they allow exceptions.
Source: A summary of Ch.5 of *FPHU*

Table 1.28. The Future Exploration of Unfolding Unconsciousness

- **In the Context of Nature**
  —Ex: the higher-dimensional space-time in hyperspace theory
  —Ex: the particle-wave interactions in quantum mechanics
  —Ex: the study of brain waves in electromagnetic theory

- **In the Context of the Mind**
  —Ex: the unconscious fantasies in psychoanalysis
  —Ex: the mind-altering drugs in biochemistry
  —Ex: the manipulation of neural activity in neurobiology

- **In the Context of Culture**
  —Ex: the correlation between anomalous experience and moral/religious/aesthetic interests in culture studies
  —Ex: the role of myths and language in epistemology

- **In the Context of Society**
  —Ex: different organizational agendas in anomalous research
  —Ex: the scholarly divide on anomalous study
  —Ex: interests and propaganda in institutioanl research
  —Ex: the transformative power of technology in research on social systems
  —Ex: the natural and non-natural selection of other worlds in exo-biology
  —Ex: the role of the post-human conscious mind in qualitative demography

Notes: The examples in each category are solely illustrative (not exhaustive), and the comparison is relative (not absolute), nor are they necessarily mutually exclusive. And some can be easily re-classified elsewhere. As generalities, they allow exceptions.
Source: A summary of Chs.2-5 of *FPHU*, in conjunction with the rest of the book

Table 1.29. Creative Techniques and Traits

- **Creative Techniques**
  - —*Comprehensiveness*
    - Ex: Broadness of Scope
    - Ex: In-Depth Analysis
    - Ex: Multifaceted Taxonomy
    - Ex: Numerous Theories
  - —*Arrangement*
    - Ex: Separation (or Subtraction)
    - Ex: Combination (or Addition)
    - Ex: Replacement
    - Ex: Reversal
    - Ex: Accommodation
    - Ex: Stretching
  - —*Serendipity*
    - Ex: Play
    - Ex: Chance

- **Creative Traits**
  - —*Openness / Risk*
    - Ex: Ability to welcome new ideas or to do new things, with risk
  - —*Discipline*
    - Ex: Ability to sacrifice whatever it takes to succeed
  - —*Resilience / Confidence*
    - Ex: Ability to take failures to mind, not to heart
  - —*Trust*
    - Ex: Ability to cooperate with others for team work, if necessary

Notes: The examples in the categories are solely illustrative (not exhaustive), and the comparison is relative (not absolute), nor are they necessarily mutually exclusive. And some can be easily re-classified elsewhere. As generalities, they allow exceptions.
Source: From *Sec.4.2* of *FPHCT*. For more details, also read the rest of the book.

Table 1.30. The Desirability of Creativity, and Its Dark Sides (Part I)

- **In Relation to Instrumental Rationality**
  —*Desirability*
    - Ex: For the sake of efficiency and effectiveness in this capitalist era of our time.

  —*Undesirability*
    - Ex: What Max Weber (1930) called the "iron cage" of capitalism, where live the "sensualists without heart, specialists without spirit"—or something which the Frankfurt School has forcefully asked us to be freed from.

- **In Relation to Substantive Rationality**
  —*Desirability*
    - Ex: For the sake of God, the King, Motherland, or other comparable ideals.

  —*Undesirability*
    - Ex: Domination and oppression of various forms—something which the moderns had struggled to free themselves from in the first place, since the dawn of modernity.

- **In Relation to Autonomous Rationality**
  —*Desirability*
    - Ex: For the sake of itself, the autonomy of creative endeavor.

  —*Undesirability*
    - Ex: The decadence of its own degeneration (e.g., the donwsides of postmodernism in our postmodern times, or what Nietzsche once called the unbearable "unreality" and "falseness" of the autonomous artist's "innermost existence"—and, in other cases, the painful suffering from different mental illnesses for those highly creative individuals).

(continued on next page)

Table 1.30. The Desirability of Creativity, and Its Dark Sides (Part II)

Notes: The examples in the categories are solely illustrative (not exhaustive), and the comparison is relative (not absolute), nor are they necessarily mutually exclusive. And some can be easily re-classified elsewhere. As generalities, they allow exceptions.
Also, I already went to great lenghts to explain the desirability and its dark sides of all these three rationalities (although there may be others too) in the two volumes of *FHC*—and, for that matter, *FCD*.
Source: From *Sec.4.9* of *FPHCT*. For more details, also read the rest of the book.

Table 1.31. Posthuman-Ism, Post-Humanism, and Trans-Humanism

- **Post-Humanism**
  —The neologism "post-human" used in my books should *not* be confused with another term which looks similar but has a totally different meaning in the literature of postmodernism, namely, "post-humanism"—which constitutes a critique of "humanism" as tradionally understood (especially, though not exclusively, in relation to the idea of progress in science and reason in the Enlightenment project). (WK 2008)
  —My works reject the project of "postmodernism" and propose the future world of what I orignally called "after-postmodernity" in *FHC* and *FCD*, for instance.

- **Trans-Humanism**
  —Also, the neologism "post-human" used in my books should *not* be confused with a similar term which is used to champion the ideology of technology for the fturue co-existence between humans and cyborgs in "trans-humanism." (WK 2008a)
  —Instead, my term "post-human" in relation to "posthuman-ism" also rejects "trans-humanism" (especially, though not exclusively, in relation to the promises of technology) and refers to something else altogether, that is, the future extinction of humans and its post-human successors in deep space and beyond unto multiverses.

- **Posthuman-Ism**
  —With these two clarifications in mind, the "post-humans" (as envisioned in my books) can take different forms, and I proposed, in my different books, some of them, such as "unfolding unconsciousness," "floating consciousness," "hyper-spatial consciousness," "thinking machines," "thinking robots," "genetically altered superior beings," "cyborgs," and others (as already analyzed in my previous works).
  —They will evolve in conjunction with other visions of mine in relation to nature, society, and culture.

Source: From *Sec.1.6* of *FPHE*. For more details, also read the rest of the book (and other books of mine).

Table 1.32. Three Great Future Transformations of the Martial Body (Part I)

- **Virtual Battle**
  —Ex: virtual fight
  —Ex: virtual memory

- **The Hyper-Martial Body**
  —*In relation to the physical dimension*
  - Ex: striking (e.g., punching, kicking, trapping, acupressure-striking, and so on in an amazing way)
  - Ex: grapping (e.g., throwing, pinning, joint-locking, and so on in an amazing way)
  - Ex: running and walking (e.g., on different surfaces)
  - Ex: jumping (e.g., through walls, trees, etc.)
  - Ex: flying (e.g., through space)
  - Ex: enduring pain (e.g., absorbing punches, kicks, and so on in an amazing way)
  - Ex: using extremely advanced hi-tech weapons
  - Ex: healing (e.g., with special energy, etc.)
  - Ex: entering (e.g., into different dimensions of space)
  - Ex: sensing (e.g., in extraordinary ways through space and time, etc.)
  - Ex: wearing hi-tech suits for defensive and offensive purposes (e.g., like a hi-tech armor)

  —*In relation to the mental dimension*
  - Ex: the ability to relax the martial body in a way that current humans cannot.
  - Ex: the ability to concentrate the martial mind in a way that current humans are not accustomed to.
  - Ex: the ability to breathe and be timely in preparing the martial body for fighting in a way that current humans are not good at.

- **The Post-Martial Floating Mind**
  —Ex: the mind without the human body
  —Ex: the quest for spirituality beyond martial arts

(continued on next page)

Table 1.32. Three Great Future Transformations of the Martial Body (Part II)

Notes: The examples in the categories are solely illustrative (not exhaustive), and the comparison is relative (not absolute), nor are they necessarily mutually exclusive. And some can be easily re-classified elsewhere. As generalities, they allow exceptions.
Source: From *Sec. 2.5.1* of *FPHMA*. See text for citations.

Table 1.33. Three Great Future Transformations of the Sexual Body

- **Virtual Pleasure**
  —Ex: virtual Sex
  —Ex: virtual Recall

- **The Hyper-Sexual Body**
  —*In relation to the physical dimension*
  - Ex: the ability to perform differenet sexual positions without the various physical limitations that humans currently have.
  - Ex: the ability to produce unusual amount of sexual energy to endure in sexual acts in a way that humans currently cannot.
  - Ex: the ability to engage in multiple sexual experiences comparable to (but different from) non-human sexuality (e.g., hermaphrodite, monoecious, sex-switching, and many other types) that current humans cannot.

  —*In relation to the mental dimension*
  - Ex: the ability to relax the sexual body in a way that current humans are not accustomed to.
  - Ex: the ability to concentrate the sexual mind in a way that current humans are not good at.
  - Ex: the ability to breathe and be patient in preparing the sexual body for sexuality in a way that current humans are not able to.

- **The Post-Sexual Floating Mind**
  —Ex: the mind without the human body
  —Ex: the quest for spirituality beyond sexuality

Notes: The examples in the categories are solely illustrative (not exhaustive), and the comparison is relative (not absolute), nor are they necessarily mutually exclusive. And some can be easily re-classified elsewhere. As generalities, they allow exceptions.
Source: From *Sec. 3.4.2* of *FPHS*. See text for more info.

Table 1.34. The Trinity of Pre-Modernity

- **Pre-Free-Spirited Pre-Modernity (Pre-Modernism) and Its Internal Split**
  —Competing worldviews and values both within and between linear centric (e.g., Islamic, Christian, Judaic, Imperial Roman) and cyclical-centric (e.g., Confucian, Taoist, Hindu, and Buddhist) orientations
  —Compare modernism with pre-modernism here in relation to the seven dimensions of human existence like the true and the holy (e.g., different versions of epistemic dogmas and religious superstitions), the everyday and the technological (e.g.,different versions of non-technophilism and non-consumerism), the beautiful/sublime (e.g., different versions of aesthetic non-autonomy), and the good and the just (e.g., different versions of moral particularism).

- **Pre-Capitalist Pre-Modernity (Pre-Modernization) and Its Own Discontents**
  —Competing versions of societal arrangements (e.g., feudalism, monarchism, and the holy order)

- **Hegemonic Pre-Modernity and Its Countervailing Forces**
  —Different power centers and their enemies (e.g., the Roman Empire and the "barbarian hordes," the "Holy Crusades" and the Muslims, the Middle Kingdom and the invading tribes, different social castes in India, and warring Greek city-states)

Notes: The examples in each category are solely illustrative (not exhaustive) nor necessarily mutually exclusive, and the comparison is relative (not absolute). As generalities, they allow exceptions. Also, it does not matter what the "base" era is in the analysis of any trinity. And in the present context, the "base" era is modernity (for instance, with its "free-spirited modernity" and the other two parts). So, for pre-modernity, the trinity takes the form of, say, "pre-free-spirited pre-modernity," together with the other two parts.
Sources: From Ch.2 of *BCIV* and also the 2 volumes of *FHC*

Table 1.35. The Trinity of Modernity (Part I)

- **Free-Spirited Modernity (Modernism) and Its Internal Split**
  —*On the True and the Holy*
    - The freedom from the dogmas of the past to the better understanding of, and union with, the world and self (Ch.3 of *FHC*)
    - Alternative discourses: about the true (e.g., anti-science discourses) and the holy (non-mainstream theologies) (Ch.3 of *FHC*)

  —*On the Technological and the Everyday*
    - The freedom from life harshness to the higher technophilic, consumeristic lifeform (Ch.2 of *FHC*)
    - Alternative discourses: about the everyday (e.g., transcendental mindsets) and the technological (e.g., Arcadianism) (Ch.2 of *FHC*)

  —*On the Good and the Just*
    - The freedom from the theo-aristocratic tyranny to the moral universality for a just society (Ch.5 of *FHC*)
    - Alternative discourses: about the just (e.g., Communism, Anarchism) and the good (e.g., Nazism/Fascism, and Zarathustrianism) (Chs.5-6 of *FHC*)

  —*On the Beautiful and the Sublime*
    - The freedom from the external distortion of aesthetic pleasure to the boundless infinity of totality in artistic autonomy (Ch.4 of *FHC*)
    - Alternative discourses: about the beautiful/sublime (e.g., kitsch and historical avant-gardism) (Ch.4 of *FHC*)

- **Capitalist Modernity (Modernization) and Its Own Discontents**
  —*During the Industrial Revolution*
    - Ex: Marx on the institution of inequality (Ch.1 of *FHC*)

  —*During the Modern Rational-Instrumental Epoch*
    - Ex: Weber on the politics of soft liberal institutions (Ch.5 of *FHC*)

  —*During the Great Depression*
    - Ex: Keynes on the myth of the free market (Chs.1-3 of *FHC*)

  —*During the Cold War*
    - Ex: Lasch on the narcissistic culture industry (Chs.2-3 of *FHC*)

(continued on next page)

Table 1.35. The Trinity of Modernity (Part II)

- **Hegemonic Modernity and Its Countervailing Forces**
  —*The Legacies of Colonialism and Imperialism*
    - Ex: European colonization of most of the modern world (Ch.1 of *FHC*)

  —*The Struggle for Decolonialization*
    - Ex: The countervailing forces of resentment, rechantment, and regionalism (Chs.1 & 6 of *FHC*)

Notes: The examples in each category are solely illustrative (not exhaustive) nor necessarily mutually exclusive, and the comparison is relative (not absolute). As generalities, they allow exceptions.
Sources: From the 2 volumes of *FHC*—and also from *FCD*

Table 1.36. The Trinity of Postmodernity

- **Free-Spirited Postmodernity (Postmodernism) and Its Internal Split**
  —*On the True and the Holy*
    - Postmodern performative turn for knowing and its enemies (Ch.3 of *FHC*)
    - Postmodern comparative theology and its opponents (Ch.3 of *FHC*)

  —*On the Technological and the Everyday*
    - Postmodern corporate technological mindset and its adversaries (Ch.2 of *FHC*)
    - Postmodern postmaterialism and its critics (Ch.2 of *FHC*)

  —*On the Good and the Just*
    - Postmodern politics of difference and its foes (Ch.5 of *FHC*)

  —*On the Beautiful and the Sublime*
    - Postmodern deconstruction and its dissenters (Ch.4 of *FHC*)

- **Capitalist Postmodernity (Postmodernization) and Its Own Discontents**
  —*During the Post-Cold War and Beyond*
    - Ex: post-Fordism and its shortcomings (Ch.6 of *FHC*; Chs.6-7 of *FCD*)

- **Hegemonic Postmodernity and Its Countervailing Forces**
  —*The Debate on the Global Village*
    - Ex: uni-civilizationalism vs. multi-civilizationalism (Ch.6 of *FHC*)

  —*The Resistance Movement*
    - Ex: rechantment and the politics of civilizational claims (e.g., Islamic, Confucian and other ethos in relation to the Same) (Ch.6 of *FHC*; Ch.10 of *FCD*)
    - Ex: resentment and the politics of resurgence (e.g., the rising Chinese superpower, the growing EU, and other players in relation to the U.S. and her allies) (Ch.6 of *FHC*; Ch.8 of *FCD*)
    - Ex: regionalism and the politics of inequality (e.g., trans- or international blocs, the North-South divide, NGO's) (Ch.6 of *FHC*; Ch.5 of *FCD*)

Notes: The examples in each category are solely illustrative (not exhaustive) nor necessarily mutually exclusive, and the comparison is relative (not absolute). As generalities, they allow exceptions.
Sources: From *FCD* and the 2 volumes of *FHC*

Table 1.37. The Trinity of After-Postmodernity

- **Free-Spirited After-Postmodernity (After-Postmodernism) and Its Internal Split**
  —The discourse of naked contingency (Ch.10 of *FCD*; Ch.4 of *FPHC*)

- **Post-Capitalist After-Postmodernity (After-Postmodernization) and Its Own Discontents**
  —Different versions of post-capitalism and post-democracy, and their enemies (Ch.10 of *FCD*; Chs.3-4 of *FPHC*)

- **Hegemonic After-Postmodernity and Its Countervailing Forces**
  —The Cyclical Progression of Hegemony in Multiverses (Chs.9-10 of *FCD*; Ch.4 of *FPHC*)

Notes: The examples in each category are solely illustrative (not exhaustive) nor necessarily mutually exclusive, and the comparison is relative (not absolute). As generalities, they allow exceptions.
Sources: From *FCD* and also *FHC*

• PART TWO •

Necessity

CHAPTER 2
NECESSITY AND ITS DISPENSABILITY

An unjust law is no law at all.
—A classical natural law maxim
(WK 2009g)

The Categoricalness of Necessity

In jurisprudence, a fundamental issue which has spent so much time and energy of legal philosophers over the ages concerns the validity of a law on the basis of some universality, relative to a given standard.

After all, what exactly is in a law which makes it necessary for us to obey?

To understand the categoricalness of this necessity in a law is the central concern of this chapter, which is to provide a comprehensive analysis of the necessity argument from the four perspectives of the mind, nature, society, and culture (in accordance to my sophisticated methodological holism, as explained in *Sec. 1.8*).

This chapter is therefore organized in four main sections, in relation to (2.2) necessity and the mind, (2.3) necessity and nature, (2.4) necessity and society, and (2.5) necessity and culture—to be examined in what follows, in that order (and summarized in *Table 2.1*).

Necessity and the Mind

Necessity, when examined from the perspective of the mind, can shed some illuminating light on the nature of law, and this can be shown by way of two case studies, namely, (2.2.1) the law of reason, and the categorical imperative, and (2.2.2) criminal law, and the maleness of violence—to be addressed hereafter, in that order.

The Law of Reason, and the Categorical Imperative

Immanuel Kant, for instance, has much to say about the law of reason in the human mind, to the extent that it can provide us the categorical imperative as a solid foundation for the law.

The Distinction between the Categorical and the Hypothetical

Kant addressed the foundational issue of moral philosophy in his three major works, namely, *Groundwork of the Metaphysics of Morals* (1785), *Critique of Practical Reason* (1788), and *Metaphysics of Morals* (1797) . (WK 2009q)

The starting point for Kant is the human faculty of "practical reason," which "is based only upon things about which reason can tell us, and not deriving any principles from experience, to reach conclusions which are able to be applied to the world of experience." (WK 2009q)

In Kant's practical reason, there is an important distinction to be made at the outset, namely, the difference between (a) the "categorical imperative" and (b) the "hypothetical imperative"—to be summarized below, in that order.

(a) The Categorical Imperative

On the one hand, the "categorical imperative" refers to the moral obligation which "is derived from the concept of duty," not from anything else, such that "categorical imperatives…are principles that are intrinsically valid; they are good in and of themselves; they must be obeyed in all situations and circumstances if our behavior is to observe the moral law." (WK 2009q)

These categorical imperatives constitutes the demands of the moral law, and it is from these categorical imperatives that "all other moral obligations are generated, and by which all moral obligations can be tested." (WK 2009q)

(b) The Hypothetical Imperative

On the other hand, the "hypothetical imperative" is different and does not constitute the demands of the moral law, because they are often pursued not as ends in themselves but as means to some ends.

For instance, "[e]nds that are based on physical needs or wants will always give for merely hypothetical imperatives. The categorical imperative, however, may be based only on something that is an 'end in itself.' That is, an end that is a means only to itself and not to some other need, desire, or purpose." (WK 2009q)

Thus, "the moral law is a principle of reason itself, and is not based on contingent facts about the world, such as what would make us happy, but to act upon the moral law which has no other motive than 'worthiness of being happy.' Accordingly,…moral obligation applies to all and only rational agents." (WK 2009q)

In this way, the hypothetical imperative, unlike the categorical imperative, does not have "pure intention" behind it, because the action based on the hypothetical imperative "is not done with the motive of duty" and thus "is without moral value." (WK 2009q)

For Kant, "every action should have pure intention behind it" in order to have moral worth; although "[h]e did not necessarily believe that the final result was the most important aspect of an action,…how the person felt while carrying out the action was the time at which value was set to the result." (WK 2009q)

With his critique of Utilitarianism in mind—Kant compared "a price" with "a dignity," as he thus wrote: "Everything has either a price or a dignity. Whatever has a price can be replaced by something else as its equivalent; on the other hand, whatever is above all price, and therefore admits of no equivalent, has a dignity. But that which constitutes the condition under which alone something can be an end in itself does not have mere relative worth, i.e., price, but an intrinsic worth, i.e., a dignity." (WK 2009q)

Three Formulations of the Categorical Imperative

Kant offered different formulations of the categorical imperative to be followed, and three major ones are, namely, (a) the first formulation (for universal law), (b) the second formulation (for the end in itself), and (c) the third formulation (for autonomy)—to be summarized hereafter, respectively. (WK 2009q)

(a) The First Formulation (for Universal Law)

In the first formulation, the task here is to check whether or not a given action can pass the test of "universal law."

Thus, the first formulation is known as the "Formula of Universal Law," which "requires that the maxims be chosen as though they should hold as universal laws of nature," as it reads: "Always act according to that maxim whose universality as a law you can at the same time will," and it is the "only condition under which a will can never come into conflict with itself." (WK 2009q)

This "universalisability test" can take five steps, as shown below: (2009q)

- "Find the agent's maxim (i.e., an action paired with its motivation). Take for example the declaration 'I will lie for personal benefit.' Lying is the action; the motivation is to fulfil some sort of desire. Paired together, they form the maxim."
- "Imagine a possible world in which everyone in a similar position to the real-world agent followed that maxim."
- "Decide whether any contradictions or irrationalities arise in the possible world as a result of following the maxim."
- "If a contradiction or irrationality arises, acting on that maxim is not allowed in the real world."
- "If there is no contradiction, then acting on that maxim is permissible, and in some instances required."

So, if a moral agent passes this test, his action has the moral worth to meet the demands of the moral law.

(b) The Second Formulation (for the End in Itself)

In the second formulation, the task here is to check whether or not a given action can pass the test of "the end in itself."

Thus, the second formulation is also known as the "Formula of the End in Itself," which requires that "the rational being, as by its nature an end and thus as an end in itself, must serve in every maxim as the condition restricting all merely relative and arbitrary ends." (WK 2009q)

This then means that a moral agent must "[a]ct with reference to every rational being (whether…[himself] or another) so that it is an end in itself in…[the] maxim," to the point that "the rational being is 'the basis of all maxims of action' and 'must be treated never as a mere means but as the supreme limiting condition in the use of all means, i.e., as an end at the same time.'" (WK 2009q)

(c) The Third Formulation (for Rational Autonomy)

And in the third formulation, the task here is to check whether or not a given action can pass the test of "autonomy."

Thus, the third formulation is called the "Formula of Autonomy," which is "a synthesis of the first two and is the basis for the 'complete determination of all maxims.' It says 'that all maxims which stem from autonomous legislation ought to harmonize with a possible realm of ends as with a realm of nature.'" (WK 2009q)

This then means that a moral agent must "act as if…[the] maxims should serve at the same time as the universal law (of all rational beings)," so that he should think of himself as exercising his rational autonomy to be "a member in the universal realm of ends." (WK 2009q)

Two Assumptions of Freedom, and the Condition of the Moral Law

But Kant was keen enough to recognize a potential serious problem here, in that the demands of the moral law in his interpretation are so strict that an ordinary mortal human being may not be free enough to meet this exceedingly high moral standard as expected from categorical imperatives so understood in the three formulations.

In order to fix this practical problem, Kant made two assumptions of freedom.

The first assumption is a kind of freedom *from* something (like "coercion")—in that Kant assumed, as the condition of the moral law, "the idea of freedom," which then allows a moral agent to choose acting morally or not. (WK 2009q) This "practical" idea of freedom refers to "the independence of our will from the 'coercion' or 'necessitation through sensuous impulses.'" (WK 2009q)

Even then, Kant also recognized that this assumption of the "practical" idea of freedom was not sufficient as the condition of the moral law, since something else was also needed.

So, the second assumption is a kind of freedom *to* something (like the attainment of "the supreme good")—in that Kant also assumed "the idea of God," to be used as "the ideal of the supreme good." (WK 2009q)

In other words, this idea of God serves as "the transcendental idea of freedom," which, unlike the "practical" idea of freedom, refers to "the question whether we must admit a power of spontaneously beginning a series of successive things or states," such that it is used as "the ideal of the supreme good." (WK 2009q)

Although Kant conceded that "we do not have the slightest ground to assume in an absolute manner… the object of this idea" of God, the idea "is necessary from the practical point of view." (WK 2009q)

Kant himself thus explained: "One cannot provide objective reality for any theoretical idea, or prove it, except for the idea of freedom, because this is the condition of the moral law, whose reality is an axiom. The reality of the idea of God can only be proved by means of this idea, and hence only with a practical purpose, i.e., to act as though…there is a God, and hence only for this purpose"—that is, to be used as "the ideal of the supreme good." (WK 2009q)

These two assumptions in regard to the practical idea of freedom and the transcendental idea of freedom in Kantian ethics thus claims that a moral agent is not only free to choose acting morally (or not) but also free to strive for "the ideal of the supreme good."

The Achilles' Heel of Kantian Jurisprudence

When translated into the language of jurisprudence, the Kantian ethics requires that a law cannot be created as a means to promote hypothetical imperatives, or something which is used as a means for something else, like "power," "wealth," "honour," "health," and other mundane desires. (WK 2009j) In fact, "such actions [based on these desires] are…the source of all manner of evil," and "[t]hey can also be extremely bad and hurtful." (WK 2009j)

Instead, a law must pass the test that "people should always be treated with respect to their personhood and dignity, and always as ends in themselves"—especially in relation to the three formulations for universal law, for the end in itself, and for rational autonomy. (WK 2009j & 2009q)

Unfortunately, Kant's solution to the practical concern with moral freedom by way of the two assumptions of freedom (i.e., practical freedom and transcendental freedom) also constitutes the Achilles' heel of the Kantian interpretaton of the law of reason.

His critics have wasted no time to question to what extent both practical freedom and transcendental freedom are possible and desirable. Consider two classic criticisms below, for illustration.

Firstly, in relation to the question of possibility, David Hume made a name of himself by famously arguing that reason by itself "could not be a ground for moral choices," because, as he thus wrote: "Reason is, and ought only to be the slave of the passions, and can never pretend to any other office than to serve and obey them." (WK 2009k; D. Hume 2003) In other words, we are not as free from our desires and passions (or independent of our impluses) as Kant naively assumed.

And secondly, in relation to the question of desirability, Arthur Schopenhauer in *On the Basis of Morality* (1965) vigorously showed that "actions are not moral when they are performed solely from duty"; any law which is based on this kind of moral duty is "cold and egoistic." (WK 2009j)

In fact, the severity of Kant's obsession with the unconditioned demands of the moral law (in his transcendental dream of the ideal of the supreme good) raises the red flag of whether or not it constitutes a form of mental neurosis which Sigmund Freud had so much warned us against, in his analysis of the "impractical moralism of the super-ego," which can degenerate into a state of mental pathology. (WK 2009r)

After all, "it is often held that Kant lived a very strict and predictable life, leading to the oft-repeated story that neighbors would set their clocks by his daily walks." (WK 2009q) John Goldthwait once argued that this account of Kant's personal life was much exaggerated and was a myth;

even then, however, Kant was known for his extremely disciplinary workaholic lifestyle. (WK 2009q; I. Kant 1961)

It is a scholarly bias, however, for a scholar (Kant) to allow his strict discipline in his eccentric personal life to be carried over into his intellectual analysis of the world around him, as if what is good for him were also true for everyone else.

A Lesson to Learn

But this is not to imply that there is nothing constructive to learn from Kantian ethics and its implications for jurisprudence.

In fact, a good illustration of something to learn from this analysis of Kantian interpretation of the law of reason is its relevance to some ontological principles in existential dialectics, and good examples include the formalness-informalness principle, the absoluteness-relativeness principle, the predictability-unpredictability principle, the explicability-inexplicability principle, the finiteness-transfiniteness principle, the preciseness-vagueness principle, the simpleness-complicatedness principle, the openness-hiddenness principle, the denseness-emptiness principle, the expansion-contraction principle, the convention-novelty principle, the evolution-transformation principle, the symmetry-asymmetry principle, the softness-hardness principle, the regression-progression principle, and the same-difference principle.

For instance, in relation to the formalness-informalness principle, if there is formalness (e.g., the formal logical requirement of consistency in Kantian ethics, in relation to the law of non-contradiction, such that one must act in accordance to one's rational autonomy, not by external influences), there is also informalness (e.g., the informal logical occurrence of inconsistency, as in the "impractical hedonism of the id" in psychoanalysis). (WK 2009j & 2009r)

In relation to the absoluteness-relativeness principle, if there is absoluteness (e.g., the absolute demand of categorical imperatives in Kantian ethics), there is relative counterpart (e.g., what is good for the Kantians in regard to the strict demands of the mroal law is not so for the Freudians in regard to the impractical moralism of the superego).

In relation to the predictability-unpredictability principle, if there is predictability (e.g., the predictable tendency of a Kantian to act out of duty, with the end in itself), there is unpredictability (e.g., the more difficult task to even predict on which particular occassions a Kantian does not succumb to external influences and when he does).

In relation to the explicability-inexplicability principle, if there is explicability (e.g., the explanation of the condition of the moral law in

Kantian ethics by appealing to the necessity of practical freedom and transcendental freedom), there is inexplicability (e.g., the inability to explain, within Kantian ethics, why moral freedom at both practical and transcendental levels are possible and desirable, other than by the stipulation that they are simply asusmed to be so).

In relation to the finitenesss-transfiniteness principle, if there is finiteness (e.g., the finiteness in the idea of a moral agent, with its mortality and vulnerability), there is transfiniteness (e.g., the transfiniteness in the idea of God, with its ideal of the supreme good, which cannot be measured in terms of a finite quantity like "a price").

In relation to the preciseness-vagueness principle, if there is preciseness (e.g., the precise identification of the three formulations of the categorical imperative), there is vagueness (e.g., the vagueness about what exactly resides in the idea of the intrinsic worth of "dignity").

In relation to the simpleness-complicatedness principle, if there is simpleness (e.g., the simple solution to the practical concern with the strict demands of the moral law by assuming both practical freedom and transcendental freedom), there is complicatedness (e.g., the complicated account of the strict demands of the moral law by questioning the extent of possibility and desirability of the two kinds of moral freedom by the critics of Kantian ethics, on the basis of other factors).

In relation to the openness-hiddenness principle, if there is openness (e.g., the open exploration of the demands of the moral law, like "rational autonomy," etc.), there is hiddenness (e.g., the hidden bias in relation to the extent of possibility and desirability of rational autonomy).

In relation to the denseness-emptiness principle, if there is denseness (e.g., the relatively denser concentration of concerns with categorical imperatives for a Kantian), there is emptiness (e.g., the relatively less dense, or more empty, concentration of concerns with hypothetical imperatives for a Kantian).

In relation to the expansion-contraction principle, if there is expansion (e.g., the relatively better developed ability of a Kantian to act out of duty in itself), there is contraction (e.g., the relatively less developed ability of a Kantian to engage in Machiavellian manipulation to serve ulterior motives).

In relation to the convention-novelty principle, if there is convention (e.g., the conventional wisdom about the utilitarian way of acting), there is novelty (e.g., the Kantian alternative novel challenge to utililiatarian consequentialism by way of his deontological ethics).

In relation to the evolution-transformation principle, if there is evolution (e.g., the natural evolution of humans to behave in the state of nature, often based on impulses), there is transformation (e.g., the technical transformation of human behaviors by way of the invention of elaborated systems of ethics and law).

In relation to the symmetry-asymmetry principle, if there is symmetry (e.g., the co-existence of different views of justice, be they Kantian, utilitarian, or else), there is asymmetry (e.g., the popularity of Kantian ethics for those in the deontological tradition of the moral law, but the more acceptance of utilitarian ethics for those in the consequentialist tradition).

In relation to the softness-hardness principle, if there is softness (e.g., the approval of the respect of human dignity in Kantian ethics), there is hardness (e.g., the strict restraint of one's impulses in Kantian ethics).

In relation to the regression-progression principle, if there is regression (e.g., the "cold" and "neurotic" aspects of Kantian ethics when implemented seriously), there is progression (e.g., the enhancement of dignity in Kantian ethics).

And in relation to the same-difference principle, if there is similarity in outcome (e.g., the discipline of human behaviors in a certain way, be it Kantian, utiliarian, or else), there is difference in outcome (e.g., the betterment of dignity in Kantian ethics, and the promotion of happiness in utilitarianism).

Criminal Law, and the Maleness of Violence

The law of reason as proposed by Kant (in the previous section) is general enough, which can be applied to any legal circumstances. But not all laws are so general.

Take the case of "criminal law" (also known as "penal law"), which is more specific to a part of public law for offenses against the state, with "the potential for unique and often severe impositions as punishment for failure to comply." (WK 2009b)

When examined from the perspective of the mind, criminal law reveals the troubling relationship between the biological maleness of violence and the principles behind criminal law.

Elements of Criminal Law

Although there are many different criminal cases to be classified, there are three major elements of criminal law which deserve consideration here, namely, (a) "actus reus" (or "guilty acts" in English)

(b) "mens rea" (or "guilty mind" in English), and (c) "strict liability (criminal)"—to be summarized below, in that order. (WK 2009b)

(a) Actus Reus

In criminal law, the Latin *actus reus* means "guilty act," which refers to "the physical element of committing a crime," because the "proof of a crime requires [the] proof of some act." (WK 2009b)

The term "act" here can be interpreted in different ways, as "it may be accomplished by an action, by threat of action, or exceptionally, by an omission to act. For example, the act of A striking B might suffice, or a parent's failure to give food to a young child also may provide the actus reus for a crime." (WK 2009b)

But in those cases involving an omission to act, "there must be a duty," which can come in all shapes and sizes; for instance, a duty can be through "contract," "a voluntary undertaking," "a blood relation with whom one lives," "one's official position," "a dangerous situation," or even the need "to help someone in distress" (in good Samaritan laws). (WK 2009b)

Under certain conditions, however, "an actus reus may be nullified by an absence of causation. For example, a crime involves harm to a person, and the person's action must be the *but for* cause and *proximate cause* of the harm. If more than one cause exists (e.g. harm comes at the hands of more than one culprit) the act must have 'more than a slight or trifling link' to the harm." (WK 2009b)

Yet, one must treat these nullifying conditions with care. For example, if a victim is already vulnerable, prior to an actus reus, does this fact make the defendant innocent? Well, the problem here is that "[c]ausation is not broken simply because a victim is particularly vulnerable. This is known as the thin skull rule. However, it may be broken by an intervening act (*novus actus interveniens*) of a third party, the victim's own conduct, or another unpredictable event." (WK 2009b)

(b) Mens Rea

Besides the "physical" element of commiting a crime (as in actus reus)—there is another element, which has to do with the mind, because the proof of a crime at times requires the proof of an "intention" to commit the "wrongful act"; thus the Latin phrase *mens rea* means "guilty mind," for the "mental" element of commiting a crime.

In criminal law, one should not confuse "intention" with "motive." For instance, "[i]f Mr. Hood robs from rich Mr. Nottingham because his motive is to give the money to poor Mrs. Marian, his 'good intentions' do not change his criminal intention to commit robbery." (WK 2009b)

Or to put it in a different way, there are two kinds of intention here, the criminal intention to rob the rich, and the moral intention to help the poor. In criminal law, it is important to consider the criminal intention (as in mens rea).

Even then, in criminal law, criminal intention can be treated in different ways, and hereafter are three well-known cases, namely, (b1) specific intent, (b2) recklessness, and (b3) negligence. (WK 2009b & 2009s)

(b1) In specific intent, a defendant can be accused of, say, "murder," if he has the "specific intent to kill [someone] or with conscious recognition that death or serious bodily harm will result." (WK 2009b)

(b2) In recklessness, however, a defendant does not have the criminal intention, although he may recognize the danger; therefore, "a lower threshold of mens rea is satisfied when a defendant recognises an act is dangerous but decides to commit it anyway. This is recklessness….In this way, the importance of mens rea has been reduced in some areas of the criminal law." (WK 2009b) The defendant, in this case, may be charged with "manslaughter," not "murder."

(b3) In negligence, a defendant has neither the specific intent nor the recognition, say, to kill or hurt someone, but commits the crime, because of an accident or a negligence on his part. (WK 2009b & 2009s) In cases like this, he can be charged with "homicide" (or more precisely, "negligent homicide").

(c) Strict Liability (Criminal)

There is a third element of commiting a crime under criminal law, and it has to do with "strict liability" which is classified neither as "mens rea" nor "actus reus" per se. (WK 2009t)

The term "strict liability" is normally used in civil law (like tort law), not in criminal law. (WK 2009b & 2009u) However, when it is used in criminal law, strict liability is a kind of liability "for which mens rea…does not have to be proven in relation to one or more elements comprising the actus reus," and "the liability is said to be strict because defendants will be convicted even though they were genuinely ignorant of one or more factors that made their acts or omissions criminal." (WK 2009t)

But strict liability is not really actus reus either, because the defendant, even when convicted, is "not…culpable in any real way, i.e. there is not even criminal negligence"—and there is "minimal stigma" attached to a person upon conviction of strict liability. (WK 2009t)

The defendant, upon conviction, is asked to compensate "for the damage and loss caused by his/her acts and omissions regardless of culpability (or fault in criminal law terms…)." (WK 2009u)

Strict liability laws are therefore "applied either in regulatory offences enforcing social behaviour where minimal stigma attaches to a person upon conviction, or where society is concerned with the prevention of harm, and wishes to maximise the deterrent value of the offence." (WK 2009t)

And they are more common in cases involving "working and safety standards" in workplaces, "the selling of alcohol to underage persons," and so on. (WK 2009t)

Objectives of Criminal Law

This concern with "the deterrent value of the offence" in strict liability now brings us to the issue concerning the objectives of criminal law, in general.

Criminal law imposes different kinds and degrees of punishment on those convicted, which can range from "capital punishment" (i.e., death sentence) through "physical or corporal punishment" (e.g., "whipping or caning") and "incarceration (i.e., jail sentence) to "government supervision (e.g., house arrest) and "fines" (e.g., "seizing money or property from a person convicted of a crime"). (WK 2009b)

Yet, all these different kinds and degrees of punishment can be classified in terms of some fundamental objectives of criminal law, and hereafter are five most often cited ones in the literature on jurisprudence, namely, (a) retribution, (b) restitution, (c) deterrence, (d) incapacitation, and (e) rehabiliation, as summarized below, in that order. (WK 2009b)

- "Retribution"—"Criminals ought to suffer in some way. This is the most widely seen goal. Criminals have taken improper advantage, or inflicted unfair detriment, upon others and consequently, the criminal law will put criminals at some unpleasant disadvantage to 'balance the scales.' People submit to the law to receive the right not to be murdered and if people contravene these laws, they surrender the rights granted to them by the law. Thus, one who murders may be murdered himself. A related theory includes the idea of 'righting the balance.'"
- "Restitution—"This is a victim-oriented theory of punishment. The goal is to repair, through state authority, any hurt inflicted on the victim by the offender. For example, one who embezzles will be required to repay the amount improperly acquired. Restitution is

commonly combined with other main goals of criminal justice and is closely related to concepts in the civil law."

- "Deterrence"—"Individual deterrence is aimed toward the specific offender. The aim is to impose a sufficient penalty to discourage the offender from criminal behavior. General deterrence aims at society at large. By imposing a penalty on those who commit offenses, other individuals are discouraged from committing those offenses."
- "Incapacitation"—"Designed simply to keep criminals away from society so that the public is protected from their misconduct. This is often achieved through prison sentences today. The death penalty or banishment have served the same purpose."
- "Rehabilitation—"Aims at transforming an offender into a valuable member of society. Its primary goal is to prevent further offense by convincing the offender that their conduct was wrong."

But then, a challenging question to ask here is, To what extent are these objectives of criminal law to be possible and desirable to be achieved, in the first place?

The Demographics of Violence

This challenging question (as asked above) is no idle academic exervise, because crimes of all kinds have been committed, time and again, in human history since time immorial, and no criminal law has ever succeeded in eliminating them or even reducing them to a considerable degree without inflctiing some great costs on both culture and society.

After all, an often quoted observation "commonly attributed to Benjamin Franklin" is that "those who would give up Essential Liberty to purchase a little Temporary Safety deserve neither Liberty nor Safety." (WK 2009v)

A good way to understand the recurrence of criminality in history is by way of the perspective of the mind, this time, in relation to the biological maleness of violence as a case study.

To start, there is a rather striking pattern in the demographics of violence so often found in different cultures and societies over the ages, in that violence concentrates more heavily among some groups of the population than others.

Consider, as an illustration, some numbers about the demographics of violence as cited below.

For instance, "an estimated 520,000 people were murdered in 2000 around the globe. Two-fifths of them were young people between the ages of 10 and 29 who were killed by other young people." (WK 2009s; T. Maugh 2002)

In the West, "nearly 90% of all murders are committed by males, with males also being the victims of 74.6% of murders (according the U.S. Department of Justice. There is a sharp peak in the age distribution of murderers between the ages of 17 and 30. People become decreasingly likely to commit a murder as they age. Incidents of children and adolescents committing murders are also extremely rare." (WK 2009s)

In fact, the murder rates may be underestimated, because "murder demographics are affected by the improvement of trauma care, leading to reduced lethality of violent assaults—thus the murder rate may not necessarily indicate the overall level of social violence." (WK 2009s; A. Harris 2002)

The Maleness of Violence

The maleness of violence in the demographics of violence can be explained from a biological perspective.

David Barash (2002), a professor of psychology at the University of Washington at Seattle, tried to explain why "human violence…is overwhelmingly perpetrated by males."

His answer is biological: "Evolutionary biology has an answer, and it emanates directly from the very definition of male and female"; and he co-authored with Judith Eve Lipton in *Gender Gap: The Biology of Male-Female Differences* to elaborate on this view. (D. Barash 2002 & 2002a)

Barash (2002) started his analysis with the observation about the so-called "killing establishment," that is, the violent world populated by "soldiers, executioners, hunters,…slaughterhouse workers," and other individuals, who are "overwhelmingly male. Underworld killers such as violent gangs are also peopled largely by men. Whenever seemingly unprovoked and deadly shootings occur in homes and workplaces, men are typically the mass murderers."

The maleness of violence is universal, because "this imbalance" is not "limited to the United States: Whether in Kosovo, Rwanda, Cambodia, the Middle East, Guatemala, or Afghanistan, when people kill and maim other people, men are nearly always the culprits. And of course, the lethal operatives of Al Qaeda and its equivalent are reliably male, as are those sent to combat them." (D. Barash 2002)

And "[s]tudies of prosecution and imprisonment records in Europe, going back several centuries, as well as examinations of modern crime statistics from the United States and around the world show that men consistently outstrip women in criminality by a ratio of at least three or four to one. When it comes to violent crimes, the difference is even greater, with the disparity increasing as the violence intensifies (simple assault versus assault and battery versus manslaughter versus homicide). The only areas, in fact, in which women commit more crimes than men are prostitution (which some would argue is not a crime but an act between consenting adults) and shoplifting." (D. Barash 2002)

This is true, even "when women are consistently aggressive, it tends to take a defensive form, as when a woman kills a man who has abused her or her children, or fights to have a murderer condemned to death….Thus, while the aggression of women tends to be reactive, men are more likely to initiate violence, to commit truly 'offensive' acts." (D. Barash 2002)

Even more extensively, this imbalance also occurs in the private sphere: "The same gender imbalance applies to the uncountable private episodes of violence that receive little national attention but are the stuff of many a personal tragedy. Admittedly, an occasional Lizzie Borden surfaces, but for every Bonnie, there are about a hundred Clydes. Male brutalizers and killers are so common, they barely make the local news, whereas their female counterparts achieve a kind of fame….Violence may or may not be as American as cherry pie, but it is as male as can be." (D. Barash 2002)

In the end, for Barash (2002), "the overall pattern is consistent: When it comes to violence, the two sexes simply are not in the same league."

Barash's explanation is based on evolutionary biology, especially in relation to "the world of sexual competition," where, "since sperm can be made in vast quantities, and with little mandated physiological follow-through, it is possible for males to have large numbers of offspring, the actual output limited by the number of females they succeed in fertilizing. By contrast, females are more likely to maximize their reproduction by producing successful offspring, rather than by outcompeting other females for the sexual attention of males." (D. Barash 2002)

Therefore, "sexual competition is a replay of fertilization itself, in which numerous males, like hyperactive spermatozoa, compete among themselves for access to females. Just as it is now clear that the egg doesn't merely passively receive suitors, it is increasingly understood that females can be active participants in their own reproduction. Nonetheless, when it comes to sperm makers, success is likely to crown those who outcompete their rivals, and so, in species after species, it is the males who are larger, nastier, more likely to be armed with lethal weaponry and a violent disposition to match." (D. Barash 2002)

Barash then concluded in this way: "Natural selection has outfitted males with the tools for success in male-male competition, much of it violent." (D. Barash 2002) And this violence is carried over to other domains of life, even when they are no longer related to sexual competiton.

A Sober Reflection

Surely, Barash's work may be too focused on the evolutionary perspective without giving due attention to social and cultural factors. After all, Ellen Ross (1981) and Rayna Rapp had argued all along that, "biological base is always experienced culturally, through a translation. The bare biological facts…do not speak for themselves; they must be expressed socially."

This critique of Barash's work aside—the larger question to ask here concerns the conventional wisdom of criminal law to curb criminal acts. If there is a biological basis for violence, with the maleness of violence here as a case study, then the objectives of criminal law (as afore-cited) are not as possible as the prosecutors and judges would like us to believe.

More even importantly, the objectives of criminal law (as afore-cited) are also not as desirable as the prosecutors and judges would want us to endorse. After all, as Friedrich Nietzsche (1969) once wrote in *The Genealogy of Morals*, what is "good" for the sheep is "bad" for the fox, and what is "good" for the fox is "evil" for the sheep.

On the basis of these two (illustrative) criticisms—the "we" vs. "they" mentality in criminal law needs to be questioned.

In addition, the analysis of the maleness of violence in relation to crimnal law can also reveal the relevance of some ontological principles in existential dialectics, and good examples include the absoluteness-relativeness principle, the predictability-unpredictability principle, the explicability-inexplicability principle, the preciseness-hardness principle, the simpleness-complicatedness principle, the openness-hiddenness principle, the denseness-emptiness principle, the expansion-contraction principle, the convention-novelty principle, the evolution-transformation principle, the symmetry-asymmetry principle, the softness-hardness principle, the regression-progression principle, and the same-difference principle.

For instance, in relation to the absoluteness-relativeness principle, if there is absoluteness (e.g., a criminal to kill someone), there is relativeness (e.g., what is good for the criminal is not necessarily so for the victim, and vice-versa).

In relation to the predictability-unpredictability principle, if there is predictability (e.g., the predictable overall pattern of violence, in that "when it comes to violence, the two sexes simply are not in the same league"), there is unpredictability (e.g., the more difficult task to predict which particular woman will end up killing a man than the other way around).

In relation to the explicability-inexplicabilitiy principle, if there is explicability (e.g., the explanation of the maleness of violence on the basis of evolutionary biology by Barash), there is inexplicability (e.g., the lack of vigorous explanation by Barash, within his biological model, on why sexual violence by males are carried over to other forms of violence).

In relation to the preciseness-vagueness principle, if there is preciseness (e.g., the precise identification of the five objectives of criminal law), there is also vagueness (e.g., the vagueness about the differences in value to be placed on each of them, depending on different cases, traditions, and situations).

In relation to the simpleness-complicatedness principle, if there is simple analysis (e.g., the simple acocunt of the maleness of violence on the basis of evolutionary biology), there is complicated counterpart (e.g., the more complicated account by the critics that "biological base is always experienced culturally, through a translation. The bare biological facts…do not speak for themselves; they must be expressed socially."

In relation to the openness-hiddenness principle, if there is openness (e.g., the open exploration of the "guilt act" and "guilty mind" in criminal law), there is hiddenness (e.g., the hidden bias in the "we" vs. "they" dichotomy behind criminal law).

In relation to the denseness-emptiness principle, if there is denseness (e.g., the relatively denser concentration of males in the "killing establishment"), there is emptiness (e.g., the relatively less dense, or more empty, concentration of females in the "killing establishment").

In relation to the expansion-contraction principle, if there is expansion (e.g., the relatively more developed skill to kill and hurt among those in the "killing establishment"), there is contraction (e.g., the relatively less developed skill to be sensitive, caring, and loving among those in the "killing establishment").

In relation to the convention-novelty principle, if there is convention (e.g.,. the conventional wisdom about the criminal to be punished in accordance to criminal law), there is novelty (e.g., the alternative novel challenge to this conventional wisdom as not being possible and desirable to the extent that the proponents would like us to believe, because of some fundamental biological differences for the maleness of violence, for instance).

In relation to the evolution-transformation principle, if there is evolution (e.g., the natural evolution of humans to live in groups, just like other social animals), there is transformtion (e.g, the technical transformation of human living together by way of the invention of criminal law and the legal institutions to enforce social order).

In relation to the symmetry-asymmetry principle, if there is symmetry (e.g., the co-existence of both males and females to commit violent crimes), there is asymmetry (e.g., the overall pattern of the maleness of violence, even although there can be violent women too).

In relation to the softness-hardness principle, if there is softness (e.g., the encouragement of "law-abiding" behaviors in society), there is hardness (e.g., the punishment of criminals in society).

In relation to the regression-progression principle, if there is regression (e.g., the "bad" consequences of criminal law for the "fox," in Nietzsche's genealogy of morals), there is progression (e.g, the "good" consequences of criminal law for the "sheep").

And in relation to the same-difference principle, if there is similarity in outcome (e.g., costs and benefits in both the criminal world and the civil world), there is difference in outcome (e.g., peace and non-violence in the civil world, and the survival of the strongest in the criminal world).

Necessity and Nature

The analysis of criminal law and its relationship with the maleness of violence from the perspective of the mind can lead us to a comparable (though different) perspective, this time, in relation to the state of nature.

In other words, when law is examined from the perspective of nature, a different debate arises, this time, about "natural law or the law of nature (Latin: *lex naturalis*)," that is, about whether or not there is "the existence of a law whose content is set by nature and that therefore has validity everywhere. The phrase natural law is opposed to the positive law (which is human-made) of a given political community, society, or nation-state, and thus can function as a standard by which to criticize that law." (WK 2009bb)

Two good illustrations can be provided hereafter, namley, (2.3.1) the laws of the jungle in nature, and social Darwinism, and (2.3.2) natural law, and Taoist anti-authoritarianism—to be addressed in what follows, in that order.

The Laws of the Jungle in Nature, and Social Darwinism

In the state of nature, where the animal kingdom is located, it is often said that the rules of the game are the laws of the jungle, which mean "anything goes," "survival of the strongest," "survival of the fittest," "eat or get eaten," or something of that tough nature. (WK 2009w)

Thomas Hobbes once famously added that, in the state of nature, life is "poore, nasty, brutish, and short." (S. Llyod 2008)

The Law Code in the Jungle of Nature

Rudyard Kipling in *The Jungle Book* (1894) beautifully wrote about "an actual law code used by wolves and other animals in the jungles of India." (WK 2009w)

This actual law code that Kipling observed in the jungles of India is about wolves and other animals, which have to struggle for survivial in a ruthless way.

As Kipling thus wrote, "this is the Law of the Jungle—as old and as true as the sky; and the Wolf that shall keep it may prosper, but the Wolf that shall break it must die….For the strength of the Pack is the Wolf, and the strength of the Wolf is the Pack….And remember the night is for hunting, and forget not the day is for sleep….Cub, when thy whiskers are grown, remember the Wolf is a hunter—go forth and get food of thine own." (WK 2009w)

But be aware, Cub, of the power of the strong and the group: "Keep peace with the Lords of the Jungle—the Tiger, the Panther, the Bear….And trouble not Hathi the Silent, and mock not the Boar in his lair. When Pack meets with Pack in the Jungle, and neither will go from the trail….Lie down till the leaders have spoken—it may be fair words shall prevail. When ye fight with a Wolf of the Pack, ye must fight him alone and afar, lest others take part in the quarrel, and the Pack be diminished by war." (WK 2009w)

Also, Cub, learn to respect the territory of others and the custom of killing: "The Lair of the Wolf is his refuge, and where he has made him his home, not even the Head Wolf may enter, not even the Council may come….If ye kill before midnight, be silent, and wake not the woods with your bay, lest ye frighten the deer from the crops, and the brothers go empty away. Ye may kill for yourselves, and your mates, and your cubs as they need, and ye can….But kill not for pleasure of killing, and SEVEN TIMES NEVER KILL MAN." (WK 2009w)

Besides, learn the custom of food sharing: "If ye plunder his Kill from a weaker, devour not all in thy pride; Pack-Right is the right of the meanest; so leave him the head and the hide. The Kill of the Pack is the meat of the Pack. Ye must eat where it lies; and no one may carry away of that meat to his lair, or he dies. The Kill of the Wolf is the meat of the Wolf. He may do what he will….But, till he has given permission, the Pack may not eat of that Kill." (WK 2009w)

And, above all, learn the hierarchy of the Pack well: "Cub-Right is the right of the Yearling. From all of his Pack he may claim full-gorge when the killer has eaten; and none may refuse him the same. Lair-Right is the right of the Mother. From all of her year she may claim one haunch of each kill for her litter, and none may deny her the same. Cave-Right is the right of the Father—to hunt by himself for his own. He is freed of all calls to the Pack; he is judged by the Council alone. Because of his age and his cunning, because of his gripe and his paw, in all that the Law leaveth open, the word of the Head Wolf is Law." (WK 2009w)

These rules, then, constitute "the Laws of the Jungle, and many and mighty are they….But the head and the hoof of the Law and the haunch and the hump is—Obey!" (WK 2009w)

Social Darwinism, and the Survival of the Fittest

But Kipling's observation about the actual law code for wolves and other animals in the jungles of India is not as systematic as the work *On the Origin of Species* in 1859 by Charles Darwin on "natural selection," which is to "explain…speciation in populations as the outcome of competition between individual organisms for limited resources popularly known as 'survival of the fittest.'" (WK 2009x)

In *Beyond Nature and Nurture* (or *BNN* in 2006), I already went to great lengths to explain the five main processes in classical Darwinian evolutionary theory (i.e., mutation, variation, inheritance, adaptation, and natural selection).

Without repeating what was written there, it suffices to add here that the term "survival of the fittest" was first coined by Anthropologist Herbert Spencer in *Principles of Biology* (1864), after reading Darwin's work, and was also exploited by Andrew Carnegie in the 1889 essay titled "The Gospel of Wealth." (WK 2009x & 2009y)

The term "social Darwinism" refers to "the claim that Darwin's theory of evolution by natural selection can be used to understand the social endurance of a nation or country," on the basis of the "survival of the fittest." (WK 2009x)

However, although "social Darwinism bears Charles Darwin's name, it is also linked today with others, notably Herbert Spencer, Thomas Malthus, and Francis Galton, the founder of eugenics. In fact Spencer was not described as a social Darwinist until the 1930s, long after his death." (WK 2009x; G. Hodgson 2004)

For instance, for Spencer, "the individual (rather than the collectivity) is the unit of analysis that evolves," and "evolution takes place through natural selection, and…it affects social as well as biological phenomena." (WK 2009x)

Malthus contributed to the social Darwinist tradition in his 1798 work *An Essay on the Principle of Population*, in which he "argued that as an increasing population would normally outgrow its food supply, this would result in the starvation of the weakest and a Malthusian catastrophe; in fact, he also suggested that "charity could exacerbate social problems." (WK 2009x)

And Galton carried social Darwinism further into the direction of heredity, in that, "just as physical traits were clearly inherited among generations of people, so could be said for mental qualities (genius and talent)," and this then means that society should "avoid over-breeding by 'less fit' members of society and the under-breeding of the 'more fit' ones." (WK 2009x)

Galton went further and even argued that "social institutions such as welfare and insane asylums were allowing 'inferior' humans to survive and reproduce at levels faster than the more 'superior' humans in respectable society, and if corrections were not soon taken, society would be awash with 'inferiors.'" (WK 2009x)

By "the second half of the 19th century, the widespread philosophy of social Darwinism dominated the thinking of many industrial tycoons of the era. They believed that because evolution was true in the biological sphere, the same methods should apply in the business world: survival of the fittest, elimination of the weak, no love for the poor." (WK 2009x)

Manifest Destiny, and the Trail of Tears

In fact, a good illustration of the social Darwinist policy for the survival of the fittest concerns the history of the American Wild West, in regard to the dealing by the U.S. federal government with the Native Indians (or the so-called "Indian question"). (WK 2009z)

The history of "the American Wild West" refers to "the period of the latter half of the 19th century, between the American Civil War and the end of the century," when "the United States expanded from coast to coast (Atlantic Ocean-to-Pacific Ocean), fulfilling its belief in Manifest Destiny," which justified the expansion as "readily apparent ('manifest') and inexorable ('destiny')." (WK 2009z & 2009aa; H. Lamar 1977)

The idea of "Manifest Destiny" speaks loudly of the ruthless survival-of-the-fittest mindset in dealing with the natives, when "the Federal government played a vital role in securing land and maintaining law and order, which allowed the expansion to proceed." (WK 2009z)

In the name of law and order, under the cover of Manifest Destiny, the infamous chapter of "the Trail of Tears" in the Native Indian history was thus written, when the U.S. federal government began to enforce, "by 1837, the 'Indian Removal policy' began to implement the act of Congress signed by Andrew Jackson in 1830. The forced march of about twenty Native American tribes included the 'Five Civilized Tribes' (Creek, Choctaw, Cherokee, Chickasaw, and Seminole). They were pushed beyond the frontier and into the 'Indian Territory' (which later became Oklahoma). Of the approximate 70,000 Indians removed, about 20% died from disease, starvation, and exposure on the route. This exodus has become known as The Trail of Tears (in Cherokee 'Nunna dual Tsuny,' 'The Trail Where they Cried'). The impact of the removals was severe. Sometimes the transplanted tribes clashed with the tribes native to the area. In addition, the Smallpox Epidemic of 1837 decimated the tribes of the Upper Missouri, weakening them, and allowing immigrants easier access to those lands." (WK 2009z; R. Utley 2003)

This policy by the U.S. federal government was justified in the name of Manifest Destiny, especially in regard to two specific claims in relation to the surivival-of-the-fittest argument in social Darwinism.

The first claim is about the "superior race" theory, in that "'inferior' peoples (i.e., natives) held land in trust until a 'superior race' came along which would be a more productive steward of the land." (WK 2009z)

And the second claim is that "the removal of natives would take them away from the contaminating influences of the frontier and help preserve their culture." (WK 2009z; A. Josephy 1965) After all, even President Andrew Jackson at the time said that "Indians had 'neither the intelligence, the industry, the moral habits, nor the desire of improvements.'" (WK 2009z; R. White 1991: 89)

Surely, these claims were just excuses for a ruthless policy towards the weak for the benefits of the strong, in a world governed by the ideology of the survival of the strongest, with no charity nor mercy towards the conquered.

Thus was the ruthless way that "the federal government [had] to deal with the 'Indian question,'" in the process of "securing land and maintaining law and order, which allowed the expansion to proceed." (WK 2009z)

In Heartfelt Retrospect

In heartfelt retrospect, this kind of "law and order" spoke volumes of the laws of the jungle in social Darwinism, with "Manifest Destiny" as an American version at the time.

This retrospect can also teach us something about the ontological principles in existential dialectics, and good examples include the absoluteness-relativeness principle, the partiality-totality priinciple, the predictability-unpredictability principle, the explicability-inexplicability principle, the preciseness-vagueness principle, the simpleness-complicatedness principle, the openness-hiddenness principle, the denseness-emptiness principle, the order-chaos priinciple, the expansion-contraction principle, the convention-novelty principle, the evolution-transformation principle, the symmetry-asymmetry principle, the softness-hardness principle, the regression-progression principle, and the same-difference principle.

For instance, in relation to the absoluteness-relativeness principle, if there is absoluteness (e.g., the absolute view of Manifest Destiny towards the conquered), there is relativeness (e.g., what is good for the U.S. federal government in regard to its policy to expand westward is not so for the Native Indians in the Trail of Tears).

In relation to the partiality-totality principle, if there is partiality (e.g., the partial perspective of each animal in the state of nature to struggle for its own existence in a given environment), there is totality (e.g., the totalistic perspective of the emergence of new species, out of the competiton among animals for existence in the evolutionary process of a given environment over time).

In relation to the predictability-unpredictability principle, if there is predictability (e.g., the predictable tendency of the U.S. government to conquer others with its history of Manifest Destiny), there is unpredictability (e.g., the more difficult task to predict at the outset the long-term success or failure of a given expansionist adventure by the U.S., be it towards the Native Indians, the Mexicans, the Philipinos, or else).

In relation to the explicability-inexplicability principle, if there is explicability (e.g., the explanation of the need of the U.S. federal government to take over the lands of the Native Indians on the basis of Manifest Destiny), there is inexplicability (e.g., the lack of explanation of why the specific claims in the Manifest Destiny are in fact true).

In relation to the preciseness-vagueness principle, if there is preciseness (e.g., the precise identificaiton of "the Laws of the Jungle" for the wolves in India by Kipling), there is vagueness (e.g., the vague treatment of the laws of the jungle by Kipling, without specifying any exceptions to the laws, or the existence of different laws for different animals).

In relation to the simpleness-complicatedness principle, if there is simple analysis (e.g., the simplistic account of "competition between individual organisms for limited resources" by the social Darwinists), there is complicated counterpart (e.g., the more complicated account of both cooperation and competition in the state of nature by the critics of social Darwinism).

In relation to the openness-hiddenness principle, if there is openness (e.g., the open exploration of the need to expand westward by the U.S. federal government), there is hiddenness (e.g., the hidden bias of the U.S. federal government to cover up this inhumane policy towards the Native Indians by way of the manipulative ideology of Manifest Destiny).

In relation to the denseness-emptiness principle, if there is denseness (e.g., the relatively denser concentration of conquests by the U.S. in the Wild West), there is emptiness (e.g., the relatively less dense, or more empty, concentration of conquests by the U.S. in Africa).

In relation to the order-chaos principle, if there is order (e.g., the existence of certain order in the state of nature, due to the laws of the jungle), there is chaos (e.g, anything goes in the state of nature, such that anything can happen and things are not so orderly even with the laws of the jungle).

In relation to the expansion-contraction principle, if there is expansion (e.g., the relatively better developed disposition of the U.S. to conquer the lesser others in its history of Manifest Destiny), there is contraction (e.g., the relatively less developed disposition of the U.S. to be non-interventionist towards the others, on average, of course).

In relation to the convention-novelty principle, if there is convention (e.g., the conventional wisdom about creation in the state of nature, as in creation theory), there is novelty (e.g., the alternative novel challenge to creation theory by the Darwinian evolutionary theory).

In relation to the evolution-transformation principle, if there is evolution (e.g., the natural evolution of animals, including humans, by way of speciation through natural selection), there is transformation (e.g., the technical transformation of human relations by way of the invention of political ideology like Manifest Destiny).

In relation to the symmetry-asymmetry principle, if there is symmetry (e.g., the co-existence of cooperation and competition among humans), there is asymmetry (e.g., the preference, for conquest and competition, of those with the belief in Manifest Destiny—but the preference, for cooperation and respect, of those with the belief in non-violence and genuine humanitarianism).

In relation to the softness-hardness principle, if there is softness (e.g., the cooperation among the wolves to live together in a pack), there is hardness (e.g., the readiness of the wolves to kill and fight, whenever needed).

In relation to the regression-progression principle, if there is regression (e.g., the infamy of the Trail of Tears in U.S. history), there is progression (e.g., the development of the Wild West, as "the U.S. federal government greatly expanded its powers" and "the nation grew from an agrarian society to an industrialized nation"). (WK 2009z)

And in relation to the same-difference principle, if there is similarity in outcome (e.g., the consolidation of power, and the maintenance of law and order, both in the Wild West and in the East Coast), there is difference in outcome (e.g., the expulsion of the British from the Eastern seaboard after the American Revolutionary War, but the removal of the Native Indians from their lands in the history of the Westward Expansion).

Natural Law, and Taoist Anti-Authoritarianism

But not all interpretations of the law of nature have to be so ruthless like the laws of the jungle in social Darwinism, with "Manifest Destiny" as an American version in the 19th century (and beyond).

A good alternative version of the law of nature concern Taoist anti-authoritarianism, as propounded by Laozi. (WK 2009cc)

Although Laozi was often thought to live in ancient China during the 6th century B.C., "[h]istorians variously contend that Laozi is a synthesis of multiple historical figures, that he is a mythical figure, or that he actually lived in the 4th century BC, concurrent with the Hundred Schools of Thought and Warring States Period." (WK 2009cc; L. Kohn 2000)

In any event, Laozi's magnum opus, the *Daodejing*, is considered as "one of the most significant treatises in Chinese cosmogony. As with most other ancient Chinese philosophers, Laozi often explains his ideas by way of paradox, analogy, appropriation of ancient sayings, repetition, symmetry, rhyme, and rhythm." (WK 2009cc)

Four Characteristics of the Tao in Nature

For Laozi, the universe follows the law of nature which can be understood in terms of "the Dao (or Tao)." (WK 2009cc)

For those in the Taoist tradition, "the Tao both precedes and encompasses the universe. As with other nondualistic philosophies, all the observable objects in the world—referred to…as 'the named' or 'the ten thousand things'—are considered to be manifestations of Tao, and can only operate within the boundaries of Tao." (WK 2009dd)

However, it is not easy to understand the "Tao," because "neither it nor its principles can ever be adequately expressed in words. It is conceived, for example, with neither shape nor form, as simultaneously perfectly still and constantly moving, as both larger than the largest thing and smaller than the smallest, because the words that describe shape, movement, size, or other qualities always create dichotomies, and Tao is always a unity." (WK 2009dd)

Yet, for the Taoists, the Tao can still be known in some ways, and hereafter are four often-cited characteristics of the Tao, namely, (a) "Tao is undifferentiated," (b) "Tao returns," (c) "Tao is subtle and quiet," and (d) "Tao is simultaneously dispassionate and nurturing"—as summarized below. (WK 2009dd)

(a) Tao Is Undifferentiated

The first characteristic of the Tao is that it is undifferentiated. So, all distinctions are superficial and "are actually relative comparisons bound together by their mutual reference. Thus, there is no such thing as 'long' except by comparison to 'short' and vice-versa; there is no such thing as 'being' except by comparison to 'non-being'. Because Tao itself has no shape or size, all comparisons fall within it, so there can never be 'real' differences. Often this is used to suggest a neutral, giving attitude." (WK 2009dd)

(b) Tao Returns

The second characteristic of the Tao is that it returns into a cycle. "Return" thus "reflects the natural cycles of the world (changing of the seasons, births of new generations)," and it also means "the natural return to quiescence that is the end result of all action….This concept is often used to argue against forceful action, on the grounds that Tao (and its manifestations) will flow back, circumvent, and eventually undo any attempts to force it into a particular path." (WK 2009dd)

(c) Tao Is Subtle and Quiet

The third characteristic of the Tao is "its unremarkable, unnoticed, everyday workings—'the softest thing in the world overcomes the hardest.' Many places in the Tao Te Ching point out that dramatic, enticing or noteworthy events may catch the eye and assume significance, but that it is the slow, slight, unobserved and continuous movement of the manifestations of Tao that actually accomplish things. In this context, practitioners are cautioned to be unobtrusive, undemanding, and unsophisticated in their actions, and to know when to let go so that the unseen workings of Tao can carry the act to its completion." (WK 2009dd)

(d) Tao Is Simultaneously Dispassionate and Nurturing

And the fourth characteristic of the Tao is that it "gives of itself wholly and completely to each" being (or manifestation of the Tao) in the world and yet "is indifferent to the disposition of mere manifestations. Birth and death and life itself, from the perspective of Tao, are only movements and transformations of form. This is often used to suggest selflessness and detachment to practitioners; compare with the Buddhist notion of anatta (no-self)." (WK 2009dd)

The Tao for a Different Jurisprudence

These characteristics of the Tao have implications for the human world, especially in the current context of the law.

To start, in the Taoist tradition, "humans have no special place within the [Tao]..., being just one of its many ('ten thousand') manifestations. People have desires and free will (and thus are able to alter their own nature)." (WK 2009cc)

Some act "naturally," but others don't. In fact, "[m]any act 'unnaturally,' upsetting the natural balance of the [Tao]....The Daodejing intends to lead students to a 'return' to their natural state, in harmony with [the Tao]....Language and conventional wisdom are critically assessed. Taoism views them as inherently biased and artificial, widely using paradoxes to sharpen the point." (WK 2009cc; B. Van Norden 2005; L. Kohn 2000)

A good way to understand this return to the natural state is the analogy given by Livia Kohn (2000), in that "[t]echnology may bring about a false sense of progress. The answer provided by Laozi is not the rejection of technology, but instead seeking the calm state of wu wei, free from desires. This relates to many statements by Laozi encouraging rulers to keep their people...'simple-minded.'" (WK 2009cc)

This "calm state of wu wei" can be "very complex" and "can mean 'not doing anything,' 'not forcing,' 'not acting,' in the theatrical sense, 'creating nothingness,' 'acting spontaneously,' and 'flowing with the moment.'" (WK 2009cc)

This vagueness aside—wu wei can be used "to explain ziran, or harmony with the [Tao]....It includes the concepts that value distinctions are ideological and seeing ambition of all sorts as originating from the same source. Laozi used the term broadly with simplicity and humility as key virtues, often in contrast to selfish action." (WK 2009cc)

When put in the context of jurisprudence, the Taoist tradition is to emphasize a system of laws which show the virtues of "simplicity," "moderation," and "humility." (WK 2009cc)

Unlike the laws of the jungle in social Darwinism for Manifest Destiny in the context of 19th century America, the Taoists would do just the opposite, in "avoiding such circumstances as war, harsh laws and heavy taxes." (WK 2009cc) The "trail of tears" would not have happened in a society governed with the Taoist system of laws which emphasize humility, moderation, and simplicity.

A Critical Look

Of course, for the critics, the problem with the Taoist system of laws concerns the possibility and desirability of its obsession with "humility, moderation, and simplicity."

Firstly, in relation to the question of possibility, it is not clear to what extent a system of laws can really be simple, in light of the highly complicated characteristics of contemporary society in the Information Age.

For instance, R. Buckminster Fuller (1938) once complained about the enormously complicated nature of contemporary patent laws, in that "the (U.S. patent) files…are so extraordinarily complex and the items so multitudinous that a veritable army of governmental servants is required to attend them….This complexity makes it inevitable that the human-equation involved in government servants relative to carelessness or mechanical limitations should occasion the granting of multitudes of 'probably' invalid patent claims." (WK 2009ee)

And in relation to the question of desirability, it is also not clear how much desirable a system of laws which is simple, moderate, and humble can really be, without being trapped into a conservative ideology of non-intervention from the state.

In fact, one often cited criticism of this Taoist view concerns the questionable consequence, when implemented, of "encouraging rulers to keep their people in 'ignorance,' or 'simple-minded'….It would not be unusual political advice if Laozi literally intended to tell rulers to keep their people ignorant," so as to make it easier to mold them into obeying the laws in that Taoist way. (WK 2009cc)

These criticism aside—the analysis of the Taoist anti-authoritarianism in the context of natural law can teach us something valuable in regard to the relevance of some ontological principles in existential dialectics, and good examples include the absoluteness-relativeness principle, the predictability-unpredictability principle, the explicability-inexplicability principle, the preciseness-vagueness principle, the simpleness-complicatedness principle, the openness-hiddenness principle, the denseness-emptiness principle, the change-constancy principle, the expansion-contraction principle, the theory-praxis principle, the convention-novelty principle, the evolution-transformation principle, the symmetry-asymmetry principle, the regression-progression principle, and the same-difference principle.

For instance, in relation to the absoluteness-relativeness principle, if there is absolute viewpoint (e.g., the absolute requirement, in Taoist jursiprudence, of a system of laws which show the virtues of "simplicity," "moderation," and "humility"), there is relative counterpart (e.g., what is good for the Taoists in regard to a a system of laws which is simple, moderate, and humble is not so for a Marxist revolutinoary who champions a heavy, and at times harsh, state intervention into the affairs of society).

In relation to the predictability-unpredictability principle, if there is predictability (e.g., the predictable tendency of a Taoist system of laws to be simple, humble, and moderate), there is unpredictability (e.g., the more difficult task to even predict to what extent a given Taoist system of laws can really be simple, in light of the highly complicated characteristics of contemporary society in the Information Age).

In relation to the explicability-inexplicability principle, if there is explicability (e.g., the Taoist explanation of the virtue of non-action on the basis that the Tao returns into a cycle, or that "the Tao…and its manifestations…will flow back, circumvent, and eventually undo any attempts to force it into a particular path"), there is inexplicability (e.g., the lack of sufficient explanation in Taoism of why exactly the Tao has to eventually return into a cycle at all, instead of moving in a straight line or somewhere else).

In relation to the preciseness-vagueness principle, if there is preciseness (e.g., the precise identification of the characteristics of the Tao, like the four major ones as discussed), there is vagueness (e.g., the essential vagueness of the "Tao," in spite of the four characteristics as identified, because "neither it nor its principles can ever be adequately expressed in words").

In relation to the simpleness-complicatedness principle, if there is simpleness (e.g., the simple Taoist view of a system of laws which is to be moderate, humble, and simple), there is complicated counterpart (e.g., the more complicated view, by the critics like Fuller, that the laws in real life can be enormously complicated, as in the case about patents).

In relation to the openness-hiddenness principle, if there is openness (e.g., the open Taoist exploration of a system of laws which can be simple, moderate, and humble), there is hiddenness (e.g., the hidden bias in the Taoist system of laws for a conservative ideology of non-intervention, or minimal intervention, from the state into the affairs of society).

In relation to the denseness-emptiness principle, if there is denseness (e.g., the relatively denser concentration of laws which can be harsh and complicated in a non-Taoist state, like a Marxist one), there is emptiness (e.g., the relatively less dense, or more empty, concentration of laws which can be harsh and complicated in a Taoist state).

In relation to the change-constancy principle, if there is change (e.g., the ever recurrent manifestations of things in nature, like the change of the seasons), there is constancy (e.g., the return of things in a cycle over time, like the cycle of the four seasons).

In relation to the expansion-contraction principle, if there is expansion (e.g., the relatively more developed capacity of an anti-authoritarian Taoist system of laws to find ways to intervene minimally into the affairs of society), there is contraction (e.g., the relatively less developed capacity of a Taoist system of laws to be highly complicated and elaborated).

In relation to the theory-praxis principle, if there is theory (e.g., the Taoist theoretical interpetation of the universe in terms of the four characterstics of the Tao), there is praxis (e.g., the practical application of the Taoist theoretical construction of the Tao for the implementation of a system of laws which are simple, humble, and moderate).

In relation to the convention-novelty principle, if there is convention (e.g., the conventional wisdom about a legal system of laws which should be complicated enough to cover all cases and harsh enough to deter violations), there is novelty (e.g, the alternative novel challenge by the Taoists, on the basis of a system of laws which is simple and moderate or non-harsh).

In relation to the evolution-transformation principle, if there is evolution (e.g., the evolution of humans to live together in groups, at time in peace and at times at war, in the state of nature), there is transformation (e.g., the technical transformation of human communities by way of the invention of jurisprudence for the formation of a system of laws for peace and order).

In relation to the symmetry-asymmetry principle, if there is symmetry (e.g., the co-existence of different systems of laws, be they simple and moderate, or complicated and harsh), there is asymmetry (e.g., the more acceptance of a simple and moderate system of laws for those who are sympathetic to Taoism, but the more popularity of a complicated and harsh system of laws for those who believe in a more authoritarian worldview).

In relation to the regression-progression principle, if there is regression (e.g., the possible abuse of a non-authoritarian Taoist system of laws to make the people "ignorant" and "simple-minded" for control), there is progression (e.g., the progress made for a less authoritarian system of laws in a Taoist community).

And in relation to the same-difference principle, if there is similarity in outcome (e.g., the molding of individual behaviors in any system of laws, be it Taoist or non-Taoist), there is difference in outcome (e.g., the less authoritarian nature of a Taoist system of laws, and the more authoritarian nature of a non-Taoist one like a Marxist system of laws).

Necessity and Society

Besides the perspectives of the mind (in *Sec. 2.2*) and nature (in *Sec. 2.3*)—a third perspective involves the role of society in relation to necessity in the context of the law.

Two illuminating case studies can be provided here, namely, (2.4.1) international public law and the International Criminal Court, and (2.4.2) constitutional law, and the balance of power—to be addressed hereafter, respectively.

International Public Law and the International Criminal Court

A growing phenomenon in the international arena concerns the institution of international public law, with its claim of universal jurisdiction over different nation-states on certain important issues—largely "due to the increase in global trade, armed conflict, environmental deterioration on a worldwide scale, awareness of human rights violations, rapid and vast increases in international transportation and a boom in global communications," especially in the 20th century and beyond. (WK 2009ff)

By definition, "public international law concerns the structure and conduct of sovereign states and intergovernmental organizations. To a lesser degree, international law also may affect multinational corporations and individuals, an impact increasingly evolving beyond domestic legal interpretation and enforcement." (WK 2009ff)

With this definition in mind, an elaboration of the nature of international public law can be provided hereafter (and also summarized in *Table 2.2*), in relation to (a) its scope, (b) its sources, (c) its interpretive problem, (d) its enforcement problem, and (e) the case study of the international criminal court in the context of the travesty of justice.

The Scope of International Public Law

At least on paper, the scope of international public law can be quite extensive, indeed, and it is also growing rapidly in the age of globalization.

Consider the following three categories of the scope of international public law for illustration.

Firstly, "international law deals with the acquisition of territory, state immunity, and the legal responsibility of states in their conduct with each other....It...includes the important functions of the maintenance of international peace and security, arms control, the pacific settlement of disputes and the regulation of the use of force in international relations. Even when the law is not able to stop the outbreak of war, it has developed principles to govern the conduct of hostilities and the treatment of prisoners." (WK 2009ff)

Secondly, "[i]nternational law is also used to govern issues relating to the global environment, the global commons such as international waters and outer space, global communications, and world trade." (WK 2009ff)

And thirdly, "[i]nternational law is similarly concerned with the treatment of individuals within state boundaries. There is thus a comprehensive regime dealing with group rights, the treatment of aliens, the rights of refugees, international crimes, nationality problems, and human rights generally." (WK 2009ff)

The Sources of International Public Law

But what gives international public law its alleged jurisdiction over different nation-states on issues as illustrated (above) in the context of the categories of its scope?

Historically, there are some important sources of international public law, which can be classified on the basis of two main groups, namely, "the agreements [treatises] among nations (*jus inter gentes*)" and "the law of nations (*jus gentium*)." (WK 2009ff & 2009ggg)

The first one, "the agreements among nations," refer to, for instance, (a) international treaties among nations. (WK 2009ff & 2009ggg) And the second one, "the law of nations," has in mind, for example, something like (b) "internatinal custom," (c) "the general principles of law," and (d) "judicial decisions and teachings." (WK 2009ff & 2009ggg)

(a) In regard to international treaties, this kind of international public law imposes "obligations" on nation-states which "expressly and voluntarily accept between themselves in treaties." (WK 2009ff)

(b) In regard to international custom, this kind of international public law "is derived from the consistent practice of States accompanied by *opinio juris*, i.e. the conviction of States that the consistent practice is required by a legal obligation....Attempts to codify customary international law picked up momentum after the Second World War with the formation of the International Law Commission (ILC), under the aegis of the United Nations. Codified customary law is made the binding interpretation of the underlying custom by agreement through treaty. For states not party to such treaties, the work of the ILC may still be accepted as custom applying to those states." (WK 2009ff)

(c) In regard to "the general principles of law," this kind of international public law refers to those principles "commonly recognized by the major legal systems of the world. Certain norms of international law achieve the binding force of peremptory norms (*jus cogens*) as to include all states with no permissible derogations." (WK 2009ff)

(d) And in regard to judicial decisions and teachings, this kind of international public law relies on "judgments of international tribunals as well as scholarly works," which "have traditionally been looked to as persuasive sources for custom in addition to direct evidence of state behavior (and they are also explicitly mentioned as such in Art. 38 of the Statute of the International Court of Justice, as subsidiary means for the determination of rules of law)." (WK 2009ff)

The Interpretative Problem of International Public Law

But these sources of international public law are not always crystally clear to everyone, and to understand them require interpretation, which can become a major point of contention among those in dispute and thus constitutes a major challenge to the naïve claim of the universal jurisdiction of internatinal public law.

Those who challenge a given interpretation of international public law can come from different parties in a dispute, and these parties can be "the protagonists" themselves, the "judicial bodies" (like "the International Court of Justice"), and so on.

This interpretive problem persists, although "the Vienna Convention on the Law of Treaties writes on the topic of interpretation that...'[a] treaty shall be interpreted in good faith in accordance with the ordinary meaning to be given to the terms of the treaty in their context and in the light of its object and purpose.'" (WK 2009ff)

Historically, there are three major approaches to interpretation in the context of international public law, which are, namely, (a) "textual," (b) "subjective," and (c) "effective"—as shown below:

- "The textual approach"—"a restrictive interpretation, which bases itself on the 'ordinary meaning' of the text; that approach assigns considerable weight to the actual text."
- "The subjective approach"—"which takes into consideration, [i] the idea behind the treaty, [ii] treaties 'in their context,' and [iii] what the writers intended when they wrote the text."
- "A third approach"—"which bases itself on interpretation 'in the light of its object and purpose,' i.e., the interpretation that best suits the goal of the treaty, also called 'effective interpretation.'"

Surely, there can be other approaches to interpretation, such as an eclectic one to combine the three, but the point here is illustrative (not exhaustive).

In addition, how these three approaches are used can also be dependent on the competing guiding principles to be appealed to, such as "monism" and "dualism." (WK 2009hhh)

In "monism," both "the internal [national] and international legal systems form a unity….International law does not need to be translated into national law. The act of ratifying the international law immediately incorporates the law into national law. International law can be directly applied by a national judge, and can be directly invoked by citizens, just as if it were national law." (WK 2009hhh)

By contrast, in "dualism," there is no inherent unity "between national and international law," and therefore, an international law needs to be translated (or accepted) into a national law for it to have legal force. (WK 2009hhh)

In other words, "[w]ithout this translation, international law does not exist as law [in accordance to dualism]….If a state accepts a treaty but does not adapt its national law in order to conform to the treaty or does not create a national law explicitly incorporating the treaty, then it violates international law. But one cannot claim that the treaty has become part of national law. Citizens cannot rely on it and judges cannot apply it. National laws that contradict it remain in force. According to dualists, national judges never apply international law, only international law that has been translated into national law." (WK 2009hhh)

These two contrastive guiding principles are also summarized in *Table 2.3*, in conjunction with other ones in the context of international law in its multifaceted classification.

The Enforcement Problem of International Public Law

But the interpretative issue here is only one major challenge to the universal claim of the universal jurisdiction of international public law. Another challenge concerns the enforceability of international public law.

The issue of enforcement becomes serious, when different nation-states are not created equal, as some are dominant powers, while others are weak ones.

Thus, this power asymmetry among differnet nation-states renders the enforcement of international public law difficult, and over time, it is quite common that "many violations of international law obligations are overlooked," for the benefits of the major powers. (WK 2009ff)

Of course, there are some mechanisms which can be used to put pressure on nation-states to comply by international public law. For example, "states try to avoid the appearance of having disregarded international obligations. States may also unilaterally adopt sanctions against one another such as the severance of economic or diplomatic ties, or through reciprocal action. In some cases, domestic courts may render judgment against a foreign state (the realm of private international law) for an injury, though this is a complicated area of law where international law intersects with domestic law." (WK 2009ff)

But these mechanisms often do not work effectively against major powers in a dispute. Consider, as an illustration hereafter, the history of the International Criminal Court (as a case study).

The Travesty of Justice, and the International Criminal Court

The case concerning the creation of the International Criminal Court (ICC) in 2002 speaks volumes of the travesty of justice in the context of international law.

(a) The International Court of Justice

To start, there was first "the International Court of Justice [ICJ], located in The Hague, Netherlands," which "was created from the Permanent Court of International Justice in 1945." (WK 2009ff)

Since its inception, there have been roughly 150 cases brought to its attention, because "the Court may give an advisory opinion on any legal question at the request of whatever body may be authorized by or in accordance with the Charter of the United Nations to make such a request." (WK 2009ff)

However, although "[t]he judgments given by the Court in these cases are binding,…it possesses no means to enforce its rulings"; moreover, quite a number of "the advisory cases brought before the court have been controversial with respect to the court's competence and jurisdiction." (WK 2009ff)

In addition, "[o]ften enormously complicated matters, ICJ cases…can stretch on for years and generally involve thousands of pages of pleadings, evidence, and the world's leading specialist public international lawyers." (WK 2009ff)

(b) The International Criminal Court

These problems of the UCJ persist, even when another international court, this time, the International Criminal Court (ICC), was created in 2002, when "its founding treaty, the Rome Statute of the International Criminal Court, entered into force." (WK 2009gg; UN 2002; AI 2002)

The offical seat of the ICC is also located in The Hague, Netherlands, but "its proceedings may take place anywhere." (WK 2009gg)

Unlike ICJ—the ICC is a permanent tribunal specifically created to have "jurisdiction over four groups of crimes, which it refers to as the 'most serious crimes of concern to the international community as a whole,'" and they are namely, (i) "the crime of genocide," (ii) "crimes against humanity," (iii) "war crimes," and (iv) "the crime of aggression." (WK 2009gg)

The statue concerning the crime of agression in (iv) is currently problematic, however, because the ICC does "not exercise its jurisdiction over the crime of aggression until such time as the states parties agree on a definition of the crime and set out the conditions under which it may be prosecuted." (WK 2009gg; UN 2002)

With this clarification aside—the ICC, at the outset, is limited in its jurisdiction in four distinctive ways, as shown below for illustration: (WK 2009gg)

- "where the person accused of committing a crime is a national of a state party (or where the person's state has accepted the jurisdiction of the court)."
- "where the alleged crime was committed on the territory of a state party (or where the state on whose territory the crime was committed has accepted the jurisdiction of the court)."
- "where a situation is referred to the court by the UN Security Council."
- where the alleged crime was "committed on or after…[the] date" of its creation, that is, in 2002.

These limited circumstances were not randomly specified but were carefully argued for by dominant powers (especially the United States) "during the negotiations that led to the Rome Statute," so that the court is not allowed to "exercise universal jurisdiction" over crimes committed by major powers (like the United States in particular).

The reason is simple enough, on the basis of legal technicality to serve the hegemonic interests of the major powers.

To start, because the UN Security Council is controlled by the five permanent members (i.e., the U.S., the U.K., China, France, and Russia) due to the existence of the veto power, no referral of a situation against any of them by the UN Security Council is possible (without it being vetoed).

In addition, the major powers refuse to sign or join the ICC, so that the ICC cannot have jurisdiction over them, because they are not part of "a state party." For instance, "China, Russia, India and the United States…are critical of the court and have not joined." (WK 2009gg)

In fact, even those who sign and join the ICC can unsign and unjoin it later. For example, later in 2002, "two of these states, the United States and Israel, 'unsigned' the Rome Statute, indicating that they no longer intend to become states parties and, as such, they have no legal obligations arising from their signature of the statute." (WK 2009gg; UN 2009; J. Bolton 2002; S. Brett 2001)

It is no wonder, therefore, that the ICC has so far "opened investigations into…situations" that involve weak states (e.g., in the non-West) and are often sponsored by major Western powers for prosecution.

For instance, the ICC has investigated cases concerning weak African countries like "Northern Uganda, the Democratic Republic of the Congo, the Central African Republic and Darfur. The court has indicted fourteen people; seven of whom remain free, two have died, and five are in custody." (WK 2009gg; ICC 2007)

But the ICC has turned a blind eye to the war crimes committed by powerful states like the U.S. and the U.K. in Iraq and Afghanistan, and Israel in Palestine, for example, because of the manipulation of legal technicality as described above.

Therefore, "critics of the court argue that there are 'insufficient checks and balances on the authority of the ICC prosecutor and judges' and 'insufficient protection against politicized prosecutions or other abuses.'" (WK 2009gg; USDS 2003)

(c) The Power Politics of the Prosecution of Crimes against Humanity

The travesty of justice to favor the major powers (or the victorious powers) and to go after the weak ones (or the defeated powers) is all the more revealed, if one looks at all the cases in which people were convicted of crimes against humanity by different international courts in the past century or so.

Hereafter are the the well-known cases of nationals in defeated (or weak) powers convicted of crimes against humanity in the past century or so. (WK 2009hh)

- Against Nazi, Fascist, and other comparable ones after WWII
  –Germany
  –Japan
  –Austria
  –France
  –Chile
  –Argentina
- Against weak African states
  –Sierra Leone
  –Rwanda
  –Ethiopia
- Against the defeated losers in former Yugoslavian states
  –Serbia
  –Bosnia and Herzegovina
  –Kosovo
  –Croatia
- Against other defeated nationals
  –Iraq
  –Haiti
  –South Africa

It is interesting to note that many of these cases of prosecution were sponsored and supported by the major powers in their campaign against the defeated (or weak) ones, for both political interests and ideological concerns.

(c1) For instance, in regard to the first category of cases (about Nazi, Fascist, and other comparable ones after WWII), the convicted individuals were Wilhelm Beiglböck, Alois Brunner, August Eigruber, Amon Göth, Maximilian Grabner, Ernst Kaltenbrunner, and Arthur Seyss-Inquart in Austria. (WK 2009jj)

In France, they were René Bousquet, Jean Leguay, Maurice Papon, and Paul Touvier in France. (WK 2009oo)

In Germany, they were Klaus Barbie, Erich Bauer, Karl Bömelburg, Martin Bormann, Adolf Eichmann, Ludwig Fischer, Hans Frank, Wilhelm Frick, Walther Funk, Karl Genzken, Hermann Göring, Waldemar Hoven,

Alfred Jodl, Wilhelm Keitel, Erhard Milch, Konstantin von Neurath, Erich Priebke, Georg-Hans Reinhardt, Joachim von Ribbentrop, Gerhard Rose, Alfred Rosenberg, Fritz Sauckel, Baldur von Schirach, Franz Schlegelberger, Albert Speer, Julius Streicher, and Ernst von Weizsäcker. (WK 2009pp)

In Japan, they were Kenji Doihara, Shunroku Hata, Hiranuma Kiichirō, Kōki Hirota, Seishirō Itagaki, Heitarō Kimura, Kuniaki Koiso, Iwane Matsui, Akira Mutō, Toshio Shiratori, and Hideki Tōjō. (WK 2009ss)

In Argentina, they were Antonio Domingo Bussi, Ramón Camps, Miguel Etchecolatz, Luciano Benjamín Menéndez, Adolfo Scilingo, and Jorge Rafael Videla. (WK 2009ii)

And in Chile, the convicted individual was Enrique Arancibia Clavel. (WK 2009ll)

(c2) In regard to the second category of cases (about weak African states), the convicted individual was Mengistu Haile Mariam in Ethiopia. (WK 2009nn)

In Rwanda, they were Jean Paul Akayesu, Théoneste Bagosora, Jean Bosco Barayagwiza, Jean Kambanda, Jean de Dieu Kamuhanda, Désiré Munyaneza, Wenceslas Munyeshyaka, Ferdinand Nahimana, Hassan Ngeze, Elizaphan Ntakirutimana, Emmanuel Rukundo, and Athanase Seromba. (WK 2009uu)

And in Sierra Leone, they were Alex Tamba Brima, Augustine Gbao, Morris Kallon, Brima Bazzy Kamara, Santigie Borbor Kanu, and Issa Sesay. (WK 2009xx)

(c3) In regard to the third category of cases (about the defeated losers in former Yugoslavian states), they were Hazim Delić and Dario Kordić in In Bosnia and Herzegovina. (WK 2009kk)

In Croatia, they were Dario Kordić and Slavko Kvaternik. (WK 2009mm)

In Kosovo, the convicted individual was Haradin Bala. (WK 2009tt)

And In Serbia, they were Radomir Kovač, Dragoljub Kunarac, Nebojša Pavković, Dragan Nikolić, Dragoljub Ojdanić, and Nikola Šainović. (WK 2009ww)

(d) And in regard to the fourth category of cases (about other defeated nationals), they were Raoul Cédras and Emmanuel Constant in Haiti. (WK 2009qq)

In Iraq, they were Awad Hamed al-Bandar, Ali Daeem Ali, Saddam Hussein, Abdullah Kadhem Roweed Al-Musheikhi, Taha Yassin Ramadan, and Barzan Ibrahim al-Tikriti. (WK 2009rr)

And in South Africa, the convicted individual was Eugene de Kock. (WK 2009yy)

In many of these cases, prosecution were carried out on the basis of power politics and ideological interests by the victorious powers that be, in their campaign against the defeated ones.

On the other hand, in none of these cases was there any national from the victorious powers who was prosecuted, except those who betrayed the hegemonic interests of the victorious powers themselves, and good examples are those individuals (as listed above) in Germany, France, and Austria after WWII who were convicted for working for the Nazis and Fascists against the Western allies.

And when the major powers invaded Iraq in early 2000's, they devastated it in the most horrific way, as already mentioned in *Sec. 1.1*, in the parlance of Tom Engelhardt (2009): "Iraq…has been devastated. The American invasion and the occupation that followed acted like whirlwinds of destruction, unraveling a land already bursting with problems and potential animosities….[P]ossibly a million or more Iraqis have died….Saddam's killing fields have been dwarfed by a fierce set of destructive American military operations as well as insurgencies…; major cities have been largely or partially destroyed, or ethnically cleansed; millions of Iraqis have been forced from their homes, becoming internal refugees or going into exile; untold numbers of Iraqis have been imprisoned, assassinated, tortured or abused; and the country's cultural heritage has been ransacked. Basic services—electricity, water, food—were terribly impaired and the economy, in the process of being privatized by the neocon overseers of the occupation, was simply wrecked. Health services were crippled…," and so on. (T. Engelhardt 2009)

In this horrific way, the American invasion and occupation of Iraq has devastated the country and its people on an enormous scale, and yet the international courts have turned a blined eye to this most heartbreaking inhumanity.

In *Beyond Democracy to Post-Democracy* (or *BDPD*), I already went to great lengths to show the horrofic crimes (e.g., war crimes, crimes of aggression, crimes of genocides, and crimes against humanity) committed by the victorious powers (like the U.S., the U.K., Israel, and others) against the others over the decades with immunity.

International law cannot touch these victorious powers, and justice has not been served for millions of innocent victims (like women, children, older folks, and others) who died, in the hands of the victorious powers in their recurrents acts of violence against the others.

It is thus insightful for D. W. Greig (1976) to once observe that "international law cannot exist in isolation from the political factors operating in the sphere of international relations." (WK 2009ff)

A Callous Fact of Life

This double standard in international law to favor the major powers which are relatively immune from being prosecuted for commiting crimes of serious offense against others and to chase after the weak and defeated losers for the power politics and idoelogical motivation of the victorious powers reveals the limited universal jurisdiction of international law.

Justice has yet to be fully served in the arena of international law.

Callous as this fact of life can be, the analysis can also teach us an invaluable lesson on the ontological principles in existential dialectics, and good examples include the formalness-informalness principle, the absoluteness-relativeness principle, the predictability-unpredictability principle, the explicability-inexplicability principle, the preciseness-vagueness principle, the simpleness-complicatedness principle, the openness-hiddenness principle, the denseness-emptiness principle, the change-constancy principle, the expansion-contraction principle, the evolution-transformation principle, the symmetry-asymmetry principle, the regression-progression principle, and the same-difference principle.

For instance, in relation to the formalness-informalness principle, if there is formalness (e.g., the formal logical requirement of consistency in prosecuting those defeated losers for crimes of most serious offense to the international community, in accordance to international law), there is also informalness (e.g., the non-formal logical inconsistency on the basis of a double standard to favor the victorious powers, in accordance to their hegemonic interests, which can change in any direction over time).

In relation to the absoluteness-relativeness principle, if there is absoluteness (e.g., the absolute demand by the victorious powers to prosecute those for crimes of most serious offense to the international community, in accordance to international law), there is relativeness too (e.g., what is good for the victorious powers to be immune from being prosecuted for their own crimes of most serious offense against the others is not so for the millions of victims who had died in the process).

In relation to the predictability-unpredictability principle, if there is predictability (e.g., the predictable tendency of international law to engage in a double standard to favor the victorious powers and to be biased against the defeated ones), there is unpredictability (e.g., the more difficult task to predict the severity of the conviction of a particular individual, because of the difficulties with respect to the competence and jurisdiction of an international court, the "often enormously complicated matters" of a given case, the different interests of the victorious powers involved, etc.).

In relation to the explicability-inexplicability principle, if there is explicability (e.g., the explanation of why the victorious powers have been relatively immune from being prosecuted for their crimes of most serious offense against the others, on the basis of legal technicality as afore-described), there is inexplicability (e.g., the lack of sufficient explanation within international law of why this kind of double standard within international law is really just).

In relation to the preciseness-vagueness principle, if there is preciseness (e.g., the precise identification of the four limited circumstances where the ICC has jurisdiction over cases concerning the "most serious crimes of concern to the international community," like "war crimes" and "the crime of aggression"), there is vagueness (e.g., the lack of a clear "definition of the crime [of aggression]" and of a clear formulation of "the conditions under which it may be prosecuted").

In relation to the simpleness-complicatedness principle, if there is simpleness (e.g., the simple but popular view that the ICC was set up to impartially provide justice against those who commit the "most serious crimes of concern to the international community"), there is the complicated counterpart (e.g., the more complicated picture of the ICC, by taking into account of its power politics, ideological motivation, and the like).

In relation to the openness-hiddenness principle, if there is openness (e.g., the open exploration of the crimes against humanity in certain countries as prosecuted by different international courts over the decades), there is hiddenness (e.g., the hidden bias of different international courts to chase after the defeated and weak powers and to turn a blind eye to the comparable but more horrific crimes committed by the victorious powers).

In relation to the denseness-emptiness principle, if there is denseness (e.g., the relatively dense concentration of cases against the defeated and weak powers in the history of international courts), there is emptiness (e.g., the relatively less dense, or more empty, concentration of cases against the victorious powers in the history of internaitonal courts).

In relation to the change-constancy principle, if there is change (e.g., the change of different international courts over time, like the creation of ICJ in 1945 and then the rise of ICC in 2002), there is constancy (e.g., the persistent constancy of a double standard in international courts to favor the victorious powers and to be biased against the weak and defeated ones).

In relation to the expansion-contraction principle, if there is expansion (e.g., the relatively better developed procedures of international courts to deal with cases against the weak powers), there is contraction (e.g., the relatively less developed procedures of international courts to confront the victorious powers over their more horrific crimes to the international community).

In relation to the evolution-transformation principle, if there is evolution (e.g., the natural evolution of humans to cope with conflicts by way of impulses and violence in the state of nature), there is transformation (e.g., the technical transformation of human conflict resolution by the invention of international law and international courts).

In relation to the symmetry-asymmetry principle, if there is symmetry (e.g., the co-existence of different nation-states over which international courts can have jurisdiction), there is asymmetry (e.g., some nation-states are more equal than others, so that there is a double standard for the dominant powers and against the weak ones, under international law).

In relation to the regression-progression principle, if there is regression (e.g., the double standard of international courts to favor the major powers), there is progression (e.g., the prosecution of those in weak and defeated powers who commit crimes of most serious offense to the international community).

And in relation to the same-difference principle, if there is similarity in outcome (e.g., the privilege of the victorious powers, and the suffering of the defeated powers, regardless of whether there are international courts or not), there is difference in outcome (e.g., in circumstances where there are international courts, "states try to avoid the appearance of having disregarded international obligations"; but when international courts do not exist or are weak, states may not even bother about the appearance, as in blunt colonialism and slavery practiced by major powers in the older days).

Constitutional Law and the Balance of Power

The concern with international law (in the previous section), especially in relation to criminal law in the international arena, is without doubt important, indeed.

Yet, there is another kind of law which is more basic, or fundamental, and that concerns constitutional law, be it domestic or international.

By definition, "constitutional law is the study of foundational or basic laws of nation states and other political organizations." (WK 2009zz)

Thus, "constitutions are the framework for government and may limit or define the authority and procedure of political bodies to execute new laws and regulations." (WK 2009zz)

But not every nation state (or political organization in general) has a written constitution, "though all such states have a *jus commune*, or law of the land, that may consist of a variety of imperative and consensual rules." (WK 2009zz)

Good examples of this kind (of the law of the land) include (i) "statutory law" (i.e., "acts of parliament"), (ii) "common law" (i.e., "judge-made law"), (iii) "custom and convention" (i.e., "long-standing practices not based on statutory or common law"), (iv) "works of authority" (i.e., "tracts by respected constitutional scholars"), and (v) even "international rules and norms." (T. Magstadt 1998; WK 2009zz)

The Functions of Constiutional Law

This qualification about written constitutions aside—constitutional law, because it is foundational, is in fact a law about the law.

In general, constitutional laws are thus "second order rulemaking," which means that they provide "rules about making rules." (WK 2009zz)

Consider three illustrations below in regard to the functions of constitutional law.

(a) Hierarchies and Relationships of Power

Firstly, constitutional law provides "rules about making rules to exercise power. It governs the relationships between the judiciary, the legislature and the executive with the bodies under its authority. One of the key tasks of constitutions within this context is to indicate hierarchies and relationships of power." (WK 2009zz)

These hierarchies and relationships of power can be based on the principle of the "balance of power," which come in different forms (e.g., unitary, federal, and confederalist or decentralized)—or, alternatively, on the principle of the "fusion of power." (WK 2009aaa & 2009bbb; T. Magstadt 1998; J. McCormick 2004)

In relation to the principle of the "balance of power," the first form concerns "a unitary state," in which "the constitution will vest ultimate authority in one central administration and legislature, and judiciary, though there is often a delegation of power or authority to local or municipal authorities." (WK 2009zz)

In a "federal" state, the "constitution…will identify the several levels of government coexisting with exclusive or shared areas of jurisdiction over lawmaking, application and enforcement." (WK 2009zz)

And in a "decentralized" (or "confederalist") state, the constitution stipulates that "the balance of power is...devolved to the subnational governments. In confederations (decentralised federations), it is more likely that the balance of power will be in favour of the sub-national level of government (that is, states or provinces)." (WK 2009aaa)

Alternatively, in relation to the principle of the "fusion of power," there is no rigid separation of power in the three branches of government. For example, in the British parlimentary system, the principle of the "fusion of power" allows that "some members of parliaments...hold cabinet positions," so that "the prime minister and his cabinet members rise and fall together." (T. Magstadt 1998)

(b) Rights of the Individual against the State

Secondly, constitutional law also lists the human rights to be protected for members in a community, and these rights are "the rights of the individual against the state." (WK 2009zz)

For instance, in the United States and France, there is "a single codified constitution, with a bill of rights. A recent example is the Charter of Fundamental Rights of the European Union which was intended to be included in the Treaty establishing a Constitution for Europe, that failed to be ratified. Perhaps the most important example is the Universal Declaration of Human Rights under the UN Charter. These are intended to ensure basic political, social and economic standards that a nation state, or intergovernmental body is obliged to provide to its citizens but many do include its governments." (WK 2009zz)

However, "some countries like the United Kingdom, have no entrenched document setting out fundamental rights; in those jurisdictions the constitution is composed of statute, case law and convention." (WK 2009zz)

(c) Parlimentary Procedures

And thirdly, constitutional law can provide "the procedure by which parliaments may legislate." (WK 2009zz)

A good illustration concerns the demand for "special majorities [which] may be required to alter the constitution. In bicameral legislatures, there may be a process laid out for second or third readings of bills before a new law can enter into force. Alternatively, there may further be requirements for maximum terms that a government can keep power before holding an election." (WK 2009zz)

And in parliamentary politics, even when there exists no clear majority, the constitution allows "the pragmatic mechanism exercised by a minor political party or other grouping whose guaranteed support may enable an otherwise minority government to obtain and hold office. This can be achieved either by the formation of a coalition government or by an assurance that any motion of no confidence in the government would be defeated." (WK 2009bbb)

The Moot Point on the Best Form of Constitutional Law

This illustrative summary of the diverse forms of provisions in a constitution has the virtue to illustrate the moot point in the debate concerning whether or not there is the best form of government (or political organization).

For instance, should constitutional law be based on the fundamental principle of the balance of power? And even should it be so, which specific form of the balance of power would be adopted instead?

In relation to the first question, the existence of the conflicting forms of government like the American presidential system (based more on the principle of the balance of power among the three different branches of government) and the British parlimentary system (based more on the principle of the fusion of power among the three different branches of government) in the realm of comparative politics nowadays should warn us against the danger of glorying one and bashing the other, depending on one's constitutional preference.

And in relation to the second question, even if one were to choose the principle of the balance of power as the foundation for a constitution, there would still be different forms to choose from, be they unitary, federalist, and decentralized (or confederalist).

For instance, the American form of the balance of power is federalist, the Japanese one is unitary, and the Canadian one is confederalist (or decentralized). (WK 2009aaa & 2009bbb; T. Magstadt 1998; J. McCormick 2004)

So, which one is the best? Should one pick the American form of government as the best, it would no doubt please the ears of the American nationalists. But would this flattering ever convince the Japanese and the Canadian counterparts that their forms of government are therefore inferior to the American one? And, of course, the reverse would also be true, should one pick the Japanese or the Canadian form of government over the American one.

In the end, it all depends on one's constitutional prefercence, this time, in regard to the specific form of the principle of the balance of power.

A Detached Perspective

The important point to remember here is to not favor one form of constitutional law against others but to show the diverse, at times conflicting, versions of constitutional law in the world today, which are contingent on the different circumstances which a people, a culture, and a society confront in a particular historical tradition.

In addition, this detached perspective can also reveal something important in regard to the ontological principles in existential dialectics, and good examples include the absoluteness-relativeness principle, the predictability-unpredictability principle, the explicability-inexplicability principle, the preciseness-vagueness principle, the simpleness-complicatedness principle, the openness-hiddenness principle, the denseness-emptiness principle, the expansion-contraction principle, the convention-novelty principle, the evolution-transformation principle, the symmetry-asymmetry principle, the regression-progression principle, and the same-difference principle.

For instance, in relation to the absoluteness-relativeness principle, if there is absolute perspective (e.g., the absolute requirement in the U.S. Constitution for the balance of power among the three branches of government), there is relative counterpart (e.g., what is good for the U.S. Constitution in regard to the balance of power among the three branches of government is not so for the British law of the land in regard to the diffusion of power among the three branches of government).

In relation to the predictability-unpredictability principle, if there is predictability (e.g., the predictable tendency of a constitutional law which is based on the principle of the balance of power to provide a check and balance among the three branches of government), there is unpredictability (e.g., the more difficult task to predict exactly which form of the balance of power, be it unitary, federalist, or confederalist, that a constitutional law will adopt, even if the principle of the balance of power is accepted, until more details about its constitution and history are known).

In relation to the explicability-inexplicability principle, if there is explicability (e.g., the explanation of a constitutional law like the U.S. Constitution which adopts the principle of the balance of power on the basis of its provision of a check and balance among the three branches of government), there is inexplicability (e.g., the lack of suficient explanation within the U.S. Constitution itself of why the alternative form like the fusion of power is not used instead to check excessive power).

In relation to the preciseness-vagueness principle, if there is preciseness (e.g., the precise identification of the possible sources of the law of the land, like statutory law, common law, custom and convention, for those governments which do not have a written constitution), there is vagueness (e.g., the lack of clear formulation of which specific sources of the law of the land is good for which specific form of government under which specific circumstances).

In relation to the simpleness-complicatedness principle, if there is simple analysis (e.g., the simple analysis of the American constitution on the basis of the balance of power among the three branches of government), there is complicated counterpart too (e.g., the more complicated analysis of the American constitution in relation to other different forms of constitution, so as to have a more comparative understanding of different possible constitutional laws).

In relation to the openness-hiddenness principle, if there is openness (e.g., the open exploration, in the American constitution, of the virtue of the balance of power for the check and balance among the three branches of government), there is hiddenness (e.g., the hidden bias of the principle of the balance of power, within the U.S. Constitution, in not including alternative principles like the fusion of power).

In relation to the denseness-emptiness principle, if there is denseness (e.g., the relatively denser concentration of the principle of the fusion of power in parlimentary forms of constitutional law like the British one), there is emptiness (e.g., the relatively less dense, or more empty, concentration of the principle of the fusion of power in presidential forms of constitutional law like the American one).

In relation to the expansion-contraction principle, if there is expansion (e.g., the relatively better developed mechanisms in parlimentary systems like the British one to allow "some members of parliaments" to "hold cabinet positions"), there is contraction (e.g., the relatively less developed mechanisms in parlimentary systems like the British one to provide a clear separation of power among the three branches of government like the American one).

In relation to the convention-novelty principle, if there is convention (e.g., the conventional wisdom in the American constitutional tradition about the virtue of the principle of the balance of power to separate the three branches of government), there is novelty (e.g., the alternative novel challenge by the parlimentary system like the British one to allow the fusion of power among the three branches of government).

In relation to the evolution-transformation principle, if there is evolution (e.g., the natural evolution of humans to live together in a group in the state of nature), there is transformation (e.g., the technical transformation of human community by way of the invention of constitutional law to "define the authority and procedure of political bodies to execute new laws and regulations").

In relation to the symmetry-asymmetry principle, if there is symmetry (e.g., the co-existence of different principles for constitutional law, like the balance of power and the fusion of power), there is asymmetry (e.g., the popularity of the principle of the balance of power in American constitutional law, but the acceptance of the principle of the fusion of power in the British tradition).

In relation to regression-progression principle, if there is regression (e.g., the drawback in the American constitutional law to not have the benefits of the British parilimentary alternative, like the formation of a coalition government), there is progression (e.g., the progress made for the check and balance among the three branches of government in the American system).

And in relation to the same-difference principle, if there is similarity in outcome (e.g., the provision of "authority and procedure of political bodies to execute new laws and regulations" in a way to avoid excessive abuse of power, be it in the American presidential system or the British parlimentary one), there is difference in outcome (e.g., the strict separation of power in the American system, but the fusion of power in the British one).

Necessity and Culture

The last perspective to be analyzed here in the context of law is from the one of culture—not solely from the perspectives of the mind, nature, and society (as shown in the previous three sections).

Two illustrative case studies are in order here, namely, (2.5.1) divine law, morality, and legal sanctions, and (2.5.2) common law, and the cultural legacy of the British Empire—to be elaborated hereafter, respectively.

Divine Law, Morality, and Legal Sanctions

The first illustration here concerns divine law and the role of religion, from the perspective of culture.

By definition, "divine law" refers to "any law (or rule) that in the opinion of believers, comes directly from the will of God (or a god). Like natural law (which may be seen as a manifestation of divine law) it is independent of the will of man, who cannot change it. However it may be revealed or not, so it may change in human perception in time through new revelation." (WK 2009cc)

The function of divine law, for the believers, is important enough for human salvation, since, as Thomas Aquinas thus argued in *Treatise on Law*, "Divine Law, as opposed to Natural Law, comes only from revelation or scripture, hence Biblical law, and is necessary for human salvation." (WK 2009cc)

Legal Sanctions, and the Moral Dimension of Divine Law

To strive for human salvation, for the believers, the divine law is universally binding and therefore needs to be obeyed, especially in relation to its moral demands.

After all, divine law represents "the will of God," and "the new Kingdom of God…was not confined to a single nation, [as] it embraced all the nations of the earth." (CE 2009) Thus, these moral demands are to be incorporated as the foundation for the law in society.

Consider, for illustration below, the moral aspects of divine law in the Catholic tradition in the context of the law.

In the Catholic tradition of interpreting divine law, there is a distinction between "the Old Law, contained in the Pentateuch, and the New Law, which was revealed by Jesus Christ and is contained in the New Testament." (CE 2009)

The divine law of the Old Testament is also known as "the Mosaic Law," because, for the believers, "Moses wrote down the Law at the direct inspiration of God. God Himself, then, is the lawgiver, Moses merely acted as the intermediary between God and His people; he merely promulgated the Law which he had been inspired to write down." (CE 2009)

For instance, one of the most amazing aspects of the Mosaic law concerns "the love of God and of one's neighbour," which "was the great precept of the Law," as "the basis of all true civilization," and it "became the clear, certain, and publicly recognized standard of moral conduct for the Jewish people, and through them for Christendom." (CE 2009)

However, this does not mean that everything in the Old Testament was written and originated by Moses himself, since "[t]here is abundant evidence in Scripture itself that many portions of the Mosaic legislation existed and were put in practice long before the time of Moses." (CE 2009)

Good examples of the practices prior to the time of Moses include "circumcision," "the religious observance of the seventh day," and the like. But these practices which were put in the Old Testament (although they were not orginated by Moses himself) are not trivial, since they are "precepts of the natural law, which can be gathered by reason from nature herself, and in fact they were known long before Moses wrote them down at the express command of God." (CE 2009)

(a) The Imperfections of the Mosaic Law, and Their Excuses

Yet, the Mosaic law, for the critics, is far from perfection, because it contains certain laws which appear rather shocking in our time, in historical retrospect. Consider the following four examples (as summarized in *Table 2.4*) for illustration, together with the excuses as exploited by the believers.

Firstly, the Mosaic law is harsh in curbing "licentious thoughts and covetous desires" broadly defined—and the excuse here is that "it was suited to the low stage of civilization to which the Israelites had at the time attained; the severe punishments which it prescribed for transgressors were necessary to bend the stiff necks of a rude people; the temporal rewards held out to those who observed the law were adapted to an unspiritual and carnal race." (CE 2009)

Secondly, the Mosaic law includes "the command given by God to exterminate certain nations, and the permission given by Him to the Israelites to spoil the Egyptians"—and the excuse here is that "the tribes of Chanaan richly deserved the fate to which they were condemned by God; and if there were innocent people among the guilty, God is the absolute Lord of life and death, and He commits no injustice when He takes away what He has given. Besides, He can make up by gifts of a higher order in another life for sufferings which have been patiently endured in this life." (CE 2009)

Thirdly, the Mosaic law allows the practice of slavery; for instance, "in Exodus 21:5-6…it is there laid down that if a Hebrew slave who has a wife and children prefers to remain with his master rather than go out free when the sabbatical year comes round, he is to be taken to the door-post and have his ear bored through with an awl, and then he is to remain a slave for life. It was a sign and mark by which he was known to be a lifelong slave." (CE 2009)

The excuse here is that "[t]he practice was doubtless already familiar to the Israelites of the time, as it was to their neighbours. The slave himself probably thought no more of the operation than does a South African beauty, when her lip or ear is pierced for the lip-ring and the ear-ring, which in her estimation are to add to her charms….It existed everywhere and although in practice it is apt to lead to many abuses, still, in the mild form in which it was allowed among the Jews, and with the safeguards prescribed by the Law, it cannot be said with truth to be contrary to sound morality." (CE 2009)

And fourthly, the Mosaic law justifies inconsistency in the enforcement of its moral codes. For instance, the cases concerning the practices of "polygamy and divorce," "usury," and the like at the time pose "serious difficulty against the holiness of the Mosaic Law…The difficulty is one which has engaged the attention of the Fathers and theologians of the Church from the beginning." (CE 2009)

The excuse here is that, in the case concerning polygamy and divorce, for instance, "[a]mid the general laxity with regard to marriage which existed among the Semitic tribes, it would have been difficult to preserve the strict law [of monogamy and marriage until death]. The importance of a rapid increase among the chosen people of God so as to enable them to defend themselves from their neighbours, and to fulfil their appointed destiny, seemed to favour relaxation. The example of some of the chief of the ancient Patriarchs was taken by their descendants as being a sufficient indication of the dispensation granted by God. With special safeguards annexed to it Moses adopted the Divine dispensation on account of the hardness of heart of the Jewish people." (CE 2009)

Therefore, so the excuses goes, "[n]either polygamy nor divorce can be said to be contrary to the primary precepts of nature. The primary end of marriage is compatible with both. But at least they are against the secondary precepts of the natural law: contrary, that is, to what is required for the well-ordering of human life. In these secondary precepts, however, God can dispense for good reason if He sees fit to do so. In so doing He uses His sovereign authority to diminish the right of absolute equality which naturally exists between man and woman with reference to marriage. In this way, without suffering any stain on His holiness, God could permit and sanction polygamy and divorce in the Old Law." (CE 2009)

In these words, biblical hermeneutics, with the help of reason, explains everything away, with whatever sophistry that reason can come up. It is no wonder that Martin Luther once said that reason is the dirty whore.

(b) The Four-Fold Reply by the Critics

Needless to say, for the critics, these excuses do not stand at all. Hereafter are four major criticisms against the theory of the divine law, also known as "the divine command theory" in the current context so understood. (WK 2009ddd)

- Firstly, the divine command theory "implies that morality is arbitrary. If divine command theory is true, morality is based merely upon God's whim. Divine Command Theory, this objection runs, entails that, if it is morally obligatory to do x, then this is in virtue of God's commanding that we do x. Thus, if God had commanded that we be cruel and dishonest, and that we not be merciful and charitable, then it would have been morally obligatory to do certain harmful (cruel and dishonest) things, and morally impermissible to do certain beneficial (merciful and eleemosynary) things. One reply to this objection denies that God would have commanded such things because, being essentially omnibenevolent, he necessarily does not command evil. Critics of divine command theory suggest that this response is a peritrope; it assumes that God knows that, say, cruelty is evil before he gives the command that, according to divine command theory, makes cruelty bad." (WK 2009ddd)
- Secondly, the divine command theory "implies that calling God good makes no sense—or, at best, that one is simply saying that God is consistent: 'God does whatever he commands.'" (WK 2009ddd)
- Thirdly, the divine command theory "commits the naturalistic fallacy. Proponents of this criticism argue that while ethics can and should specify the non-moral properties that make things good, it is always a mistake to use non-moral terms in giving the meaning of the word 'good'. If I ask why I shouldn't commit murder, the divine command answer is: 'because God commands you not to,' but I can then ask why I should do what God commands. If the answer is that God created me, I can ask why I should obey my creator, and so on. This is not a matter of motivation, but of the explanation of the normativity of morality." (WK 2009ddd)
- Finally, the divine command theory does not answer "the epistemological question of how one comes to know the will of God. Most religions point to their scriptures for answers, but it is still possible to question whether these really state the will of God. Furthermore, few if any religions claim to have texts detailing their deity's will concerning every possible situation. These gaps often concern situations that the writers of ancient religious scriptures couldn't have foreseen, such as those involving advanced technologies, especially biological and medical ones. Because of these problems, critics claim that one can never be sure if a person, including oneself, who claims to know God's will actually does know, or is lying, mistaken, or mad (or indeed if God has subsequently

> changed his mind, though this possibility is ruled out by many notions of God)." (WK 2009ddd)

Surely, these counter-criticisms by the critics have rarely convinced the believers to abandon their dogmatic way of obeying the divine law in any major way, no matter what.

(b) The Rejoinder by the Believers, and Some Persistant Problems

For instance, the believers would answer the critics by providing the following responses. (WK 2009ddd) However, for the critics, the responses fail to prove anything.

- Firstly, "many proponents of divine command theory 'bite the bullet,' agreeing with the point the critic is making but arguing that it is not a problem with the theory. For example, writers like William of Ockham argue that if God had commanded murder, then murder would indeed have been morally obligatory. Indeed, Ockham goes so far as to say that God could change the moral order at any time. Thus Ockham embraces divine command theory wholeheartedly; his view has been characterized as being that 'God's command is good' is analytically true....It is also possible to bite the bullet regarding the naturalistic fallacy by arguing that defining morality in non-moral terms is not a fallacy at all." (WK 2009ddd)
  But, for the critics, this "biting the bullet" is question-begging, since it only insists but does not prove that "God's command is good" is in fact true (other than the trivial stipulation by definition).
- Secondly, another way to defend God's command is the approach suggested by Duns Scotus, who suggested that, "for one set of moral values at least, God could not have commanded otherwise because they are necessary (omnipotence, of course, means being able to do anything, but the logically impossible is essentially nonsensical, and not part of anything). However, this would mean that necessity, not God, is the source of objective morality. God is reduced to a passer-on of moral laws....Thus, for example, that murder is wrong is a truth, and though God commanded us not to murder he couldn't have done otherwise, nor can he revoke his command....This is similar to a more recent approach developed by Richard Swinburne." (WK 2009ddd)
  But for the critics, this reponse by Scotus and Swinburne that "God is reduced to a passer-on of moral laws" is also question-begging, since one can continue and ask, Why are these moral laws (passed on by God) necessary at all? One cannot simply appeal to God again, at this

stage of the argument, because God is already reduced to a passer-on of moral laws.

- Thirdly, another modified response is by R.M. Adams, who "distinguishes between two meanings of ethical terms like 'right' and 'wrong': the meaning that Adams explains in roughly emotivist terms, and the meaning that has its place in religious discourse (that is, commanded or forbidden by God). Because God is benevolent, the two meanings coincide; God is, however, free to command other than he has done, and if he had chosen to command, for example, that murder was morally right, then the two meanings would break apart. In that case, even the religious believer would be forced to accept that it was correct to say both that murder was wrong and that God commanded us to commit murder." (WK 2009ddd)
  Again, for the crirics, this response by Adams is also question-begging, because it does not explain why it is justified for a person to be inconsistent in accepting that murder is wrong, in the emotivist meaning, but to commit murder anyway, in the prescriptivist meaning. The moral self thus becomes inherently fragmentary.
- Fourthly, another response is by Saint Thomas Aquinas, who "claimed that God creates moral norms that reflect his own essence, meaning that his demands are not arbitrary. In this case, it would become necessary to examine the essence of God." (WK 2009ddd)
  But, for the critics, this response by Aquinas is no better, since it is question-begging about how one can know for sure the essence of God and why it is necessary to accept his demands in the first place.
- Finally, another response is the conventional view that, for instance, "from a Christian viewpoint, man, as made in God's image, conform also to his sense of morality. Therefore 'good' and 'bad' are relevant to God, and our sense of what is good or bad corresponds to God's sense of good and bad." (WK 2009ddd)
  Again, for the critics, this conventional Christian answer is question-begging too, since it does not prove that "man" is "made in God's image," especially for those in the tradition of evolutinary theory (not creation theory), and also does not justify or explain why it is necessary to conform to God's sense of morality at all, when man is not God, even if made in God's image.

In the end, the universality of divine law remains problematic, when it is subject to a closer scrutiny. So, its relevance to legal sanctions in the context of the legal institutioin in society remains problematic at best.

A Critical Look from both Sides

It should be stressed, however, that this critical assessment of the divine law in the context of the law does not mean to reject a sacral (religious) treatment of the law in favor of a more secular alternative.

On the contrary, the point here is to not endorse either of the two sides in the debate, while learning something from them (without, however, integrating them, since they are not compatible in some fundamental ways).

In fact, a good way to show this critical look from both sides is to reveal its relevance to some ontological principles in existential dialectics, and good examples include the formalness-informalness principle, the absoluteness-relativeness principle, the predictability-unpredictability principle, the explicability-inexplicability principle, the preciseness-vagueness principle, the simpleness-complicatedness principle, the openness-hiddenness principle, the denseness-emptiness principle, the change-constancy principle, the expansion-contraction principle, the theory-praxis principle, the convention-novelty principle, the evolution-transformation principle, the symmetry-asymmetry principle, the softness-hardness principle, the regression-progression principle, and the same-difference principle.

For instance, in relation to the formalness-informalness principle, if there is formalness (e.g., the formal logical requirement of consistency in moral codes, as in "the Golden Rule," which "demands that one's actions conform to one's own standard"), there is informalness (e.g., the non-formal allowance of inconsistency in the Mosaic law, in regard to moral laxity in the context of polygamy and divorce). (WK 2009j)

In relation to the absoluteness-relativeness principle, if there is absolute viewpoint (e.g., the absolute command of God in the Mosaic law "to exterminate certain nations, and the permission given by Him to the Israelites to spoil the Egyptians"), there is relative counterpart (e.g., what is good for the Israelites in regard to the extermination of certain nations and tribes is not so for those nations and tribes as the victims).

In relation to the predictability-unpredictability principle, if there is predictability (e.g., the predictable tendency of the Israelites to obey the Mosaic law), there is unpredictability (e.g., the more difficult task to predict which specific questionable practices can be successfully excused over time for circumstantial reasons, in relation to the Mosaic law).

In relation to the explicability-inexplicability principle, if there is explicability (e.g., the explanation by Scotus and Swinburne of why "God could not have commanded otherwise" on the basis that "necessity, not God, is the source of objective morality"), there is inexplicaiblity (e.g., the lack of sufficient explanation by Scotus and Swinburne, since one can continue and ask, Why are these moral laws passed on by God necessary in the first place?).

In relation to the preciseness-vagueness principle, if there is preciseness (e.g., the precise identification of the commandments to be obeyed in the Mosaic law, like "the love of God and of one's neighbour"), there is vagueness (e.g., the lack of clear formulation of the specific circumstances in the Mosaic law when these commandments can be observed or violated, for instance, in relation to certain nations and tribes, or of how harsh is harsh in dealing with "licentious thoughts and covetous desires").

In relation to the simpleness-complicatedness principle, if there is simple analysis (e.g., the simple view of the Mosaic law as the "standard of moral conduct for the Jewish people, and through them for Christendom"), there is complicated counterpart (e.g., the more complicated analysis of the Mosaic law in relation to its historical contingency and multifaceted imperfections).

In relation to the openness-hiddenness principle, if there is openness (e.g., the open exploration of love in the Mosaic law, in special relation to God and one's neighbors), there is hiddenenss (e.g., the hidden bias in the Mosaic law in regard to its dark sides, which are to be "excused" by "the Fathers and theologians of the Church from the beginning").

In relation to the denseness-emptiness principle, if there is denseness (e.g., the relatively denser concentration of regulations of the "acts of the people of God," be they "civil, ceremonial, and moral," in a comprehensive way, in the Mosaic law), there is also emptiness (e.g., the relatively less dense, or more empty, concentration in the Mosaic law of "the humanitarian and sentimental canons of the twentieth century"). (CE 2009)

In relation to the change-constancy principle, if there is change (e.g., the ever new responses by the religious believers to defend their faith and practices in response to the criticisms by the critics), there is constancy (e.g., the recurrent question-beggingness of the ever new responses by the believers).

In relation to the expansion-contraction principle, if there is expansion (e.g., the relatively better developed ability of the believers to engage in biblical hermeneutics in order to make ever new excuses), there is contraction (e.g, the relatively lesser developed ability of the believers to utilize the empiricist approach to knowledge as often found among scientists).

In relation to the theory-praxis principle, if there is theory (e.g., the theoretical construction of divine law), there is praxis (e.g., the practical application of the divine command theory for moral conducts in everyday life).

In relation to the convention-novelty principle, if there is convention (e.g., the conventional wisdom, among the believers, that divine law represents the will of God), there is novelty (e.g.., the alternative novel challenge to the conventional wisdom concernng the divine command theory by R.M. Adams for a modified divine command theory, such that one could accept that murder is wrong and commit murder anyway, should God so dictate).

In relation to the evolution-transformation principle, if there is evolution (e.g., the natural evolution of humans to behave in certain ways in the state of nature, be they about the law of the jungle or else), there is transformation (e.g, the technical transformation of human behaviors by way of the invention of moral codes in relation to divine law).

In relation to the symmetry-asymmetry principle, if there is symmetry (e.g., the co-existence of the theory of the divine law and the classical evolutionary theory), there is asymmetry (e.g., the acceptance of the divine command theory by the believers in the bible, and the more popularity of evolutinary theory among scientists).

In relaiton to the softness-hardness principle, if there is softness (e.g., the promised reward of salvation to those who obey divine law), there is hardness (e.g., the severe punishment against those who violate divine law).

In relation to the regression-progression principle, if there is regression (e.g., the abuses and excuses in the history of the Mosaic law to justify slavery, moral laxity, the extermination of certain nations and tribes, and gruesome punishment), there is progression (e.g., the progress made in relation to the love of God and one's neighbors).

And in relation to the same-difference principle, if there is similarity in outcome (.e.g., the occurrence of violence and abuse in history, with or without the Mosaic law, albeit in different ways), there is difference in outcome (e.g., the selective treatment of certain nations, tribes, and peoples, depending on the moral codes and legal sanctions in question, as shown by the allowance to engage in usury with foreigners among the Isralites, but the disallowance of such a practice at all among the Christians). (CE 2009)

Common Law, and the Cultural Legacy of the British Empire

Another way to illustrate the cultural influence on the development of the law is by way of external cultural diffusion into a country over time.

In the current context of necessity in relation to the law, it is often said that the common law is gaining more acceptance around the world, to the extent that "the common law…is crucial to understanding almost all important areas of law" and thus enjoys the privilege of some version of universality.

But, to what extent is this claim really true?

A good point of departure to answer this question is to begin by analyzing what the common law tradition is not and what it is—to be summarized in what follows (and also in *Table 2.5*).

What the Common Law Tradition Is Not

To start, there are different legal traditions, and two major ones in the Western world are "common law" and "civil law," although in the rest of the world, there can be others, like "Islamic law," "socialist law," and the rest.

The term "common law" refers to "law developed by judges through decisions of courts and similar tribunals (called case law), rather than through legislative statutes [for "statutory law"] or executive action [for "regulatory law"], and to corresponding legal systems that rely on precedential case law." (WK 2009fff)

There are three main features which set the common law tradition apart from others, as shown below. (WK 2009fff)

(a) Common Law Is Not Statutory Law, Regulatory Law, etc.

The first main feature of the common law tradition is that its authority to promulgate a law is not through congressional or parlimentary legislation (as in "statutory law") nor executive action (as in "regulaory law") but through judiciary decisions in courts and other tribunals. (WK 2009fff; B. Garner 2001; J. Salmond 1907)

This distinction can be further made into two finer points, namely, (a) "pure common law arising from the traditional and inherent authority of courts to say what the law is, even in absence of an underlying statute" (e.g., "most criminal law and procedural law before the 20th century, and even today, most of contract law and the law of torts"), and (b) "court decisions that decide the fine boundaries and distinctions in law promulgated by other bodies, such as judicial interpretations of the

Constitution, of statutes, and of regulations." (WK 2009fff; B. Garner 2001)

(b) Common Law Is Not Civil Law, Islamic Law, Socialist Law, etc.

The second main feature of the common law tradition is that it "differentiates 'common law' jurisdictions and legal systems from 'civil law' or 'code' jurisdictions. Common law systems place great weight on court decisions, which are considered 'law' with the same force of law as statutes." (WK 2009fff; B. Garner 2001)

On the other hand, "in civil law jurisdictions (the legal tradition that prevails in, or is combined with common law in, almost all non-Islamic, non-common law countries), judicial precedent is given relatively less weight (which means that a judge deciding a given case has more freedom to interpret the text of a statute independently, and less predictably), and scholarly literature is given relatively more." (WK 2009fff)

An excellent example here concerns "the Napoleonic code" which "expressly forbade French judges from pronouncing the law. As a rough rule of thumb, common law systems trace their history to England, while civil law systems trace their history to Roman law." (WK 2009fff)

However, this distinction between common law and civil law should be taken with care, since "the differences between common and civil law jurisdictions are gradually becoming smaller, as common law jurisdictions enact statutes that cover areas formerly left to the common law, and civil law courts give increasing weight to precedent." (WK 2009fff)

In addition, there are also other law traditions, such as Islamic law (based on the divine law as revealed in the Koran), Socialist law (based on the principle of equality as in Marxism), and Chinese law (based on the principle of harmony as in Confucianism and the principle of simplicity as in Taoism).

(c) Common Law Is Not Equity

And the third main feature of the common law tradition is that "common law" (or "law," in short) is not "equity." (WK 2009fff; B. Garner 2001; J. Salmond 1907)

The distinction between law and equity can be made in four major ways, in what follows. (WK 2009eee & 2009fff)

Firstly, a court of "law" is more for awarding "money damages," whereas a court of "equity" is more for issuing injunctions.

For instance, "before 1873, England had two parallel court systems: courts of 'law' that could only award money damages and recognized only the legal owner of property, and courts of 'equity' that could issue injunctive relief (that is, a court order to a party to do something, give something to someone, or stop doing something) and recognized trusts of property. This split propagated to many of the colonies, including the United States." (WK 2009fff)

However, this distinction is increasingly blurred, because contemporary legal systems tend to merge them into one. For instance, "most jurisdictions, including the U.S. federal system and most states, have merged the two courts. Additionally, even before the separate courts were merged together, most courts were permitted to apply both law and equity, though under potentially different procedural law." (WK 2009fff; M. Friedman 2005)

Even then, however, "the historical distinction between 'law' and 'equity' remains important today." (WK 2009fff)

Secondly, a "legal" title is more about ownership, whereas an "equitable" title is more about trust.

For instance, this distinction is important in property law, trust law, and others, because "the same article of property often has a 'legal title' and an 'equitable title,' and these two groups of ownership rights may be held by different people." (WK 2009fff)

Thirdly, a court of "law" is more likely to have a "jury trial," whereas a court of "equity" is more likely to have a "judge trial."

For instance, in the United States, it is "the Seventh Amendment" which provides the "right to a jury trial," and the determination of this fact is "necessary to resolution of a 'common law' claim"; otherwise, "the issue will be decided by a judge," in relation to "what the law is" and to "equity." (WK 2009fff)

And fourthly, in cases of "law," there is "the standard of review and degree of deference given by an appellate tribunal to the decision of the lower tribunal under review" on a *de novo* basis, that is, "'as if new' from scratch by the appellate tribunal"—whereas, in cases of "equity," the standard of review is on the basis of any "abuse of discretion." (WK 2009fff)

This is true, even though the use of "discretion" is often considerd as an advantage of "equity" over "common law," because it is to "mitigate the rigor of common law," by "allowing courts to use their discretion and apply justice fairly, in accordance with natural law," for instance. (WK 2009eee)

What the Common Law Tradition Is

But to say what the common law tradition is not is not the same as saying what it is.

There are five main features which characterize the common law tradition.

(a) The Common Law Is Slow in Adjudication

Firstly, the procedure of a common law adjudication is slow, relatively speaking.

In other words, "in a common law jurisdiction several stages of research and analysis are required to determine what 'the law is' in a given situation. First, one must ascertain the facts. Then, one must locate any relevant statutes and cases. Then one must extract the principles, analogies and statements by various courts of what they consider important to determine how the next court is likely to rule on the facts of the present case. Later decisions, and decisions of higher courts or legislatures carry more weight than earlier cases and those of lower courts. Finally, one integrates all the lines drawn and reasons given, and determines what 'the law is.' Then, one applies that law to the facts." (WK 2009fff)

(b) The Common Law Is Incremental in Change

Secondly, the common law tradition is incremental in change, relatively speaking—and therefore conservative, by comparison.

There are two good reasons for the incremental malleability of the common law. (WK 2009fff) The first reason is that "common law courts are not absolutely bound by precedent, but can (when extraordinarily good reason is shown) reinterpret and revise the law, without legislative intervention, to adapt to new trends in political, legal and social philosophy." (WK 2009fff) And the second reason is that "the common law evolves through a series of gradual steps, that gradually works out all the details, so that over a decade or more, the law can change substantially but without a sharp break, thereby reducing disruptive effects." (WK 2009fff)

In contrast, in statutory law, for instance, "the legislative process is very difficult to get started, as legislatures tend to delay action until a situation is totally intolerable. For these reasons, legislative changes tend to be large, jarring and disruptive (sometimes positively, sometimes negatively, and sometimes with unintended consequences)." (WK 2009fff)

(c) The Common Law Is Important in Many Important Areas of Law

Thirdly, the common law is important in many "important areas of law." (WK 2009fff)

For instance, "in England and Wales and in most states of the United States, the basic law of contracts, torts and property do not exist in statute, but only in common law (though there may be isolated modifications enacted by statute). In almost all areas of the law (even those where there is a statutory framework, such as contracts for the sale of goods, or the criminal law), legislature-enacted statutes generally give only terse statements of general principle, and the fine boundaries and definitions exist only in the common law." (WK 2009fff)

Therefore, "to find out what the precise law is that applies to a particular set of facts, one has to locate precedential decisions on the topic, and reason from those decisions by analogy. To consider but one example, the First Amendment to the United States Constitution states 'Congress shall make no law respecting an establishment of religion, or prohibiting the free exercise thereof'—but interpretation (that is, determining the fine boundaries, and resolving the tension between the 'establishment' and 'free exercise' clauses) of each of the important terms was delegated by Article III of the Constitution to the judicial branch, so that the current legal boundaries of the Constitutional text can only be determined by consulting the common law." (WK 2009fff; G. Hughes 1996)

(d) The Common Law Values Less Legal Treatises/Academic Works

Fourthly, the common law tradtion puts less emphasis on the role of "legal treatises" and "academic writings."

This relative dismissal in the common law tradition is at odds with the greater attention to "legal treatises" and "academic writings" in the civil law tradition.

In other words, "in common law jurisdictions, legal treatises compile common law decisions, and state overarching principles that (in the author's opinion) explain the results of the cases. However, in common law jurisdictions, treatises are not the law, and lawyers and judges tend to use these treatises as only 'finding aids' to locate the relevant cases. In common law jurisdictions, scholarly work is seldom cited as authority for what the law is. When common law courts rely on scholarly work, it is almost always only for factual findings, policy justification, or the history and evolution of the law, but the court's legal conclusion is reached through analysis of relevant statutes and common law, seldom scholarly commentary." (WK 2009fff)

In contrast, the civil law tradition puts more value on legal treatises and academic writings, in that "the writings of law professors are given significant weight by courts. In part, this is because civil law decisions traditionally were very brief, sometimes no more than a paragraph stating who wins and who loses. The rationale has to come from somewhere else, and the academy often filled that role. As civil law court decisions move in the direction of common law reasoning, it is possible that this balance may shift." (WK 2009fff)

(e) The Common Law Is Precise and Reliable

And fifthly, the common law tends to be precise (and therefore serves as "a foundation for commercial economies"). (WK 2009fff)

The reason is that "there is common law to give reasonably precise guidance on almost every issue," so "parties (especially commercial parties) can predict whether a proposed course of action is likely to be lawful or unlawful." (WK 2009fff)

As an illustration, "many commercial contracts are more economically efficient, and create greater wealth, because the parties know ahead of time that the proposed arrangement, though perhaps close to the line, is almost certainly legal. Newspapers, taxpayer-funded entities with some religious affiliation, and political parties can obtain fairly clear guidance on the boundaries within which their freedom of expression rights apply." (WK 2009fff; M. Yeo 2006)

The Historical Legacy of the Common Law Tradition

These characteristics of the common law tradition have much to say about its strengths (not just weaknesses) as a legal system; after all, the fact that the common law is crucial for many important areas of law and even serves as the foundation for commercial economies speaks for itself about the adoptability by a sizable number of countries around the world.

Yet, there is another important reason for the wide-spread influence of the common law tradition, and this other reason has much to do with the cultural diffusion of the British Empire in modern times, especially in relation to its legal system known as the common law legal system.

In fact, it is no exaggeration to say that "every country which has been colonised at some time by England, Great Britain, or the United Kingdom uses common law." (WK 2009fff)

The only exceptions are those places which "had been formerly colonised by other nations, such as Quebec (which follows French law to some extent), South Africa and Sri Lanka (which follow Roman Dutch law), where the prior civil law system was retained to respect the civil rights of the local colonists. India's system of common law is also a mixture of English law and the local Hindu law, except in the state of Goa which retains the Portuguese civil code." (WK 2009fff)

In Nicaragua, as another example, its "legal system also is a mixture of the English Common Law and the Civil Law through the influence of British administration of the Eastern half of the country from the mid-1600s until about 1905, the William Walker period from about 1855 through 1857, USA interventions/occupations during the period from 1909 to 1933, the influence of USA institutions during the Somoza family administrations (1933 through 1979) and the considerable importation between 1979 and the present of USA culture and institutions." (WK 2009fff)

In general, "the common law constitutes the basis of the legal systems of: England and Wales, Northern Ireland, Ireland, federal law in the United States and the law of individual U.S. states (except Louisiana), federal law throughout Canada and the law of the individual provinces and territories (except Quebec), Australia (both federal and individual states), New Zealand, South Africa, India, Malaysia, Brunei, Pakistan, Singapore, Hong Kong, and many other generally English-speaking countries or Commonwealth countries (except Malta and Scotland)." (WK 2009fff)

A Note of Caution

Lest any misunderstanding hastily occurs, the claim about the cultural influence of the British Empire on its former colonies around the world in relation to this common law tradition does not suggest that the common law is better than any other legal systems or that the historical legacy of colonialism and imperialism is therefore justified.

Quite on the contrary, as this is something that I already went to great lengths to explain in the 2 volumes of *The Future of Human Civilization* (or *FHC*), the Western colonial legacy in modern times constitutes part of what I called "hegemonic modernity," with both negative and positive effects to be considered.

The important point to remember here in the context of the law from the perspective of culture concerns how and why culture has a role to play in shaping the legal system of a society over time, such that any claim of legal universality remains problematic, precisely because of the historical contingency in the outcome of the development of a legal system.

And the case study of the cultural diffusion of the common legal system by the British Empire to its former colonies around the world precisely shows the historical contingency of the rise of the common law tradition in question, besides other factors like its strengths, not just weaknesses (as indicated above).

In fact, another way to show this note of caution in analysis is by way of illustrating the usefulness of the present discussion to the understanding of some ontological principles in existential dialectics, and good examples include the absoluteness-relativeness principle, the predictability-unpredictability principle, the explicability-inexplicability, the preciseness-vagueness principle, the simpleness-complicatedness principle,the openness-hiddenness principle, the denseness-emptiness principle, the slowness-quickness principle, the expansion-contraction principle, the convention-novelty principle, the evolution-transformation principle, the symmetry-asymmetry principle, the regression-progression principle, and the same-difference principle.

For instance, in relation to the absoluteness-relativeness principle, if there is absolute viewpoint (e.g., the insistence of the common law tradition for a slow process of adjudication), there is relative counterpart (e.g., what is important for the common law tradition in regard to the slow process of adjudication is not so for the civil law tradition to allow flexibility and discretion for abrupt changes).

In relation to the predictability-unpredictability principle, if there is predictability (e.g., the predicable tendency of the common law tradition to be incremental in change over time), there is unpredictability (e.g., the more difficult task to predict when exactly the common law tradition will undergo abrupt, substantial changes "when extraordinarily good reason is shown" in extraordinary circumstances).

In relation to the explicability-inexplicability principle, if there is explicability (e.g., the explanation of some successful commerical economies with good entrepreneurship on the basis of their adoption of the common law traditon, which is reliable), there is inexplicability (e.g., the lack of sufficient explanation, within this argument for the success of the common law tradition, of why some other countries like China used to have successful commerce with good entrepreneurship in its long history, but without the adoption of the common law tradition).

In relation to the preciseness-vagueness principle, if there is preciseness (e.g., the precise identification of some essential features which characterize the common law tradition), there is vagueness (e.g., the relatively vague characterization of how exactly slow, incremental, and precise the common law tradition is, as compared with other traditions).

In relation to the simpleness-complicatedness principle, if there is simple analysis (e.g., the simple analysis of the common law tradition, in that it is different from other ones, like Islamic law, civil law, etc.), there is complicated counterpart (e.g., the more complicated analysis by John Makdisi of "the Islamic Origins of the Common Law"). WK 2009fff; J. Makdisi 1999; M. Devichand 2008)

In relation to the openness-hiddenness principle, if there is openness (e.g., the open exploration of the slow, incremental aspects of the common law to serve justice better), there is hiddenness (e.g., the hidden bias of the slow, incremental nature of the common law towards a conservative ideological orientation).

In relation to the denseness-emptiness principle, if there is denseness (e.g., the relatively denser concentration of cases in the common law tradition which are slowly and precisely considered), there is emptiness (e.g., the relativley less dense, or more empty, concentration of cases in the common law tradition which are quickly and discretively considered).

In relation to the slowness-quickness principle, if there is slowness (e.g., the relatively slow procedure of adjudication in the common law tradition), there is quickness (e.g., the relatively less slow, or faster, procedure of consideration in the civil law tradition).

In relation to the expansion-contraction principle, if there is expansion (e.g., the relatively better developed procedures in the common law tradition to handle cases slowly, incrementally, and precisely), there is contracton (e.g., the relatively less developed procedures in the common law tradition to handles cases which require fast and revolutionary actions).

In relation to the convention-novelty principle, if there is convention (e.g., the conventional wisdom of the common law tradition to be fundamentally different from other traditions like the civil law tradition, the Islamic law tradition, etc.), there is novelty (e.g., the alternative novel challenge by John Makdisi about "the Islamic Origins of the Common Law").

In relation to the evolution-transformation principle, if therre is evolution (e.g., the natural evolution of humans to resolve conflicts in a rough way in the state of nature), there is transformtion (e.g., the technical transformaton of human conflict resolution by way of the invention of the common law tradition, which is slow, incremental, and precise in its process).

In relation to the symmetry-asymmetry principle, if there is symmetry (e.g., the co-existence of different legal traditions, like the common law, the civil law, etc.), there is asymmetry (e.g., the more acceptance of the common law tradition in the U.S. and the U.K., for instance, but the more popularity of the civil law tradition in continental Europe, for instance).

In relation to the regression-progression principle, if there is regression (e.g., the forceful cultural diffusion of the common law tradition by the British Empire to its colonies, during the notorious days of Western colonialism and imperialism), there is progression (e.g., the progress made in the development of a systemaic legal tradition like the common law).

And in relation to the same-difference principle, if there is similarity in outcome (e.g., the outcome of all legal traditions to provide law and order, albeit in different ways), there is difference in outcome (e.g., the differences among different legal traditions in outcome, be they about incremental changes in the common law tradition and the relatively more abrupt ones in the civil law tradition).

The Hypotheticalness of Necessity

This comprehensive analysis of necessity from the four persectives of the mind, nature, society, and culture in this chapter is to show the different ways in which the clam for the universality of the law is both possible and desirable, but not to the extent that the ideologues would like us to believe.

Necessity thus has its own hypotheticalness, contingent on the multiple factors of the mind, nature, society, and culture (as illustrated in this chapter). In other words, necessity is dispensable.

But then this then leads us to the issue of contingency itself, as it is another side of the same coin.

With this in mind, let's now turn to Chapter Three for an analysis of contingency, and its mortality.

Table 2.1. Necessity and Its Dispensability

- **Necessity and the Mind**
  —Ex: the law of reason, and the categorical imperative
  —Ex: criminal law, and the maleness of violence

- **Necessity and Nature**
  —Ex: the laws of the jungle in nature, and social Darwinism
  —Ex: natural law, and Taoism

- **Necessity and Society**
  —Ex: international public law and the International Criminal Court
  —Ex: constitutional law and the balance of power

- **Necessity and Culture**
  —Ex: divine law, morality, and legal sanctions
  —Ex: common law, and the cultural legacy of the British Empire

Notes: The examples in the categories are solely illustrative (not exhaustive), and the comparison is relative (not absolute), nor are they necessarily mutually exclusive. And some can be easily re-classified elsewhere. As generalities, they allow exceptions.
Source: A summary of Ch.2 of *FPHLAW*

Table 2.2. Main Characteristics of International Law

- **In Relation to Its Types**
  —Ex: international public law
  —Ex: international private law

- **In Relaiton to Its Sources**
  —The body of treatises (*jus inter gentes*)
    - Ex: international treaties among nations

  —The law of nations (*jus gentium*)
    - Ex: judicial decisions
    - Ex: international custom
    - Ex: judicial teachings
    - Ex: the general principles of law

- **In Relation to Its Interpretive Approaches**
  —Ex: textual
  —Ex: subjective
  —Ex: effective

- **In Relation to Its Guiding Principles**
  —Ex: monism
  —Ex: dualism

Notes: The categories and its examples are solely illustrative (not exhaustive), and the comparison is relative (not absolute), nor are they necessarily mutually exclusive. And some can be easily re-classified elsewhere. As generalities, they allow exceptions.
Source: From *Sec. 2.4.1* of *FPHLAW*

Table 2.3. The Varieties of Principles Behind the Law (Part I)

- **In Relation to Different Laws**
  - —*Public Law*
    - Constitutional Law (*Sec. 1.2*)
      - –Ex: balance of power (*Sec. 2.4.2*)
      - –Ex: fusion of power (*Sec. 2.4.2*)
    - Criminal Law (*Sec. 1.2*)
      - –Ex: retribution (*Sec. 2.2.2*)
      - –Ex: restitution (*Sec. 2.2.2, Sec. 3.5.1*)
      - –Ex: deterrence (*Sec. 2.2.2*)
      - –Ex: incapacitation (*Sec. 2.2.2*)
      - –Ex: rehabilitation (*Sec. 2.2.2*)
    - Administrative Law (*Sec. 1.2*)
      - –Ex: due process (*Sec. 3.5.2*)
      - –Ex: fairness (against ultra vires) (*Sec. 3.5.2*)
  - —*Private Law*
    - Property Law (*Sec. 1.2*)
      - –Ex: labor product (*Sec. 3.4.1*)
      - –Ex: communality (*Sec. 3.4.1*)
      - –Ex: first posssession (*Sec. 3.4.1*)
    - Tort Law (*Sec. 1.2, Sec. 3.5.1*)
      - –Ex: care (in relation to negligence) (*Sec. 3.2.2*)
      - –Ex: care (in relation to nuisance) (*Sec. 3.2.2*)
    - Contract Law (*Sec. 1.2*)
      - –Ex: promissory obligation (*Sec. 3.5.1*)
      - –Ex: economic benefits (*Sec. 3.5.1)*
    - Trust Law (*Sec. 1.2*)
      - –Ex: equity (*Sec. 2.5.2*)

(continued on next page)

Table 2.3. The Varieties of Principles Behind the Law (Part II)

- **In Relation to Different Legal Traditons**
  - —*Common Law Tradition* (*Sec. 2.5.2*)
    - Ex: precedents (*Sec. 2.5.2*)
    - Ex: incrementality (*Sec. 2.5.2*)
  - —*Civil Law Tradition* (*Sec. 2.5.2*)
    - Ex: flexibility (*Sec. 2.5.2*)
    - Ex: discretion (*Sec. 2.5.2*)
  - —*Islamic Law Tradition* (*Sec. 1.4*)
    - Ex: the will of God (in divine law) (*Sec. 2.5.1*)
  - —*Socialist Law Tradition* (*Sec. 3.4.1*)
    - Ex: equality (*Sec. 3.4.1*)
  - —*Chinese Law Tradition* (*Sec. 2.3.2*)
    - Ex: harmony (in Confucianism) (*Sec. 2.3.2*)
    - Ex: simplicity (in Taoism) (*Sec. 2.3.2*)

- **In Relation to Different Boundaries of the Law**
  - —*International Law* (*Sec. 1.2*)
    - Ex: monism (*Sec. 2.4.1*)
    - Ex: dualism (*Sec. 2.4.1*)
  - —*National Law* (*Sec. 1.2*)
    - Ex: sovereignty (*Sec. 2.4.1*)

- **In Relation to Different Sociological Analyses of Law**
  - —*Approach to Law*
    - Ex: the rise of legal rationalism in modern times (*Sec. 3.4.2*)
  - —*Integration of Society in Law*
    - Ex: the growth of restitutive law in modern times (*Sec. 3.4.2*)

Notes: The examples in the categories are solely illustrative (not exhaustive), and the comparison is relative (not absolute), nor are they necessarily mutually exclusive. And some can be easily re-classified elsewhere. As generalities, they allow exceptions.
Source: From Chs.1-3 of *FPHLAW*

Table 2.4. The Debate on the Divine Law: The case of the Mosaic Law (Part I)

- **The Defense of Its Weaknesses**
  - –Ex: the Mosaic law is harsh in curbing "licentious thoughts and covetous desires" broadly defined—and the excuse here is that "it was suited to the low stage of civilization to which the Israelites had at the time attained." (CE 2009)
  - –Ex: the Mosaic law includes "the command given by God to exterminate certain nations, and the permission given by Him to the Israelites to spoil the Egyptians"—and the excuse here is that "the tribes of Chanaan richly deserved the fate to which they were condemned by God; and if there were innocent people among the guilty, God is the absolute Lord of life and death, and He commits no injustice when He takes away what He has given." (CE 2009)
  - –Ex: the Mosaic law allows the practice of slavery—and the excuse here is that "[t]he practice was doubtless already familiar to the Israelites of the time, as it was to their neighbours." (CE 2009)
  - –Ex: the Mosaic law justifies inconsistency in the enforcement of its moral codes, like the cases concerning the practices of "polygamy and divorce," "usury," and the like—and the excuse here is that, in the case concerning polygamy and divorce, for instance, "[a]mid the general laxity with regard to marriage which existed among the Semitic tribes, it would have been difficult to preserve the strict law [of monogamy and marriage until death]. The importance of a rapid increase among the chosen people of God so as to enable them to defend themselves from their neighbours, and to fulfil their appointed destiny, seemed to favour relaxation." (CE 2009)

(continued on next page)

**Table 2.4. The Debate on the Divine Law:
The case of the Mosaic Law
(Part II)**

- **The Critiique of Its Weaknesses**
  - –Ex: the divine command theory "implies that morality is arbitrary. If divine command theory is true, morality is based merely upon God's whim." (WK 2009ddd)
  - –Ex: the divine command theory "implies that calling God good makes no sense—or, at best, that one is simply saying that God is consistent: 'God does whatever he commands.'" (WK 2009ddd)
  - –Ex: the divine command theory "commits the naturalistic fallacy. Proponents of this criticism argue that while ethics can and should specify the non-moral properties that make things good, it is always a mistake to use non-moral terms in giving the meaning of the word 'good'." (WK 2009ddd)
  - –Ex: the divine command theory does not answer "the epistemological question of how one comes to know the will of God. Most religions point to their scriptures for answers, but it is still possible to question whether these really state the will of God." (WK 2009ddd)

Notes: The examples in the categories are solely illustrative (not exhaustive), and the comparison is relative (not absolute), nor are they necessarily mutually exclusive. And some can be easily re-classified elsewhere. As generalities, they allow exceptions.
Source: From *Sec. 2.5.1* of *FPHLAW*

Table 2.5. Main Characteristics of the Common Law Tradition

- **What the Common Law Tradition Is Not**
  —Ex: common law is not statutory law, regulatory law, etc.
  —Ex: common law is not civil law, Islamic law, Socialist law, etc.
  —Ex: common law is not equity

- **What the Common Law Tradition Is**
  —Ex: the common law is slow in adjudication
  —Ex: the common law is incremental in change
  —Ex: the common law is important in many important areas of law
  —Ex: the common law values less legal treatises / academic works
  —Ex: the common law is very precise and reliable

Notes: The examples in the categories are solely illustrative (not exhaustive), and the comparison is relative (not absolute), nor are they necessarily mutually exclusive. And some can be easily re-classified elsewhere. As generalities, they allow exceptions.
Source: From *Sec. 2.5.2* of *FPHLAW*

• PART THREE •

Contingency

CHAPTER 3
CONTINGENCY AND ITS MORTALITY

> International law seems to me nae better than a systematized and legalized scheme o' rape, robbery, piracy, incendiarism, and murder.
> —Victor Kiernan (1982:154)

The Expediency of Contingency

If necessity has its dispensability, what then is the fate of contingency?

The appeal of contingency is its practical expediency, be it in the context of the law or not. But there is a price to pay, namely, its temporality, which comes and goes as time passes.

To understand the nature of contingency in the context of the law better, it is important to provide a comprehensive analysis from the four perspectives of the mind, nature, society, and culture (which are so proposed, in accordance to my sophisticated methodological holism, as explained in *Sec. 1.8*), just as the analysis of necessity was similarly treated in Chapter Two.

This chapter is thus divided in four main sections, in relation to (3.2) contingency and the mind, (3.3) contingency and nature, (3.4) contingency and society, and (3.5) contingency and culture—to be examined, respectively, hereafter (and summarized in *Table 3.1*).

Contingency and the Mind

The issue of contingency, when looked from the perspective of the mind, can reveal something illustrative about the nature of contingency. And this illustration can be shown by way of two case studies, namely, (3.2.1) analytical jurisprudence, and Hume's naturalistic fallacy, and

(3.2.2) tort law and its controversy—to be analyzed in what follows, in that order.

Analytical Jurisprudence, and Hume's "Is-Ought" Problem

As introduced in *Sec. 1.3*, there is a major approach to jurisprudence, namely, "analytical jurisprudence," which "is a legal theory that draws on the resources of modern analytical philosophy to try to understand the nature of law. Since the boundaries of analytical philosophy are somewhat vague, it is difficult to say how far it extends. H. L. A. Hart was probably the most influential writer in the modern school of analytical jurisprudence, though its history goes back at least to Jeremy Bentham." (WK 2009iii)

Legal Positivism vs. Legal Formalism

However, "analytical jurisprudence," especially in its dominant school of thought known as "legal positivism," should not be confused with a seemingly comparable term like "legal formalism," which is merely about the "mechanical, algorithmic process" in legal reasoning; instead, for those in analytical jurisprudence (especially in "legal positivism"), "legal formalism is fundamentally mistaken as a theory of law," because it confuses "what is" with "what ought to be." (WK 2009iii)

The dominant school of thought known as analytical jurisprudence, that is, legal positivism, makes three major claims: (WK 2009lll)

- "There is no inherent or necessary connection between the validity conditions of law and ethics or morality"
- "Laws are rules made, whether deliberately or unintentionally, by human beings"
- "Laws must follow the rules of determinism"

In other words, the task of "analytical jurisprudence" is to "clarify," not to advocate any specific law. Therefore, "analytic, or 'clarificatory' jurisprudence uses a neutral point of view and descriptive language when referring to the aspects of legal systems. This was a philosophical development that rejected natural law's fusing of what law is and what it ought to be." (WK 2009iii)

In this way, analytic jurisprudence is more concerned with clarifying questions like "What are laws?," "What is the law?," and so on—with "legal positivism is the dominant theory, although there are a growing number of critics, who offer their own interpretations." (WK 2009iii)

Analytic jurisprudence, especially in the context of legal positivism, therefore tries to understand better the nature of logical reasoning in the human mind, so as to avoid the trap in which the mind can fall, in invalidly infering what "ought to be" from what "is," in a fallacious way.

Hume's "Is-Ought" Problem

This distinction between "what is" and "what ought to be" in logical reasoning for the human mind is something that "David Hume famously argued in *A Treatise of Human Nature*," in that "people invariably slip between describing that the world is a certain way to saying therefore we ought to conclude on a particular course of action." (WK 2009iii)

As Hume thus wrote, "in every system of morality, which I have hitherto met with, I have remark'd, that the author proceeds for some time in the ordinary ways of reasoning, and establishes the being of a God, or makes observations concerning human affairs; when all of a sudden I am surpriz'd to find, that instead of the usual copulations of propositions, is, and is not, I meet with no proposition that is not connected with an ought, or an ought not." (WK 2009kkk)

But, for Hume, this is not logically valid, because, "as a matter of pure logic, one cannot conclude that we ought to do something merely because something is the case. So analysing and clarifying the way the world is must be treated as a strictly separate question to normative and evaluative ought questions." (WK 2009iii)

Serious Implications for the Law

But then this "is-ought" problem as a fallacious way of logical reasoning in the human mind has serious implications for how to ground the foundation of law.

In other words, one can then ask, Why should a law be therefore normative, only because one understands what the law is (or what its foundation is)?

Consider two main examples of works by some well-known scholars on law and morality, who had committed this fallacy.

Firstly, one good example here conerns the appeal to "natural law," which, upon scrutniy, is not logically valid. As a reminder, the topic about "natural law" was already discussed in Chapter Two, especially in the context of social Darwinism (in *Sec. 2.3.1*), Taoism (in *Sec. 2.3.2*), and divine law (in *Sec. 2.5.1*).

With this reminder in mind—G. E. Moore in his 1903 book *Principia Ethica* used the term "naturalistic fallacy" in the context of ethics, to refer a formal fallacy "whenever a philosopher attempts to prove a claim about ethics by appealing to a definition of the term 'good' in terms of one or more natural properties (such as 'pleasant,' 'more evolved,' 'desired,' etc.)." (WK 2009jjj)

And Jeremy Bentham, in the context of in law and morality, "found that when people discuss problems and issues they talk about how they wish it would be as opposed to how it actually is. This can be seen in discussions of natural law and positive law. Bentham criticized natural law theory because in his view it was a naturalistic fallacy, claiming that it described how things ought to be instead of how things are." (WK 2009jjj)

For example, Bentham was critical to "social Darwinism from the theory of evolution by natural selection," since what is "natural" (or what "is" in evolution by natural selection) does not logically imply that it is "good" (or that it "ought to be"). (WK 2009jjj) Bentham even once called natural law "nonsense upon stilts." (WK 2009lll)

Conversey, there is also the reverse of naturalistic fallacy, when one tries to argue, in the reverse direction, that "the immorality of survival of the fittest implies the theory of evolution is false….Jeremy Bentham…indicated the is-ought problem in order to identify…[alternative non-fallacious] theories of morality and law." (WK 2009jjj)

And the second example concerns the appeal to "divine law" (which, as a reminder, was already analyzed in Chapter Two, especially in the context of the Mosaic law in *Sec. 2.5.1*).

The probem with the appeal to "divine law" is that, while "those who "propose supernaturalist origins of morality" are aware of the potential problem of "is/ought incommensurability" and even "assert [that] these similarities between ethical rules and natural biological behavior are just coincidental," they "fail…to elucidate morality since the supernaturalist must additionally show how we are to choose between competing supernatural ethical systems without appealing to naturalistic principles." (WK 2009kkk)

Therefore, the "supernaturalist approach to ethics appears arbitrary and has no explanatory advantage"—in the context of naturalistic fallacy (or, more generally, the "is-ought" problem). (WK 2009kkk)

This "is-ought" problem has thus much to do with logical reasoning in the human mind, in that the mind can at times trick us to infer what "ought to be" from what "is," in a fallacious way.

Some Criticisms against the "Is-Ought" Problem

However, there are some scholars who have been quite critical to this view of the "is-ought" problem and proposed their alternative views instead, for a different way to derive what "ought to be" from what "is." But do they really succeed in resolving the "is-ought" problem as claimed?

Consider three main examples below, for illustration.

Firstly, John Searle (1964 & 1995) tried to show that "an 'ought' can actually be derived from an 'is,' with the example that "the act of making a promise places one under an obligation by definition, and that such an obligation amounts to an 'ought'....Searle has...developed the concept of institutional facts." (WK 2009kkk)

Yet, the problem with Searle's argument is that this ony means that social institutions impose an value on the act of making a promise, that is, by attaching an value to the act of making a promise, with legal sanctions like threat and punishment if violated.

But, contrary to what Searle claimed, this still does not imply that this "ought" can indeed be logically derived from an "is"—but only that an intermediary external agency like the legal institution comes to attach the value (the "ought") to the act of making a promise (the "is"), which is enforced with the threat of punishment if violated. So, there is still no logical inference between the "ought" and the "is"; instead, there is only an empirical relationship between the 'ought' and the "is" through an intermediary external agency, which is contingent on society and culture, for instance, but not grounded on logic.

Secondly, another argument involves "many modern naturalistic philosophers" who "believ[e] an 'ought' can derive from an 'is' whenever we analyze goal-directed behavior, and a statement of the form 'In order for A to achieve goal B, A ought to do C' exhibits no category error and may be factually verified or refuted." (WK 2009kkk)

Yet, the problem with this second argument is that "this doesn't really address the problem, since the 'goal' is an implied ought. The argument would amount to nothing more than deriving an ought from an ought." (WK 2009kkk)

Thirdly, Alasdair MacIntyre (1981) offered another argument, in that "because ethical language developed in the West in the context of a recognition of a human telos--an end or goal--our inherited moral language, including terms such as 'good' and 'bad,' have functioned, and function, to evaluate the way in which certain behaviors facilitate the achievement of the telos. In an evaluative capacity, therefore, 'good' and 'bad carry moral weight without committing a category error." (WK 2009kkk)

Yet, the problem with MacIntyre's argument is that it suffers from the two criticisms (as indicated above) at the same time, in that the goal or end is already an implied ought and that different cultures impose certain values on certain acts, through an intermediary external agency (like a legal institution) between an "ought" and an "is," to be enforced with the threat of punishment if violated. But in both instances, there is still no logical inference of an "ought" from an "is."

A Detached Reflection

This disagreement between those who advocate the logical derivation of an "ought" from an "is," on the one hand, and those who criticize it, on the other hand, only shows us why even the contingency argument is limited, dependent on specific schools of thought in analytical jurisprudence.

In addition, this summary of the debate can also show us the relevance of some ontological principles in existential dialectics, and some good examples include the absoluteness-relativeness principle, the predictability-unpredictability principle, the explicability-inexplicability principle, the preciseness-vagueness principle, the simpleness-complicatedness principle, the openness-hiddenness principle, the denseness-emptiness principle the expansion-contraction principle, the theory-praxis principle, the convention-novelty principle, the evolution-transformation principle, the symmetry-asymmetry principle, the softness-hardness principle, the regression-progression principle, and the same-difference principle.

For instance, in relation to the absoluteness-relativeness principle, if there is absolute viewpoint (e.g., the claim by social Darwinists about the normativeness of the law on the basis of natural selection), there is relative counterpart (e.g., what is good for the social Darwinists in regard to natural selection as the normative foundation for the law is not so for the legal positivists which question such a connection).

In relation to the predictability-unpredictability principle, if there is predictability (e.g., the predictable tendency of the legal positivists to reject any necessary logical connection between an "ought" and an "is" in the law), there is unpredictability (e.g., the more difficult task to predict the particular direction of a given legal case that a legal positivist will pursue, because there are numerous schools of thought in legal positivism like the ones by Jeremy Bentham, John Austin, Hans Kelsen, H.L.A. Hart, Joseph Raz, and others).

In relation to the explicability-inexplicability principle, if there is explicability (e.g., the explanation, by Hume, of the invalidity of the foundation for certain laws on the basis of a questionable logical inference of an "ought" from an "is"), there is inexplicability (e.g., the lack of sufficient explanation within Hume's argument of why there exists an empirical, though not logical, relationship between an "ought"and an "is" in some laws, backed with a threat of punishment by a legal institution as an external intermediary agency).

In relation to the preciseness-vagueness principle, if there is preciseness (e.g., the precise identification of three major claims of legal positivism), there is vagueness (e.g., the lack of clear formulation of the three major claims of legal positivism by themselves, as the words in the claims have different meanings and interpretations, dependent on a particular legal positivist; for instance, the word "determinism" for John Austin has more to do with the use of threat in legal sanctions, as in contract law, but, for H. L. Hart, such an interpretation "was analogous to a gunman backing up his demands with a threat of violence"). (WK 2009lll)

In relation to the simpleness-complicatedness principle, if there is simple analysis (e.g., the simple view, as in social Darwinism, that what is good in the state of nature for animals to compete for the survival of the fittest is also good in society for humans), there is complicated counterpart (e.g., the more complicated critique of social Darwinism by Jeremey Bentham that natural law commits the naturalistic fallacy in the context of the "is-ought" problem, in order to propose a non-fallacious theory of law and morality, based on utiliarianism).

In relation to the openness-hiddenness principle, if there is openness (e.g., the open exploration of the logical fallacy in the "is-ought" problem by the legal positivists), there is hiddeness (e.g., the hidden bias of the legal positivists in its separating the law from ethics or morality, while accepting the law as "posited by lawmakers"). (WK 2009lll)

In relation to the denseness-emptiness principle, if there is denseness (e.g, the relatively denser concentration of laws as "posited by lawmakers" which are accepted by the legal positivists), there is emptiness (e.g., the relatively less dense, or more empty, concentration of laws based on ethics or morality, which are accepted by the legal positivists).

In relation to the expansion-contraction principle, if there is expansion (e.g., the relatively more developed aspects of a legal system based on legal positivism which are more text-based, so as "to remove any metaphysics from the science of law by providing a totally internally-defined system with an entirely sufficient set of meanings"), there is contraction (e.g., the relatively less developed aspects of a legal system based on legal positivism which are more context-based, as in legal realists, who look for "the meaning of any given law…one might bring to the suggestions of the text"). (WK 2009lll)

In relation to the theory-praxis principle, if there is theory (e.g., the theoretical construction of the "is-ought" problem), there is praxis (e.g., the practical application of the "is-ought" problem by the legal positivists to get rid of any moral or ethical influence on the law, which is to be posited by lawmakers instead, not by moralists).

In relation to the convention-novelty principle, if there is convention (e.g., the conventional wisdom about the law to be based on moral, divine, or other claims), there is novelty (e.g., the alternative novel challenge by the legal positivists to question any normative basis of the law, be it moral, divine, or else, and to replace it with a more positivist foundation as posited by lawmakers).

In relation to the evolution-transformation principle, if there is evolution (e.g., the evolution of humans in the state of nature to behave in certain ways), there is transformation (e.g., the technical transformation of human behaviors by way of the invention of legal positivism for laws to be posited by lawmakers).

In relation to the symmetry-asymmetry principle, if there is symmetry (e.g., the co-existence of different laws with different foundations, be they natural, divine, or legal-positivist), there is asymmetry (e.g., the more acceptance of the foundation for the law on the basis of natural law by social Darwinists, but the more popularity of the foundation for the law on the basis of decisions by lawmakers by legal positivists).

In relation to the softness-hardness principle, if there is softness (e.g., the praise of individuals for good behaviors according to the law), there is hardness (e.g., the threat of punishment of individuals for bad behaviors according to the law).

In relation to the regression-progression principle, if there is regression (e.g., a consequence of the legal positivist argument is that the laws as posited by lawmakers tend to be amoral), there is progression (e.g., the progress made in eliminating the abuse of any fallacious connection between natural law and the law, as revealed in the notorious legacy of social Darwinism against the weak and the poor).

And in relation to the same-difference principle, if there is similarity in outcome (e.g., the control of human behaviors in certain ways, regardless of the foundation for the law which is natural, divine, or legal-positivist), there is difference in outcome (e.g., the consequence of laws based on legal positivism to be amoral, and the consequence of laws based on natural law to be naturalist).

Tort Law and Its Controversy

A different way to examine the issue of contingency in the context of the law from the perspective of the mind is to understand the nature of tort law in regard to the issue of intentionality (and its counterpart, non-intentionality) in the human mind.

To start, "tort law," by definition, "is a body of law that addresses, and provides remedies for, civil wrongs not arising out of contractual obligations. A person who suffers legal damages may be able to use tort law to receive compensation from someone who is legally responsible, or liable, for those injuries. Generally speaking, tort law defines what constitutes a legal injury and establishes the circumstances under which one person may be held liable for another's injury." (WK 2009mmm; G. White 2003)

Thus, tort law differs both from contract law and criminal law, as the word "tort" is "the Norman word for a 'wrong.' As traditionally used, this kind of wrong is distinct from a contractual or criminal wrong." (WK 2009mmm; G. White 2003)

In addition, tort law involves both "intentional acts [nuisant acts] and accidents [negligent acts]….In contrast to criminal law (in which the offense is against the State and the State is the plaintiff), in tort law, the offense is against a person and that person is the plaintiff." (WK 2009mmm)

For analysis, tort law can therefore be classified in two main categories, namely, (a) intentional torts, and (b) unintentional torts, to be summarized hereafter, in that order.

This issue of intentionality (and its counterpart, non-intentionality) is a question concerning the human mind in the context of the law.

Intentional Torts

The first category of tort law covers "intentional torts," which refer to "any intentional acts that are reasonably foreseeable to cause harm to an individual, and that do so." (WK 2009mmm)

There are two major subcategories of intentional torts, namely, (a) "torts against the person" (e.g., "assault, battery, false imprisonment, intentional infliction of emotional distress, and fraud"), and (b) torts against the property of an individual, or in short, "property torts" (e.g., "trespass to land, trespass to chattels, and conversion"). (WK 2009mmm)

(a) In relation to torts against the person—cases like this often overlap with cirminal cases. For instance, "in English law an assault is both a crime and a tort (a form of trespass to the person)." (WK 2009mmm)

In a civil case, "a tort allows a person, usually the victim, to obtain a remedy that serves their own purposes (for example by the payment of damages to a person injured in a car accident, or the obtaining of injunctive relief to stop a person interfering with their business)." (WK 2009mmm)

But in a criminal case, the same event is treated in a different way, since "criminal actions...are pursued not to obtain remedies to assist a person—although often criminal courts do have power to grant such remedies—but to remove their liberty on the state's behalf. That explains why incarceration is usually available as a penalty for serious crimes, but not usually for torts." (WK 2009mmm)

One consequence of this overlap between civil law and criminal law in torts is that a given case can yield two different outcomes, with their resultant controversy. For instance, "in the O. J. Simpson murder trial, the jury were not convinced beyond reasonable doubt that O. J. Simpson had committed the crime of murder, but a later civil trial, the jury in that case felt that he did satisfy the balance of probabilities threshold required to prove the tort of wrongful death." (WK 2009mm)

Anyone who knows well the O.J. Simpson case understands the notorious controversy surrounding it.

(b) And in relation to property torts, cases like this can also overlap with criminal law, although they are less so, by comparison—and have their own distinctive problems.

Consider, for illustration, the case concerning property torts.

In property torts, one well known principle here concerns "nuisance," which "is traditionally used in three ways: (1) to describe an activity or condition that is harmful or annoying to others (e.g., indecent conduct, a rubbish heap or a smoking chimney); (2) to describe the harm caused by the before-mentioned activity or condition (e.g., loud noises or objectionable odors); and (3) to describe a legal liability that arises from the combination of the two. The law of nuisance was created to stop such bothersome activities or conduct when they unreasonably interfered either with the rights of other private landowners (i.e., private nuisance) or with the rights of the general public (i.e., public nuisance)." (WK 2009mmm; J. Gray 2009)

There are some major problems with property torts, however. Hereafter are two examples.

Firstly, the first problem is that the use of intentional torts is not always effective for the plaintiff, as it can work in both ways, sometimes favorable to the plaintiff but sometimes to the defendant.

For instance, "the case of Jones v Powell (1629)" favors the defendant, where "[a] brewery made stinking vapors which wafted onto neighbors' property, damaging his papers. As he was a landowner, the neighbor sued in nuisance for this damage. But Whitelocke J, speaking for the Court of the King's Bench, said that because the water supply was contaminated, it was better that the neighbor's documents were risked. He said 'it is better that they should be spoiled than that the common wealth stand in need of good liquor.' Nowadays, interfering with neighbors' property is not looked upon so kindly." (WK 2009mmm)

On the other hand, "the case of Rylands v. Fletcher" favors the plaintiff, where "a dam burst into a coal mine shaft. So a dangerous escape of some hazard, including water, fire, or animals means strict liability in nuisance. This is subject only to a remoteness cap, familiar from negligence when the event is unusual and unpredictable. This was the case where chemicals from a factory seeped through a floor into the water table, contaminating East Anglia's reservoirs." (WK 2009mmm)

And secondly, the scope of property torts is also subject to disagreement. For instance, "free market environmentalists would like to expand tort damage claims into pollution (i.e. toxic torts) and environmental protection." (WK 2009mmm) But major firms in the corporate world often object to such an expansion of tort damage claims.

Unintentional Torts

Unlike intentional torts (as described above)—unintentional torts are different, because they refer to "the existence of a breach of duty of care owed by one person to another," even when the incident is not intentional and involves "negligence." (WK 2009mmm)

For instance, one famous example of negligence so understood concerns "the case of Donoghue v. Stevenson, where Mrs. Donoghue consumed part of a drink containing a decomposed snail while in a public bar in Paisley, Scotland and claimed that it had made her ill. The snail was not visible, as the bottle of ginger beer in which it was contained was opaque." (WK 2009mmm)

However, "neither her friend, who bought it for her, nor the shopkeeper who sold it were aware of its presence. The manufacturer was Mr. Stevenson, whom Mrs. Donoghue sued for damages for negligence. She could not sue Mr. Stevenson for damages for breach of contract because there was no contract between them." (WK 2009mmm)

Yet, "the majority of the members of the House of Lords agreed (3-2) that Mrs. Donoghue had a valid claim, but disagreed as to why such a claim should exist. Lord MacMillan thought this should be treated as a new product liability case. Lord Atkin argued that the law should recognise a unifying principle that we owe a duty of reasonable care to our neighbors. He quoted the Bible in support of his argument, specifically the general principle that 'thou shalt love thy neighbor.'" (WK 2009mmm)

In general, "negligence" can refer to five different elements, as shown below: (WK 2009mmm & 2009nnn)

- "Duty of care"
- "Breach of duty"
- "Factual causation" (e.g., "breach causing harm in fact")
- "Legal causation" (e.g., "breach being a proximate or not too remote a cause, in law")
- "Damage"

But "negligence" so understood in uninentional torts has its own problems. Hereafter are two major examples for illustration.

Firstly, these five elements of negligence can be re-classified in different ways; for instance, they can be re-classified in terms of three elements (e.g., "conduct, causation and damages"), four elements (e.g., "duty, breach, causation and pecuniary damages") or five elements (e.g., "duty, breach, actual cause, proximate cause, and damages"). (WK 2009nnn)

Secondly, the elements of negligence are also subject to different interpretations as to how they are to be understood. Consider two illustrations below.

The first illustration concerns the first element, that is, what precisely is meant by the "duty of care" in the first element? There are different answers, depending on different cases. In "the case of Caparo v. Dickman (1990)," as an illustration, it requires the test of three specific things, namely, "(1) [the incident must be] reasonably foreseeable, (2) there must be a relationship of proximity between the plaintiff and defendant and (3) it must be 'fair, just and reasonable' to impose liability." (WK 2009nnn)

Even then, however, these three specific things "as guidelines for the courts in establishing a duty of care" are not universal, as "much of the principle is still at the discretion of judges." (WK 2009nnn)

And the second illustration concerns the fifth element, that is, what exactly counts as "damage"? In general, "damage may be physical, purely economic, both physical and economic (loss of earnings following a personal injury), or reputational (in a defamation case)." (WK 2009nnn)

Even then, the specific list of damages has different interpretations in different cases. For instance, "in English law, the right to claim for purely economic loss is limited to a number of 'special' and clearly defined circumstances, often related to the nature of the duty to the plaintiff as between clients and lawyers, financial advisers, and other professions where money is central to the consultative services." (WK 2009nnn)

Other cases may expand the list of damages to cover, say, "emotional distress"; even then, there is no universal agreement on this. For instance, in general, a "plaintiff could recover for emotional distress caused by injury, but only if it accompanied a physical or pecuniary injury. A claimant who suffered only emotional distress and no pecuniary loss would not recover for negligence." (WK 2009nnn)

However, some recent cases challenged this interpretation, as some "courts have recently allowed recovery for a plaintiff to recover for purely emotional distress under certain circumstances. The state courts of California allowed recovery for emotional distress alone—even in the absence of any physical injury…." (WK 2009nnn)

This disagreement is all the more intensified, when, in some cases, the "damages" or "losses" in question "cannot be quantified exactly in monetary terms (the actual pain, suffering, and loss of amenity caused by the negligent act), as well as expected future losses from the date of trial (e.g. continuing pain and suffering, and loss of earnings)." (WK 2009nnn)

Conflicting Claims about the Aims of Tort Law

As if there were not enough problems in tort law—another serious kind of problem in tort law concerns its aims. In other words, what are the aims of tort law?

Precisely here, different "scholars and lawyers have identified conflicting aims...[of] the law of tort." (WK 2009mmm)

For instance, in "The Aims of the Law of Tort" (1951), "Glanville Williams saw four possible bases on which different torts rested: appeasement, justice, deterrence and compensation." (WK 2009mmm)

Other scholars, however, like "a group of legally oriented economists and economically oriented lawyers emphasized incentives and deterrence, and identified the aim of tort as being the efficient distribution of risk. They are often described as the law and economics movement. Ronald Coase, one of the movement's principal proponents, submitted, in his article *The Problem of Social Cost* (1960), that the aim of tort should be to reflect as closely as possible liability where transaction costs should be minimized." (WK 2009mmm)

It is therefore no wonder that different scholars in different legal communities call for a reform of tort law in different ways, which reflect, in a way, the disagreement among legal scholars on the fundamental aims of tort law.

For instance, some legal scholars in New Zealand "call…for reform [and] stress the difficulties encountered by potential claimants. Because of all people who have accidents, only some can find solvent defendants from which to recover damages in the courts, P. S. Atiyah has called the situation a 'damages lottery.' Consequently, in New Zealand, the government in the 1960's established a no-fault system of state compensation for accidents. Similar proposals have been the subject of Command Papers in the UK and much academic debate." (WK 2009mmm)

On the other hand, in the United States, the call for reform tends to be more minimalist, in that its proponents "have tended to be for drastic limitation on the scope of tort law, [for] a minimisation process on the lines of economic analysis. Anti-trust damages have come under special scrutiny, and many people believe the availability of punitive damages generally are a strain on the legal system." (WK 2009mmm)

A Constructive View

These disagreements in multiple fronts on different issues about tort law reflect the controversial nature of contingency in tort law, and the analysis here is not to favor any side against any others in the debate.

The point to remember here is to illustrate the contentious aspects of the contingency argument, dependent on different views and interpretations about intentionality (and its absence, that is, non-intentionality) in the context of the law, from the perspective of the mind.

In fact, this illustration is also useful for the understanding of some ontological principles in existential dialectics, and good examples include the absoluteness-relativenesss principle, the predictability-unpredictability principle, the explicability-inexplicability principle, the preciseness-vagueness principle, the simpleness-complicatedness principle, the openness-hiddenness principle, the denseness-emptiness principle, the convention-novelty principle, the evolution-transformation principle, the symmetry-asymmetry principle, the regression-progression principle, and the same-difference principle.

For instance, in relation to the absoluteness-relativeness principle, if there is absolute viewpoint (e.g., the legal reform in New Zealand in regard to the "no-fault system of state compensation for accidents," which the country prefers, as opposed to other ones), there is relative one too (e.g., what is important for the legal reform in New Zealand in regard to the "no-fault system of state compensation for accidents" is not so for the legal reform in the U.S. in regard to a "drastic limitation on the scope of tort law").

In relation to the predictability-unpredictability principle, if there is predictability (e.g., the predictable tendency of unintentional tort law to focus on the principle of care in relation to negligence), there is unpredictability (e.g., the more difficult task to predict the outcome of a given unintentional tort case, since in negligence, "the event is unusual and unpredictable").

In relation to the explicability-inexplicability principle, if there is explicability (e.g., the explanation, by Ronald Coase, of the aim of tort law on the basis of the minimization of transaction costs in liability), there is inexplicability (e.g., the lack of sufficient explanation in Coase's argument of why the fundamental assumptions in the explanation, namely, property rights, efficient and identical use of resources, transaction costs in bargaining, perfect competition and information, and wealth and income effects, are valid, as critically pointed out by Steve Kangas). (WK 2009; S. Kangas 2008)

In relation to the preciseness-vagueness prnciple, if there is preciseness (e.g., the precise identification of the five elements of "negligence"), there is vagueness (e.g., the vague formulation of what exactly these five elements are to mean, as there are various court interpretations about them).

In relation to the simpleness-complicatedness principle, if there is simpleness (e.g., the simple listing of different aims of tort law), there is complicatedness (e.g., the more complicated account of the aims of tort law on the basis of conflicting claims among different scholars and of different calls for reforms in different countries).

In relation to the opennes-hiddenness principle, if there is openness (e.g., the open exploration of the role of transaction costs in cases concerning nuisance in property torts by Ronald Coase), there is hiddenness (e.g., the hidden bias of Coase's argument, which represents the recurrent conservative ideology of free market as advocated by "economists and lawyers including Milton Friedman and Gary Becker," in their vocal call for "deregulation and privatisation," against "state regulation or what they see as restrictions on the operation of free market"). (WK 2009; S. Jakoby 2005)

In relation to the denseness-emptiness principle, if there is denseness (e.g., the relatively denser concentration of concerns with transaction costs, by scholars who are in the law and economics movement), there is emptiness (e.g., the relatively less dense, or more empty, concentration of concerns with drastic government intervention in tort law, by scholars in the law and economics movement).

In relation to the convention-novelty principle, if there is convention (e.g., the conventional wisdom about the aims of tort law in the context of appeasement, justice, etc.), there is novelty (e.g., the alternative novel challenge to the conventional wisdom on torts by Coase and others, by suggesting that tort law should be about the minimization of transaction costs for the efficient distribution of risk).

In relation to the evolution-transformation principle, if there is evolution (e.g., the evolution of humans to commit acts of negligence from time to time in the state of nature), there is transformation (e.g., the technical transformation of human dealing with negligence by way of the invention of unintentional tort law).

In relation to the symmetry-asymmetry principle, if there is symmetry (e.g., the co-existence of different views on the aims of tort law, be it about the one for free market or the one for government regulation), there is asymmetry (e.g., the more acceptance of the view on the aims of tort law by way of the free market, by those in the law and economics movement; but the more popularity of the view on the aims of tort law by way of government intervention, by the critics like Steve Kangas).

In relation to the regression-progression principle, if there is regression (e.g., the blind faith in the free market to minimize transacton costs in torts, by those in the law and economics movement, without questioning its invalid assumptions, for the critics), there is progression (e.g., the progress made to make us aware of the role of transaction costs in dealing with torts).

And in relation to the same-difference principle, if there is similarity in outcome (e.g., both advantages and disadvantages of different legal reforms in the context of tort law, be it about the one in New Zealand or the one in the U.S.), there is differrence in outcome (e.g., the focus on the "no-fault system of state compensation for accidents" in the case of New Zealand, but the concern with "drastic limitation on the scope of tort law, [for] a minimisation process on the lines of economic analysis" in the U.S.).

Contingency and Nature

The issue of contingency can also be analyzed from a different perspective, this time, in relation to nature, so as to further understand its limitations.

An illuminating case study here concerns the pheonomenon of the will to power (affecting many living species in nature) and its impact on the law—to be examined below.

The Will to Power in Nature, and the Law

The idea about the will to power in nature has been closely studied by different scholars over time.

Consider first some examples below (which are summarized in *Table 3.2*).

The Varieties of the Will to Power

Firstly, Arthur Schopenhauer proposed what he called the "will to live," in order to explain why "the universe and everything in it is driven by a primordial will to live, which results in all living creatures' desire to avoid death and procreate. For Schopenhauer, this will is the most fundamental aspect of realiy." (WK 2009ooo)

Secondly, Roger Joseph Boscovich suggested the idea of "centers of force," in his rejection of the idea of "materialistic atomism," in order to explain that there are different centers of force in nature, with each of them fighting for its existence. (WK 2009ooo; G. Whitlock 1996)

In fact, "Boscovich's theory of centers of force was prominent in Germany at the time. Boscovich's theory 'is echoed in Immanuel Kant's *Metaphysical Foundations of Natural Science*, which reduces matter to force altogether. Kant's view, in turn, became very influential in German physics through the work of Hermann von Helmholtz and his followers." (WK 2009ooo; L. Anderson 1994)

Thirdly, Wilhelm Roux proposed the idea of "the struggle of parts in the organism" in 1881, in his critical response to classical Darwinian theory. (WK 2009ooo)

Influenced by Ernst Haeckel, Roux argued for the idea of "internal struggle," or "the struggle for existence occurred at the cellular level," in that "the various cells and tissue struggle for finite resources, so that only the strongest survive. Through this mechanism, the body grows stronger and better adapted." (WK 2009ooo; G. Moore 2002; W. Müller-Lauter 1999)

Fourthly, Léon Dumont suggested in 1875 the idea of "pleasure in the expansion of power," in that "pleasure is related to increases in force," especially in relation to "intellectual beings, since, according to Dumont, pain and pleasure require a coming to consciousness and not just a sensing." (WK 2009ooo; R. Small 2001)

Fifthly, William Rolph, in 1884, advanced the idea of "insatiability and assimilation" for life expansion (as an alternative to the Darwinian idea of the struggle for existence), in that "all life seeks primarily to expand itself. Organisms fulfill this need through assimilation, trying to make as much of what is found around them into part of themselves, for example by seeking to increase intake and nutriment. Life forms are naturally insatiable in this way." (WK 2009ooo; T. Brobjer 1997)

And sixthly, Karl Wilhelm von Nägeli, in 1884, argued for the "perfection principle," or the "drive towards complexity," in that life in nature tends to "greater complexity" over time, such that, "with a military metaphor,…a more complex, complicatedly ordered idioplasma would usually defeat a simpler rival. In other words, he is also arguing for internal evolution, similar to Roux, except emphasizing complexity as the main factor instead of strength." (WK 2009ooo; A. Horn 2005)

Nietzsche's Idea of the Will to Power

These illustrative examples of scholars who had proposed different versions of the will to power in nature are important for the understanding of Friedrich Nietzsche's idea of the will to power.

In fact, the scholars (as introduced above) had influenced Nietzsche's thinking on the will to power in one way or the other.

For instance, "Dumont's pleasure in the expansion of power, Roux's internal struggle, Nägeli's drive towards complexity, and Rolph's principle of insatiability and assimilation are fused together into the biological side of Nietzsche's theory of will to power, which is developed in a number of places in his published writings." (WK 2009ooo; G. Moore 2002)

Thus, "[h]aving derived the 'will to power' from three anti-Darwin evolutionists, as well as Dumont, it seems appropriate that [Nietzsche]… should use his 'will to power' as an anti-Darwinian explanation of evolution. He expresses a number of times [as in *Beyond Good and Evil*, §13; *The Gay Science*, §349; and *The Genealogy of Morality*, II:12] the idea that adaptation and the struggle to survive is a secondary drive in the evolution of animals, behind the desire to expand one's power—the will to power." (WK 2009ooo)

In addition, "[i]nfluenced by his earlier readings of Boscovich,…[Nietzsche] began to develop a physics of the Will to Power. The idea of matter as centers of force is translated into matter as centers of will to power. Nietzsche wanted to slough off the theory of matter, which he viewed as a relic of the metaphysics of substance." (WK 2009ooo; L. Williams 1996; G. Whitlock 1996)

Even more daringly, Nietzsche went further and "developed an equally elusive theory of the 'eternal recurrence of the same' and much speculation on the physical possibility of this idea and the mechanics of its actualization recur in his later notebooks, which becomes tied with his theory of will to power as a potential physics integrated with the 'eternal recurrence of the same.' Nietzsche appeared to imagine a physical universe of perpetual struggle and force, which successively completes its cycle and returns to the beginning again and again." (WK 2009ooo)

The Problem of Interpretation Revisited

Yet, there are multiple interpretations of Nietzsche's work on the will to power. Consider, for illustration, four main examples below.

Firstly, some scholars argued that the Nietzschean will to power is a psychological principle in its essence, and the reason for this interpretation is that "Nietzsche applies it most frequently to human behavior." (WK 2009ooo)

Secondly, other scholars proposed an alternative interpretation, in that the Nietzschean will to power is a cosmic force, "as a more general force, underlying all reality not just human behavior—thus making it more directly analogous to Schopenhauer's will to live." (WK 2009ooo) And the reason for this interpretation is that Nietzsche argued, in *The Will to Power*, that the "world is the will to power—and nothing besides!" (WK 2009ooo)

Thirdly, still other scholars "upheld a biological interpretation of the Nietzschean will to power," making it equivalent with some kind of social Darwinism," and the reason for this interpretation is that "the concept was appropriated by some Nazis like Alfred Bäumler, etc., who may have drawn influence from it or used it to justify their expansive quest for power and world domination." (WK 2009ooo)

And fourthly, some other scholars suggested a more pragmatic interpretation of the Nietzschean will to power, and the reason for this interpretation is that, when compared with "Schopenhauer's will to live," which "Schopenhauer thought…was what was most real in the universe, Nietzsche can be understood as claiming only that the will to power is a particularly useful principle for his purposes." (WK 2009ooo)

The Will to Power, and the Law

With this caution about the mutltiple interpretations of the Nietzschean will to power in mind—what then can be said about the will to power in the context of jurisprudence?

Although Nietzsche did not offer any analysis of the law in depth or provided his own theory of jurisprudence, his idea of the will to power (together with his supporting one concerning the idea of etnernal recurrence) could tell us something interesting about their implications for a potential Nietzschean jurisprudence.

To start, because of Nietzsche's rejection of classical Darwinism (especially in relation to the evolutionary claim about the struggle for survival), law in society is often regarded as being based on "herd morality" for survival, not for expansion. (J. Linarelli 2004)

Thus, for Nietzsche, what is understood as law in conventional jurisprudence serves "primarily for society and can harm persons striving for a noble morality. Nietzsche would ask us to develop a new jurisprudence that preserves freedom to overcome, to pursue noble morality. Positive law can be constructed in such a way because Nietzsche viewed norms embodied in morals and law as social constructions." (J. Linarelli 2004)

In this way, "Nietzsche would prefer a legal system that disables and avoids ressentiment, that would promote human freedom in a pluralist setting without interpersonal comparisons. Nietzsche's normative vision is that we should fundamentally re-evaluate law and other social systems and reorient towards a noble morality." (J. Linarelli 2004)

This re-evaluation of the law is important, because "a fundamental aspect of the human condition that law seeks to address is which sorts of inequality deserve legal redress and which do not. Hence, constitutional law mandating equal protection and due process, statutes prohibiting discrimination and cases interpreting these statutes, and the recent affirmative action cases are but examples of the ongoing dialogue between law and society on what sorts of inequalities are permissible and which are not." (J. Linarelli 2004)

Nietzsche's answer to this important question of equality is that some existing forms of equality in society are essentially dictatorial, in the name of "equality." For instance, "in *Thus Spoke Zarathustra*, in a section entitled 'On the Tarantulas,' Nietzsche metaphorically describes 'preachers of equality' as tarantulas whose 'secretly vengeful' ways make the soul whirl with revenge.' Nietzsche's main concern seems to be about dictatorial preferences: 'You preachers of equality, the tyrannomania of impotence clamors thus out of you for equality: your most secret ambitions to be tyrants thus shroud themselves in words of virtue' [or] 'I do not wish to be mixed up and confused with these preachers of equality.'" (J. Linarelli 2004)

Surely, these kinds of passages would be "easily misconstrued to suggest that Nietzsche was anti-liberal, racist," but "Nietzsche's conception of will to power does not mean that the strong should subjugate the weak, or that there are inherent inequalities among peoples." (J. Linarelli 2004)

Instead, Nietzsche would propose two different ways to understand equality under the law.

Firstly, "the striving for equality is a search for the unattainable. People are different and can choose. Some will seek a noble life while others will practice ressentiment and bad conscience. If people are free they will make choices about which path to take." (J. Linarelli 2004)

And secondly, "equality is overrated," in that, "in response to the democratic consolidation that started to take hold in Europe in the nineteenth century, Nietzsche is essentially asking the question 'Is that all there is?' To Nietzsche, equality works much like Christianity, to sap the life out of people, to make them comfortable, complacent, and to furnish incentives to compare their lot with others, even if their state of affairs is dismal, rather than to strive for a higher order on their own, without reference to what others have or do not have." (J. Linarelli 2004)

In this way, "Nietzsche's vision of rule of law is classical, in the sense that law is supposed to promote human freedom, to stop or deter one person or a group of persons from imposing their morality upon others, to prohibit or reduce arbitrary activities that would permit preying of one person on another." (J. Linarelli 2004)

In so doing, Nietzsche is critical to the utilitarians in regard to their happiness of the greatest number, as he once bitingly wrote about them: "utilitarians 'are right so rarely that it is really pitiful.'" (J. Linarelli 2004; P. Berkowitz 1990)

This critique is especially relevant nowadays, for these "'English [utilitarian] psychologists'...bears particular relevance for critiquing law and economics, currently the dominant research agenda in the legal academy....Nietzsche's complaints about utilitarianism shed light on the scope and force of economic analysis of law." (J. Linarelli 2004)

After all, for Nietzsche, "what is good (or, in economic terms, 'a good') has nothing to do with utility [which is good for herd or slave morality in the pursuit of preservation]"; instead, "Nietzsche looks to the origins of the good in noble morality," not in herd morality. (J. Linarelli 2004)

The Problems with the Will to Power behind the Law

Yet, a potential Nietzschean jurisprudence so understood is not without serious problems, especially in its treatment of equality.

Consider two main criticisms below, for illustration.

Firstly, Nietzsche's treatment of equality is "vague." (J. Linarelli 2004)

For instance, one the one hand, it is clear that Nietzsche would not have "much interest in the minimum fairness standard of treating like cases alike…Treating like cases alike does not impose the straight jacket that everyone must be the same; it only says that everyone must be treated the same if they are the same." (J. Linarelli 2004)

On the other hand, it is not clear what exactly is the "same" or "alike" or not, in a Nietzschean jurisprudence; after all, even in conventional jurisprudence, this issue of "same" or "alike" is already "the subject of volumes of law on permissible and impermissible categories of difference. For example, to discriminate against entry to university on the basis of race is impermissible because it treats applicants differently, on the basis of an impermissible category. Race discrimination produces impermissible inequality….But to discriminate against entry to a university on the basis of SAT scores is permissible because it treats applicants differently on the basis of a permissible category, success on a standardized test." (J. Linarelli 2004)

Thus, "Nietzsche does not 'solve' the question how to determine which value should be permitted and which should not. Rather, his answer would be that this is all well and good but that such interpersonal comparisons are largely beside the point of overcoming, a commitment to the noble life." (J. Linarelli 2004)

And secondly, Nietzsche's treatment of equality has been criticized as "anti-liberal," "racist," "Nazi," and so on.

For instance, there are passages in his works which seem to suggest this bias, as in "For to me, justice speaks thus: 'Men are not equal.' Nor shall they become equal! What would my love of the overman be if I spoke otherwise?" (J. Linarelli 2004)

For his defenders, however, although "there are other more obvious and regrettable racist and sexist passages in Nietzsche's works,…[t]he problem with many Nietzsche interpretations…is selective misquoting." (J. Linarelli 2004)

Yet, for the critics like Jacques Derrida (1984:24), the defenders of Nietzsche have yet to explain convincingly "why the only teaching institution or the only beginning of a teaching institution that ever succeeded in taking as its model the teaching of Nietzsche on teaching will have been a Nazi one."

Another Assessment

This introduction to two sides in the debate is to not favor any of them but to learn about the issue of contngency in the context of law, which is to be understood in different ways, varying from one thinker to another, from one ideology to another, from one tradition to another, or from one age to another.

That said, the discussion can also shed some revealing light on some ontological principles in existential dialectics, and some examples include, say, the absoluteness-relativeness principle, the predictability-unpredictability principle, the explicability-inexplicability principle, the preciseness-vagueness principle, the simpleness-complicatedness principle, the openness-hiddenness principle, the denseness-emptiness principle, the expansion-contraction principle, the theory-praxis principle, the convention-novelty principle, the evolution-transformation principle, the symmetry-asymmetry principle, the regression-progression principle, and the same-difference principle.

For instance, in relation to the absoluteness-relativeness principle, if there is absolute viewpoint (e.g., the herd mentality to treat all individuals as equal, even if they are not the same, according to Nietzsche), there is relative counterpart (e.g., what is good for the herds is not so for the nobles, according to Nietzsche).

In relation to the predictability-unpredictability principle, if there is predictability (e.g., the predictable tendency in herd morality to value existential preservation, not power expansion), there is unpredictability (e.g., the inability within herd morality to predict what others who do not accept herd morality will likely do in a particular case).

In relation to the explicability-inexplicability principle, if there is explicability (e.g., the explanation, by Wilhelm Roux, of life in nature on the basis of "internal struggle," or "the struggle for existence occurred at the cellular level"), there is inexplicability (e.g., the lack of sufficient explanation, within Roux's framework, of life in nature not at the cellular level, like the classical Darwinian theory on natural selection and Rolph's idea of "insatiability and assimilation" for life expansion).

In relation to the preciseness-vagueness principle, if there is preciseness (e.g., the precise identification of Nietzsche's two-fold answer to the notion of equality), there is vagueness (e.g., the vague aspects of Nietzsche's answer to the notion of equality, as it does not resolve the issue concernng which categories of difference are permissible and which ones are impermissible).

In relation to the simpleness-complicatedness principle, if there is simple analysis (e.g., the simple analysis of Nietzsche's will to power for a new jurisprudence which allows the flourishing of noble morality, not just herd morality), there is also complicatedness (e.g., the more complicated analysis of the origins of Nietzsche's will to power on the multifaceted historical influence by previous scholars on his work).

In relation to the openness-hiddenness principle, if there is openness (e.g., the open exploration of the will to power in nature by Nietzsche), there is hiddenness (e.g., the hidden bias in Nietzsche's idea of the will to power against competing views like the Darwinian, utilitarian, Christian, or else).

In relation to the denseness-emptiness principle, if there is denseness (e.g., the relatively denser concentration of normative concerns with striving for equality, in jurisprudence based on herd morality), there is emptiness (e.g., the relatively less dense, or more empty, concentration of normative concerns with striving for difference, in jurisprudence based on herd morality).

In relation to the expansion-contraction principle, if there is expansion (e.g., the relatively more developed aspects of a legal system, which is based on utiliarianism, to promote utility maximization and the happiness of the greatest number), there is contraction (e.g., the relatively less developed aspects of a legal system, which is based on utiliarianism, to promote power expansion and difference).

In relation to the theory-praxis principle, if there is theory (e.g., the theoretical construction of the democratic idea of equality), there is praxis (e.g., the application of the democratic idea of equality for affirmative action programs).

In relation to the convention-novelty principle, if there is convention (e.g., the conventional wisdom about the classical Darwinian evolutionary theory), there is novelty (e.g., the alternative novel challenge to the classical Darwinian evolutionary theory by thinkers like Roux in regard to the idea of "internal struggle" or Dumont in regard to the idea of "pleasure in the expansion of power").

In relation to the evolution-transformation principle, if there is evolution (e.g., the natural evolution of humans to live together by certain behaviors in the state of nature), there is transformation (e.g, the technical transformation of human living together by way of the inventon of a legal institution for law and order).

In relation to the symmetry-asymmetry principle, if there is symmetry (e.g., the co-existence of different versions of equality, be it utilitarian, Nietzschean, or else), there is asymmetry (e.g., the popularity of utilitarian jurisprudence among those in the law and economics movement, but the more acceptance of Nietzschean jurisprudence among the Nazis during the Third Reich).

In relation to the regression-progression principle, if there is regression (e.g., the abuse by the Nazis in using Nietzsche's idea of the will to power for its teaching institution), there is progression (e.g., the progress made in making us aware of the dark side of egalitarianism in suppressing difference, especially towards the overmen, for Nietzsche).

And in relation to the same-difference principle, if there is similarity in outcome (e.g., the promotion of equality in different versions of jursiprudence, be they utiliarian, Christian, or else), there is difference in outcome (e.g., the emphases on the greatest number in utilitarian jurisprudence, or on the herds in the Christian version).

Contingency and Society

Besides the perspectives of the mind (in *Sec. 3.2*) and nature (in *Sec. 3.3*)—the third perspective to analyze the issue of contingency in the context of the law concerns the role of society.

Two important case studies can be provided here, namely, (3.4.1) property law, and copyright violation, and (3.4.2) sociological analysis, and the law—to be analyzed hereafter, respectively.

Property Law, and Copyright Violation

The term "property" in property law refers to "any physical or intangible entity that is owned by a person or jointly by a group of persons. Depending on the nature of the property, an owner of property has the right to consume, sell, rent, mortgage, transfer, exchange or destroy his or her property, and/or to exclude others from doing these things." (WK 2009qqq; BD 2009; AHD 2009; WN 2009)

Surely, there are other definitions of "property" besides the one shown here, so the above definition is used solely as a convenient tool to start the present discussion of property law. (WK 2009ppp)

With this clarification in mind, property can be understood in terms of its conceptual classification, property rights, and theoretical debate, together with the case study of copyright violation—as will be addressed in what follows, in that order (and summarized in *Table 3.3*).

The Classification of Property

Property, in general, can be classified in terms of two main categories, namely, (a) "public property" (viz., "any property that is controlled by a state or by a whole community") and (b) "private property" (viz., "any property that is not public property" and "may be under the control of a single person or by a group of persons jointly"). (WK 2009qqq; J. Schrems 2004)

Another way to classify property is to understand its different types, such as "real property (land)," "personal property (physical possessions belonging to an person)," "private property (property owned by legal persons or business entities)," "public property (state owned or publicly owned and available possessions)," and even "intellectual property (exclusive rights over artistic creations, inventions, etc.)." (WK 2009qqq)

However, these terms in the classification are more for the common law tradition. But different terms may be used in other (non-common law) traditions; for instance, "[i]n the civil law system, there is a division between movable and immovable property. Movable property roughly corresponds to personal property, while immovable property corresponds to real estate or real property." (WK 2009ppp)

The Rights to Use Property

The above classification of property already implies some property rights, which are often guided by some principles which include, for example, the following rights: (WK 2009qqq)

- "control of the use of the property"
- "the right to any benefit from the property" (e.g., "mining rights")
- "a right to transfer or sell the property"
- "a right to exclude others from the property"

However, these traditional property rights do not suggest the following: (WK 2009qqq)

- "uses that unreasonably interfere with the property rights of another private party (the right of quiet enjoyment)"
- "uses that unreasonably interfere with public property rights, including uses that interfere with public health, safety, peace or convenience"

Yet, there are two qualifications to this discussion of "property rights."

Firstly, "property rights" in property law should not be confused with "contractual rights" in contract law.

This distinction is important, because "[p]roperty rights are rights over things enforceable against other persons. By contrast, contractual rights are rights enforceable against particular persons." (WK 2009ppp

This is true, even though "[p]roperty rights…may arise from a contract, so there is an overlap between the two systems of rights. In relation to the sale of land, for example, two sets of legal relationships exist alongside one another: the personal right to sue for damages on the contract, and the proprietary right exercisable over the thing." (WK 2009ppp)

And secondly, "property rights" should not be confused with "personal rights."

By definition, "personal rights" refer to "the rights that a person has over their own body. Among personal rights are associated rights to protect and safeguard the body, most obviously protected by the torts of assault and battery. Furthermore, aspects of personality are protected, such as a person's reputation, by the tort of defamation, and legislation protecting the privacy of individuals." (WK 2009rrr)

This distinction is important, because the existence of "property rights" by itself does not automatically guarantee that some individuals have the "personal rights" to own property and to not be owned by others as slaves, prostitutes, and the like.

For instance, in relation to the personal right to own property—it used to be the case in "[i]n the past [that] groups lacking political power have often been disqualified from the benefits of property. In an extreme form this has meant that persons have become 'objects' of property right, legally 'things,' or chattels….More commonly, marginalised groups have been denied legal rights to own property. These include Jews in England and married women in Western societies until the late 19th century." (WK 2009ppp)

And in relation to the personal right to not be owned by others—"the dividing line between personal rights and property rights is not always easy to draw. For instance, is one's reputation property which can be commercially exploited by affording property rights to it? The question of the proprietary character of personal rights is particularly relevant in the case of rights over human tissue, organs and other body parts." (WK 2009ppp) This concern with "human tissue, organs, and other body parts" is also relevant to the cases concerning slavery, prostitution, and the like.

This dispute about rights raises a more fundamental theoretical question here concerns what constitutes a legimitate defense of property rights, to be enforced by society.

This discussion then lead us to the controversical dispute on what exactly constitutes the foundation for property law.

The Unsettled Theoretical Debate on the Foundation for Property Law

The theoretical debate on ownership is to provide a foundation for property law.

Unfortunately, there is no universal agreement on such a theoretical foundation, which is contingent on a given ideological orientation, which varies from one thinker to another, from one culture to another, and from one era to another.

This contingency of the theoretical debate on ownership for the foundation for property law can be analyzed in terms of two major groups, namely, (a) the right wing of the ideological spectrum and (b) the left wing of the ideological spectrum—as shown below, in that order.

(a) The Right Wing of the Ideological Spectrum

In this category, there are different thinkers to be introduced. Although they do not share the same views on all aspects of property ownership, they all stress the private ownership of property, albeit in different degrees.

Consider, for illustration, three examples below, namely, (a1) the "first possession theory of property," (a2) the "labor theory of property," and (a3) the "customs and convention" theory of property.

(a1) Firstly, there is the "first possession theory of property," which boldly claims that "ownership [of] something is seen as justified simply by someone seizing something before someone else does." (WK 2009qqq; G. Oppy 2005)

Jean-Jacques Rousseau (1984) once criticized this theory as naive in a famous passage: "The first man who, having fenced in a piece of land, said 'This is mine,' and found people naive enough to believe him, that man was the true founder of civil society. From how many crimes, wars, and murders, from how many horrors and misfortunes might not any one have saved mankind, by pulling up the stakes, or filling up the ditch, and crying to his fellows: Beware of listening to this impostor; you are undone if you once forget that the fruits of the earth belong to us all, and the earth itself to nobody." (WK 2009vvv)

(a2) Secondly, there is "the labor theory of property," which suggests that "you own your own life, and it follows that you must own the products of that life, and that those products can be traded in free exchange with others." (WK 2009qqq)

For instance, Ayn Rand (1957), in *Atlas Shrugged*, vocally wrote in defense of private ownership under the law: "Just as man can't exist without his body, so no rights can exist without the right to translate one's rights into reality, to think, to work and keep the results, which means: the right of property." (WK 2009qqq)

John Locke (1986), in *The Second Treatise on Civil Government*, thus wrote: "Every man has a property in his own person. This nobody has a right to, but himself." (WK 2009qqq) And this is so, "when one mixes one's labor with nature, one gains ownership of that part of nature with which the labor is mixed, subject to the limitation that there should be 'enough, and as good, left in common for others.'" (WK 2009qqq; WN 2009)

Frédéric Bastiat (1944), in *The Law*, argued that "[l]ife, liberty, and property do not exist because men have made laws. On the contrary, it was the fact that life, liberty, and property existed beforehand that caused men to make laws in the first place." (WK 2009qqq)

Adam Smith (1977), in *Wealth of Nations*, argued that "the expectation of profit from 'improving one's stock of capital' rests on private property rights. It is a belief central to capitalism that property rights encourage the property holders to develop the property, generate wealth, and efficiently allocate resources based on the operation of the market. From this evolved the modern conception of property as a right which is enforced by positive law, in the expectation that this would produce more wealth and better standards of living." (WK 2009qqq)

(a3) And thirdly, there is the "customs and convention" theory of property, in that "there are property rights because of and to the extent that the existing law, supported by social customs, secure them." (WK 2009qqq)

David Hume, for instance, believed that "existing customs should not lightly be disregarded, because they have come to be what they are as a result of human nature." (WK 2009qqq)

Other scholars, especially those in anthropology, had studied "ownership and possession" in different cultures on the basis of the "custom and regulation," in which context "[property] law…can meaningfully be applied."

For instance, by customs and convention, "[m]any {Cherokee] tribal cultures balance individual ownership with the laws of collective groups: tribes, families, associations and nations." (WK 2009qqq) And, "historically all property was owned by the monarch and it devolved through feudal land tenure or other feudal systems of loyalty and fealty." (WK 2009ppp)

(b) The Left Wing of the Ideological Spectrum

In this group, there are also different thinkers to be introduced. Like those in the right-wing of the ideological spectrum, they do not share the same views on all aspects of property ownership.

But unlike those in the right-wing of the ideological spectrum, they are critical to the private ownership of property, albeit in different degrees.

Consider, for illustration, three examples below, namely, (b1) the "libertarian socialist" theory of property, (b2) the "socialist" theory of property, and (b3) the "communist" theory of property.

(b1) Firstly, there is the "libertarian socialist" theory of property, in that the "libertarian socialists generally accepts property rights, but with a short abandonment time period. In other words, a person must make (more or less) continuous use of the item or else he loses ownership rights. This is usually referred to as 'possession property' or 'usufruct.' Thus, in this usufruct system, absentee ownership is illegitimate, and workers own the machines they work with." (WK 2009qqq)

(b2) Secondly, there is the "socialist" theory of property, in that the "socialists"—unlike the libertarian socialists—in general, are critical to the very idea of private ownership of property, "stating, among other things, that the cost of defending property is higher than the returns from private property ownership, and that even when property rights encourage the property-holder to develop his property, generate wealth, etc., he will only do so for his own benefit, which may not coincide with the benefit of other people or society at large." (WK 2009qqq)

(b3) And thirdly, there is the "communist" view of property, in that the "communists" go even further and advocate that "only collective ownership of the means of production through a polity (though not necessarily a state) will assure the minimization of unequal or unjust outcomes and the maximization of benefits, and that therefore private property (which in communist theory is limited to capital) should be abolished." (WK 2009qqq)

Karl Marx (1948) and his followers argued, for instance, that "the creation of private property will always benefit one class over another, giving way to domination through the use of this private property. Communists are naturally not opposed to personal property which is '[h]ard-won, self-acquired, self-earned' [as stated in the Communist Manifesto]...by members of the proletariat." (WK 2009qqq)

Surely, the communist view is not without problems. A good critique comes from Aristotle (2009), who, in *Politics*, exposed the "tragedy of the commons," when he wrote that "that which is common to the greatest number has the least care bestowed upon it. Every one thinks chiefly of his own, hardly at all of the common interest; and only when he is himself concerned as an individual….If they do not share equally enjoyments and toils, those who labor much and get little will necessarily complain of those who labor little and receive or consume much. But indeed there is always a difficulty in men living together and having all human relations in common, but especially in their having common property." (WK 2009qqq)

The Controversial Application of Property Law for Copyright Violation

The unsettled theoretical debate on ownership for the foundation for property law can be seen more clearly when examined in a case study concerning the controverisal use of property law to deal with copyright violation.

The term "copyright infringement (or copyright violation)" refers to "the unauthorized use of material that is covered by copyright law, in a manner that violates one of the copyright owner's exclusive rights, such as the right to reproduce or perform the copyrighted work, or to make derivative works." (WK 2009sss)

In the United States, for instance, it is the "United States copyright law" which determines what constitutes copyright violation. (WK 2009ttt)

(a) Four Defenses to Copyright Violation

Under the U.S. copyright law, there are several guidelines which allow defenses to copyright violation. (WK 2009sss)

Consider the following examples of defenses to copyright violation, for illustration. (WK 2009sss)

- Independent Creation

  "A defendant in an infringement action may rebut the presumption of copying by a showing of independent creation. It is possible for an author to create a work independently while bearing similarities to another. If access is not established, there is no copying, even if there is a striking similarity between the two works. For this reason, corporations will destroy or return unsolicited mailings from authors as a policy."
- Trivial Use

  "The legal doctrine of *de minimis non curat lex*, 'the law does not care about trivial things,' provides a *de minimis* copying defense against infringement. When the plaintiff establishes only a trivial use of the copyrighted work by the defendant, there is no infringement."

- Sale Doctrine
  "The first sale doctrine is a defense to infringement of the distribution right. It permits a lawful purchaser of a copyrighted work to resell or otherwise dispose of it. This, however, is not a defense to the reproduction right."
- Fair Use
  "Fair use is an affirmative defense, but its application will vary greatly depending on the facts and circumstances of the case. Courts apply a four part balancing test examining the scope of infringement, the effect on the copyright owner's rights (e.g. his or her ability to sell the work), the amount of the work copied, and the purpose of the infringement."

Even then, these defenses to copyright violation can also be interpreted in different ways, which vary from one particular case to another, from one legal system to another, and from one historical era to another—as explained below.

(b) The Contingent Nature of Legal Interpretation

For instance, in relation to different cases, "[c]ourts [in the U.S.] have held that a non-commercial use is not fair use when it has a substantial market effect"; in other words, "courts are more receptive to arguments regarding the effect on the copyright owner's market or potential market," when a particular case has "a small-scale impact" than a large one. (WK 2009sss)

In relation to different legal traditions, while "fair use is used mainly in the United States…[o]ther common law jurisdictions [unlike the one in the U.S.] have the more rigidly defined defence of fair dealing." (WK 2009sss)

And in relation to different historical eras, "the passage of the No Electronic Theft Act (NET Act)" in 1976 changed the "U.S. copyright law …to allow for the civil and criminal prosecution of persons allegedly engaged in copying of copyrighted works without permission that did not result in personal financial gain." (WK 2009sss)

This change is historic, since it used to be the case that "the criminal copyright law required infringement to be for financial gain. Among other things, the NET Act altered the definition of financial gain to include bartering and trading. In addition, under this U.S. law, members of software piracy groups could also be prosecuted for participation in a criminal enterprise." (WK 2009sss)

(c) The Controversial Case against YouTube

This contingent nature of legal interpretation is more revealing in the particular case of copyright violation against the online company known as *YouTube*.

YouTube is a popular "video sharing website on which users can upload and share videos. Three former PayPal employees created YouTube in February 2005….The company is based in San Bruno, California, and uses Adobe Flash Video technology to display a wide variety of user-generated video content, including movie clips, TV clips, and music videos, as well as amateur content such as video blogging and short original videos. Most of the content on YouTube has been uploaded by individuals, although media corporations including CBS, the BBC, UMG and other organizations offer some of their material via the site, as part of the YouTube partnership program." (WK 2009uuu; J. Hopkins 2006; T. Weber 2009)

The controversy began when YouTube failed "to ensure that its videos respect the law of copyright. At the time of uploading a video, YouTube users are always shown a screen with the following message: 'Do not upload any TV shows, music videos, music concerts or commercials without permission unless they consist entirely of content you created yourself.'" (WK 2009uuu)

In spite of this advice, "there are still many unauthorized clips from television shows, films and music videos on YouTube. YouTube does not view videos before they are posted online, and it is left to copyright holders to issue a takedown notice under the terms of the Digital Millennium Copyright Act." (WK 2009uuu; R. Marsden 2009)

Because of this violation, "organizations including Viacom, Mediaset and the English Premier League have filed lawsuits against YouTube, claiming that it has done too little to prevent the uploading of copyrighted material. Viacom, demanding US$1 billion in damages, said that it had found more than 150,000 unauthorized clips of its material on YouTube that had been viewed 'an astounding 1.5 billion times.'" (WK 2009uuu; BBC 2008; CNN 2008; DT 2008)

YouTube's defense was to appeal to the principles of trivial use and fair use, in that it did not copy any of the copyrighted materials themselves (at least only in a trivial way in terms of listing) and that it was the users which posted them, mainly for non-commerical use (by sharing). In addition, YouTube also claimed that it "goes far beyond its legal obligations in assisting content owners to protect their works." (WK 2009uuu)

In the end, YouTube won and lost in this legal case.

On the one hand, YouTube won, in that, "[i]n August 2008, a U.S. court ruled that copyright holders cannot order the removal of an online file without first determining whether the posting reflected fair use of the material. The case involved Stephanie Lenz from Gallitzin, Pennsylvania, who had made a home video of her 13-month-old son dancing to Prince's song 'Let's Go Crazy' and posted the 29-second video on YouTube." (WK 2009uuu; SFC 2008)

On the other hand, YouTube lost in this case, at least on two counts.

The first count is that, "[s]ince Viacom filed its lawsuit, YouTube has introduced a system called Video ID, which checks uploaded videos against a database of copyrighted content with the aim of reducing violations." (WK 2009uuu; BBC 2009a; YT 2008)

And the second count is that, "in July 2008, Viacom won a court ruling requiring YouTube to hand over data detailing the viewing habits of every user who has watched videos on the site....U.S. District Court Judge Louis Stanton...ordered YouTube to hand over documents totalling around 12 terabytes of data." (WK 2009uuu)

This decision "led to concerns that the viewing habits of individual users could be identified through a combination of their IP addresses and login names. The decision was criticized by the Electronic Frontier Foundation, which called the court ruling 'a set-back to privacy rights.'" (WK 2009uuu; BBC 2008b)

But the larger concern here, for the critics, raises the fundamental question concerning the foundation for property law. It is therefore no wonder that, in the current case study of copyright violation, "[a]nti-copyright advocates and other critics of intellectual property [e.g., musical compositions, novels, computer programs, etc.] dispute the concept of intellectual property." (WK 2009qqq)

In fact, this constitutes a major reason that intellectual property is neither popular nor "widely recognized or enforced." (WK 2009qqq)

A Fresh Rejoinder

This discussion of the controversial case of copyright violation involving YouTube in the larger context of the foundation for property law is to not favor any ideological orientation about ownership in general but to learn from them in an overall perspective, especially in regard to the issue of contingency of property law and its limits.

This overall perspective can also be understood in relation to the ontological principles in existential dialectics, and good example include, say, the absoluteness-relativeness principle, the predictability-unpredictability principle, the explicability-inexplicability principle, the preciseness-vagueness principle, the simpleness-complicatedness principle, the openness-hiddenness principle, the denseness-emptiness principle, the expansion-contraction principle, the theory-praxis principle, the convention-novelty principle, the evolution-transformation principle, the symmetry-asymmetry principle, the regression-progression principle, and the same-difference principle.

For instance, in relation to the absoluteness-relativeness principle, if there is absolute viewpoint (e.g., the "first possession theory of property" to allow someone to claim a property by seizing it first), there is relative counterpart (e.g., what is good for the first claimer who believes in the "first possession theory of property" for exclusive private property is not so for the communist who believes in the "communist" theory of property for common ownership).

In relation to the predictability-unpredictability principle, if there is predictability (e.g., the predictable tendency of someone who believes in the "labor theory of property" to claim a property after mixing his labor with it), there is unpredictability (e.g., the more difficult task to predict how much "there should be 'enough, and as good, left in common for others'," in a particular case of someone who accepts the "labor theory of property").

In relation to the explicability-inexplicability principle, if there is explicability (e.g., the explanation, by someone in the "customs and convention" theory of property, of a property ownership to be legitimate, on the basis of certain customs and convention in the community), there is inexplicability (e.g., the lack of sufficient explanation, within the "customs and convention" theory of property, of why customs and convention are just in the first place, especially when "all property was owned by the monarch and it devolved through feudal land tenure or other feudal systems of loyalty and fealty").

In relation to the preciseness-vagueness principle, if there is preciseness (e.g., the precise identification of traditional property rights in property law), there is vagueness (e.g., the vague formulation of the traditional property rights, because it does not clearly resolve the issue concerning "the proprietary character of personal rights…over human tissue, organs and other body parts").

In relation to the simpleness-complicatedness principle, if there is simpleness (e.g., the simple analysis of the defenses to copyright violation in terms of four principles), there is complicatedness (e.g., the more complicated analysis of the defenses to copyright violation by accounting for the varieties of interpretation, depending on different particular cases, legal traditions, and historical eras).

In relation to the openness-hiddenness principle, if there is openness (e.g., the open exploration of the option for collective ownership in the communist theory of property), there is hiddenness (e.g., the hidden bias, in the communist theory of property, of its ideological preference for drastic equality, as opposed to other more conservative alternatives).

In relation to the denseness-emptiness principle, if there is denseness (e.g., the relatively denser concentration of public property in a communist society), there is also emptiness (e.g., the relatively less dense, or more empty, concentration of public property in a capitalist society).

In relation to the expansion-contraction principle, if there is expansion (e.g., the relativley more developed ability and inclination of individuals in a capitalist society to care for their private properties), there is contraction (e.g., the relatively less developed ability and inclination of individuals in a capitalist society to care for the public properties).

In relation to the theory-praxis principle, if there is theory (e.g., the theoretical construction of Marxist communism), there is praxis (e.g., the practical application of Marxist communism to build a new society in Soviet times).

In relation to the convention-novelty principle, if there is convention (e.g., the conventional wisdom about property ownership in accordance to the "customs and convention" view of property), there is novelty (e.g., the alternative novel challenge to the conventional view of property by the Marxists in terms of a new theory of collective ownership for the interests of the proletariat).

In relation to the evolution-transformation principle, if there is evolution (e.g., the natural evolution of humans to live and share property within small groups in the state of nature), there is transformation (e.g, the technical transformation of human sharing of property within groups by way of the invention of the "labor theory of property" for the rise of capitalism).

In relation to the symmetry-asymmetry principle, if there is symmetry (e.g., the co-existence of different theories of property in history), there is asymmetry (e.g., the popularity of the "communist" theory of property in the Soviet Union, but the acceptance of the "labor theory of property" in capitalist America).

In relation to the regression-progression principle, if there is regression (e.g., the tragedy of the commons in the Soviet Union), there is progression (e.g., the reduction of inequality in the Soviet Union).

And in relation to the same-difference principle, if there is similarity in outcome (e.g., the justification of how to distribute property in human society throughout history, albeit in different ways, depending on different thinkers, legal traditions, and historical eras), there is difference (e.g., the more use of private property in capitalist society, but the more use of public property in communist society).

Sociological Analysis, and the Law

A different way to explore the issue of contingency in relation to law has to do with the sociology of law, especially on the rise and fall of certain legal institutions over time.

The study of the sociology of law is a sub-field of sociology (and, for that matter, legal studies), which "examines the interaction of law with other aspects of society, such as the effect of legal institutions, doctrines, and practices on other social phenomena and vice versa. Some of its areas of inquiry include the social development of legal institutions, the social construction of legal issues, and the relation of law to social change." (WK 2009vvv; D. Jary 1995)

Three major phenomena in the study of the sociology of law are illustrative in revealing the historical contingency of the development of law in modern times, namely, (a) the rise of legal rationalism, (b) the growth of restitutive law, and (c) other sociological analyses of law—to be introduced hereafter, in that order.

The Rise of Legal Rationalism in Modern Times

The first major phenomenon in the modern historical development of law has to do with the rise of what Max Weber called "legal rationalism," which refers to "the formal rationalization of law on the basis of general procedures that are applied equally and fairly to all. Modern rationalized law is…codified and impersonal in its application." (WK 2009www)

This scientific study of law in modern times reflects Weber's "external approach to law" to study "the empirical characteristics of law, as opposed to the internal perspective of the legal sciences and the moral approach of the philosophy of law." (WK 2009www)

Hereafter are two illustrations of "legal ratonalism" in action, namely, in relation to (a1) leadership and (a2) bureaucracy in the modern world.

(a1) In Relation to Leadership in the Modern World

Weber differentiated three ideal types of leadership, domination, and authority in history, as shown below: (WK 2009xxx; W. Mommsen 1992)

- "charismatic domination" (e.g., "familial and religious)"
- "traditional domination" (e.g., "patriarchs, patrimonalism, feudalism)"

- “legal domination” (e.g., “modern law and state, bureaucracy)”

It is the third type, namely, legal rationalism, which has come to dominate the modern scene, especially in relation to its social institutions (like the law, the bureaucracy, and the state in a broad sense).

The reason for the failure of the first two types to carry on their continued dominance to the modern world is that both suffer from their own weaknesses.

For instance, in relation to the first type of domination, namely, “charismatic domination”—the problem here concerns “the instability of charismatic authority,” which so often “inevitably forces it to 'routinize' into a more structured form of authority” (like the third type). (WK 2009xxx)

In relation to the second type of domination, namely, “traditional domination”—the problem here concerns “sufficient resistance to a master” which so often “can lead to a 'traditional revolution,'” with the consequence of eventually moving into the third type too. (WK 2009xxx)

Therefore, in relation to the third type of domination, namely, “legal domination”—Weber argued for “an inevitable move towards a rational-legal structure of authority, utilising a bureaucratic structure. Thus this theory can be sometimes viewed as part of the social evolutionism theory. This ties to his broader concept of rationalisation by suggesting the inevitability of a move in this direction.” (WK 2009xxx; R. Bendix 1977)

(a2) In Relation to Bureaucracy in the Modern World

This utilization of “a bureaucratic structure” in the legal-rational form of authority then leads to Weber’s “critical study of the bureaucratisation of society, the rational ways in which formal social organizations apply the ideal type characteristics of a bureaucracy.” (WK 2009xxx)

For Weber, “to achieve the maximum benefits of the bureaucratic design,…an organization must have the following characteristics,” as shown below: (M. Matteson 2005: 545)

- “All tasks will be divided into highly specialized jobs.”
- “Each task is performed accordingly to a system of abstract rules to ensure uniformity and coordination of different tasks.”
- “Each member or office of the organization is accountable for job performance to one, and only, manager. Managers hold their authority because of their expert knowledge and because it’s delegated from the top of the hierarchy. An unbroken chain of command exists.”

- "Each employee of the organization relates to other employees and clients in an impersonal, formal manner, maintaining a social distance with subordinates and clients. The purpose of this practice is to ensure that personalities and favoritism do not interfere with efficient accomplishment of the organization's objectives."
- "Employment in the bureaucratic organization is based on technical qualifications and is protected against arbitrary dismissal. Similarly, promotions are based on seniority and achievement. Employment in the organization is viewed as a lifelong career, and a high degree of loyalty is engendered."

In fact, "it was Weber who began the studies of bureaucracy and whose works led to the popularization of this term. Many aspects of modern public administration go back to him, and a classic, hierarchically organized civil service of the Continental type is called 'Weberian civil service,' although this is only one ideal type of public administration and government," as analyzed in his work *Economy and Society* (1978).

However, as I already explained in Chapter 2 of *The Future of Post-Human Organization* (or *FPHO*), the bureaucratisation of the organizational world has its dark side too, because "a work with a high degree of the division of labor can yield boredom (because of its monotonous nature for each smaller standardized piece of work), centralization can stifle competition and autonomy, and the formalization of rules can encourage red tape and general frustration."

Weber was aware of this dark side of bureaucratisation, and this is something that "he did not particularly like himself—he only thought it particularly efficient and successful. In this work, Weber outlines a description, which has become famous, of rationalization (of which bureaucratisation is a part) as a shift from a value-oriented organization and action (traditional authority and charismatic authority) to a goal-oriented organization and action (legal-rational authority)." (WK 2009xxx; M. Sashkin 2002)

The consequence of this shift, for Weber, "is a 'polar night of icy darkness,' in which increasing rationalization of human life traps individuals in an 'iron cage' of rule-based, rational control." (WK 2009xxx; G. Ritzer 2004)

The Growth of Restituive Law in Modern Times

The second major phenomenon in the modern historical development of law concerns what Emile Durkheim regarded as the evolution of "mechanical solidarity" towards "organic solidarity," especially in relation to (b1) repressive law versus restitutive law and (b2) eogism versus human dignity. (WK 2009www)

(b1) Repressive Law versus Restitutive Law

For Durkheim, an important impact of the evolution from a mechanical solidarity to an organic one in modern society has to do with the "transformation from repressive law to restitutive law" in modern times. (WK 2009www)

The distinction between "mechanical solidarity" and "organic solidarity" here refers to the fact that, since "[l]aw is an indicator of the mode of integration of a society," it "can be mechanical, among identical parts, or organic, among differentiated parts such as in industrialized societies." (WK 2009www)

However, "[o]ver the course of history, law undergoes a transformation from repressive law to restitutive law. Restitutive law operates in societies in which there is a high degree of individual variation and emphasis on personal rights and responsibilities." (WK 2009www)

The distinction between repressive law and restitutive law is "characterised by their sanctions…, as a direct reflection of types of social solidarity. The study of law was therefore of interest to sociology for what it could reveal about the nature of solidarity." (WK 2009yyy)

(b2) Egosim versus Human Dignity

The distinction (above) is important, since, insofar as "law (both civil and criminal) is an expression and guarantee of society's fundamental values," for Durkheim, "modern law increasingly expresses a form of moral individualism—a value system that is, in his view, probably the only one universally appropriate to modern conditions of social solidarity." (WK 2009yyy; R. Cotterrell 1999)

In this way, "individualism" constitutes "the basis of human rights and of the values of individual human dignity and individual autonomy. It is to be sharply distinguished from selfishness and egoism, which for Durkheim are not moral stances at all. Many of Durkheim's closest followers, such as Marcel Mauss, Paul Fauconnet and Paul Huvelin also specialised in or contributed to the sociological study of law." (WK 2009yyy)

The reason for this second distinction between human dignity and egoism is that Durkheim is well aware of the danger of excessive individualism in modern times.

In fact, this was precisely what happened in modern times, when, as I already went to great lengths to explain in the 2 volumes *The Future of Human Civilization* (or *FHC*), where I wrote that, "with the death of God qua the breakdown of traditional laws and norms which used to hold society together within a communal and kinship structure, the social bondage among individuals in modern times was disrupted into what Durkheim called the anomic state." (P. Baofu 2000; V. Parrillo 1985; E.B.1994)

In this "Durkheimian anomic state, separate domains of minimal selves pursue their own narrow interests and interact with others on a contractual belonging in a community without a collective idea so understood, any more than society can exist apart from individuals." (P. Baofu 2000: Ch.3)

This is thus the dark side of individualism in organic solidarity.

Other Sociological Analyses of Law

These two major phenomena in the modern historical development of law are by no means exhaustive but solely illustrative for the purpose at hand.

For instance, hereafter are some other views concerning the modern historical development of law, as debated by different scholars: (WK 2009www)

Firstly, there is the view that law is a form of social control.

For illustration, Talcott Parsons argued that "law is conceived as an essential mechanism of social control....Critical sociologists developed a perspective of law as an instrument of power." (WK 2009www)

However, for the critics like Philip Selznick, "modern law became increasingly responsive to a society's needs and had to be approached morally as well." (WK 2009www)

Secondly, there is the view that law is rigid in communicating with other social institutions.

For illustration, Niklas Luhmann claimed that "law as unable to communicate with other social institutions because of the rigidity of its binary code of guilty/innocent." (WK 2009www)

However, for the critics like Jurgen Habermas, "the law can do a better job as a 'system' institution' by representing more faithfully the interests of everyday people in the 'lifeworld.'" (WK 2009www)

And thirdly, there is the view that law is a social field for symbolic and cultural violence.

For instance, Pierre Bourdeiu argued that law is the new "professional habitus of the lawyer." (WK 2009www) By "habitus," Bourdieu referred to "a system of dispositions (lasting, acquired schemes of perception, thought and action). The individual agent develops these dispositions in response to the objective conditions it encounters. In this way Bourdieu theorizes the inculcation of objective social structures into the subjective, mental experience of agents." (WK 2009www)

Through habitus, for Bourdieu, "social classes, especially the ruling and intellectual classes, preserve their social privileges across generations despite the myth that contemporary post-industrial society boasts equality of opportunity and high social mobility, achieved through formal education." (WK 2009zzz)

This constitutes a new form of violence, or what he called "symbolic violence," which means "the imposition of categories of thought and perception upon dominated social agents who then take the social order to be just." (WK 2009zzz) Thus, law is the new "social field in which actors struggle for cultural, symbolic and economic capital and in so doing develop the reproductive professional habitus of the lawyer." (WK 2009www)

However, for the critics, Bourdieu's talk of symbolic violence is biased in its leftist exaggeration of the illegitimacy of the social order under the law. After all, why is an imposition of thoughts and perceptions necessarily (always) unjust, other than by definition?

A More Balanced Viewpoint

This introduction to the different sociological analyses of law has the virtue to show us the contingency of the legal institution in its historical development over time, be it about the approach to law (e.g., the rise of legal-rationalism in modern times), the mode of integration (e.g., the growth of restittuive law), the nature of social mechanism (e.g., social control of law), the flexibility of communication (e.g., the rigidity of the binary code of guilty/innocent under the law), or the form of capital (e.g., the violence of symbolic capital).

And the disagreements among different scholars on these sociological analyses also speak volumes about the limits of contingency in the context of the law.

In addition, the introduction can also shed some light on some ontological principles of existential dialectics, and some good examples include the formalness-informalness principle, the absoluteness-relativeness principle, the predictability-unpredictability principle, the explicability-inexplicability principle, the preciseness-vagueness principle, the simpleness-complicatedness principle, the openness-hiddenness principle, the denseness-emptiness principle, the expansion-contraction principle, the convention-novelty prnciple, the evolution-transformation principle, the symmetry-asymmetry principle, the softness-hardness principle, the regression-progression principle, and the same-difference principle.

For instance, in relation to the formalness-informalness principle, if there is formalness (e.g., the formal logical requirement of the binary code of guilty/innocent under the law), there is informalness (e.g., Luhmann's more informal view about going beyond this narrow logical dichotomy of guilty/innocent under the law).

In relation to the absoluteness-relativeness principle, if there is absoluteness (e.g., the absolute viewpoint in the older days of mechanical solidarity, when identicalness, not difference, was expected), there is relativeness (e.g., what is good for those in mechanical solidarity to celebrate identicalness is not so for those in organic solidarity to celebrate difference).

In relation to the predictability-unpredictability principle, if there is predictability (e.g., the predictable tendency of those in orgnanic solidarity to value individualism), there is unpredictability (e.g., the more difficult task to predict exactly when individualism could degenerate into anomie in which particular way).

In relation to the explicability-inexplicability principle, if there is explicability (e.g., the explanation, by Bourdieu, of symbolic violence on the basis of "the imposition of categories of thought and perception upon dominated social agents who then take the social order to be just," when it is not really so), there is inexplicability (e.g., the lack of sufficient explanation, within Bourdieu's framework, of why an imposition is necessarily unjust, other than by definition).

In relation the preciseness-vagueness principle, if there is preciseness (e.g., the precise, clear distinction betwene egoism and human dignity in individualism, according to Durkheim), there is vagueness (e.g., the vagueness in the formulation of what human dignity is supposed to mean, as it can be subject to different interpretations).

In relation to the simpleness-complicatedness principle, if there is simpleness (e.g., the simple analysis of the main characteristics of legal-rationalism in relation to organizational structure), there is complicatedness (e.g., the more complicated analysis of the nature of bureaucracy in terms of its multifaceted relationships with the law, the state, and its dark side too).

In relation to the openness-hiddenness principle, if there is openness (e.g., the open exploration of symbolic capital and its violence by Bourdieu), there is hiddenness (e.g., the hidden leftist bias in Bourdieu's analysis of symbolic violence because of its exaggeration of the illegitimacy of the existing social order).

In relation to the denseness-emptiness principle, if there is denseness (e.g., the relatively denser concentration of legal-rational organizations in the modern lifeworld), there is emptiness (e.g., the relatively less dense, or more empty, concentration of traditional authority in modern organizational lifeworld).

In relation to the expansion-contraction principle, if there is expansion (e.g., the relatively more developed procedures in a legal-rational organization to be precise and impersonal), there is contraction (e.g., the relativley less developed procedures in legal-rational organizations to allow discretion in decision-making).

In relation to the convention-novelty principle, if there is convention (e.g., the conventional wisdom about law for social order), there is novelty (e.g., the alternative novel challenge to the conventional wisdom about law for social order by Bourdieu, in that it can be a field of symbolic violence).

In relation to the evolution-transformation principle, if there is evolution (e.g., the natural evolution of humans to live together in groups sometimes in peace and some other times in conflict, in the state of nature), there is transformation (e.g., the technical transformation of human living together by way of the invention of legal-rationalism as a form of domination and authority).

In relation to the symmetry-asymmetry principle, if there is symmetry (e.g., the co-existence of different forms of authority in history), there is asymmetry (e.g., the more relevance of charismatic authority in familial and religious contexts, but the more importance of legal-rational authority in modern law, bureaucracy, and the state in a broad sense).

In relation to the softness-hardness principle, if there is softness (e.g., the charm of a charismatic leader towards his followers), there is hardness (e.g., the punishment of those who violate charismatic domination).

In relation to the regression-progression principle, if there is regression (e.g., the "polar night of icy darkness" in the bureaucratisation of the modern world), there is progression (e.g, the progress made in improviing organizaitonal efficiency).

And in relation to the same-difference principle, if there is similarity in outcome (e.g.., the use of law, be it traditional or legal-rational, for instance, to provide social order, in accordance to Weber), there is difference (e.g.., the appeal to tradition in traditional domination, but the use of legal-rationality in legal-rational domination).

Contingency and Culture

The last perspective to be considered here in regard to the issue of necessity in the context of law has to do with culture—not just the mind, nature, and society (as shown in the previous three sections).

Two illustrative case studies are in order here, namely, (3.5.1) contract law, and the tradition of promise, and (3.5.2) administrative law, and the comparative analysis of traditions—to be addressed in what follows, respectively.

Contract Law, and the Tradition of Promise

The word "contract" in contract law refers to "a binding legal agreement that is enforceable in a court of law. That is to say, a contract is an exchange of promises for the breach of which the law will provide a remedy." (WK 2009aaaa; A. Sullivan 2003)

Contract law then "is based on the principle expressed in the Latin phrase *pacta sunt servanda* (usually translated 'pacts must be kept,' but more literally 'agreements are to be kept')." (WK 2009aaaa; H. Wehberg 1959)

With this definition in mind, contract law can be analyzed in relation to its different aspects like (a) the three categories of obligation, (b) the five elements of a contract, (c) the five conditions for challenging a contract, (d) the three special circumstance concerning a contract, and (e) the theoretical debate on the basis of contract law—to be analyzed hereafter, in that order (and summarized in *Table 3.4*).

The Three Categories of Obligation

In contract theory, contract is part of the law of obligations, which can be classified in terms of three main categories, namely, (a1) promissory obligation, (a2) tort obligation, and (a3) restitutionary obligation.

(a1) In relation to promissory obligation—when a promise is made, a breach of the promise will oblige the promiser, under the law, to "provide a remedy" to the promisee. (WK 2009aaaa)

Thus, "contractual liability" in a breach of promise means the failure "to make things better (by not rendering the expected performance)." (WK 2009aaaa)

(a2) In relation to tort obligation—the tort liability here differs from contractual liability, in that "obligations in tort…are based on the wrongful infliction of harm to certain protected interests, primarily imposed by the law, and typically owed to a wider class of persons." (WK 2009aaaa)

In other words, while "contractual liability…is generally for failing to make things better (by not rendering the expected performance), liability in tort is generally for action (as opposed to omission) making things worse." (WK 2009aaaa)

Tort obligations are thus covered by tort law (as already discussed in *Sec. 3.2.2*), not contract law.

(a3) And in relation to restitutionary obligations—the restitutionary liability here differs from both tort liability and contractual liability, in that it is "based on the unjust enrichment of the defendant at the plaintiff's expense," which means that the defendant had unjustly taken or retained "the benefit of the plaintiff's money or work." (WK 2009aaaa) In cases like this, "a party unjustly enriched…may be required to provide restitution for unjust enrichment." (WK 2009aaaa)

Restitution can fall under the jurisdiction of criminal law, contract law, or else.

With these three categories of obligation in mind—promise in contract law is therefore a form of obligations and can be classified as "part of a general law of obligations," which include promise, tort, and restitution.

The Five Elements of a Contract

This distinction among promise, tort, and restitution aside—the formation of a contract can include five possible major elements to be considered in a court of contract law, namely, (b1) offer and acceptance, (b2) consideration and estoppel, (b3) intention to be legally bound, (b4) third parties, and (b5) formalities and writing—to be summarized hereafter, respectively.

(b1) Offer and Acceptance

The first element of a contract is about "offer and acceptance," in that "one party makes an offer for an arrangement that another accepts. This can be called a 'concurrence of wills' or 'ad idem' (meeting of the minds) of two or more parties." (WK 2009aaaa)

There are two clarifications here, however.

Firstly, "[t]here must be evidence that the parties had each from an objective perspective engaged in conduct manifesting their assent, and a contract will be formed when the parties have met such a requirement." (WK 2009aaaa)

However, "[a]n objective perspective means that it is only necessary that somebody gives the impression of offering or accepting contractual terms in the eyes of a reasonable person, not that they actually did want to form a contract." (WK 2009aaaa)

And secondly, "[o]ffer and acceptance does not always need to be expressed orally or in writing. An implied contract is one in which some of the terms are not expressed in words." (WK 2009aaaa)

An implied contract so understood can mean "in fact" or "in law." In other words, "a contract which is implied in fact is one in which the circumstances imply that parties have reached an agreement even though they have not done so expressly." (WK 2009aaaa)

By contrast, "a contract which is implied in law is also called a quasi-contract, because it is not in fact a contract; rather, it is a means for the courts to remedy situations in which one party would be unjustly enriched were he or she not required to compensate the other." (WK 2009aaaa)

However, even with these two clarifications in mind—the concept of offer and acceptance "is somewhat contested. The obvious objection is that a court cannot read minds and the existence or otherwise of agreement is judged objectively, with only limited room for questioning subjective intention....In the U.S., the general rule is that in 'case of doubt, an offer is interpreted as inviting the offeree to accept either by promising to perform what the offer requests or by rendering the performance, as the offeree chooses.'" (WK 2009aaaa)

(b2) Consideration and Estoppel

The second element of a contract is about "consideration" (also known as "the price of a promise"), in that "both parties to a contract must bring something to the bargain" and "that both parties must confer some benefit or detriment." (WK 2009aaaa)

In general, there are three rules governing consideration, as shown below: (WK 2009aaaa)

- "Consideration must be real, but need not be adequate."
  "For instance,...contracts in which the consideration of one party greatly exceeds that of another may nevertheless be held invalid for lack of real consideration....Such contracts may also be held invalid for other reasons such as fraud, duress, or being contrary to public policy."
- "Consideration must not be from the past."
  "For instance, in Eastwood v. Kenyon, the guardian of a young girl obtained a loan to educate the girl and to improve her marriage prospects. After her marriage,...the guardian could not enforce the

promise because taking out the loan to raise and educate the girl was past consideration—it was completed before the husband promised to repay it."

- "Consideration must move from the promisee."
 "For instance, it is good consideration for person A to pay person C in return for services rendered by person B. If there are joint promisees, then consideration need only to move from one of the promisees."

But the requirement of this second element in the formation of a contract is controversial, since its origins can be traced back to the older days in the Middle Ages, together with the old-fashioned idea of "free will" in the 18th century. (WK 2009aaaa)

In fact, in civil law systems, "consideration" so understood is no longer needed; instead, "an exchange of promises, or a concurrence of wills alone, rather than an exchange in valuable rights is the correct basis." (WK 2009aaaa)

And even in common law systems, "the concept of *culpa in contrahendo*, a form of 'estoppel', is increasingly used to create obligations during pre-contractual negotiations. Estoppel is an equitable doctrine that provides for the creation of legal obligations if a party has given another an assurance and the other has relied on the assurance to his detriment." (WK 2009aaaa)

(b3) Intention to be Legally Bound

The third element of a contract is about "intention to be legally bound." (WK 2009aaaa)

This sounds obvious, but under contract law, it is not necessarily so, because intention can be enforceable in some others but not in others. In other words, intention may not be serious enough in certain circumsances.

For example, a non-enforceable case can be found in "Balfour v. Balfour," where, "using contract-like terms, Mr. Balfour had agreed to give his wife £30 a month as maintenance while he was living in Ceylon (Sri Lanka). Once he left, they separated and Mr. Balfour stopped payments. Mrs. Balfour brought an action to enforce the payments. At the Court of Appeal, the Court held that there was no enforceable agreement as there was not enough evidence to suggest that they were intending to be legally bound by the promise." (WK 2009aaaa)

On the other hand, an enforceable case can be found in "Merritt v. Merritt," where "the court distinguished the case from Balfour v. Balfour because Mr. and Mrs. Merritt, although married again, were estranged at the time the agreement was made. Therefore any agreement between them was made with the intention to create legal relations." (WK 2009aaaa)

(b4) Third Parties

The fourth element of a contract is about "third parties," subject to the "doctrine of privity of contract," which suggests that "only those involved in striking a bargain would have standing to enforce it" and therefore third parties are generally not part of the contract. (WK 2009aaaa)

However, "in recent years the rule of privity has eroded somewhat and third party beneficiaries have been allowed to recover damages for breaches of contracts they were not party to." (WK 2009aaaa)

For instance, "[i]n cases where facts involve third party beneficiaries or debtors to the original contracting party," they "have been allowed to be considered parties for purposes of enforcement of the contract....The recent tests applied by courts have been the test of benefit and the duty owed test .The duty owed test looks to see if the third party was agreeing to pay a debt for the original party and whereas the benefit test looks to see if circumstances indicate that the promisee intends to give the beneficiary the benefit of the promised performance." (WK 2009aaaa)

(b5) Formalities and Writing

And the fifth element of a contract is about "formalities and writing," in two important ways.

Firstly, an oral contract can be as valid as a written one, as "any contract that uses words, spoken or written, is a verbal contract." (WK 2009aaaa)

And secondly, a contract can also be "non-verbal, non-oral," such that it is "implied by the acts of the parties" and thus "can be either implied in fact or implied in law." (WK 2009aaaa)

However, this fifth element of a contract is also subject to disagreement. Here are two illustrations of disagreement.

The first illustration of disagreement is that an oral contract may be unenforceable in cases "involving large amounts of money or real estate. For example, in the U.S., generally speaking, a contract is unenforceable if it violates...statutes which require certain contracts to be in writing. An example...is an oral contract for the sale of a motorcycle for US$5,000 in a jurisdiction which requires a contract for the sale of goods over US $500 to be in writing to be enforceable." (WK 2009aaaa)

The second illustration of disagreement is that an oral contract may be abused because of "false allegations"; for instance, "the point of the Statute of Frauds is to prevent false allegations of the existence of contracts that were never made, by requiring formal (i.e. written) evidence of the contract." (WK 2009aaaa)

Even then, not every country accepts the same requirement of certain formalities and writing of a contract. For instance, "in Australia and many, if not all, jurisdictions which have adopted the common law of England, for contracts subject to legislation equivalent to the Statute of Frauds, there is no requirement for the entire contract to be in writing." (WK 2009aaaa) This is true, even though, "for property transactions there must be a note or memorandum evidencing the contract, which may come into existence after the contract has been formed." (WK 2009aaaa)

The Five Conditions for Challenging a Contract

The five possible elements of a contract only tell us the possible requirements which are needed for the formation of a contract.

However, other conditions are also needed, so as to prevent a contract from being "voidable" (as in "fraud in inducement"), or even "void" (as in "fraud in the factum").

There are five possible conditions to be considered hereafter, namely, (c1) misrepresentation, (c2) mistake, (c3) duress and undue influence, (c4) incapacity, and (c5) illegality.

(c1) Misrepresentation

The first condition for challenging a contract is about "misrepresentation," which refers to "a false statement of fact made by one party to another party and has the effect of inducing that party into the contract." (WK 2009aaaa)

There are two distinctions to be made here.

Firstly, misrepresentation can be either "fraud in the factum" or "fraud in inducement." (WK 2009aaaa)

On the one hand, "[f]raud in the factum focuses on whether the party in question knew they were creating a contract. If the party did not know that they were entering into a contract, there is no meeting of the minds, and the contract is void." (WK 2009aaaa)

On the other hand, "[f]raud in inducement focuses on misrepresentation attempting to get the party to enter into the contract. Misrepresentation of a material fact (if the party knew the truth, that party would not have entered into the contract) makes a contract voidable." (WK 2009aaaa)

Secondly, misrepresentation can be either "by words" or "by conduct." (WK 2009aaaa)

For instance, in "Gordon v. Selico," this distinction is made, in that a misrepresentation can be "either by words or by conduct, although not everything said or done is capable of constituting a misrepresentation. Generally, statements of opinion or intention are not statements of fact in the context of misrepresentation. If one party claims specialist knowledge on the topic discussed, then it is more likely for the courts to hold a statement of opinion by that party as a statement of fact." (WK 2009aaaa)

In any event, a consequence of "misrepresentation allows for a remedy of rescission and sometimes damages depending on the type of misrepresentation." (WK 20009aaaa)

(c2) Mistake

The second condition for challenging a contract is about "mistake," which means "an incorrect understanding by one or more parties to a contract and may be used as grounds to invalidate the agreement." (WK 2009aaaa)

In the common law tradition, there are three types of mistake in contract, namely, (i) unilateral mistake, (ii) mutual mistake, and (iii) common mistake. (WK 2009aaaa)

(i) In a "unilateral mistake"—only one party makes a mistake "as to the terms or subject-matter. The courts will uphold such a contract unless it was determined that the non-mistaken party was aware of the mistake and tried to take advantage of the mistake. It is also possible for a contract to be void if there was a mistake in the identity of the contracting party. An example is in Lewis v. Avery where Lord Denning MR held that the contract can only be avoided if the plaintiff can show that, at the time of agreement, the plaintiff believed the other party's identity was of vital importance." (WK 2009aaaa)

(ii) In a "mutual mistake"—both both parties make a mistake "as to the terms" of the contract, but in a different way; for instance, "[e]ach believes they are contracting to something different. The court usually tries to uphold such a mistake if a reasonable interpretation of the terms can be found. However, a contract based on a mutual mistake in judgement does not cause the contract to be voidable by the party that is adversely affected." (WK 2009aaaa)

(iii) And in a "common mistake"—both parties make the same mistake about "the facts. This is demonstrated in the case of Bell v. Lever Brothers Ltd., which established that common mistake can only void a contract if the mistake of the subject-matter was sufficiently fundamental to render its identity different from what was contracted, making the performance of the contract impossible." (WK 2009aaaa) (c3) Duress and Undue Influence

The third condition for challenging a contract is about (i) "duress" and (ii) "undue influence." (WK 2009aaa)

(i) In "duress"—the situation here refers to a "threat of harm made to compel a person to do something against his or her will or judgment; esp., a wrongful threat made by one person to compel a manifestation of seeming assent by another person to a transaction without real volition."

For instance, the case of "Barton v. Armstrong" is about duress, because "Armstrong threatened to kill Barton if he did not sign a contract, so the court set the contract aside." (WK 2009aaaa)

Therefore, "[an] innocent party wishing to set aside a contract for duress to the person need only to prove that the threat was made and that it was a reason for entry into the contract; the burden of proof then shifts to the other party to prove that the threat had no effect in causing the party to enter into the contract. There can also be duress to goods and sometimes, the concept of 'economic duress' is used to vitiate contracts." (WK 2009aaaa)

(ii) In "undue influence"—the situation here refers to "an equitable doctrine that involves one person taking advantage of a position of power over another person. The law presumes that in certain classes of special relationship, such as between parent and child, or solicitor and client, there will be a special risk of one party unduly influencing their conduct and motives for contracting. As an equitable doctrine, the court has the discretion to vitiate such a contract. When no special relationship exists, the general rule is whether there was a relationship of such trust and confidence that it should give rise to such a presumption." (WK 2009aaaa)

(c4) Incapacity

The fourth condition for challenging a contract is about "incapacity," in that " the capacity of either natural or artificial persons to either enforce contracts, or have contracts enforced against them, is restricted." (WK 2009aaaa)

Three common examples of incapacity are, namely, (i) "very small children may not be held to bargains they have made, on the assumption that they lack the maturity to understand what they are doing," (ii) "errant employees or directors may be prevented from contracting for their company, because they have acted ultra vires (beyond their power)," and (iii) "people who are mentally incapacitated, either by disability or drunkenness." (WK 2009aaaa)

In cases of incapacity like this, "the law limits or bars a person from engaging in specified activities," and "any agreements or contracts to do so are either voidable or void for incapacity. The law on capacity can serve either a protective function or can be a way of restraining people who act as agents for others." (WK 2009aaaa)

(c5) Illegality

And the fifth condition for challenging a contract is about "illegality," in that a "contract is void if it is based on an illegal purpose or contrary to" the law or public policy in question. (WK 2009aaaa)

For instance, in the case of "Royal Bank of Canada v. Newell," the contract of a husband with a bank was voided, when his wife "forged her husband's signature on 40 checks, totaling over $58,000. To protect her from prosecution, her husband signed a letter of intent prepared by the bank in which he agreed to assume 'all liability and responsibility' for the forged checks. However, the agreement was unenforceable, and struck down by the courts because of its essential goal, which was to 'stifle a criminal prosecution.' Because of the contract's illegality, and as a result voided status, the bank was forced to return the payments made by the husband." (WK 2009aaaa)

There are other (comparable) cases, which "include contracts agreeing to work for less than minimum wage and forfeiting the right to workman's compensation in cases where workman's compensation is due." (WK 2009aaaa)

However, there are also borderline cases; for illustration, "[i]n the U.S., one unusual type of unenforceable contract is a personal employment contract to work as a spy or secret agent. This is because the very secrecy of the contract is a condition of the contract (in order to maintain plausible deniability). If the spy subsequently sues the government on the contract over issues like salary or benefits, then the spy has breached the contract by revealing its existence. It is thus unenforceable on that ground, as well as the public policy of maintaining national security (since a disgruntled agent might try to reveal all the government's secrets during his/her lawsuit)." (WK 2009aaaa)

Three Special Circumstances concerning a Contract

However, these five possible conditions for challenging a contract do not cover some special circumstances concernng a contract, and three good examples include (d1) uncertainty, (d2) incompleteness, and (d3) severance—to be summarized below.

Under the law, "an agreement to agree does not constitute a contract," because there can be special circumstances when the agreement contains clauses which are "uncertain" and "incomplete," especially when the parties in question cannot "agree on key issues, which may include such things as price or safety," and other contentious issues. (WK 2009aaaa)

However, in special circumstances like this, "a court will attempt to give effect to commercial contracts where possible, by construing a reasonable construction of the contract." (WK 2009aaaa)

For instance, "[c]ourts may…look to external standards, which are either mentioned explicitly in the contract or implied by common practice in a certain field. In addition, the court may also imply a term; if price is excluded, the court may imply a reasonable price, with the exception of land, and second-hand goods, which are unique." (WK 2009aaaa)

And even in the worst case scenarios, when "all options in resolving its true meaning [of an uncertain and incomplete agreement] have failed, it may be possible to sever and void just those affected clauses if the contract includes a severability clause. The test of whether a clause is severable is an objective test—whether a reasonable person would see the contract standing even without the clauses." (WK 2009aaaa)

The Theoretical Debate on the Basis of Contract Law

Yet, the discussion of the categories of obligation, the elements of a contract, the conditions for challenging a contract, and the special circumstances concerning a contract (in the previous four sub-sections) has left out some of the most foundational questions for contract law, and one of them is, Why are contracts to be enforced at all?

Precisely here, there is no universal agreement among different scholars of contract theory. Consider, for illustration, the following four examples to show the conflicting theoretical claims in the debate.

Firstly, there is the economic theory of contract, in that people are motivated to perform what they promise, because of "the economic benefits of enforcing bargains." (WK 2009aaaa)

Secondly, there is the theory of promissory obligation, in that, as argued by Charles Fried (1981) in *Contract as Promise*, "the purpose of contract law is to enforce promises." (WK 2009aaaa) As already addressed in *Sec. 3.2.1*—John Searle (1964 & 1995) also made a comparable point, when he claimed that "the act of making a promise places one under an obligation by definition, and that such an obligation amounts to an 'ought.'" (WK 2009kkk)

Thirdly, there is the "efficient breach" theory of contract, which focuses more on "questions of transaction cost" and efficiency improvement and is related to the law and economics movement. (WK 2009aaaa) For instance, as already addressed in *Sec. 1.4*— Ronald Coase

(1960) claimed that "the law ought to…be guided by the most efficient solution," so as to minimize transaction costs. (WK 2009)

And fourthly, there are the writings of "legal realists and critical legal studies theorists," especially in relation to some "Marxist and feminist interpretations of contract." (WK 2009aaaa) For instance, two major claims of critical legal theorists are that, firstly, "at the end of the day, all 'law is politics'" and that, secondly, "far more often than is usually suspected the law tends to serve the interests of the wealthy and the powerful by protecting them against the demands of the poor and the subaltern (women, ethnic minorities, the working class, indigenous peoples, the disabled, homosexuals etc.) for greater justice." (WK 2009bbbb) A Marxist critical interpretation of contract law, in this sense, is to point out the phenomenon of class struggle and domination embedded in the legal institution for the class exploitation of the dominated one.

So, which of these theories should one choose to defend or criticize contract law?

A Caveat againt Ideological Contamination

Interesting as each of these theories is, they are not necessarily compatible, as they look at the world with different vantage points of interpretation and value preference.

The introduction to them here is to not favor any one of them against the others; the point here is to learn from them all, in relation to their conflicting views, which also reveal the nature of contingency in the business of interpreting contract law, varying from case to case and from tradition to tradition.

In addition, these conflicting views, together with the analysis of the nature of contract (earlier in the previous four sub-sections), reveal something more fundamental in relation to some ontological principles in existential dialectics, and good examples include the absoluteness-relativeness principle, the predictability-unpredictability principle, the explicability-inexplicability principle, the preciseness-vagueness principle, the simpleness-complicatedness principle, the openness-hiddenness principle, the denseness-emptiness principle, the expansion-contraction principle, the convention-novelty principle, the evolution-transformation principle, the symmetry-asymmetry principle, the softness-hardness principle, the regression-progression principle, and the same-difference principle.

For instance, in relation to the absoluteness-relativeness principle, if there is absoluteness (e.g., the absolute vantage point of a party to misrepresent a fact in a contract to another party to take advantage of him), there is also relativeness (e.g., what is beneficiary for one party to misrepresent a fact in a contract for his advantage is not so for the other party who is misled in accepting the contract at his own disadvantage).

In relation to the predictability-unpredictability principle, if there is predictability (e.g., the predictable tendency of a contract to have the element of "intention to be legally bound"), there is unpredictability (e.g., the more difficult task to preduct which particular cases of contract are enforceable and which ones are not, as courts over time can interprete "intention" in different ways, like the non-enforceable case of "Balfour v. Balfour" and the enforceable one of "Merritt v. Merritt").

In relation to the explicability-inexplicability principle, if there is explicability (e.g., the explanation, in accordance to the economic theory of contract, of a contract to be enforced, on the basis of "economic benefits"), there is inexplicability (e.g., the lack of sufficient explanation, within the economic theory of contract, of why this appeal to "economic benefits" is necessarily justified as "fair," especially for the critics like the Marxists).

In relation to the preciseness-vagueness principle, if there is preciseness (e.g., the precise identification of the five elements of a contract), there is vagueness (e.g.., the lack of clear formulation of the exact meanings in regard to the five elements of a contract, such that different courts offer different interpretations about them over time).

In relation to the simpleness-complicatedness principle, if there is simpleness (e.g., the simple analysis of the formation of a contract in terms of five elements), there is complicatedness (e.g., the more complicated analysis of the five elements of a contract by making all kinds of distinctions and qualifcations, like "explicit" vs. "implied," "in fact" vs. "in law," "oral" vs. "written," "verbal" vs. "non-verbal," and "enforceable intention" vs. "non-enforceable intention," and the like).

In relation to the openness-hiddenness principle, if there is openness (e.g., the open exploration of the foundation for contract law in terms of minimizing transaction costs, as in the efficiency theory of contract by Coase), there is also hiddenness (e.g., the hidden bias of the efficiency theory of contract in downplaying other important factors like exploitation and domination as pointed out by the critics like the Marxists and the feminists).

In relation to the denseness-emptiness principle, if there is densenss (e.g., the relatively denser concentration of market-oriented concerns in contract law based on mainstream economic theories), there is emptiness (e.g., the relatively less dense, or more empty, concentration, in contract law based on mainstream economic theories, of alternative concerns based on morality, politics, or else as pointed out by the critics).

In relation to the expansion-contraction principle, if there is expansion (e.g,. the relatively more developed mechanisms in contract law based on mainstream economic theories to solve issues of efficiency), there is contraction (e.g., the relatively less developed mechanisms in contract law based on mainstream economic theories to handle the more anti-establishment issues like exploitation, domination, and the like).

In relation to the convention-novelty principle, if there is convention (e.g., the conventional wisdom about "third parties," subject to the "doctrine of privity of contract"), there is novelty (e.g., the alternative novel challenge to "the doctrine of privity" by more recent court decisions "where facts involve third party beneficiaries or debtors to the original contracting party" are introduced and third parties "have been allowed to be considered parties for purposes of enforcement of the contract").

In relation to the evolution-transformation principle, if there is evolution (e.g., the natural evolution of humans making agreements in the state of nature), there is transformation (e.g, the technical transformation of human agreements by way of the invention of contract law to formally enforce promissory obligations).

In relation to the symmetry-asymmetry principle, if there is symmetry (e.g., the co-existence of different views on the requirement of "consideration" in the formation of a contract, be they in the common law tradition or in the civil law tradition), there is asymmetry (e.g., the more dispensability of the requirement of "consideration" in the civil law tradition, but the requirement of "consideration" in the common law tradition in a different way, that is, through the use of "the concept of *culpa in contrahendo*, a form of 'estoppel'...to create obligations during pre-contractual negotiations").

In relation to the softness-hardness principle, if there is softness (e.g., the provision of remedy in contract law), there is hardness (e.g., the imposition of restitution in contract law).

In relation to the regression-progression principle, if there is regressioin (e.g., the abuse of an oral contract by "false allegations of the existence of contracts"), there is progression (e.g., the progress made to enforce contracts, be they oral or written). (WK 2009aaaa)

And in relation to the same-difference prnciple, if there is similarity in outcome (e.g., the provision of explanation in understanding the foundation for contract law, by different theories of contract), there is difference in outcome (e.g., the understanding of contract law on the basis of promissory obligation in the theory proposed by Charles Fried, but the understanding of contract law on the basis of class exploitation and domination in the Marxist theory of contract).

Administrative Law from Different Traditions

Another way to study the issue of contingency in the context of law from the perspective of culture is the comparative analysis of administrative law in different traditions.

The term "administrative law" refers to "the body of law that governs the activities of administrative agencies of government....Administrative law is considered a branch of public law." (WK 2009cccc)

As part of public law, "administrative law expanded greatly during the twentieth century, as legislative bodies worldwide created more government agencies to regulate the increasingly complex social, economic and political spheres of human interaction." (WK 2009cccc)

A good way to understand the main characteristics of administrative law is to address (a) administrative decisions, (b) administrative powers, and (c) administrative principles—to be summarized hereafter (and also in *Table 3.5*).

Administrative Decisions

Administrative law concerns "with the decision-making of administrative units of government (e.g., tribunals, boards or commissions) that are part of a national regulatory scheme in such areas as police law, international trade, manufacturing, the environment, taxation, broadcasting, immigration and transport." (WK 2009cccc)

However, the particular decisions that admnistrative law in a given culture deals more with vary from one legal system to another.

In the United States, for instance, administrative law tends to have more to say, relatively speaking, about issues on taxation and agriculture. In fact, in the U.S., "[t]axation decisions are the decisions based on administrative law that are most often contested in courts," and "the agricultural sector is one of the most heavily regulated sectors in the U.S. economy, as it is regulated in various ways at the international, federal, state, and local levels." (WK 2009cccc)

It is no wonder that, for instance, "administrative law is a significant component of the discipline of Agricultural Law" in the U.S., and "the United States Department of Agriculture and its myriad agencies such as the Agricultural Marketing Service are the primary sources of regulatory activity....An extensive treatment of the administrative laws and regulations pertaining to the agricultural sector is provided by the The

National Agricultural Law Center in its Administrative Law Reading Room." (WK 2009cccc)

By contrast, in the European legal tradition, things are a bit different. For instance, in the European Union, the most often contested decisions in courts concerning administrative law have to do with such issues as "dispensation of monetary benefits," "environmental licenses," "building inspection," "taxation," "child custody," "involuntary commitment," "immigration decisions," and "summary public payments (other than fines imposed by general courts)." (WK 2009dddd)

Therefore, administrative law in the European Union has a different focus which differs from the one in the United States.

Administrative Powers

This contrastive focus of administrative law aside—administrative law also specifies the administrative powers of the administrative agencies of government.

In the United States, these powers are granted on the basis of the "statutes enacted by the Congress that exist outside of the federal executive departments but are still part of the executive branch. Congress has also created some special judicial bodies known as Article I tribunals to handle some areas of administrative law." (WK 2009cccc) These statutes must be consistent with the U.S. Constitution, of course. (WK 2009eeee)

For instance, in the United States, the three most important administrative powers allowed under administrative law are (b1) enforcement, (b2) adjudication, and (b3) rulemaking (or legislation).

(b1) Enforcement

The first power granted to administrative agencies is to "enforce" or "'execute' administrative goals (through agency enforcement personnel)." (WK 2009cccc)

In order to prevent any abuse of power, because "the United States Constitution sets no limits on this tripartite authority of administrative agencies, Congress enacted the APA to establish fair administrative law procedures to comply with the constitutional requirements of due process." (WK 2009cccc)

(b2) Adjudication

The second power granted to administrative agencies has to do with adjudication.

The nature of "adjudication" differs from that of "rulemaking" (or "legislating" (as will be discussed in the next section), because, by definition under administrative law, "adjudication" refers to "an agency process for the formulation of an order," and the word "order" means "the whole or part of a final disposition…of an agency in a matter other than rule making but including licensing." (WK 2009eeee)

According to the Londoner/Bimetallic definition, adjudication tends to have the following three characteristics: (WK 2009eeee)

- "Involving a small number of people"
- "Individuals involved are specially affected by the act"
- "Decision based on the facts of an individual case, rather than policy concerns"

For instance, in the case of "Londoner v. City and County of Denver," there was an adjudication "involving a tax levied on residents of a particular street without affording them the opportunity to have their objections heard in person." (WK 2009eeee)

But in the case of "Bi-Metallic Investment Co. v. State Board of Equalization," there was the rulemaking "involving a tax levied on the entire city of Denver." (WK 2009eeee)

With this distinction between adjudication and rulemaking in mind—under administrative law in the U.S., "[t]here are two ways that an individual can attain the right to a hearing in an adjudicative proceeding. First, the Due Process clause of the 5th Amendment or 14th Amendment can require that a hearing be held if the interest that is being adjudicated is sufficiently important or if, without a hearing, there is a strong chance that the petitioner will be erroneously denied that interest. A hearing can also be required if a statute somehow mandates the agency to hold formal hearings when adjudicating certain issues." (WK 2009eeee)

(b3) Rulemaking (or Legislating)

And the third power granted to administrative agencies is to "make rules" or "promulgate rules that have the effect of substantive law." (WK 2009eeee)

This power of rulemaking "stems from the agency's organic statute, and extends to all regulations necessary to carry out the purposes of the Act, rather than being limited to powers expressly granted by the statute. The power extends to substantive rules as well as procedural rules." (WK 2009eeee)

There are three types of rulemaking to remember, as shown below: (WK 2009eeee)

- "Formal Rulemaking"
  This "is rulemaking for which the organic statute requires that rules be 'made on the record after agency opportunity for hearing,' and for which the APA prescribes particular procedures; the phrase is required for formal rulemaking; simply requiring that rules be made 'after a hearing' does not trigger the requirements of formal rulemaking."
- "Informal Rulemaking"
  This "is rulemaking for which no procedural requirements are prescribed in the organic statute, and for which the APA requires notice and comment."
- "Hybrid Rulemaking"
  This "is rulemaking for which particular procedural requirements beyond notice and comment [are needed], but not rising to the level of formal rulemaking."

However, rulemaking is not unlimited, as there are contingent constraints on it. Consider the following examples.

Firstly, rulemaking is subject to different allowance in different states. For instance, "many states, such as Kentucky, have been less willing to allow their agencies to promulgate rules with the effect of substantive law." (WK 2009eeee)

Secondly, "agencies may not promulgate retroactive rules unless expressly granted such power by the organic statute," as shown in the case of "Bowen v. Georgetown University Hospital, 488 U.S. 204 (1988)." (WK 2009eeee)

Thirdly, "[t]he choice of whether to promulgate rules or proceed with ad hoc adjudicative decisions rests in the informed discretion of agencies," as shown in the case of "SEC v. Chenery Corp., 332 U.S. 194 (1947)." (WK 2009eeee)

Fourthly, "the rules themselves are not arbitrary or capricious," as shown in the case of "Heckler v. Campbell, 461 U.S. 458 (1983)." (WK 2009eeee)

And fifthly, "[a]gencies must abide by their own rules and regulations," as shown in the case of "Accardi v. Shaughnessy, 347 U.S. 260 (1954)." (WK 2009eeee)

Administrative Principles

These contingent constraints concerning "arbitariness" or "consistentcy" then bring us to the fundamental issue concerning the administrative principles governing administrative law.

In general, "administrative decision-making bodies are often controlled by larger governmental units," and "their decisions could be reviewed by a court of general jurisdiction under some principle of judicial review." (WK 2009eeee)

To start, "judicial review" should not be confused with an "appeal." In a judicial review, "the Court will only look at the method in which the decision was arrived at"; but in an appeal, "the correctness of the decision itself will be under question. This difference is vital in appreciating administrative law in common law countries." (WK 2009eeee)

Yet, judicial review does not operate in a vacuum but is based on some admiinistrative principles, and good examples for illustration include (c1) due process and (c2) fairness (against ultra vires).

(c1) Due Process

In the United States, "the terms *law of the land* and *due process* were used somewhat interchangeably," and due process is guaranteed by two amendments to the U.S. Constitution, namely, "the Fifth Amendment" (where "due process is applicable only to actions of the federal government") and "the Fourteenth Amendment" (where due process is "expressly applied to the states"). (WK 2009ffff)

There are two distinctions to be made here, namely, (i) enumerated (explicit) due process right vs. unenumerated (implicit) due process right and (ii) procedural due process vs. substantive due process.

(i) In relation to "enumerated due process right" vs. "unenumerated due process right"—the first part, that is, 'enumerated due process right," refers to specified constraint under the U.S. Constitution against "not only…the executive and judicial branches, but additionally…the legislative branch"; therefore, "[i]n case a person is deprived of liberty by a process that conflicts with some provision of the Constitution, then the Due Process Clause normally prescribes the remedy: restoration of that person's liberty." (WK 2009ffff)

By contrast, the second part, that is, "unenumerated due process right," refers to "unwritten requirements from the Due Process Clause, regarding both procedure as well as substance" that the courts may extract by different interpretations. This second part of due process is controversial, for two reasons, namely, that "[the distinction between substance and procedure is difficult in both theory and practice to establish," and that "the substantive component of due process has proven to be even more controversial than the procedural component, because it gives the Court considerable power to strike down state and federal statutes that criminalize various activities." (WK 2009ffff)

This then leads us to the second distinction, that is, between procedural due process and substantive due process (as explained below).

(ii) In relation to "procedural due process" vs. "substantive due process"—the first part, that is, "procedural due process," refers to "the concept of 'fundamental fairness'" at the basic level." (WK 2009ffff)

This "fundamental fairness" requires the need to follow legal procedures, so that "it includes an individual's right to be adequately notified of charges or proceedings, the opportunity to be heard at these proceedings," and the requirement "that the person or panel making the final decision over the proceedings be impartial in regards to the matter before them." (WK 2009ffff)

In the United States, this fundamental fairness for procedural due process right is "generally governed by explicit guarantees of procedural rights under the Bill of Rights. Most of these rights have been incorporated under the Fourteenth Amendment to the States….In criminal cases, many of these due process protections overlap with procedural protections provided by the Eighth Amendment to the United States Constitution, which guarantees reliable procedures that protect innocent people from being executed, which would be tantamount to cruel and unusual punishment." (WK 2009ffff)

By contrast, the second part, that is, "substantive due process," refers to "liberty-based due process challenges which seek certain outcomes instead of merely contesting procedures and their effects; in such cases, the Supreme Court recognizes a constitutionally-based 'liberty' which then renders laws seeking to limit said 'liberty' either unenforceable or limited in scope." (WK 2009ffff; G. White 2000)

For the critics, however, these decisions concerning "liberty" and "those fundamental rights that are 'implicit in the concept of ordered liberty'" are controversial, because "just what those rights are is not always clear, nor is the Supreme Court's authority to enforce such unenumerated rights clear." (WK 2009ffff; B. Hawkins 2006)

For instance, "critics of substantive due process claim that the doctrine began, at the federal level, with the infamous 1857 slavery case of Dred Scott v. Sandford. Advocates of substantive due process acknowledge that the doctrine was employed in Dred Scott, but claim that it was employed incorrectly." (WK 2009ffff)

But then, how can one make sure that substantial due process right is not employed incorrectly?

These critics are known as "originalists," and "originalism is usually linked to opposition against substantive due process rights, and the reasons for that can be found in the following explanation that was endorsed unanimously by the Supreme Court in a 1985 case: '[W]e must always bear in mind that the substantive content of the [Due Process] Clause is suggested neither by its language nor by preconstitutional history; that content is nothing more than the accumulated product of judicial interpretation of the Fifth and Fourteenth Amendments.'" (WK 2009ffff)

(c2) Fairness (against Ultra Vires)

Administrative powers can also be limited by judicial review on the basis of another principle of justice, namely, in relation to fairness against "ultra vires," which "is a Latin phrase that literally means 'beyond the powers.' Its inverse is called *intra vires*, meaning 'within the powers.' It is used as a legal term in a number of common law contexts." (WK 2009gggg)

In the context of administrative law, "ultra vires" can be used against administrative powers "in a narrow or broad sense. Narrow ultra vires applies if an administrator did not have the substantive power to make a decision or it was wrought with procedural defects. Broad ultra vires applies if there is an abuse of power (e.g., *Wednesbury* unreasonableness or bad faith) or a failure to exercise an administrative discretion (e.g., acting at the behest of another or unlawfully applying a government policy). Either doctrine may entitle a claimant to various prerogative writs, equitable remedies or statutory orders if they are satisfied." (WK 2009gggg)

In general, there are five broad categories of "ultra vires" to be used against administrative powers, as shown below: (WK 2009eeee)

- "The regulation is an unconstitutional delegation of power (under current case law, courts almost never invalidate a regulaton on this ground)."
- "The organic statute explicitly denies authority (but note that failure to grant authority in later legislative efforts is not dispositive)."
- "The regulation is not based on factual findings."
- "The regulation is not pursuant to serving the 'public convenience, interest, or necessity.'"
- "The regulation is outside the agency's statutory purpose as articulated in its organic statute."

However, these broad categories can also be subject to different interpretations by different courts over time. After all, for the critics, how could the "infamous 1857 slavery case of Dred Scott v. Sandford" be possible in the first place? And why did the courts not consider this case at the time as a case of "ultra vires" or, alternatively, a violation of due process?

Other scholars like Mark Elliott (1999) tried to modify the "ultra vires doctrine for administrative law, placing it firmly in the correct constitutional setting," so as to minimize any abuse. (WK 2009gggg)

Even then, for the critics, the most fundamental question remains unanswered, What exactly is justce in the first place, such that everyone can agree, be it about procedural due process vs. substantive due process, enumerated due process right vs. unenumerated due process right, *ultra vires* vs. *intra vires*, and the like?

The contingency of justice by itself does not make justice look any better, since its limits can be notorious, as shown by the "infamous 1857 slavery case of Dred Scott v. Sandford."

A Revealing Exercise

This larger theoretical debate on the nature of justice is precisely where different sides in the debate conflict with each other, as it has been so in the human condition since time immemorial.

Yet, this unanswered question does not render the current discusion here pointless, since much can still be learned from different sides in regard to administrative law, especially in relation to the issue of contingency and its limits in the context of law.

This current discussion can also teach us something about the ontological principles in existential dialectics, and good examples include the absoluteness-relativeness principle, the predictability-unpredictability principle, the explicability-inexplicability principle, the preciseness-vagueness principle, the simpleness-complicatedness principle, the openness-hiddenness priinciple, the openness-emptiness principle, the expansion-contraction principle, the theory-praxis principle, the conventioin-novelty principle, the evolution-transformation principle, the symmetry-asymmetry principle, the regression-progression principle, and the same-difference principle.

For instance, in relation to the absoluteness-relativeness principle, if there is absoluteness (e.g., the absolute perspective of the originalists to reject substantive due process for a stricter interpretation of the constitution), there is also relativeness (e.g., what is acceptable for the proponents of substantive due process is not so for the originalists who are against it).

In relation to the predictability-unpredictability principle, if there is predictability (e.g., the predictable tendency of admiinistrative agencies to enforce, adjudicate, or make rules), there is unpredictability (e.g., the more difficult task to predict when a particular administrative decision, though justified at the time, will not end up criticized later on as a violation of due process, or even an infamous case of ultra vires).

In relation to the explicability-inexplicability principle, if there is explicability (e.g., the explanation of the foundation for due process on the basis of some fundamental justice at the basic level), there is inexplicability (e.g, the lack of sufficient explanation, within the theory of fundamental justice, of why this justification of justice at the fundamental level, be it about procedures or rights, is really justified, as questioned by the critics).

In relation to the preciseness-vagueness principle, if there is preciseness (e.g.., the precise identification of substantive due process in relation to the idea of "constitutionally-based 'liberty'"), there is vagueness (e.g., the lack of clear formulation of what exactly this idea of "constitutionally-based 'liberty'" is, because "just what those rights are is not always clear").

In relation to the simpleness-complicatedness prnciple, if there is simpleness (e.g., the simple analysis of due process in terms of enumerated due process right vs. unenumerated due process right and procedural due process vs. substantive due process), there is complicatednes (e.g., the more complicated analysis of due process in terms of different interpretations and views about this simple distinction of due process).

In relation to the openness-hiddenness principle, if there is openenss (e.g., the open exploration of the substantive nature of due process, not just its procedural one), there is hiddenness (e.g., the hidden bias of the idea of substantive due process, in its advocation of an activist expansion of administrative and judiciary power).

In relation to the expansion-contraction principle, if there is expansion (e.g., the relatively more developed mechanism to strictly follow guidelines in administrative law based on the tradition of enumerated due process right), there is contraction (e.g., the relatively less developed mechanism to extract alternative interpretations from administrative law, if based on the tradition of enumerated due process right).

In relation to the theory-praxis principle, if there is theory (e.g., the theoretical construction of due process), there is praxis (e.g., the practical application of due process for "the 1857 slavery case of Dred Scott v. Sandford").

In relation to the convention-novelty principle, if there is convention (e.g., the conventional wisdom about due process as understood by the originalists), there is novelty (e.g., the alternative novel challenge to this conventional originalist wisdom by those for substantive due process).

In relation to the evolution-transformation principle, if there is evolution (e.g., the natural evolution of humans to follow primitive patterns of behavior in the state of nature), there is transformation (e.g., the technical transformation of human patterns of behavor by way of the invention of administrative law for due process and fairness against ultra vires).

In relation to the symmetry-asymmetry principle, if there is symmetry (e.g., the co-existence of different views about due process, be they procedural vs. substantive, enumerated vs. unenumerated, etc.), there is asymmetry (e.g., the popularity of procedural due process among the originalists, but the acceptance of substantive due process among its proponents).

In relation to the regression-progression principle, if there is regression (e.g., the 1857 infamous slavery case of "Dred Scott v. Sandford" in the name of due process), there is progression (e.g., the more awareness of the downside of legal interpretations, as even the "[a]dvocates of substantive due process acknowledge that the doctrine was employed in Dred Scott, but claim that it was employed incorrectly").

And in relation to the same-difference principle, if there is similarity in outcome (e.g., the use and misuse of legal decisions, be they with due process or without it), there is difference in outcome (e.g., the regret, later on, about the misuse of due process, in the case involving due process, but the likely absence of such later formal acknowledgement in the case without the appeal to due process).

The Temporality of Contingency

This last perspective of culture in regard to the issue of contingency in the context of law adds to the insight concerning the use and misuse of contingency—not just from the perspective of the mind, nature, and society (as shown in the earlier three sections).

This comprehensive analysis of the nature of contingency and its abuse from the four persectives of the mind, nature, society, and culture in this chapter is to illustrate the different ways in which contingency is both possible and desirable, but not to the extent that the proponents would like us to believe.

The expdiency of contingency, in the context of law, has its downside too, which constitutes its limits. Thus are contingency and its temporality, if seen from both sides of the same coin.

With the ending of this chapter in mind, what then can be concluded in regard to justice, especially in the relation to its necessity and contingency?

This is the question which is to be answered in the next chapter, that is, Chapter Four, the concluding chapter, to which we now turn.

Table 3.1. Contingency and Its Mortality

- **Contingency and the Mind**
  —Ex: analytical jurisprudence, and Hume's "is-ought" problem
  —Ex: tort law and its controversy

- **Contingency and Nature**
  —Ex: the will to power in nature, and the law

- **Contingency and Society**
  —Ex: property law, and copyright violation
  —Ex: sociological analysis, and the law

- **Contingency and Culture**
  —Ex: contract law, and the tradition of promise
  —Ex: administrative law and the comparative analysis of traditions

Notes: The examples in the categories are solely illustrative (not exhaustive), and the comparison is relative (not absolute), nor are they necessarily mutually exclusive. And some can be easily re-classified elsewhere. As generalities, they allow exceptions.
Source: A summary of Ch.3 of *FPHLAW*

Table 3.2. Different Versions of the Will to Power in Nature

- **Arthur Schopenhauer**
  —The will to live
- **Roger Joseph Boscovich**
  —The struggle among the centers of force
- **Wilhelm Roux**
  —The internal struggle for existence at the cellular level
- **Leon Dumont**
  —The pleasure in the expansion of power
- **William Rolph**
  —The insatiability and assimilation for life expansion
- **Karl Wilhelm von Nägeli**
  —The drive towards complexity
- **Friedrich Nietzsche**
  —The will to power for noble morality

Notes: The examples are solely illustrative (not exhaustive), and the comparison is relative (not absolute), nor are they necessarily mutually exclusive. And some can be easily re-classified elsewhere. As generalities, they allow exceptions.
Source: From *Sec. 3.3.1* of *FPHLAW*

Table 3.3. Main Characteristics of Property Law

- **The Classification of Property**
  —Ex: private property
  —Ex: public property

- **The Rights to Use Property**
  —Ex: "control of the use of the property"
  —Ex: "the right to any benefit from the property"
  —Ex: "a right to transfer or sell the property"
  —Ex: "a right to exclude others from the property"

- **The Theoretical Debate on the Foundation for Property Law**
  —*The Right Wing of the Ideological Spectrum*
    - Ex: the "first possession theory of property"
    - Ex: the "labor theory of property"
    - Ex: the "customs and convention" theory of property

  —*The Left Wing of the Ideological Spectrum*
    - Ex: the "libertarian socialist" theory of property
    - Ex: the "socialist" theory of property
    - Ex: the "communist" theory of property

- **Four Defenses to Copyright Violation**
  —Ex: independent creation
  —Ex: trivial use
  —Ex: sale doctrine
  —Ex: fair use

Notes: The categories and examples are solely illustrative (not exhaustive), and the comparison is relative (not absolute), nor are they necessarily mutually exclusive. And some can be easily re-classified elsewhere. As generalities, they allow exceptions.
Source: From *Sec. 3.4.1* of *FPHLAW*. See text for citations.

Table 3.4. Main Characteristics of Contract Law

- **The Categories of Obligation**
  —Ex: promissory obligation
  —Ex: tort obligation
  —Ex: restitutionary obligation

- **The Elements of a Contract**
  —Ex: offer and acceptance
  —Ex: consideration and estoppel
  —Ex: intention to be legally bound
  —Ex: third parties
  —Ex: formalities and writing

- **The Conditions for Challenging a Contract**
  —Ex: misrepresentation
  —Ex: mistake
  —Ex: duress and undue influence
  —Ex: incapacity
  —Ex: illegality

- **Special Circumstances concerning a Contract**
  —Ex: uncertainty
  —Ex: incompleteness
  —Ex: severance

- **Different Theories of Contract**
  —Ex: economic benefits
  —Ex: promissory obligation
  —Ex: transaction costs
  —Ex: exploitation and domination

Notes: The categories and examples are solely illustrative (not exhaustive), and the comparison is relative (not absolute), nor are they necessarily mutually exclusive. And some can be easily re-classified elsewhere. As generalities, they allow exceptions.
Source: From *Sec. 3.5.1* of *FPHLAW*. See text for citations.

Table 3.5. Main Characteristics of Administrative Law

- **Administrative Decisions**
  —Ex: "taxation"
  —Ex: "dispensation of monetary benefits"
  —Ex: "building inspection"
  —Ex: "environmental licenses"
  —Ex: "child custody"
  —Ex: "immigration decisions"
  —Ex: "involuntary commitment"
  —Ex: "summary public payments"

- **Administrative Powers**
  —Ex: enforcement
  —Ex: adjudication
  —Ex: rulemaking (or legislation)

- **Administrative Principles**
  —Ex: due process
  —Ex: fairness (against ultra vires)

Notes: The categories and examples are solely illustrative (not exhaustive), and the comparison is relative (not absolute), nor are they necessarily mutually exclusive. And some can be easily re-classified elsewhere. As generalities, they allow exceptions.
Source: From *Sec. 3.5.2* of *FPHLAW*. See text for citations.

• PART FOUR •

Conclusion

CHAPTER 4
CONCLUSION—THE FUTURE OF LAW

In every system of morality, which I have hitherto met with, I have always remark'd, that the author proceeds for some time in the ordinary ways of reasoning, and establishes the being of a God, or makes observations concerning human affairs; when all of a sudden I am surpriz'd to find, that instead of the usual copulations of propositions, is, and is not, I meet with no proposition that is not connected with an ought, or an ought not.

—David Hume (WK 2009kkk)

The Rethinking of Law

The analyses of necessity (in Chapter Two) and contingency (in Chapter Three) allow us to rethink the very extent of the possibility and desirability of necessity and contingency in the history of law.

This is especially so, when put in the context of the conventional wisdom that law is to conscientiously punish the "bad" doers and reward the "good" ones—such that, where there is the rule of law, peace and order are to be expected, so that "the rule of law is better than the rule of any individual" (as already introduced in *Sec. 1.1*).

Contrary to the conventional wisdom conveniently held by many in human history, the rule of law has its other side which has not yet been systematically understood, such that the rule of law is neither possible nor desirable to the extent that the defenders of the legal institution would like us to believe.

Lest any misunderstanding hastily occurs, this is not to imply that the rule of law is absolutely useless, or that the literature in jurisprudence (and other related fields like political philosohy, ethics, law and economics, and the sociology of law) should be dismissed because of their scholarly irrelevance. Of course, neither of these two extreme views is reasonable either.

Instead, this book is to provide an alternative (better) way to understand the nature of law, in relation to its necessity and contingency in the context of justice—while learning from different approaches in the literature but without favoring any one of them (nor integrating them, since they are not necessarily compatible with each other).

In the process, this book offers a new theory to transcend the existing approaches in the literature in a new direction (different from the convenience of the conventional wisdom about the rule of law).

This new theory is called *the reconstruction theory of law* and has three distinctive features to remember.

Firstly, it makes good use of all theoretical approaches in the literature on law (like the necessity argument and the contingency argument)—especially from the most comprehensive combined perspectives of the mind, nature, society, and culture.

Secondly, as it is the case for many other theories of mine in my previous books, my theory here does not heavily favor any specific theory over others in the literature, nor trying to integrate them (as they are not necessarily compatible with each other).

And thirdly, it contains eleven major theses, namely, (a) the first thesis: the absoluteness-relativeness principle, (b) the second thesis: the predictability-unpredictability principle, (c) the third thesis: the explicability-inexplicability principle, (d) the fourth thesis: the preciseness-vagueness principle, (e) the fifth thesis: the simpleness-complicatedness principle, (f) the sixth thesis: the openness-hiddenness principle, (g) the seventh thesis: the evolution-transformation principle, (h) the eighth thesis: the symmetry-asymmetry principle, (i) the nineth thesis: the regression-progression principle, (j) the tenth thesis: the same-difference principle, and (k) the eleventh thesis: the post-human reconstruction—to be summarized shortly in this chapter.

In the end, there is no justice without injustice (as first proposed in *FHC*), in accordance to existential dialectics—and it will be transcended.

This seminal project, if successful, will fundamentally change the way that we think about the nature of law, from the combined perspectives of the mind, nature, society, and culture, with enormous implications for the human future and what I originally called its "post-human" fate.

Other Relevant Principles

Lest misunderstanding hastily occurs (as this is something that I regularly did in my previous books, *almost verbatim*), it should be clarified at the outset that, if other ontological principles in existential dialectics (other than the ten as listed in the eleven theses) are not explicitly included in the listing of the theses in the Table of Contents, it is not because they are not important, but merely because they are not as equally relevant as the others in the current case study (in terms of the number of citations of each principle in the book), although different case studies will, of course, reveal different degrees of relevance of the principles.

Even then, in some cases (like this one), the difference between any two given principles, for instance, in terms of the number of citations in a book, is rather small, so the reason in those cases is more aesthetic (than otherwise), because it looks nicer to list only 10 theses for 10 principles (than 21 theses for all of the 21 principles) in the Table of Contents.

This is true, even if different studies of the same kind can yield different views about the degree of relevance for each ontological principle, depending on the specific nature of a research in question, needless to say. So, if a different author analyzes the subject matter in a different way, the relevance of the ontological principles will be different.

After all, the symmetry-asymmetry principle already implies that not all principles are equally relevant in any topic under examination, as they are not created equal for all cases under all circumstances (which would be an extreme view, of course).

In any event, the relevancy of other principles (besides the ones as already listed in the theory above) for the present study can be summarized below, in relation to the five categories of ontological principles in existential dialectics.

In the Category of Method

Firstly, in regard to the formalness-informalness principle (on the formal requirements of logical systems), if there is formalmess (e.g., the formal logical requirement of consistency in Kantian ethics, in relation to the law of non-contradiction, such that one must act in accordance to one's rational autonomy, not by external influences, in *Sec. 2.2.1*; the formal logical requirement of consistency in prosecuting those defeated losers for crimes of most serious offense to the international community, in accordance to international law, in *Sec. 2.4.1*; the formal logical requirement of consistency in moral codes, as in "the Golden Rule," which "demands that one's actions conform to one's own standard," in *Sec. 2.5.1*; and the formal logical requirement of the binary code of guilty/innocent under the law, in *Sec. 3.4.2*), there is informalness too (e.g., the informal logical occurrence of inconsistency, as in the "impractical hedonism of the id" in psychoanalysis, in *Sec. 2.2.1*; the non-formal logical inconsistency on the basis of a double standard to favor the victorious powers, in accordance to their hegemonic interests, which can change in any direction over time, in *Sec. 2.4.1*; the non-formal allowance of inconsistency in the Mosaic law, in regard to moral laxity in the context of polygamy and divorce, in *Sec. 2.5.1*; and Luhmann's more informal view about going beyond this narrow logical dichotomy of guilty/innocent under the law, in *Sec. 3.4.2*).

And secondly, in regard to the partiality-totality principle (on the relationships between whole and parts), if there is partial analysis (e.g., the partial perspective of each animal in the state of nature to struggle for its own existence in a given environment, in *Sec. 2.3.1*), there is also holistic analysis (e.g., the totalistic perspective of the emergence of new species, out of the competiton among animals for existence in the evolutionary process of a given environment over time, in *Sec. 2.3.1*).

In the Category of Structure

Firstly, in regard to the finiteness-transfiniteness principle (on the nature of numbers), if there is finiteness (e.g., the finiteness in the idea of a moral agent, with its mortality and vulnerability, in *Sec. 2.2.1*), there is also transfiniteness (e.g., the transfiniteness in the idea of God, with its ideal of the supreme good, which cannot be measured in terms of a finite quantity like "a price," in *Sec. 2.2.1*).

And secondly, in regard to the denseness-emptiness principle (on the distribution of entities in space)), on the one hand, there is denseness (e.g., the relatively denser concentration of concerns with categorical imperatives for a Kantian, in *Sec. 2.2.1*; the relatively denser concentration of males in the "killing establishment," in *Sec. 2.2.2*; the relatively denser concentration of conquests by the U.S. in the Wild West, in *Sec. 2.3.1*; the relatively denser concentration of laws which can be harsh and complicated in a non-Taoist state, like a Marxist one, in *Sec. 2.3.2*; the relatively dense concentration of cases against the defeated and weak powers in the history of international courts, in *Sec. 2.4.1*; the relatively denser concentration of the principle of the fusion of power in parlimentary forms of constitutional law like the British one, in *Sec. 2.4.2*; the relatively denser concentration of regulations of the "acts of the people of God," be they "civil, ceremonial, and moral," in a comprehensive way, in the Mosaic law, in *Sec. 2.5.1*; the relatively denser concentration of cases in the common law tradition which are slowly and precisely considered, in *Sec. 2.5.2*; the relatively denser concentration of laws as "posited by lawmakers" which are accepted by the legal positivists, in *Sec. 3.2.1*; the relatively denser concentration of concerns with transaction costs, by scholars who are in the law and economics movement, in *Sec. 3.2.2*; the relatively denser concentration of normative concerns with striving for equality, in jurisprudence based on herd morality, in *Sec. 3.3.1*; the relatively denser concentration of public property in a communist society, in *Sec. 3.4.1*; the relatively denser concentration of legal-rational organizations in the modern lifeworld, in *Sec. 3.4.2*; and the relatively denser concentration of market-oriented concerns in contract law based on mainstream economic theories, in *Sec. 3.5.1*).

On the other hand, there is also emptiness (e.g., the relatively less dense, or more empty, concentration of concerns with hypothetical imperatives for a Kantian, in *Sec. 2.2.1;* the relatively less dense, or more empty, concentration of females in the "killing establishment," in *Sec. 2.2.2*; the relatively less dense, or more empty, concentration of conquests by the U.S. in Africa, in *Sec. 2.3.1*; the relatively less dense, or more empty, concentration of laws which can be harsh and complicated in a Taoist state, in *Sec. 2.3.2*; the relatively less dense, or more empty, concentration of cases against the victorious powers in the history of internaitonal courts, in *Sec. 2.4.1*; the relatively less dense, or more empty, concentration of the principle of the fusion of power in presidential forms of constitutional law like the American one, in *Sec. 2.4.2*; the relatively less dense, or more empty, concentration in the Mosaic law of "the humanitarian and sentimental canons of the twentieth century," in *Sec. 2.5.1*; the relativley less dense, or more empty, concentration of cases in the common law tradition which are quickly and discretively considered, , in *Sec. 2.5.2*; the relatively less dense, or more empty, concentration of laws based on ethics or morality, which are accepted by the legal positivists, in *Sec. 3.2.1*; the relatively less dense, or more empty, concentration of concerns with drastic government intervention in tort law, by scholars in the law and economics movement, in *Sec. 3.2.2*; the relatively less dense, or more empty, concentration of normative concerns with striving for difference, in jurisprudence based on herd morality, in *Sec. 3.3.1*; the relatively less dense, or more empty, concentration of public property in a capitalist society, in *Sec. 3.4.1*; the relatively less dense, or more empty, concentration of traditional authority in modern organizational lifeworld, in *Sec. 3.4.2*; and the relatively less dense, or more empty, concentration, in contract law based on mainstream economic theories, of alternative concerns based on morality, politics, or else as pointed out by the critics, in *Sec. 3.5.1*).

In the Category of Process

Firstly, in regard to the change-constancy principle (on the alteration of things), if there is change (e.g., the ever recurrent manifestations of things in nature, like the change of the seasons, in *Sec. 2.3.2*; the change of different international courts over time, like the creation of ICJ in 1945 and then the rise of ICC in 2002, in *Sec. 2.4.1*; and the ever new responses by the religious believers to defend their faith and practices in response to the criticisms by the critics, in *Sec. 2.5.1*), there is constancy (e.g., the return of things in a cycle over time, like the cycle of the four seasons, in *Sec. 2.3.2*; the persistent constancy of a double standard in international courts to favor the victorious powers and to be biased against the weak and defeated ones, in *Sec. 2.4.1*; and the recurrent question-beggingness of the ever new responses by the believers, in *Sec. 2.5.1*).

Secondly, in relation to the order-chaos principle (on the pattern of things), if there is order (e.g., the existence of certain order in the state of nature, due to the laws of the jungle, in *Sec. 2.3.1*), there is chaos (e.g., anything goes in the state of nature, such that anything can happen and things are not so orderly even with the laws of the jungle, in *Sec. 2.3.1*).

Thirdly, in regard to the slowness-quickness principle (on the speed of change), if there is slowness (e.g., the relatively slow procedure of adjudication in the common law tradition, in *Sec. 2.5.2*), there is quickness too (e.g., the relatively less slow, or faster, procedure of consideration in the civil law tradition, in *Sec. 2.5.2*).

And fourthly, in relation to the expansion-contraction principle (on the growth of things), on the one hand, there is expansion (e.g., the relatively better developed ability of a Kantian to act out of duty in itself, in *Sec. 2.2.1*; the relatively more developed skill to kill and hurt among those in the "killing establishment," in *Sec. 2.2.2*; the relatively better developed disposition of the U.S. to conquer the lesser others in its history of Manifest Destiny, in *Sec. 2.3.1*; the relatively more developed capacity of an anti-authoritarian Taoist system of laws to find ways to intervene minimally into the affairs of society, in *Sec. 2.3.2*; the relatively better developed procedures of international courts to deal with cases against the weak powers, in *Sec. 2.4.1*; the relatively better developed mechanisms in parlimentary systems like the British one to allow "some members of parliaments" to "hold cabinet positions," in *Sec. 2.4.2*; the relatively better developed ability of the believers to engage in biblical hermeneutics in order to make ever new excuses, in *Sec. 2.5.1*; the relatively better developed procedures in the common law tradition to handle cases slowly, incrementally, and precisely, in *Sec. 2.5.2*; the relatively more developed aspects of a legal system based on legal positivism which are more text-based, so as "to remove any metaphysics from the science of law by providing a totally internally-defined system with an entirely sufficient set of meanings," in *Sec. 3.2.1*; the relatively more developed aspects of a legal system, which is based on utiliarianism, to promote utility maximization and the happiness of the greatest number, in *Sec. 3.3.1*; the relativley more developed ability and inclination of individuals in a capitalist society to care for their private properties, in *Sec. 3.4.1*; the relatively more developed procedures in a legal-rational organization to be precise and impersonal, in *Sec. 3.4.2*; the relatively more developed mechanisms in contract law based on mainstream economic theories to solve issues of efficiency, in *Sec. 3.5.1*; and the relatively more developed mechanism to strictly follow guidelines in administrative law based on the tradition of enumerated due process right, in *Sec. 3.5.2*).

On the other hand, there is contraction (e.g., the relatively less developed ability of a Kantian to engage in Machiavellian manipulation to serve ulterior motives, in *Sec. 2.2.1*; the relatively less developed skill to be sensitive, caring, and loving among those in the "killing establishment," in *Sec. 2.2.2*; the relatively less developed disposition of the U.S. to be non-interventionist towards the others, on average, of course, in *Sec. 2.3.1*; the relatively less developed capacity of a Taoist system of laws to be highly complicated and elaborated, in *Sec. 2.3.2*; the relatively less developed procedures of international courts to confront the victorious powers over their more horrific crimes to the international community, in *Sec. 2.4.1*; the relatively less developed mechanisms in parlimentary systems like the British one to provide a clear separation of power among the three branches of government like the American one, in *Sec. 2.4.2*; the relatively lesser developed ability of the believers to utilize the empiricist approach to knowledge as often found among scientists in *Sec. 2.5.1*; the relatively less developed procedures in the common law tradition to handles cases which require fast and revolutionary actions, in *Sec. 2.5.2*; the relatively less developed aspects of a legal system based on legal positivism which are more context-based, as in legal realists, who look for "the meaning of any given law…one might bring to the suggestions of the text," in *Sec. 3.2.1*; the relatively less developed aspects of a legal system, which is based on utiliarianism, to promote power expansion and difference, in *Sec. 3.3.1*; the relatively less developed ability and inclination of individuals in a capitalist society to care for the public properties, in *Sec. 3.4.1*; the relativley less developed procedures in legal-rational organizations to allow discretion in decision-making, in *Sec. 3.4.2*; the relatively less developed mechanisms in contract law based on mainstream economic theories to handle the more anti-establishment issues like exploitation, domination, and the like, in *Sec. 3.5.1*; and the relatively less developed mechanism to extract alternative interpretations from administrative law, if based on the tradition of enumerated due process right, in *Sec. 3.5.2*).

In the Category of Agency

Firstly, in regard to the theory-praxis principle (on the duality of knowledge), if there is theoretical construction (e.g., the Taoist theoretical interpetation of the universe in terms of the four characterstics of the Tao, in *Sec. 2.3.2*; the theoretical construction of divine law, in *Sec. 2.5.1*; the theoretical construction of the "is-ought" problem, in *Sec. 3.2.1*; the theoretical construction of the democratic idea of equality, in *Sec. 3.3.1*; the theoretical construction of Marxist communism, in *Sec. 3.4.1*; and the theoretical construction of due process, in *Sec. 3.5.2*), there is also its practical application (e.g., the practical application of the Taoist theoretical construction of the Tao for the implementation of a system of laws which are simple, humble, and moderate, in *Sec. 2.3.2*; the practical application of the divine command theory for moral conducts in everyday life, in *Sec. 2.5.1*; the practical application of the "is-ought" problem by the legal positivists to get rid of any moral or ethical influence on the law, which is to be posited by lawmakers instead, not by moralists, in *Sec. 3.2.1*; the application of the democratic idea of equality for affirmative action programs, in *Sec. 3.3.1*; the practical application of Marxist communism to build a new society in Soviet times, in *Sec. 3.4.1*; and the practical application of due process for "the 1857 slavery case of Dred Scott v. Sandford," in *Sec. 3.5.2*).

Secondly, in regard to the convention-novelty principle (on the nature of creative thinking), on the one hand, there is convention (e.g., the conventional wisdom about the utilitarian way of acting, in *Sec. 2.2.1*; the conventional wisdom about the criminal to be punished in accordance to criminal law, in *Sec. 2.2.2*; the conventional wisdom about creation in the state of nature, as in creation theory, in *Sec. 2.3.1*; the conventional wisdom about a legal system of laws which should be complicated enough to cover all cases and harsh enough to deter violations, in *Sec. 2.3.2*; the conventional wisdom in the American constitutional tradition about the virtue of the principle of the balance of power to separate the three branches of government, in *Sec. 2.4.2*; the conventional wisdom, among the believers, that divine law represents the will of God, in *Sec. 2.5.1*; the conventional wisdom of the common law tradition to be fundamentally different from other traditions like the civil law tradition, the Islamic law tradition, etc., in *Sec. 2.5.2*; the conventional wisdom about the law to be based on moral, divine, or other claims, in *Sec. 3.2.1*; the conventional wisdom about the aims of tort law in the context of appeasement, justice, etc., in *Sec. 3.2.2*; the conventional wisdom about the classical Darwinian evolutionary theory, in *Sec. 3.3.1*; the conventional wisdom about property ownership in accordance to the "customs and convention" view of property, in *Sec. 3.4.1*; the conventional wisdom about law for social order, in *Sec. 3.4.2*; the conventional wisdom about "third parties," subject to the "doctrine of privity of contract," in *Sec. 3.5.1*; and the conventional wisdom about due process as understood by the originalists, in *Sec. 3.5.2*).

On the other hand, there is novelty (e.g., the Kantian alternative novel challenge to utililiatarian consequentialism by way of his deontological ethics, in *Sec. 2.2.1*; the alternative novel challenge to this conventional wisdom as not being possible and desirable to the extent that the proponents would like us to believe, because of some fundamental biological differences for the maleness of violence, for instance, in *Sec. 2.2.2*; the alternative novel challenge to creation theory by the Darwinian evolutionary theory, in *Sec. 2.3.1*; the alternative novel challenge by the Taoists, on the basis of a system of laws which is simple and moderate or non-harsh, in *Sec. 2.3.2*; the alternative novel challenge by the parlimentary system like the British one to allow the fusion of power among the three branches of government, in *Sec. 2.4.2*; the alternative novel challenge to the conventional wisdom concernng the divine command theory by R.M. Adams for a modified divine command theory, such that one could accept that murder is wrong and commit murder anyway, should God so dictate, in *Sec. 2.5.1*; the alternative novel challenge by John Makdisi about "the Islamic Origins of the Common Law," in *Sec. 2.5.2*; the alternative novel challenge by the legal positivists to question any normative basis of the law, be it moral, divine, or else, and to replace it with a more positivist foundation as posited by lawmakers, in *Sec. 3.2.1*; the alternative novel challenge to the conventional wisdom on torts by Coase and others, by suggesting that tort law should be about the minimization of transaction costs for the efficient distribution of risk, in *Sec. 3.2.2*; the alternative novel challenge to the classical Darwinian evolutionary theory by thinkers like Roux in regard to the idea of "internal struggle" or Dumont in regard to the idea of "pleasure in the expansion of power," in *Sec. 3.3.1*; the alternative novel challenge to the conventional view of property by the Marxists in terms of a new theory of collective ownership for the interests of the proletariat, in *Sec. 3.4.1*; the alternative novel challenge to the conventional wisdom about law for social order by Bourdieu, in that it can be a field of symbolic violence, in *Sec. 3.4.2*; the alternative novel challenge to "the doctrine of privity" by more recent court decisions "where facts involve third party beneficiaries or debtors to the original contracting party" are introduced and third parties "have been allowed to be considered parties for purposes of enforcement of the contract," in *Sec. 3.5.1*; and the alternative novel challenge to this conventional originalist wisdom by those for substantive due process, in *Sec. 3.5.2*).

And thirdly, in regard to the softness-hardness principle (on the force of change), if there is softness (e.g., the approval of the respect of human dignity in Kantian ethics, in *Sec. 2.2.1*; the encouragement of "law-abiding" behaviors in society, in *Sec. 2.2.2*; the cooperation among the wolves to live together in a pack, in *Sec. 2.3.1*; the promised reward of salvation to those who obey divine law, in *Sec. 2.5.1*; the praise of individals for good behaviors according to the law, in *Sec. 3.2.1*; the charm of a charismatic leader towards his followers, in *Sec. 3.4.2*; and the provision of remedy in contract law, in *Sec. 3.5.1*), there is also hardness (e.g., the strict restraint of one's impulses in Kantian ethics, in *Sec. 2.2.1*; the punishment of criminals in society, in *Sec. 2.2.2*; the readiness of the wolves to kill and fight, whenever needed, in *Sec. 2.3.1*; the severe punishment against those who violate divine law, in *Sec. 2.5.1*; the threat of punishment of individuals for bad behaviors according to the law, in *Sec. 3.2.1*; the punishment of those who violate charismatic domination, in *Sec. 3.4.2*; and the imposition of restitution in contract law, in *Sec. 3.5.1*).

1st Thesis: The Absoluteness-Relativeness Principle

With these other principles in mind—the first thesis refers to the absoluteness-relativeness principle (on the multiplicity of things) in the category of "method" in existential dialectics, which was first proposed in *FPHK*, in that there is the multiplicity of things in reality, be they about entities, qualities (or properties), and relationships. And, if there is something absolute, there is likewise something relative.

Both absoluteness and relativeness here are also relevant to different modalities often cited in the literature on ontology, such as possibility (e.g., something "can" happen) and its opposite (e.g., impossibility), probability (e.g., something "will" happen) and its opposite (e.g., improbability), and necessity (e.g., something "should" happen) and its opposite (e.g., contingency).

For instance, on the one hand, there are absolute viewpoints (e.g., the absolute demand of categorical imperatives in Kantian ethics, in *Sec. 2.2.1*; a criminal to kill someone, in *Sec. 2.2.2*; the absolute view of Manifest Destiny towards the conquered, iin *Sec. 2.3.1*; the absolute requirement, in Taoist jursiprudence, of a system of laws which show the virtues of "simplicity," "moderation," and "humility," in *Sec. 2.3.2*; the absolute demand by the victorious powers to prosecute those for crimes of most serious offense to the international community, in accordance to international law, in *Sec. 2.4.1*; the absolute requirement in the U.S. Constitution for the balance of power among the three branches of government, in *Sec. 2.4.2*; the absolute command of God in the Mosaic law "to exterminate certain nations, and the permission given by Him to the Israelites to spoil the Egyptians," in *Sec. 2.5.1*; the insistence of the common law tradition for a slow process of adjudication, in *Sec. 2.5.2*; the claim by social Darwinists about the normativeness of the law on the basis of natural selection, in *Sec. 3.2.1*; the legal reform in New Zealand in regard to the "no-fault system of state compensation for accidents," which the country prefers, as opposed to other ones, in *Sec. 3.2.2*; the herd mentality to treat all individuals as equal, even if they are not the same, according to Nietzsche, in *Sec. 3.3.1*; the "first possession theory of property" to allow someone to claim a property by seizing it first, in *Sec. 3.4.1*; the absolute viewpoint in the older days of mechanical solidarity, when identicalness, not difference, was expected, in *Sec. 3.4.2*; the absolute vantage point of a party to misrepresent a fact in a contract to another party to take advantage of him, in *Sec. 3.5.1*; and the absolute perspective of the originalists to reject substantive due process for a stricter interpretation of the constitution, in *Sec. 3.5.2*).

On the other hand, there are likewise relative counterparts (e.g., what is good for the Kantians in regard to the strict demands of the mroal law is not so for the Freudians in regard to the impractical moralism of the superego, in *Sec. 2.2.1*; what is good for the criminal is not necessarily so for the victim, and vice-versa, in *Sec. 2.2.2*; what is good for the U.S. federal government in regard to its policy to expand westward is not so for the Native Indians in the Trail of Tears, in *Sec. 2.3.1*; what is good for the Taoists in regard to a a system of laws which is simple, moderate, and humble is not so for a Marxist revolutinoary who champions a heavy, and at times harsh, state intervention into the affairs of society, in *Sec. 2.3.2*; what is good for the victorious powers to be immune from being prosecuted for their own crimes of most serious offense against the others is not so for the millions of victims who had died in the process, in *Sec. 2.4.1*; what is good for the U.S. Constitution in regard to the balance of power among the three branches of government is not so for the British law of the land in regard to the diffusion of power among the three branches of government, in *Sec. 2.4.2*; what is good for the Israelites in regard to the extermination of certain nations and tribes is not so for those nations and tribes as the victims, in *Sec. 2.5.1*; what is important for the common law tradition in regard to the slow process of adjudication is not so for the civil law tradition to allow flexibility and discretion for abrupt changes, in *Sec. 2.5.2*; what is good for the social Darwinists in regard to natural selection as the normative foundation for the law is not so for the legal positivists which question such a connection, in *Sec. 3.2.1*; what is important for the legal reform in New Zealand in regard to the "no-fault system of state compensation for accidents" is not so for the legal reform in the U.S. in regard to a "drastic limitation on the scope of tort law," in *Sec. 3.2.2*; what is good for the herds is not so for the nobles, according to Nietzsche, in *Sec. 3.3.1*; what is good for the first claimer who believes in the "first possession theory of property" for exclusive private property is not so for the communist who believes in the "communist" theory of property for common ownership, in *Sec. 3.4.1*; what is good for those in mechanical solidarity to celebrate identicalness is not so for those in organic solidarity to celebrate difference, in *Sec. 3.4.2*; what is beneficiary for one party to misrepresent a fact in a contract for his advantage is not so for the other party who is misled in accepting the contract at his own disadvantage, in *Sec. 3.5.1*; and what is acceptable for the proponents of substantive due process is not so for the originalists who are against it, in *Sec. 3.5.2*).

However, it should be stressed (as this is something that I regularly did in my previous books, *almost verbatim*) that there are different shades of gray (or different degrees of truth) in the two opposites, and the classification is not necessarily mutually exclusive either. In fact, even when some combinations of the two occur, they only end up sharing the same dialectic relationship, but in a different degree.

Also, there are some other relationships (as a kind of family resemblance) which have something in common with the principle, but they are not exactly the same but only more or less comparable, which varies from case to case. Good examples of family resemblance in relation to the principle are uniformity-diversity, internalness-externalness, and so forth.

2nd Thesis: The Predictability-Unpredictability Principle

The second thesis is called the predictability-unpredictability principle (on the occurrence of events) in the category of "method" in existential dialectics (which was first proposed in *FC* and, later, other books of mine), in that both predictability and unpredictability have a major role to play in the occurrence of things, so that neither determinism nor indeterminism wins the centuries-old fight.

There are events which are predictable, just as there are those which are not. Or what is regarded as unpredictable at one point in time may turn out to be predictable later, and, conversely, what is deemed as predictable may turn out to not be so predictable. Even in predictability, outcomes are subject to uncertainty, the degree of which varies from case to case.

For instance, on the one hand, there is predictability (e.g., the predictable tendency of a Kantian to act out of duty, with the end in itself, in *Sec. 2.2.1*; the predictable overall pattern of violence, in that "when it comes to violence, the two sexes simply are not in the same league," in *Sec. 2.2.2*; the predictable tendency of the U.S. government to conquer others with its history of Manifest Destiny, in *Sec. 2.3.1*; the predictable tendency of a Taoist system of laws to be simple, humble, and moderate, in *Sec. 2.3.2*; the predictable tendency of international law to engage in a double standard to favor the victorious powers and to be biased against the defeated ones, in *Sec. 2.4.1*; the predictable tendency of a constitutional law which is based on the principle of the balance of power to provide a check and balance among the three branches of government, in *Sec. 2.4.2*; the predictable tendency of the Israelites to obey the Mosaic law, in *Sec. 2.5.1*; the predicable tendency of the common law tradition to be incremental in change over time, in *Sec. 2.5.2*; the predictable tendency of the legal positivists to reject any necessary logical connection between an "ought" and an "is" in the law, in *Sec. 3.2.1*; the predictable tendency of unintentional tort law to focus on the principle of care in relation to negligence, in *Sec. 3.2.2*; the predictable tendency in herd morality to value existential preservation, not power expansion, in *Sec. 3.3.1*; the predictable tendency of someone who believes in the "labor theory of property" to claim a property after mixing his labor with it, in *Sec. 3.4.1*; the predictable tendency of those in orgnanic solidarity to value individualism, in *Sec. 3.4.2*; the predictable tendency of a contract to have the element of "intention to be legally bound," in *Sec. 3.5.1*; and the predictable tendency of admiinistrative agencies to enforce, adjudicate, or make rules, in *Sec. 3.5.2*).

On the other hand, there is unpredictability (e.g., the more difficult task to even predict on which particular occassions a Kantian does not succumb to external influences and when he does, in *Sec. 2.2.1*; the more difficult task to predict which particular woman will end up killing a man than the other way around, in *Sec. 2.2.2*; the more difficult task to predict at the outset the long-term success or failure of a given expansionist adventure by the U.S., be it towards the Native Indians, the Mexicans, the Philipinos, or else, in *Sec. 2.3.1*; the more difficult task to even predict to what extent a given Taoist system of laws can really be simple, in light of the highly complicated characteristics of contemporary society in the Information Age, in *Sec. 2.3.2*; the more difficult task to predict the severity of the conviction of a particular individual, because of the difficulties with respect to the competence and jurisdiction of an international court, the "often enormously complicated matters" of a given case, the different interests of the victorious powers involved, etc., in *Sec. 2.4.1*; the more difficult task to predict exactly which form of the balance of power, be it unitary, federalist, or confederalist, that a constitutional law will adopt, even if the principle of the balance of power is accepted, until more details about its constitution and history are known, in *Sec. 2.4.2*; the more difficult task to predict which specific questionable practices can be successfully excused over time for circumstantial reasons, in relation to the Mosaic law, in *Sec. 2.5.1*; the more difficult task to predict when exactly the common law tradition will undergo abrupt, substantial changes "when extraordinarily good reason is shown" in extraordinary circumstances, in *Sec. 2.5.2*; the more difficult task to predict the particular direction of a given legal case that a legal positivist will pursue, because there are numerous schools of thought in legal positivism like the ones by Jeremy Bentham, John Austin, Hans Kelsen, H.L.A. Hart, Joseph Raz, and others, in *Sec. 3.2.1*; the more difficult task to predict the outcome of a given unintentional tort case, since in negligence, "the event is unusual and unpredictable," in *Sec. 3.2.2*; the inability within herd morality to predict what others who do not accept herd morality will likely do in a particular case, in *Sec. 3.3.1*; the more difficult task to predict how much "there should be 'enough, and as good, left in common for others'," in a particular case of someone who accepts the "labor theory of property," in *Sec. 3.4.1*; the more difficult task to predict exactly when individualism could degenerate into anomie in which particular way, in *Sec. 3.4.2*; the more difficult task to preduct which particular cases of contract are enforceable and which ones are not, as courts over time can interprete "intention" in different ways, like the non-enforceable case of "Balfour v. Balfour" and the enforceable one of "Merritt v. Merritt," in *Sec. 3.5.1*; and the more difficult task to predict when a particular administrative decision, though justified at the time, will not end up criticized later on as a violation of due process, or even an infamous case of ultra vires, in *Sec. 3.5.2*).

Again, it should be stressed, however, that there are different shades of gray (or different degrees of truth) in the two opposites, and the classification is not necessarily mutually exclusive either. In fact, even when some combinations of the two occur, they only end up sharing the same dialectic relationship, but in a different degree.

Also, there are some other relationships (as a kind of family resemblance) which have something in common with the principle, but they are not exactly the same but only more or less comparable, which varies from case to case. Good examples of family resemblance in relation to the principle are sureness-arbitrariness, and so forth.

3rd Thesis: The Explicability-Inexplicability Principle

The third thesis is called the explicability-inexplicability principle (on the underlying mechanisms of things) in the category of "method" in existential dialectics (which was proposed in *FPHU* and other books of mine), in that both explicability and inexplicability are part of the understanding of things.

This principle tells us the dual nature of the research dilemma, in that, if reality can be explained in some ways, it also has its other ways which are not quite explainable, at a given point in time.

For instance, on the one hand, there is explicability (e.g., the explanation of the condition of the moral law in Kantian ethics by appealing to the necessity of practical freedom and transcendental freedom, in *Sec. 2.2.1*; the explanation of the maleness of violence on the basis of evolutionary biology by Barash, in *Sec. 2.2.2*; the explanation of the need of the U.S. federal government to take over the lands of the Native Indians on the basis of Manifest Destiny, in *Sec. 2.3.1*; the Taoist explanation of the virtue of non-action on the basis that the Tao returns into a cycle, or that "the Tao…and its manifestations…will flow back, circumvent, and eventually undo any attempts to force it into a particular path," in *Sec. 2.3.2*; the explanation of why the victorious powers have been relatively immune from being prosecuted for their crimes of most serious offense against the others, on the basis of legal technicality as afore-described, in *Sec. 2.4.1*; the explanation of a constitutional law like the U.S. Constitution which adopts the principle of the balance of power on the basis of its provision of a check and balance among the three branches of government, in *Sec. 2.4.2*; the explanation by Scotus and Swinburne of why "God could not have commanded otherwise" on the basis that "necessity, not God, is the source of objective morality," in *Sec. 2.5.1*; the explanation of some successful commerical economies with good entrepreneurship on the basis of their adoption of the common law traditon, which is reliable, in *Sec. 2.5.2*; the explanation, by Hume, of the invalidity of the foundation for certain laws on the basis of a questionable logical inference of an "ought" from an "is," in *Sec. 3.2.1*; the explanation, by Ronald Coase, of the aim of tort law on the basis of the minimization of transaction costs in liability, in *Sec. 3.2.2*; the explanation, by Wilhelm Roux, of life in nature on the basis of "internal struggle," or "the struggle for existence occurred at the cellular level," in *Sec. 3.3.1*; the explanation, by someone in the "customs and convention" theory of property, of a property ownership to be legitimate, on the basis of certain customs and convention in the community, in *Sec. 3.4.1*; the explanation, by Bourdieu, of symbolic violence on the basis of "the imposition of categories of thought and perception upon dominated social agents who then take the social order to be just," when it is not really so, in *Sec. 3.4.2*; the explanation, in accordance to the economic theory of contract, of a contract to be enforced, on the basis of "economic benefits," in *Sec. 3.5.1*; and the explanation of the foundation for due process on the basis of some fundamental justice at the basic level, in *Sec. 3.5.2*).

On the other hand, there is inexplicability (e.g., the inability to explain, within Kantian ethics, why moral freedom at both practical and transcendental levels are possible and desirable, other than by the stipulation that they are simply asusmed to be so, in *Sec. 2.2.1*; the lack of vigorous explanation by Barash, within his biological model, on why sexual violence by males are carried over to other forms of violence, in *Sec. 2.2.2*; the lack of explanation of why the specific claims in the Manifest Destiny are in fact true, in *Sec. 2.3.1*; the lack of sufficient explanation in Taoism of why exactly the Tao has to eventually return into a cycle at all, instead of moving in a straight line or somewhere else, in *Sec. 2.3.2*; the lack of sufficient explanation within international law of why this kind of double standard within international law is really just, in *Sec. 2.4.1*; the lack of suficient explanation within the U.S. Constitution itself of why the alternative form like the fusion of power is not used instead to check excessive power, in *Sec. 2.4.2*; the lack of sufficient explanation by Scotus and Swinburne, since one can continue and ask, Why are these moral laws passed on by God necessary in the first place?, in *Sec. 2.5.1*; the lack of sufficient explanation, within this argument for the success of the common law tradition, of why some other countries like China used to have successful commerce with good entrepreneurship in its long history, but without the adoption of the common law tradition, in *Sec. 2.5.2*; the lack of sufficient explanation within Hume's argument of why there exists an empirical, though not logical, relationship between an "ought"and an "is" in some laws, backed with a threat of punishment by a legal institution as an external intermediary agency, in *Sec. 3.2.1*; the lack of sufficient explanation in Coase's argument of why the fundamental assumptions in the explanation, namely, property rights, efficient and identical use of resources, transaction costs in bargaining, perfect competition and information, and wealth and income effects, are valid, as critically pointed out by Steve Kangas, in *Sec. 3.2.2*; the lack of sufficient explanation, within Roux's framework, of life in nature not at the cellular level, like the classical Darwinian theory on natural selection and Rolph's idea of "insatiability and assimilation" for life expansion, in *Sec. 3.3.1*; the lack of sufficient explanation, within the "customs and convention" theory of property, of why customs and convention are just in the first place, especially when "all property was owned by the monarch and it devolved through feudal land tenure or other feudal systems of loyalty and fealty," in *Sec. 3.4.1*; the lack of sufficient explanation, within Bourdieu's framework, of why an imposition is necessarily unjust, other than by definition, in *Sec. 3.4.2*; the lack of sufficient explanation, within the economic theory of contract, of why this appeal to "economic benefits" is necessarily justified as "fair," especially for the critics like the Marxists, in *Sec. 3.5.1*; and the lack of sufficient explanation, within the theory of fundamental justice, of why this justification of justice at the fundamental level, be it about procedures or rights, is really justified, as questioned by the critics, in *Sec. 3.5.2*).

Once more, it should be stressed, however, that there are different shades of gray (or different degrees of truth) in the two opposites, and the classification is not necessarily mutually exclusive either. In fact, even when some combinations of the two occur, they only end up sharing the same dialectic relationship, but in a different degree.

Also, there are some other relationships (as a kind of family resemblance) which have something in common with the principle, but they are not exactly the same but only more or less comparable, which varies from case to case. Good examples of family resemblance in relation to the principle are underlyingness-regularness, and so forth.

4rd Thesis: The Preciseness-Vagueness Principle

The fourth thesis is called the preciseness-vagueness principle (on the refinement of things) in the category of "structure" in existential dialectics (which was first out worked out in *FIA*), in that both preciseness and vagueness are important, not that one is better than the other, but that both are used, in different degrees of preference, in accordance to the contextual application from the perspectives of nature, the mind, culture, and society.

For instance, on the one hand, there is preciseness (e.g., the precise identification of the three formulations of the categorical imperative, in *Sec. 2.2.1*; the precise identification of the five objectives of criminal law, in *Sec. 2.2.2*; the precise identificaiton of "the Laws of the Jungle" for the wolves in India by Kipling, in *Sec. 2.3.1*; the precise identification of the characteristics of the Tao, like the four major ones as discussed, in *Sec. 2.3.1*; the precise identification of the four limited circumstances where the ICC has jurisdiction over cases concerning the "most serious crimes of concern to the international community," like "war crimes" and "the crime of aggression," in *Sec. 2.4.1*; the precise identification of the possible sources of the law of the land, like statutory law, common law, custom and convention, for those governments which do not have a written constitution, in *Sec. 2.4.2*; the precise identification of the commandments to be obeyed in the Mosaic law, like "the love of God and of one's neighbor," in *Sec. 2.5.1*; the precise identification of some essential features which characterize the common law tradition, in *Sec. 2.5.2*; the precise identification of three major claims of legal positivism, in *Sec. 3.2.1*; the precise identification of the five elements of "negligence," in *Sec. 3.2.2*; the precise identification of Nietzsche's two-fold answer to the notion of equality, in *Sec. 3.3.1*; the precise identification of traditional property rights in property law, in *Sec. 3.4.1*; the precise, clear distinction betwene egoism and human dignity in individualism, according to Durkheim, in *Sec. 3.4.2*; the precise identification of the five elements of a contract, in *Sec. 3.5.1*; and the precise identification of substantive due process in relation to the idea of "constitutionally-based 'liberty,'" in *Sec. 3.5.2*).

On the other hand, there is vagueness (e.g., the vagueness about what exactly resides in the idea of the intrinsic worth of "dignity," in *Sec. 2.2.1*; the vagueness about the differences in value to be placed on each of them, depending on different cases, traditions, and situations, in *Sec. 2.2.2*; the vague treatment of the laws of the jungle by Kipling, without specifying any exceptions to the laws, or the existence of different laws for different animals, in *Sec. 2.3.1*; the essential vagueness of the "Tao," in spite of the four characteristics as identified, because "neither it nor its principles can ever be adequately expressed in words," in *Sec. 2.3.1*; the lack of a clear "definition of the crime [of aggression]" and of a clear formulation of "the conditions under which it may be prosecuted," in *Sec. 2.4.1*; the lack of clear formulation of which specific sources of the law of the land is good for which specific form of government under which specific circumstances, in *Sec. 2.4.2*; the lack of clear formulation of the specific circumstances in the Mosaic law when these commandments can be observed or violated, for instance, in relation to certain nations and tribes, or of how harsh is harsh in dealing with "licentious thoughts and covetous desires," in *Sec. 2.5.1*; the relatively vague characterization of how exactly slow, incremental, and precise the common law tradition is, as compared with other traditions, in *Sec. 2.5.2*; the lack of clear formulation of the three major claims of legal positivism by themselves, as the words in the claims have different meanings and interpretations, dependent on a particular legal positivist; for instance, the word "determinism" for John Austin has more to do with the use of threat in legal sanctions, as in contract law, but, for H. L. Hart, such an interpretation "was analogous to a gunman backing up his demands with a threat of violence," in *Sec. 3.2.1*; the vague formulation of what exactly these five elements are to mean, as there are various court interpretations about them, in *Sec. 3.2.2*; the vague aspects of Nietzsche's answer to the notion of equality, as it does not resolve the issue concernng which categories of difference are permissible and which ones are impermissible, in *Sec. 3.3.1*; the vague formulation of the traditional property rights, because it does not clearly resolve the issue concerning "the proprietary character of personal rights…over human tissue, organs and other body parts," in *Sec. 3.4.1*; the vagueness in the formulation of what human dignity is supposed to mean, as it can be subject to different interpretations, in *Sec. 3.4.2*; the lack of clear formulation of the exact meanings in regard to the five elements of a contract, such that different courts offer different interpretations about them over time, in *Sec. 3.5.1*; and the lack of clear formulation of what exactly this idea of "constitutionally-based 'liberty'" is, because "just what those rights are is not always clear," in *Sec. 3.5.2*).

Once more, it should be stressed, however, that there are different shades of gray (or different degrees of truth) in the two opposites, and the classification is not necessarily mutually exclusive either. In fact, even when some combinations of the two occur, they only end up sharing the same dialectic relationship, but in a different degree.

Also, there are some other relationships (as a kind of family resemblance) which have something in common with the principle, but they are not exactly the same but only more or less comparable, which varies from case to case. Good examples of family resemblance in relation to the principle are clarity-ambiguity, directness-indirectness, and the like.

5th Thesis: The Simpleness-Complicatedness Principle

The fifth thesis refers to the simpleness-complicatedness principle (on the interconnection among things) in the category of "structure" in existential dialectics (which was first out worked out in *FIA*), in that both simpleness and complicatedness are vital, without favoring one over the other, and each is utilized, depending on the basis of the perspectives of nature, the mind, culture, and society.

For instance, on the one hand, there is simple analysis (e.g., the simple solution to the practical concern with the strict demands of the moral law by assuming both practical freedom and transcendental freedom, in *Sec. 2.2.1*; the simple acocunt of the maleness of violence on the basis of evolutionary biology, in *Sec. 2.2.2*; the simplistic account of "competition between individual organisms for limited resources" by the social Darwinists, in *Sec. 2.3.1*; the simple Taoist view of a system of laws which is to be moderate, humble, and simple, in *Sec. 2.3.2*; the simple but popular view that the ICC was set up to impartially provide justice against those who commit the "most serious crimes of concern to the international community," in *Sec. 2.4.1*; the simple analysis of the American constitution on the basis of the balance of power among the three branches of government, in *Sec. 2.4.2*; the simple view of the Mosaic law as the "standard of moral conduct for the Jewish people, and through them for Christendom," in *Sec. 2.5.1*; the simple analysis of the common law tradition, in that it is different from other ones, like Islamic law, civil law, etc., in *Sec. 2.5.2*; the simple view, as in social Darwinism, that what is good in the state of nature for animals to compete for the survival of the fittest is also good in society for humans, in *Sec. 3.2.1* the simple listing of different aims of tort law, in *Sec. 3.2.2*; the simple analysis of Nietzsche's will to power for a new jurisprudence which allows the flourishing of noble morality, not just herd morality, in *Sec. 3.3.1*; the simple analysis of the defenses to copyright violation in terms of four principles, in *Sec. 3.4.1*; the simple analysis of the main characteristics of legal-rationalism in relation to organizational structure, in *Sec. 3.4.2*; the simple analysis of the formation of a contract in terms of five elements, in *Sec. 3.5.1*; and the simple analysis of due process in terms of enumerated due process right vs. unenumerated due process right and procedural due process vs. substantive due process, in *Sec. 3.5.2*).

On the other hand, there is also complicated counterpart (e.g., the complicated account of the strict demands of the moral law by questioning the extent of possibility and desirability of the two kinds of moral freedom by the critics of Kantian ethics, on the basis of other factors, *in Sec. 2.2.1*; the more complicated account by the critics that "biological base is always experienced culturally, through a translation. The bare biological facts…do not speak for themselves; they must be expressed socially," in *Sec. 2.3.1*; the more complicated account of both cooperation and competition in the state of nature by the critics of social Darwinism, in *Sec. 2.3.1*; the more complicated view, by the critics like Fuller, that the laws in real life can be enormously complicated, as in the case about patents, in *Sec. 2.3.2*; the more complicated picture of the ICC, by taking into account of its power politics, ideological motivation, and the like, in *Sec. 2.4.1*; the more complicated analysis of the American constitution in relation to other different forms of constitution, so as to have a more comparative understanding of different possible constitutional laws, in *Sec. 2.4.2*; the more complicated analysis of the Mosaic law in relation to its historical contingency and multifaceted imperfections, in *Sec. 2.5.1*; the more complicated analysis by John Makdisi of "the Islamic Origins of the Common Law," in *Sec. 2,5,2*; the more complicated critique of social Darwinism by Jeremey Bentham that natural law commits the naturalistic fallacy in the context of the "is-ought" problem, in order to propose a non-fallacious theory of law and morality, based on utiliarianism, in *Sec. 3.2.1*; the more complicated account of the aims of tort law on the basis of conflicting claims among different scholars and of different calls for reforms in different countries, in *Sec. 3.2.2*; the more complicated analysis of the origins of Nietzsche's will to power on the multifaceted historical influence by previous scholars on his work, in *Sec. 3.3.1*; the more complicated analysis of the defenses to copyright violation by accounting for the varieties of interpretation, depending on different particular cases, legal traditions, and historical eras, in *Sec. 3.4.1*; the more complicated analysis of the nature of bureaucracy in terms of its multifaceted relationships with the law, the state, and its dark side too, in *Sec. 3.4.2*; the more complicated analysis of the five elements of a contract by making all kinds of distinctions and qualifcations, like "explicit" vs. "implied," "in fact" vs. "in law," "oral" vs. "written," "verbal" vs. "non-verbal," and "enforceable intention" vs. "non-enforceable intention," and the like, in

Sec. 3.5.1; and the more complicated analysis of due process in terms of different interpretations and views about this simple distinction of due process, in *Sec. 3.5.2*).

Again, it should be stressed, however, that there are different shades of gray (or different degrees of truth) in the two opposites, and the classification is not necessarily mutually exclusive either. In fact, even when some combinations of the two occur, they only end up sharing the same dialectic relationship, but in a different degree.

Also, there are some other relationships (as a kind of family resemblance) which have something in common with the principle, but they are not exactly the same but only more or less comparable, which varies from case to case. Good examples of family resemblance in relation to the principle are inflexibility-flexibility, standardization-specialization, imperfectness-perfectness, superficiality-depth, shallowness-deepness, and the like.

6th Thesis: The Openness-Hiddenness Principle

The sixth thesis refers to the openness-hiddenenss principle (on the detection of things) in the category of "structure" in existential dialectics (which was already worked out in my previous books, especially in *FPHU*), in that reality has its hidden face, just as it is open to outside view in some other ways.

For instance, on the one hand, there is openness (e.g., the open exploration of the demands of the moral law, like "rational autonomy," etc., in *Sec. 2.2.1*; the open exploration of the "guilt act" and "guilty mind" in criminal law, in *Sec. 2.2.2*; the open exploration of the need to expand westward by the U.S. federal government, in *Sec. 2.3.1*; the open Taoist exploration of a system of laws which can be simple, moderate, and humble, in *Sec. 2.3.2*; the open exploration of the crimes against humanity in certain countries as prosecuted by different international courts over the decades, in *Sec. 2.4.1*; the open exploration, in the American constitution, of the virtue of the balance of power for the check and balance among the three branches of government, in *Sec. 2.4.2*; the open exploration of love in the Mosaic law, in special relation to God and one's neighbors, in *Sec. 2.5.1*; the open exploration of the slow, incremental aspects of the common law to serve justice better, in *Sec. 2.5.2*; the open exploration of the logical fallacy in the "is-ought" problem by the legal positivists, in *Sec. 3.2.1*; the open exploration of the role of transaction costs in cases concerning nuisance in property torts by Ronald Coase, in *Sec. 3.2.2*; the open exploration of the will to power in nature by Nietzsche, in *Sec. 3.3.1*; the open exploration of the option for collective ownership in the communist theory of property, in *Sec. 3.4.1*; the open exploration of symbolic capital and its violence by Bourdieu, in *Sec. 3.4.2*; the open exploration of the foundation for contract law in terms of minimizing transaction costs, as in the efficiency theory of contract by Coase, in *Sec. 3.5.1*; and the open exploration of the substantive nature of due process, not just its procedural one, in *Sec. 3.5.2*).

On the other hand, there is also hiddenness (e.g., the hidden bias in relation to the extent of possibility and desirability of rational autonomy, in *Sec. 2.2.1*; the hidden bias in the "we" vs. "they" dichotomy behind criminal law, in *Sec. 2.2.2*; the hidden bias of the U.S. federal government to cover up this inhumane policy towards the Native Indians by way of the manipulative ideology of Manifest Destiny, in *Sec. 2.3.1*; the hidden bias in the Taoist system of laws for a conservative ideology of non-intervention, or minimal intervention, from the state into the affairs of society, in *Sec. 2.3.2*; the hidden bias of different international courts to chase after the defeated and weak powers and to turn a blind eye to the comparable but more horrific crimes committed by the victorious powers, in *Sec. 2.4.*1; the hidden bias of the principle of the balance of power, within the U.S. Constitution, in not including alternative principles like the fusion of power, in *Sec. 2.4.2*; the hidden bias in the Mosaic law in regard to its dark sides, which are to be "excused" by "the Fathers and theologians of the Church from the beginning," in *Sec. 2.5.1*; the hidden bias of the slow, incremental nature of the common law towards a conservative ideological orientation, in *Sec. 2.5.2*; the hidden bias of the legal positivists in its separating the law from ethics or morality, while accepting the law as "posited by lawmakers," in *Sec. 3.2.1*; the hidden bias of Coase's argument, which represents the recurrent conservative ideology of free market as advocated by "economists and lawyers including Milton Friedman and Gary Becker," in their vocal call for "deregulation and privatisation," against "state regulation or what they see as restrictions on the operation of free market," in *Sec. 3.2.2*; the hidden bias in Nietzsche's idea of the will to power against competing views like the Darwinian, utilitarian, Christian, or else, in *Sec. 3.3.1*; the hidden bias, in the communist theory of property, of its ideological preference for drastic equality, as opposed to other more conservative alternatives, in *Sec. 3.4.1*; the hidden leftist bias in Bourdieu's analysis of symbolic violence because of its exaggeration of the illegitimacy of the existing social order, in *Sec. 3.4.2*; the hidden bias of the efficiency theory of contract in downplaying other important factors like exploitation and domination as pointed out by the critics like the Marxists and the feminists, in *Sec. 3.5.1*; and the hidden bias of the idea of substantive due process, in its advocation of an activist expansion of administrative and judiciary power, in *Sec. 3.5.2*).

Again, it should be stressed, however, that there are different shades of gray (or different degrees of truth) in the two opposites, and the classification is not necessarily mutually exclusive either. In fact, even when some combinations of the two occur, they only end up sharing the same dialectic relationship, but in a different degree.

Also, there are some other relationships (as a kind of family resemblance) which have something in common with the principle, but they are not exactly the same but only more or less comparable, which varies from case to case. Good examples of family resemblance in relation to the principle are overtness-covertness, publicness-privateness, openness-closedness, and so on.

7th Thesis: The Evolution-Transformation Principle

The seventh thesis is the evolution-transformation principle (on the multiple kinds of agency). in the category of "agency" in existential dialectics (which was first worked out in *FAE* and then in other books of mine).

This principle—and the symmetry-asymmetry principle, for instance—are both about agency. More precisely, the word "agency," in a formal definition, refers to "a person or thing through which power is exerted or an end is achieved." (MWD 2007) It therefore does not have to necessarily involve an intelligent lifeform.

Because of this dual meaning in agency, the evolution-transformation principle is more concerned with *the kind of agency*, that is, both about the *evolution* in the state of nature (e.g., an object of natural beauty) and the *transformation* in the world of intelligent lifeforms (e.g., a work of art).

In classical Darwinian evolutionary theory (as more detailedly analyzed in *BNN*), evolution is "blind." But in the human world, change often takes place because of the conscious intervention of humans in transforming society and culture, just to cite two instances.

And the transformative part of the principle precisely refers to the other dimension in the dual meaning of agency, in giving technology (as invented by intelligent lifeforms like humans and, soon, post-humans) a major role to play in the change of the world, which is something that I extensively analyzed in *FHC* in the context of the technophilic lifeworld, espeically though not exclusively since modern times.

For instance, on the one hand, there is evolution (e.g., the natural evolution of humans to behave in the state of nature, often based on impulses, in *Sec. 2.2.1*; the natural evolution of humans to live in groups, just like other social animals, in *Sec. 2.2.2*; the natural evolution of animals, including humans, by way of speciation through natural selection, in *Sec. 2.3.1*; the evolution of humans to live together in groups, at time in peace and at times at war, in the state of nature, in *Sec. 2.3.2*; the natural evolution of humans to cope with conflicts by way of impulses and violence in the state of nature, in *Sec. 2.4.1*; the natural evolution of humans to live together in a group in the state of nature, in *Sec. 2.4.2*; the natural evolution of humans to behave in certain ways in the state of nature, be they about the law of the jungle or else, in *Sec. 2.5.1*; the natural evolution of humans to resolve conflicts in a rough way in the state of nature, in *Sec. 2.5.2*; the evolution of humans in the state of nature to behave in certain ways, in *Sec. 3.2.1*; the evolution of humans to commit acts of negligence from time to time in the state of nature, in *Sec. 3.2.2*; the natural evolution of humans to live together by certain behaviors in the state of nature, in *Sec. 3.3.1*; the natural evolution of humans to live and share property within small groups in the state of nature, in *Sec. 3.4.1*; the natural evolution of humans to live together in groups sometimes in peace and some other times in conflict, in the state of nature, in *Sec. 3.4.2*; the natural evolution of humans making agreements in the state of nature, in *Sec. 3.5.1*; and the natural evolution of humans to follow primitive patterns of behavior in the state of nature, in *Sec. 3.5.2*).

On the other hand, there is transformation (e.g., the technical transformation of human behaviors by way of the invention of elaborated systems of ethics and law, in *Sec. 2.2.1*; the technical transformation of human living together by way of the invention of criminal law and the legal institutions to enforce social order, in *Sec. 2.2.2*; the technical transformation of human relations by way of the invention of political ideology like Manifest Destiny, in *Sec. 2.3.1*; the technical transformation of human communities by way of the invention of jurisprudence for the formation of a system of laws for peace and order, in *Sec. 2.3.2*; the technical transformation of human conflict resolution by the invention of international law and international courts, in *Sec. 2.4.1*; the technical transformation of human community by way of the invention of constitutional law to "define the authority and procedure of political bodies to execute new laws and regulations," in *Sec. 2.4.2*; the technical transformation of human behaviors by way of the invention of moral codes in relation to divine law, in *Sec. 2.5.1*; the technical transformaton of human conflict resolution by way of the invention of the common law tradition, which is slow, incremental, and precise in its process, in *Sec. 2.5.2*; the technical transformation of human behaviors by way of the invention of legal positivism for laws to be posited by lawmakers, in *Sec. 3.2.1*; the technical transformation of human dealing with negligence by way of the invention of unintentional tort law, in *Sec. 3.2.2*; the technical transformation of human living together by way of the inventon of a legal institution for law and order, in *Sec. 3.3.1*; the technical transformation of human sharing of property within groups by way of the invention of the "labor theory of property" for the rise of capitalism, in *Sec. 3.4.1*; the technical transformation of human living together by way of the invention of legal-rationalism as a form of domination and authority, in *Sec. 3.4.2*; the technical transformation of human agreements by way of the invention of contract law to formally enforce promissory obligations, in *Sec. 3.5.*1; and the technical transformation of human patterns of behavor by way of the invention of administrative law for due process and fairness against ultra vires, in *Sec. 3.5.2*).

Again, it should be stressed, however, that there are different shades of gray (or different degrees of truth) in the two opposites, and the classification is not necessarily mutually exclusive either. In fact, even when some combinations of the two occur, they only end up sharing the same dialectic relationship, but in a different degree.

Also, there are some other relationships (as a kind of family resemblance) which have something in common with the principle, but they are not exactly the same but only more or less comparable, which varies from case to case. Good examples of family resemblance in relation to the principle are inorganicness-volition, nonwillingness-willingness, naturalness-technologicalness, naturalness-nonnaturalness, and so on.

8th Thesis: The Symmetry-Asymmetry Principle

The eighth thesis is labeled as the symmetry-asymmetry principle (on the relationships among existents) in the category of "agency" in existential dialectics (which was also already worked out in my previous books), in that there is no asymmetry without symmetry.

For instance, the Same can be symmetric and asymmetric towards the Others. But in case of asymmetry (as analyzed in *BDPD*), oppression and self-oppression can occur. So, when the Same is asymmetric towards the Others, the Same can also be relatively asymmetric towards itself in self-oppression, just as the Others can be likewise towards themselves. The subsequent oppressiveness is dualistic, as much by the Same against the Others and itself, as by the Others against the Same and themselves. Both oppression and self-oppression can be achieved by way of downgrading differences between the Same and the Others and of accentuating them.

This is true, even though not all forms of asymmetry have to be about oppression and self-oppression.

In addition, from Chapter Three of *FPHG*, symmetry is not perfect, to be understood in an approximate sense under many life circumstances. With this clarification in mind, hereafter are some empirical examples.

For instance, on the one hand, there is symmetry (e.g., the co-existence of different views of justice, be they Kantian, utilitarian, or else, in *Sec. 2.2.1*; the co-existence of both males and females to commit violent crimes, in *Sec. 2.2.2*; the co-existence of cooperation and competition among humans, in *Sec. 2.3.1*; the co-existence of different systems of laws, be they simple and moderate, or complicated and harsh, in *Sec. 2.3.2*; the co-existence of different nation-states over which international courts can have jurisdiction, in *Sec. 2.4.1*; the co-existence of different principles for constitutional law, like the balance of power and the fusion of power, in *Sec. 2.4.2*; the co-existence of the theory of the divine law and the classical evolutionary theory, in *Sec. 2.5.1*; the co-existence of different legal traditions, like the common law, the civil law, etc., in *Sec. 2.5.2*; the co-existence of different laws with different foundations, be they natural, divine, or legal-positivist, in *Sec. 3.2.1*; the co-existence of different views on the aims of tort law, be it about the one for free market or the one for government regulation, in *Sec. 3.2.2*; the co-existence of different versions of equality, be it utilitarian, Nietzschean, or else, in *Sec. 3.3.1*; the co-existence of different theories of property in history, in Sec. *3.4.1*; the co-existence of different forms of authority in history, in *Sec. 3.4.2*; the co-existence of different views on the requirement of "consideration" in the formation of a contract, be they in the common law tradition or in the civil law tradition, in *Sec. 3.5.1*; and the co-existence of different views about due process, be they procedural vs. substantive, enumerated vs. unenumerated, etc., in *Sec. 3.5.2*).

On the other hand, there is also asymmetry (e.g., the popularity of Kantian ethics for those in the deontological tradition of the moral law, but the more acceptance of utilitarian ethics for those in the consequentialist tradition, in *Sec. 2.2.1*; the overall pattern of the maleness of violence, even although there can be violent women too, in *Sec. 2.2.2*; the preference, for conquest and competition, of those with the belief in Manifest Destiny—but the preference, for cooperation and respect, of those with the belief in non-violence and genuine humanitarianism, in *Sec.*

2.3.1; the more acceptance of a simple and moderate system of laws for those who are sympathetic to Taoism, but the more popularity of a complicated and harsh system of laws for those who believe in a more authoritarian worldview, in *Sec. 2.3.2*; some nation-states are more equal than others, so that there is a double standard for the dominant powers and against the weak ones, under international law, in *Sec. 2.4.1*; the popularity of the principle of the balance of power in American constitutional law, but the acceptance of the principle of the fusion of power in the British tradition, in *Sec. 2.4.2*; the acceptance of the divine command theory by the believers in the bible, and the more popularity of evolutinary theory among scientists, in *Sec. 2.5.1*; the more acceptance of the common law tradition in the U.S. and the U.K., for instance, but the more popularity of the civil law tradition in continental Europe, for instance, in *Sec. 2.5.2*; the more acceptance of the foundation for the law on the basis of natural law by social Darwinists, but the more popularity of the foundation for the law on the basis of decisions by lawmakers by legal positivists, in *Sec. 3.2.1*; the more acceptance of the view on the aims of tort law by way of the free market, by those in the law and economics movement; but the more popularity of the view on the aims of tort law by way of government intervention, by the critics like Steve Kangas, in *Sec. 3.2.2*; the popularity of utilitarian jurisprudence among those in the law and economics movement, but the more acceptance of Nietzschean jurisprudence among the Nazis during the Third Reich, in *Sec. 3.3.1*; the popularity of the "communist" theory of property in the Soviet Union, but the acceptance of the "labor theory of property" in capitalist America, in *Sec. 3.4.1*; the more relevance of charismatic authority in familial and religious contexts, but the more importance of legal-rational authority in modern law, bureaucracy, and the state in a broad sense, in *Sec. 3.4.2*; the more dispensability of the requirement of "consideration" in the civil law tradition, but the requirement of "consideration" in the common law tradition in a different way, that is, through the use of "the concept of *culpa in contrahendo*, a form of 'estoppel'…to create obligations during pre-contractual negotiations," in *Sec. 3.5.1*; and the popularity of procedural due process among the originalists, but the acceptance of substantive due process among its proponents, in *Sec. 3.5.2*).

Again, for the last time, it should be stressed, however, that there are different shades of gray (or different degrees of truth) in the two opposites, and the classification is not necessarily mutually exclusive either. In fact, even when some combinations of the two occur, they only end up sharing the same dialectic relationship, but in a different degree.

Also, there are some other relationships (as a kind of family resemblance) which have something in common with the principle, but they are not exactly the same but only more or less comparable, which varies from case to case. Good examples of family resemblance in relation to the principle are strength-weakness, balance-extremity, harmoniousness-unharrmoniousness, potence-impotence, reflexiveness-unreflexiveness, and something like that.

9th Thesis: The Regression-Progression Principle

The nineth thesis is referred to as the regression-progression princple (on the direction of history) in the category of "outcome" in existential dialectics (which was also already worked out in my previous books), in that neither the cyclical nor the linear views are adequate for explaining many phenomena at all levels.

History progresses to more advanced forms, but with a regressive touch. Examples include no freedom without unfreedom, no equality without inequality, and no civilization without barbarity. This is not an inevitable law, but merely a highly likely empirical trend.

For instance, on the one hand, there is regression (e.g., the "cold" and "neurotic" aspects of Kantian ethics when implemented seriously, in *Sec. 2.2.1*; the "bad" consequences of criminal law for the "fox," in Nietzsche's genealogy of morals, in *Sec. 2.2.2*; the infamy of the Trail of Tears in U.S. history, in *Sec. 2.3.1*; the possible abuse of a non-authoritarian Taoist system of laws to make the people "ignorant" and "simple-minded" for control, in *Sec. 2.3.2*; the double standard of international courts to favor the major powers, in *Sec. 2.4.1*; the drawback in the American constitutional law to not have the benefits of the British parilimentary alternative, like the formation of a coalition government, in *Sec. 2.4.2*; .the abuses and excuses in the history of the Mosaic law to justify slavery, moral laxity, the extermination of certain nations and tribes, and gruesome punishment, in *Sec. 2.5.1*; the forceful cultural diffusion of the common law tradition by the British Empire to its colonies, during the notorious days of Western colonialism and imperialism, in *Sec. 2.5.2*; a consequence of the legal positivist argument is that the laws as posited by lawmakers tend to be amoral, in *Sec. 3.2.1*; the blind faith in the free market to minimize transacton costs in torts, by those in the law and economics movement, without questioning its invalid assumptions, for the critics, in *Sec. 3.2.2*; the abuse by the Nazis in using Nietzsche's idea of the will to power for its teaching institution, in *Sec. 3.3.1*; the tragedy of the commons in the Soviet Union, in *Sec. 3.4.1*; the "polar night of icy darkness" in the bureaucratisation of the modern world, in *Sec. 3.4.2*; the abuse of an oral contract by "false allegations of the existence of contracts," in *Sec. 3.5.1*; and the 1857 infamous slavery case of "Dred Scott v. Sandford" in the name of due process, in *Sec. 3.5.2*).

On the other hand, there is progress (e.g., the enhancement of dignity in Kantian ethics, in *Sec. 2.2.1*; the "good" consequences of criminal law for the "sheep," in *Sec. 2.2.2*; the development of the Wild West, as "the U.S. federal government greatly expanded its powers" and "the nation grew from an agrarian society to an industrialized nation," in *Sec. 2.3.1*; the progress made for a less authoritarian system of laws in a Taoist community, in *Sec. 2.3.2*; the prosecution of those in weak and defeated powers who commit crimes of most serious offense to the international community, in *Sec. 2.4.1*; the progress made for the check and balance among the three branches of government in the American system, in *Sec. 2.4.2*; the progress made in relation to the love of God and one's neighbors, in *Sec. 2.5.1*; the progress made in the development of a systemaic legal tradition like the common law, in *Sec. 2.5.2*; the progress made in eliminating the abuse of any fallacious connection between natural law and the law, as revealed in the notorious legacy of social Darwinism against the weak and the poor, in *Sec. 3.2.1*; the progress made to make us aware of the role of transaction costs in dealing with torts, in *Sec. 3.2.2*; the progress made in making us aware of the dark side of egalitarianism in suppressing difference, especially towards the overmen, for Nietzsche, in *Sec. 3.3.1*; the reduction of inequality in the Soviet Union, in *Sec. 3.4.1*; the progress made in improviing organizaitonal efficiency, in *Sec. 3.4.2*; the progress made to enforce contracts, be they oral or written, in *Sec. 3.5.1*; and the more awareness of the downside of legal interpretations, as even the "[a]dvocates of substantive due process acknowledge that the doctrine was employed in Dred Scott, but claim that it was employed incorrectly," in *Sec. 3.5.2*).

Again, it should be stressed, however, that there are different shades of gray (or different degrees of truth) in the two opposites, and the classification is not necessarily mutually exclusive either. In fact, even when some combinations of the two occur, they only end up sharing the same dialectic relationship, but in a different degree.

Also, there are some other relationships (as a kind of family resemblance) which have something in common with the principle, but they are not exactly the same but only more or less comparable, which varies from case to case. Good examples of family resemblance in relation to the principle are decline-growth, and so forth.

10th Thesis: The Same-Difference Principle

The tenth thesis is referred to as the same-difference princple (on the metamorphosis of change) in the category of "outcome" in existential dialectics (which was worked out in *ALD* and other books of mine), in that an entity, as it evolves over time, can be both different from and similar to its opposing alternatives and does not have to be solely more different from them over time.

Opposites are not absolute in a black-or-white fashion; so, an entity can become relatively more similar to (or more different from) its opposite over time.

This is further constrained by another principle, that is, the symmetry-asymmetry principle about the relationships among existents under the category about agency in existential dialectics, in that if there is symmetry (equality) between two entities, there is likewise asymmetry (inequality) emerging in a different way.

For instance, on the one hand, there is similarity in outcome (e.g., the discipline of human behaviors in a certain way, be it Kantian, utiliarian, or else, in *Sec. 2.2.1*; costs and benefits in both the criminal world and the civil world, in *Sec. 2.2.2*; the consolidation of power, and the maintenance of law and order, both in the Wild West and in the East Coast, in *Sec. 2.3.1*; the molding of individual behaviors in any system of laws, be it Taoist or non-Taoist, in *Sec. 2.3.2*; the privilege of the victorious powers, and the suffering of the defeated powers, regardless of whether there are international courts or not, in *Sec. 2.4.1*; the provision of "authority and procedure of political bodies to execute new laws and regulations" in a way to avoid excessive abuse of power, be it in the American presidential system or the British parlimentary one, in *Sec. 2.4.2*; the occurrence of violence and abuse in history, with or without the Mosaic law, albeit in different ways, in *Sec. 2.5.1*; the outcome of all legal traditions to provide law and order, albeit in different ways, in *Sec. 2.5.2*; the control of human behaviors in certain ways, regardless of the foundation for the law which is natural, divine, or legal-positivist, in *Sec. 3.2.1*; both advantages and disadvantages of different legal reforms in the context of tort law, be it about the one in New Zealand or the one in the U.S., in *Sec. 3.2.2*; the promotion of equality in different versions of jursiprudence, be they utiliarian, Christian, or else, in *Sec. 3.3.1*; the justification of how to distribute property in human society throughout history, albeit in different ways, depending on different thinkers, legal traditions, and historical eras, in *Sec. 3.4.1*; the use of law, be it traditional or legal-rational, for instance, to provide social order, in accordance to Weber, in *Sec. 3.4.2*; the provision of explanation in understanding the foundation for contract law, by different theories of contract, in *Sec. 3.5.1*; and the use and misuse of legal decisions, be they with due process or without it, in *Sec. 3.5.2*).

On the other hand, there is difference in outcome (e.g., the betterment of dignity in Kantian ethics, and the promotion of happiness in utilitarianism, in *Sec. 2.2.1*; peace and non-violence in the civil world, and the survival of the strongest in the criminal world, in *Sec. 2.2.2*; the expulsion of the British from the Eastern seaboard after the American Revolutionary War, but the removal of the Native Indians from their lands in the history of the Westward Expansion, in *Sec. 2.3.1*; the less authoritarian nature of a Taoist system of laws, and the more authoritarian nature of a non-Taoist one like a Marxist system of laws, in *Sec. 2.3.2*; in circumstances where there are international courts, "states try to avoid the appearance of having disregarded international obligations"; but when international courts do not exist or are weak, states may not even bother about the appearance, as in blunt colonialism and slavery practiced by major powers in the older days, in *Sec. 2.4.1*; the strict separation of power in the American system, but the fusion of power in the British one, in *Sec. 2.4.2*; the selective treatment of certain nations, tribes, and peoples, depending on the moral codes and legal sanctions in question, as shown by the allowance to engage in usury with foreigners among the Isralites, but the disallowance of such a practice at all among the Christians, in *Sec. 2.5.1*; the differences among different legal traditions in outcome, be they about incremental changes in the common law tradition and the relatively more abrupt ones in the civil law tradition, in *Sec. 2.5.2*; the consequence of laws based on legal positivism to be amoral, and the consequence of laws based on natural law to be naturalist, in *Sec. 3.2.1*; the focus on the "no-fault system of state compensation for accidents" in the case of New Zealand, but the concern with "drastic limitation on the scope of tort law, [for] a minimisation process on the lines of economic analysis" in the U.S., in *Sec. 3.2.2*; the emphases on the greatest number in utilitarian jurisprudence, or on the herds in the Christian version, in *Sec. 3.3.1*; the more use of private property in capitalist society, but the more use of public property in communist society, in *Sec. 3.4.1*; the appeal to tradition in traditional domination, but the use of legal-rationality in legal-rational domination, in *Sec. 3.4.2*; the understanding of contract law on the basis of promissory obligation in the theory proposed by Charles Fried, but the understanding of contract law on the basis of class exploitation and domination in the Marxist theory of contract, in *Sec. 3.5.1*; and the regret, later on, about the misuse of due process, in the case involving due process, but the likely absence of such later formal acknowledgement in the case without the appeal to due process, in Sec. 3.5.2).

Again, it should be stressed, however, that there are different shades of gray (or different degrees of truth) in the two opposites, and the classification is not necessarily mutually exclusive either. In fact, even when some combinations of the two occur, they only end up sharing the same dialectic relationship, but in a different degree.

Also, there are some other relationships (as a kind of family resemblance) which have something in common with the principle, but they are not exactly the same but only more or less comparable, which varies from case to case. Good examples of family resemblance in relation to the principle are homogeneity-heterogeneity, and so forth.

11th Thesis: The Post-Human Reconstruction

The eleventh thesis is about the role of "post-humans," which I originally proposed in my previous books, starting with the first book titled *The Future of Human Civilization* in 2000 and all others afterwards.

As already pointed out in *Sec. 1.8*, I need to emphasize, as this is something that I used to repeat (*almost verbatim*) from my previous books, two clarifications here about the term "post-human" as a neologism in my works.

Firstly, the word "post-human" here should *not* be confused with another term which looks similar but has a totally different meaning in the literature of postmodernism, namely, "post-humanism"—which constitutes a critique of "humanism" as tradionally understood (especially, though not exclusively, in relation to the idea of progress in science and reason in the Enlightenment project). (WK 2008)

My works reject the project of "postmodernism" and propose the future world of what I orignally called "after-postmodernity" in *FHC* and *FCD*, for instance.

And secondly, the word "post-human" here should also *not* be confused with a similar term which is used to champion the ideology of technology for the future co-existence between humans and cyborgs in "trans-humanism." (WK 2008a)

Instead, my term "post-human" in relation to "posthuman-ism" also rejects "transhumanism" (especially, though not exclusively, in relation to the promises of technology) and refers to something else altogether, that is, the future extinction of humans and its post-human successors in deep space and beyond unto multiverses.

With these two clarifications in mind (as summarized in *Table 1.31*)—the post-human reconstruction can be analyzed in relation to two main directions, based on the analysis in this book so far (and also on the visions as already worked out in my previous books).

Firstly, the "post-human" reconstruction of law will take guidance from the reconstruction theory of law in three distinctive ways, namely, (a) in relation to the analysis of the necessity and contingency of law, (b) in relation to the four perspectives of the mind, nature, society, and culture, and (c) in relation to the need to transcend justice (as will be clarified in the next section).

In the end, there is no justice without injustice (as first proposed in Ch. 5 of *FHC*), in accordance to existential dialectics.

And secondly, the post-human reconstruction of law will likely have to confront the new challenges as posed by the long-term civilizational development of intelligent life in the distant future, both here on this planet Earth and elsewhere in deep space until multiverses—such that justice will be transcended too.

I already worked out, in my numerous books, what these new challenges will be and provide different original visions to meet them—especially, in regard to the future evolutions of the mind (e.g., "floating consciousness," "hyper-spatial consciousness," "unfolding unconsciousness," "thinking machines," "thinking robots," "genetically altered superior beings," "cyborgs," and others), of nature (e.g., the "alteration of space-time," the "creation of new matter-energy," "selective geometry," and the like), of society (e.g., virtual organizations, different versions of "post-capitalism" and "post-democracy," the movement of "cyclical progression" at both structural and systemic levels, "ambivalent technology," and so forth), and of culture (e.g., the rise of "post-civilization," "transformative aesthetic experience," "contrastive mathematical-logic," and the whatnot) in history (e.g., the age of "after-postmodernity"), in the context of my approaches in relation to methodology (e.g., "sophisticated methodologial holism") and ontology (e.g., "existential dialectics").

Of course, the examples (as listed above) are not exhaustive but illustrative, since my numerous books have worked out many other visions (as already roughly summarized in *Sec.1.7* and *Sec. 1.8*).

Many, though not all, of my visions on the mind, nature, society, culture, history, methodology, and ontology (as cited above) are summarized in the tables as shown in Chapter One and Chapter Four.

With these visions of mine in mind—what then can be said about the future of law in relation to justice?

Beyond Justice

This post-human reconstruction of law to transcend intelligent life in a new direction (based on my visions in relation to the mind, nature, society, and culture as already worked out in my previous books) has implications for a more profound question in the context of law—What is justice?

The relatively primitive civilizational level in human history since time immemorial (by future standards), in light of myriad problems confronting the struggle for existence with nature, has forced humans to be obsessed with the question of justice among themselves—just as the obsession with the struggle for existence has greatly constrained animals in the state of nature since the beginning of life on earth. After all, so many lives have been lost in human history in the name of justice, just as so much suffering since time immemorial has been endured by so many, all hoping that justice will be served one day.

However, the first answer to the question is that the necessity and contingency of law are neither possible nor desirable to the extent that the proponents from both opposing sides in all human history hitherto existing would want us to believe. In the end, there is no justice without injustice (as first proposed in Ch. 5 of *FHC*), in accordance to existential dialectics.

And the second answer is that, in the very long haul of civilizational history for intelligent life, both on earth and, later, even more importantly, in deep space unto multiverses, the deeper question is less about what justice is (or what justice is not)—but more about how and why justice is to be transcended altogether into different higher spiritual concerns.

For instance, in Chapter 10 of *The Future of Capitalism and Democracy* (2002), I already explained why and how there will be more spiritual transformations to come, especially in relation to the two value ideals of (i) transcending freedom in floating existence and (ii) transcending equality in the rivalry of cosmic hegemony.

Even then, these two value ideals constitute only a form of transcendent state of higher spiritual concerns, with other more ideals to come in the distant future, especially when considered in conjunction with other future transformations of the mind, nature, society, and culture (as already addressed in my other books on numerous topics).

In the end, justice does not have to be necessary and contingent, as it can be transcended altogether into different higher spiritual concerns in more distant histories that our current relatively prmitive world has never known. Welcome, therefore, to the post-human world beyond justice—for better and for worse, to be judged, however, by the power that be (and all those) in the post-human future.

Table 4.1. Sophisticated Methodological Holism (Part I)

• "My methodological holism implies the partiality-totality principle in the ontology of existential dialectics (see the table on the partiality-totality principle for summary), which is against the varieties of (a) reductionism and (b) reverse-reductionism, in relation to (i) concept, (ii) theory, (iii) methodology, and (iv) ontology." (*FC*)

• "[M]y methodological holism here is not opposed to methodological individualism but includes it (and, for that matter, other methodologies too)…." (*FPHC*) For this reason (and others too, as summarized hereafter), my version of methodological holism is sophisticated—not vulgar as sometimes used by inapt scholars using the same term. (*FC*)

• "[M]y methodological holism does not democratically presume that all levels are equally valid, as all levels are not created equal. In other words, in relation to issue X, level A may be more relevant than level B, but in relation to Y, level B can be more relevant than level A instead." (*FPHC*) One excellent example of this vulgar democratic presumption is what I called in *BNN* "the compromise fallacy." (*FC*)

• My methodological holism does not presume that a lower level of analysis is more important than a higher level, solely because the former serves as the foundation for the latter—and vice versa, for that matter. One excellent example of this reductionistic presumption is what I called in *FPHST* "the foundation fallacy." (*FPHST*, *FC*)

(continued on next page)

Table 4.1. Sophisticated Methodological Holism (Part II)

• "[M]y methodological holism does not make any a-priori postulation that there must be a definite (and, for that matter, indefinite) number of levels" in any analysis. (*FPHC*) Nor does it dogmatically require that there must be a certain combination of levels of analysis in a given inquiry. (*FC*)

• "[M]ethodological holism, in my usage, does not assume that all levels…can necessarily be integrated, since methodological holism is not aimed to search for the holy grail of 'an integral theory…' (as is the case for Wilber). In other words, it allows that sometimes some levels may experience irreducible gaps between them, to be understood, at best, as empirical correlations, not as causal relations…." (*FPHC*)

• "[D]ifferent levels may overlap and even interact with each other in a given context (but sometimes may not), and the fact that I even proposed different ways of re-classifying the levels (whenever needed) in *FDC* reinforces this point….The dual danger here is either forcefully making different levels interact when they are just different (or, metaphorically speaking, apples and oranges) or inappropriately ignoring their interactions when some situations instead require them." (*FPHC*)

• "[T]o understand different levels from their own (unique) perspectives (as required by my methodological holism) is not the same as trying to reduce them to a preferred level in the process of learning from other levels. This second kind of multidisciplinary work is not genuine and does no justice to the unique complexities and merits inherent at each level." (*FPHC*)

(continued on next page)

Table 4.1. Sophisticated Methodological Holism (Part III)

• "[My] methodological holism walks a fine line between the artificial classification (separation) of levels and the simultaneous incorporation of them, if only for the sake of human scholarly endeavor. It should be reminded that nature does not impose upon itself the academic classification of the levels of analysis as humans have. The enterprise of classification is therefore anthropocentric." (*FPHC*)

• "[M]y methodological holism advocates neither epistemic subjectivism nor epistemic non-subjectivism (e.g., realism, idealism, and historicism), neither epistemic relativism (e.g., subjectivism, historicism) nor epistemic absolutism (e.g., realism, positivism), neither epistemic reductionism nor epistemic emergencism, and neither epistemic objectivism (e.g., realism, idealism) nor epistemic historicism....Neither does methodological holism, in my usage, accept the false meta-conceptual dichotomy between nominalism and realism....These false dichotomies...are to be transcended. In other words, methodological holism does not fully accept epistemic realism, positivism (a form of epistemic idealism), historicism, subjectivism, and reductionism in epistemology and philosophy of science but learns from the strengths and weaknesses of all of the opposing approaches without siding with any of them...." (*FPHC*)

• "Sophisticated methodological holism is subject to the constraints as imposed by the syntax of existential dialectics (e.g., the partiality-totality principle and the predictability-unpredictability principle). Even in predictability, outcomes are subject to uncertainty, the degree of which varies from case to case." (*FC*)

(continued on next page)

Table 4.1. Sophisticated Methodological Holism (Part IV)

• "Sophisticated methodological holism—when applied, especially though not exclusively, as illustrated in my numerous works—can enrich the understanding of reality in some distinctive ways. Here are three examples (as revealed in each of my books)." (*FPHCT*; *FPHL*)

—"Firstly, it provides a comprehensive analysis of a subject matter, from which much can be learned about reality," "both in relation to the perspectives of the mind, nature, society, and culture and also in relation to a new classification of the subject matter."

—"Secondly, it suggests some visions of the future in relation to the subject matter in question."

—"And thirdly, it proposes some insights on meta-theory (e.g., methodology and ontology) in general—with the clear understanding, however, of the dilemma of specific vs. general ontology (as shown in the table on the syntax of existential dialectics in the context of the dilemma of ontology). For this very reason, all of these ways are important, without reducing one into the analysis of another."

• In the end, my meta-theory (both sophisticated methodological holism and existential dialectics) serves as a foundation to unify all domains of knowledge into *an unified theory of everything* (by way of some ontological principles and the comprehensive perspectives of the mind, nature, society, and culture). This is so, without commiting the sins of reductionism and reverse-reductionism (as often seen in many holistic approaches, with the fad of sysems approach—be it about systems theory, chaos theory, complexity theory, or else—as a most recent notorious example, which I debunked in *The Future of Complexity*). My distinctive approach makes good use of different schools of thought without favoring any of them nor trying to integrate them (as they are not necessarily compatible with each other), so as to adjust for subjectivity, diversity, conflict, and complexity, for example. In this sense, the word "unified" does not have to mean integrative approach, in a narrow sense, nor systems approach, in a broad one, both of which I reject while learning from them. (*FPHS*)

Sources: A summary of *Sec.1.2* in *FPHC*—and also from *BNN*, *FPHST*, *ALD*, *FC*, *FPHCT*, and the rest of all other books of mine. See the books for more detail.

Table 4.2. On Reductionism and Reverse-Reductionism (Part I)

- **The Partiality-Totality Principle**
  —The partiality-totality principle in the ontology of existential dialectics targets against the varieties of reductionism and reverse-reductionism (as already worked out in my previous books).

- **Against the Varieties of Reductionism**
  —*Conceptual Reductionism*
  - Some illustrative instances involve myriad dualities like mind vs. body, self vs. world, democracy vs. non-democracy, and the like (as already addressed in *FHC*, *FPHC*, and *BDPD*, for instance).

  —*Theoretical Reductionism*
  - A fascinating case study concerns what I originally called "the foundation fallacy" in *FPHST*, in any attempt to naively understand space-time from the physical perspective as the foundation and, consequently, to dangerously dismiss other perspectives.
  - In *FAE*, I elaborated further these versions of reductionism in the literature on aesthetics (e.g., form vs. content, representation vs. expression, critics vs. artists, and externalism vs. internalism).
  - In *FIA*, I revealed other forms of reductionism in the literature on information architecture (e.g., the constructivist argument).
  - In *FPHU*, I showed the persistent legacy of reductionism, this time, in the literature on anomalous experience (e.g., the obsession with physics, chemistry, and biology for explaining anomalous experience).
  - In *FPHE*, I examined another case of reductionism in action, in the context of engineering (e.g., technical constraints vs. normative constraints).
  - In *FPHMM*, I elaborated one more version of reductionism, in relation to the three domains of communication (e.g., the competing views on sending, connecting, and receiving).
  - In *FPHCT*, I explored another version of reductionism, in relation to invention and innovation (e.g., the bio-psychological argument vs. the socio-cultural arguments).

(continued on next page)

Table 4.2. On Reductionism and Reverse-Reductionism (Part II)

- **Against the Varieties of Reductionism *(cont'd)***
  - —*Theoretical Reductionism (cont'd)*
    - In *FPHG*, I identify another version of reductionism, in relation to infinity, symmetry, and dimensionality (e.g., the Euclidean argument vs. the non-Euclidean arguments).
    - In *FPHUP*, I analyzed another version of reductionism, in relation to density and void (e.g., the engineering argument and the ecology argument).
    - In *FPHL*, I examined another version of reductionism, in relation to structure and context (e.g., the structuralist argument and the contextualist argument).
    - In *PFHO*, I explored another version of reductionism, in relation to communcation, decision-making, and leadership (e.g., the rational-system argument vs. the natural-system argument).
    - In *PFHMA*, I revealed another version of reductionism, in relation to the martial body and spirit (e.g., the spiritual argument vs. the materialist argument vs. the defensive argument).
    - In *PFHS*, I analyzed another version of reductionism, in relation to the sexual body and spirit (e.g., the naturalist argument vs. the constructivist argument).
    - And in *PFHLAW*, I scrutize another version of reductionism, in relation to law (e.g., the necessity argument vs. the contengency argument).
  - —*Methodological Reductionism*
    - A good instance concerns the debate between different versions of qualitative and quantitative methods (as already analyzed in *FC* and also *FHC*). In *FPHML*, I examined similar reductionism, this time, in the literature on mathematical logic (e.g., the obsession with consistency, soundness, and completeness).
  - —*Ontological Reductionism*
    - An excellent example is the debate between emergentism and reductionism in complexity theory and also in psychology (as elaborated in *FPHC*, in the context of Being and Becoming).

(continued on next page)

Table 4.2. On Reductionism and Reverse-Reductionism (Part III)

- **Against the Varieties of Reverse-Reductionism**
  —*Conceptual* Reverse-Reductionism
  - Any concept of "art" (e.g., fine art, cave art, outsider art, junk art) is deemed acceptable in postmodernism (as already addressed in Ch.4 of *FHC*).

  —*Theoretical Reverse-Reductionism*
  - There are numerous art and literary theories co-exist. Take the case of literature, as there are now Literary Structuralism, Marxist Literary Criticism, New Criticism, Phenomenology, Hermeneutics, Language-Game Literary Criticism, Feminist Literary Criticism, Reception Theory, Reader Response Criticism, Poststructuralism, Semiotics, Pyschoanalytic Literary Criticism, just to cite some well-known ones, with no one being said to be better than any others (as detailedly analyzed in Ch.4 of *FHC*). (S. Raman 1997) In *BNN*, I even introduced "the compromise fallacy" as another good illustration of theoretical reverse-reductionism, in misleadingly treating both genetic and environmental approaches as equally valid.

  —*Methodological Reverse-Reductionism*
  - There is the "anything-goes" mentality in postmodernism (e.g., doing art without praxis, doing art with praxis, and doing art by sublation), as analyzed in Ch.4 of *FHC*.

  —*Ontological Reverse-Reductionism*
  - There are likewise no privileged ontology, and the door is open for anything in postmodernism (e.g., the equal status of the ontology of Being vs. that of Becoming, as already addressed in Ch.4 of *FHC*—and also in *FPHC)*. In *FAE*, I also introduced another version of reverse-reductionism, that is, "the pluralist fallacy," in the context of understanding aesthetic experience, for instance—although this fallacy has been committed not exclusively in relation to the ontological level (but also at the conceptual, theoretical, and methodological ones).

Sources: From my previous books.

Table 4.3. The Concepton of Existential Dialectics (Part I)

- **Sets and Elements**
  - —Sets
    - Ex: the Same
    - Ex: the Others
  - —Elements
    - Ex: whites in 20th century America (in the set of "the Same")
    - Ex: Iraq during the U.S. invasion in 2003 (in the set of "the Others")

- **Relations, Operations, Functions**
  - —Relations (e.g., "belongs," "equals to," "is greater than")
    - Ex: symmetric interactions within the Same (or the Others)
    - Ex: asymmetric interactions between the Same and the Others
  - —Operations (e.g., "and," "or," "not," "if…then")
    - Ex: if the Same oppresses the Others, it will also oppress itself.
    - Ex: the Same is not the Others.
  - —Functions (e.g., goals)
    - Ex: the Same is hegemonic in relation to the Others.

- **Truth Values**
  - —"1" if True (in Symbolic Logic)
    - Ex: the proposition that imperial Japan was hegemonic to China during WWII
  - —"0" if False (in Symbolic Logic)
    - Ex: the proposition that Grenada invaded France in 2003
  - —"1" & "0" if Both True and False (in Dialectic Logic)
    - Ex: the proposition that the rabbit-duck picture refers to a duck
  - —"~1" & "~0" if Neither True Nor False (or N/A, in Dialectic Logic)
    - Ex: the proposition that God really exists

(continued on next page)

Table 4.3. The Conception of Existential Dialectics (Part II)

- **Axioms, Postulates, Theorems, Principles**
  - —Axioms
    - Ex: the reflexive axiom—"any quantity is equal to itself"
  - —Postulates
    - Ex: the SSS postulate—"if the three sides of a triangle are congruent to their corresponding parts, then the triangles are congruent"
  - —Theorems (and Principles) in Existential Dialectics
    - <u>In Relation to Method</u>
      - –#1: The formalness-informalness principle
      - –#2: The absoluteness-relativeness principle
      - –#3: The partiality-totality principle
      - –#4: The predictability-unpredictability principle
      - –#5: The explicability-inexplicability principle
    - <u>In Relation to Structure</u>
      - –#6: The finiteness-transfiniteness principle
      - –#7: The preciseness-vagueness principle
      - –#8: The simpleness-complicatedness principle
      - –#9: The openness-hiddenness principle
      - –#10: The denseness-emptiness principle
    - <u>In Relation to Process</u>
      - –#11: The change-constancy principle
      - –#12: The order-chaos principle
      - –#13: The slowness-quickness principle
      - –#14: The expansion-contraction principle
    - <u>In Relation to Agency</u>
      - –#15: The theory-praxis principle
      - –#16: The convention-novelty principle
      - –#17: The evolution-transformation principle
      - –#18: The symmetry-asymmetry principle
      - –#19: The softness-hardness principle
    - <u>In Relation to Outcome</u>
      - –#20: The regression-progression principle
      - –#21: The same-difference principle

(continued on next page)

Table 4.3. The Conception of Existential Dialectics (Part III)

Notes: The categories and examples in each are solely illustrative (not exhaustive). The comparison is also relative (not absolute), nor are they mutually exclusive. As generalities, they allow exceptions.
Sources: Starting from Ch.6 of *BCPC* and also from other books of mine

Table 4.4. The Syntax of Existential Dialectics I: The Principles (Part I)

• **In Relation to Method**

—*The Formalness-Informalness Principle*
(On the Formal Requirements of Logical Systems)

- The formal requirements of a logical system (e.g., consistency, soundness, and completeness) have both usefulness and non-usefulness, to the extent that, if there are formal systems requiring them, there are alternative ones which do not. Thus, it does *not* exclude classical logics but simply goes beyond both classical and non-classical logics, while learning something from each.
- For instance, existential dialectics can make use of both classical logics under certain conditions (e.g., especially, though not exclusively, when they are clear-cut, etc.) and non-classical logics under alternative conditions (especially, though not exclusively, when they are "unknown," "irrelevant," "ambiguous," "possible," with "different degrees of truth," empirically inconsistent in a desirable way, etc.). (WK 2008u)
- Family resemblance: e.g., logicalness-nonlogicalness, etc.
- Sources: From *FPHML*. See also other books of mine (from that point on).

—*The Explicability-Inexplicability Principle*
(On the Underlying Mechanisms of Things)

- Both explicability and inexplicability are part of the understanding of things.
- This principle tells us the duality of the research dilemma, in that, if reality can be explained in some ways, it also has its other ways which are not quite explainable, at a given point in time.
- Family resemblance: e.g., underlyingness-regularness, etc.
- Sources: Especially from *FPHU*—and also *FPHC*. See also other books of mine (from that point on).

(continued on next page)

Table 4.4. The Syntax of Existential Dialectics I: The Principles (Part II)

- **In Relation to Method *(cont'd)***

—*The Predictability-Unpredictability Principle*
(On the Occurrence of Events)

- Both predictability and unpredictability have a major role to play in the occurrence of things, so that neither determinism nor indeterminism wins the centuries-old fight.
- There are events which are predictable, just as there are those which are not. Or what is regarded as unpredictable at one point in time may turn out to be predictable later, and, conversely, what is deemed as predictable may turn out to not be so predictable. Even in predictability, outcomes are subject to uncertainty, the degree of which varies from case to case.
- Family resemblance: e.g., sureness-arbitrariness, etc.
- Sources: Especially from *FC*. See also other books of mine (from that point on).

—*The Partiality-Totality Principle*
(On the Relationships between Whole and Parts)

- The whole is not the sum of the parts.
- Any inquiry about a phenomenon in the work is to guard against the varieties of (a) reductionism and (b) reverse-reductionism.
- Reductionism and reverse-reductionism can be (i) conceptual, (ii) theoretical, (iii) methodological, and (iv) ontological.
- Family resemblance: e.g., individualisticness-holisticness, partness-wholeness, analysis-synthesis, etc.
- Sources: Especially from *FC*. See also other books of mine (from that point on).

(continued on next page)

Table 4.4. The Syntax of Existential Dialectics I: The Principles (Part III)

- **In Relation to Method *(cont'd)***

—*The Absoluteness-Relativeness Principle*
(On the Multiplicity of Things)

- There is the multiplicity of things in reality, be they about entities, qualities (or properties), and relationships, such that what is acceptable from one standpoint may not be so from another. For instance, if there is something absolute, there is likewise something relative.
- Both absoluteness and relativeness here are also relevant to different modalities often cited in the literature on ontology, such as possibility (e.g., something "can" happen) and its opposite (e.g., impossibility), probability (e.g., something "will" happen) and its opposite (e.g., improbability), and necessity (e.g., something "should" happen) and its opposite (e.g., contingency).
- Family resemblance: e.g., uniformity-diversity, internalness-externalness, etc.
- Sources: From *FPHK*. See also other books of mine (from that point on).

(continued on next page)

Table 4.4. The Syntax of Existential Dialectics I: The Principles (Part IV)

• In Relation to Structure

—*The Finiteness-Transfiniteness Principle*
(On the Nature of Numbers)

- If there are finite things, there are likewise transfinite ones.
- To avoid confusion, my usage of the word "transfinite" here differs radically from the one used by Cantor (and other mathematicians) for "relative" infinity—and is more limited, in light of the problems confronting any attempt to understand the idea of infinity, be it by intuition, imagination, and conception (as detailedly analyzed in *Sec. 2.2.3* of *FPHG*).
- Instead, by "transfinity," I allow numbers which can be many times larger—or smaller, for that matter—than the finite things that we encounter in daily life, but they do not have to be related to the idea of infinity at all (which may not exist).
- Of course, there may be some *borderline* cases, in which it is not clear whether the number in question is transfinite (in my usage) or simply a mathematical convenience. A good example of a borderline case is the Planck unit of length for "the smallest space possibly measured in nature," which is "less than billionths of trillionths of trillionths of an inch" (or something like 1.6×10^{-35} meters).
- That said—my usage of "transfinity" can also resolve (or better, dissolve) an age-old problem in philosophy known as "Zeno's paradoxes" (as already explained in *Sec. 2.2.3* of *FPHG*).
- Family resemblance: e.g., boundedness-quasiunboundedness, smallness-largeness, etc.
- Source: From *FPHG*. See also other books of mine (from that point on).

(continued on next page)

Table 4.4. The Syntax of Existential Dialectics I: The Principles (Part V)

- **In Relation to Structure *(cont'd)***

—*The Simpleness-Complicatedness Principle*
(On the Interconnection among Things)

- Both simpleness and complicatedness are vital, without favoring one over the other, in that each is utilized, depending on the basis of the perspectives of nature, the mind, culture, and society. And even when a combination of them is preferred, the dilemma is only shifted to a combinational degree of concern.
- In relation to taxonomy, simpleness has its heuristic usefulness, just as complicatedness has its realistic representation, for instance. And in relation to network, simpleness has its economical attractiveness, just as complicatedness has its practical reliability, for instance.
- Family resemblance: e.g., inflexibility-flexibility, standardization-specialization, imperfectness-perfectness, superficiality-depth, shallowness-deepness, etc.
- Sources: Especially from *FIA*. See also my later books.

—*The Preciseness-Vagueness Principle*
(On the Refinement of Things)

- Both preciseness and vagueness are important, not that one is better than the other, but that both are used, in different degrees of preference, in accordance to the contextual application from the perspectives of nature, the mind, culture, and society. Even when both are used in a combination, the dilemma is shifted instead to one of combinational concern.
- In relation to taxonomy, preciseness has its taxonomic clarity, just as vagueness has its classificatory flexibility, for instance. And in relation to network, vagueness has its explorative liberty, just as preciseness has its conceptual definitiveness, for instance.
- Family resemblance: e.g., clarity-ambiguity, directness-indirectness, etc.
- Sources: Especially from *FIA*. See also my later books.

(continued on next page)

Table 4.4. The Syntax of Existential Dialectics I: The Principles (Part VI)

- **In Relation to Structure** ***(cont'd)***

—*The Openness-Hiddenness Principle*
(On the Detection of Things)

- This principle suggests that reality has its hidden face, just as it is open to outside view in some other ways.
- For instance, in the context of anomalous experience, certain aspects of reality concerning anomalous experience can be open for examination (e.g., the experiment with SPECT images, the transmission of telepathemic bit, and the use of metonymies and metaphors). Other aspects, however, remain hidden, and examples include the elusive deeper nature of spiritual reality in the intangible realm, the undetectability of different branched universes, the underlying mechanisms of signals traveling between different folds of physical space-time, and the dependence on language and the bias for science and logic).
- Family resemblance: e.g., overtness-covertness, publicness-privateness, openness-closedness, etc.
- Sources: Especially from *FPHU*. See also my later books.

—*The Denseness-Emptiness Principle*
(On the Distribution of Entities in Space)

- Both density and void are needed, in relation to the mind, nature, culture, and society, albeit in different ways.
- Lest any misunderstanding occurs, the term "void" is used here only as an approximation of emptiness (depending on the degree of the lack of density), since, in physics, it is well known that "empty" space is not really empty all the way, because it can be full of energy (e.g., random quantum fluctuations at the sub-atomic level, and, for that matter, dark energy in the universe) and matter (e.g., different versions of sub-atomic particles, and, for that matter, dark matter in the universe).
- Family resemblance: e.g., fullness-voidness, nearness-farness, etc.
- Sources: First worked out in *FPHUP*. See also my later books.

(continued on next page)

Table 4.4. The Syntax of Existential Dialectics I: The Principles (Part VII)

• **In Relation to Process**

—*The Expansion-Contraction Principle*
(On the Growth of Things)

- Entities in the world can both expand in some ways and contract in other ones, as part of their nature
- For instance, in the context of anomalous experience, one of its most fascinating expressions is none other than the analysis of different causes of the slow but steady expansion (and, furthermore, if put in a different way, unfolding) of unconsciousness.
- Family resemblance: e.g., conquest-autarky, rise-fall (or up-down), etc.
- Sources: Especially from *FPHU*. See also my later books.

—*The Slowness-Quickness Principle*
(On the Speed of Change)

- Both slowness and quickness co-exist, with their own internal tension, to the extent that each fights for its own relevance with the other, in accordance to the perspectives of nature, the mind, culture, and society, without one being the victor and the other being the vanquished in the long haul. Even when both are chosen in other cases, this dilemma is only transferred into something else with a combinational character.
- In relation to taxonomy, quickness has its efficient usability, just as slowness has its aesthetic appeal, for instance. And in relation to network, quickness has its adventurous readiness, just as slowness has its risk-adverse convenience, for instance.
- Family resemblance: e.g., inconvenience-convenience, passiveness-activenessness, gradualness-abruptness, etc.
- Sources: Especially from *FIA*. See also my later books.

(continued on next page)

**Table 4.4. The Syntax of Existential Dialectics I:
The Principles
(Part VIII)**

• In Relation to Process *(cont'd)*

—The Change-Constancy Principle
(On the Alteration of Things)
- Change occurs over time, although constancy is also allowed.
- Asymmetry undergoes changes over time, so does symmetry.
- Old players fade away, and new ones emerges, with ever new causes and ever new forms.
- Family resemblance: e.g., dynamicness-staticness, instability-stability, etc.
- Sources: First named in *BCPC*. Especially from *FHC*, *FCD*, and *FPHC*. See also other books of mine (from that point on).

—The Order-Chaos Principle
(On the Pattern of Things)
- Both order and chaos are vital in the process of change in the world. The preference for order is biased, since it does not give sufficient attention to the vital role of chaos in the transformation of the world (without somehow reducing it for the understanding of order).
- The scientific search for order in the world is often a hidden bias in its ontological obsession with order, since chaos is often treated as the "bad" guy, with order as the "good" guy (for the end goal of science).
- Neither order nor chaos is the final end of the world, and one is not to be treated as the means for the other in the transformation of things. Both are fundamental in their recurrent dialectical interactions with each other over time, without reducing one for the other.
- Family resemblance: e.g., lawfulness-disorder, etc.
- Sources: Especially from *FC*. See also my later books.

(continued on next page)

Table 4.4. The Syntax of Existential Dialectics I: The Principles (Part IX)

- **In Relation to Agency**

—*The Softness-Hardness Principle*
(On the Force of Change)

- This has to do with *the force of change* under the category about agency in existential dialectics, in that any change by an agent, be it organic (like humans) or non-organic (like natural objects), can occur in a forceful (aggressive) or gentle (pacific) way, which can come in all shapes and sizes, of course.
- Family resemblance: e.g., peacefulness-violence, cooperation-competition, etc.
- Sources: Especially from *ALD*. See also my later books.

—*The Theory-Praxis Principle*
(On the Duality of Knowledge))

- This has to do with the duality of knowledge in existential dialectics, in that, if there is theoretical construction, there is likewise its practical application, both technical and normative.
- Family resemblance: e.g., discovery-application, knowledge-action, etc.
- Source: Especially from *FPHE*. See also my later books.

(continued on next page)

Table 4.4. The Syntax of Existential Dialectics I: The Principles (Part X)

• **In Relation to Agency** ***(cont'd)***

—*The Symmetry-Asymmetry Principle*
(On the Relationships among Existents)

- There is no symmetry without asymmetry.
- For instance, the Same can be symmetric and asymmetric towards the Others. But in case of asymmetry, oppression and self-oppression can occur. So, when the Same is asymmetric towards the Others, the Same can also be relatively asymmetric towards itself in self-oppression, just as the Others can be likewise towards themselves.
- The subsequent oppressiveness is dualistic, as much by the Same against the Others and itself, as by the Others against the Same and themselves.
- Both oppression and self-oppression can be achieved by way of downgrading differences between the Same and the Others and of accentuating them.
- This is true, even though not all forms of asymmetry have to be about oppression and self-oppression.
- In addition, from Chapter Three of *FPHG*, symmetry is not perfect, to be understood in an approximate sense under many life circumstances.
- Family resemblance: e.g., strength-weakness, balance-extremity, harmoniousness-unharrmoniousness, potence-impotence, reflexiveness-unreflexiveness, etc.
- Sources: From all my books, starting with *FHC*. First named in *BCPC*. See, for instance, *FCD* for more details on the Same and the Others.

(*continued on next page*)

**Table 4.4. The Syntax of Existential Dialectics I:
The Principles
(Part XI)**

• **In Relation to Agency *(cont'd)***

—*The Evolution-Transformation Principle*
(On the Multiple Kinds of Agency)

• This principle (and the symmetry-asymmetry principle) are both about *the agency of change*. The word "agency," in a formal definition, refers to "a person or thing through which power is exerted or an end is achieved." (MWD 2007b) It therefore does not have to necessarily involve an intelligent lifeform.
• Because of this dual meaning in agency, the evolution-transformation principle is more concerned with *the multiple kinds of agency*, that is, both about the *evolution* in the state of nature (e.g., an object of natural beauty) and the *transformation* in the world of intelligent lifeforms (e.g., a work of art, an air-conditioner, etc.).
• And the transformative part of the principle precisely refers to the other dimension in the dual meaning of agency, in giving technology a major role to play in the change of the world, which is something that I extensively analyzed in *FHC* in the context of the technophilic lifeworld, espeically though not exclusively since modern times.
• Family resemblance: e.g., inorganicness-volition, nonwillingness-willingness, naturalness-technologicalness, naturalness-nonnaturalness, etc.
• Sources: Especially from *FAE*. See also other books of mine.

(*continued on next page*)

Table 4.4. The Syntax of Existential Dialectics I: The Principles (Part XII)

• **In Relation to Agency** ***(cont'd)***

—*The Convention-Novelty Principle*
(On the Nature of Creative Thinking)

- If there is conventional wisdom, there is likewise novel challenge, to the extent that both convergent and divergent thinking are part of life.
- In addition, in this context of the convention-novelty principle, there are, in the absence of better words, what I want to call (a) *creative techniques* and (b) *creative traits*, which, when satisfied—in relation to the larger context of the mind, nature, society, and culture—can be used to enhance creative works. The list of creative techniques and traits (as summarized in *Table 4.1* of *FPHCT*) are not exhaustive, of course, but the examples here constitute a great beginning of understanding the structure of creative thinking.
- Yet, lest the reader gets carried away by the euphoria about creative thinking in our time, it should be reminded that creative thinking has its own possibilities and limits (as shown in *Table 2.1* of *FPHCT* on invention), just as it has its own promises and pitfalls (as shown in *Table 3.1* of *FPHCT* on innovation). In the end, it should also be stressed that creative thinking has its own desirability and dark sides (as shown in *Table 4.2* of *FPHCT*).
- This has important daily implications for an average individual, and the word "average" here allows different degrees of variation from one individual to another in a population, at any given point in history.
- Family resemblance: e.g., convergence-divergence, normalness-nonnormalness, etc.
- Sources: First from *FPHCT*. See also my later books.

(*continued on next page*)

Table 4.4. The Syntax of Existential Dialectics I: The Principles (Part XIII)

• In Relation to Outcome

—The Regression-Progression Principle
(On the Direction of History)

• Neither the cyclical nor the linear views are adequate for explaining many phenomena at all levels.
• History progresses to more advanced forms, but with a regressive touch. Examples include no freedom without unfreedom, no equality without inequality, and no civilization without barbarity.
• This is not an inevitable law, but merely a highly likely empirical trend.
• Family resemblance: e.g., decline-growth, etc.
• Sources: From all my books, starting with *FHC*. First named in *BCPC*.

—The Sameness-Difference Principle
(On the Metamorphosis of Change)

• An entity, as it evolves over time, can be both different from and similar to its opposing alternatives and does not have to be solely more different from them over time.
• Opposites are not absolute in a black-or-white fashion; so, an entity can become relatively more similar to (or more different from) its opposite over time.
• Family resemblance: e.g., homogeneity-heterogeneity, etc.
• Sources: Especially from ALD. See also my later books.

Notes: The features in each principle are solely illustrative (not exhaustive). The comparison is also relative (not absolute), nor are they mutually exclusive. As generalities, they allow exceptions.

Table 4.5. The Syntax of Existential Dialectics II: The Principles as Short Cuts (Part I)

• The principles should be treated with caution, lest misunderstanding occurs, since they do not constitute rigid dualities (or dichotomies).

• The reason is that each pair in an ontological principle consists of two opposites, which are, however, merely short cuts both for multiple variations and degrees, as well as for different interactions with multiple other entities unlike them. In this light, each pair can end up having hundred (or even thousand, if not more) different versions, which interact with hundred (or even thousand, if not more) other entities. There are two clarifications here.

• Firstly, this conception of shortcuts is not mutually exclusive nor absolute, in that the opposites can come in all shapes and sizes, with different degrees. For instance, by analogy, just as there are different degrees of the two colors "white" and "black"—there are likewise different degrees of the opposites in each ontological pair, to the extent that there can be multiple entities (not only two) interacting with each other in each pair.

• And secondly, this conception of shortcuts do not ignore other possible entities in interacting with the two opposites (with their different versions) in each pair. For instance, by analogy, there are not only the two colors "white" and "black" as opposites, since there are other colors too besides them like "yellow," "green," "purple," or else. The same logic can be applied to each ontological pair, in that they also interact with other entities, not with only two of them (with their different versions).

• Therefore, with these two clarifications in mind—each pair in an ontological principle serves only as an abbreviation for something more complicated and, therefore, although it contains two opposites, it should not be confused as a duality (dualism).

(continued on next page)

Table 4.5. The Syntax of Existential Dialectics II: The Principles as Short Cuts (Part II)

• Existential dialectics rejects any dualism (or dichotomy) as too rigid and instead allows the multiplicity of entities, to the extent that between the two opposites in each pair exist many other alternatives to choose from. They are named in that short form for aesthetic elegance, instead of listing all possible entities between the two opposites in the title.

• To be dialectic is to go beyond any rigid dichotomy and transcend into something different altogether in the long haul. One may be tempted to call the dialectic logic here with a different name like existential "multilectics" (instead of "dialectics"), but this naming is incorrect (or even misleading), for the two reasons aforestated.

• After all, each ontological pair come in all shapes and sizes (with different degrees) and do not exist by themselves but also interact with other entities unlike them. The virtue of revealing an ontological pair is to show how they relate within themselves (in multiple versions) and also interact with others unlike them (also in multiple versions).

• This will be clear in the table on "the dialectic constraints imposed by the principles."

Source: From Ch.1 of *FPHK*

Table 4.6. The Syntax of Existential Dialectics III: The Principles as Family Resemblances

• Each ontological principle is generic, with some other comparable ontological pairs to be put in the same family (like a *family resemblance*). Ludwig Wittgenstein (1953) once suggested the idea of "family resemblance" in explaining different games classified under the same family called *games*.

• Why should, for instance, playing football and chess as playing "games," when it is well understood that football is not the same as chess? The answer is that, although each game is different and has different rules, many of them (though not all) share, more or less, some commonalites (e.g., scoring as necessary for winning).

• And this is so, even though some games share more than some others in any given selection of critieria, and no two games are exactly identical. So, his point here is that there is no essential core which is common to all games, and the best that one can look for is some characteristics which are common to many (but not all) games. (A. Biletzki 2006)

• By the same logic—in the previous section on selection criteria, the flexibility-inflexibility pair can be put in the family resemblance of the simpleness-complicatedness principle, although the two pairs are not exactly identical. Likewise, the directness-indirectness pair can be put in the family resemblance of the preciseness-vagueness principle, although, again, the two pairs are not exactly identical.

• In this sense, which specific pair in a family should be used to designate the name of the family can be at times a bit arbitrary, but with good reason.

• For illustration, in the context of method, the partiality-totality principle can take the different form like individualisticness-holisticness, just as the explicability-inexplicability principle can take the different form like underlyingness-regularness—although each two pairs are not exactly identical and have slightly different meanings and usages. A more comprehensive listing of this family resemblance for all other principles is shown in the table on the syntax of existential dialectics.

Source: From Ch.1 of *FPHK*

Table 4.7. The Syntax of Existential Dialectics IV: The Dialectic Constraints Imposed by the Principles (Part I)

- **Co-Existent and Asymmetric**
  - —The principles, as they constitute the syntax of existential dialectics, are dialectic in character, such that, when they are applied, they impose dialectic constraints on how reality is to be understood. Consider, say, the symmetry-asymmetry principle as an illustration here, in order to summarize two main characters of the dialectic constraints in question.
  - —Firstly, to be dialectic here is to go beyond the narrow dichotomies (and, for that matter, any rigid multi-dimensional classificatory scheme), be they about "self" vs. "world," "freedom" vs. "unfreedom," "barbarity" vs. "civilization," "individuality" vs. "communality," and so on.
  - —One way to do so (to go beyond) is to consider them all in terms of co-existence (without favoring one over the rest). For instance, my theory of "post-civilization" (to be summarized later in the section on the pragmatics of existential dialectics) is to go beyond barbarity and civilization in terms of understanding barbarity and civilization as being co-existent. And the same logic can be said in relation to my theories of "post-democracy," "post-capitalsm," and others (also to be introduced later in the section on the pragmatics of existential dialectics), in regard to freedom vs. unfreedom, equality vs. inequality, communality vs. individuality, spirituality vs. materiality, and so on.
  - —But to consider them all (in the dichotomies—and, for that matter, in any rigid multi-dimensional classifactory schme) as co-existent is not the same as to imply that the opposites in any classificatory scheme are all equal, since, in accordance to the symmetry-asymmetry principle (as an illustration here), if they are equal in terms of being considered as co-existent, they are asymmetric in terms of being unequal in dialectic interaction (e.g., X can be more dominant than Y in case A, or Y is more dominant than X in case B).

(continued on next page)

Table 4.7. The Syntax of Existential Dialectics IV: The Dialectic Constraints Imposed by the Principles (Part II)

—For this reason, there are different versions of "post-democracy" and "post-capitalism" in my theories. As an illustration, in version I of the theory of post-democracy, freedom is more dominant than equality, whereas in version II of the theory of post-democracy, equality is more so than freedom.
—But this "X more than Y" has to be understood in the context of dialectic logic (not in conventional logic), in that both "X" and "Y" are important in post-democracy (in the context of dialectic logic), but in an asymmetry way. By contrast, in conventional logic, it often favors one over the other—be it in regard to privileging freedom over equality in Fascism, favoring freedom relatively more than equality in Liberal Democracy, or favoring equality relatively more than freedom in Socialist Democracy. In the latter two cases (about Liberal Democracy and Socialist Democracy), the difference between dialectic logic and conventional logic can be one in degree, not in kind—in this sense, albeit not in other senses.
—The same logic can be said about the relatonships between individuality and communality, between spirituality and materiality, and between formal legalism and informal legalism in the different versions of my theory of post-capitalism.

• **Transcendent**
—Secondly, to be dialectic is to go beyond the narrow dichotomies (and, for that matter, any rigid multi-dimensional classificatory scheme) in another way, this time, in a transcendent way, that is, in exploring other possibilities or even other issues not considered within the narrow confines of narrow dichotomies (and, for that matter, any rigid multi-dimensional classificatory scheme).

(continued on next page)

Table 4.7. The Syntax of Existential Dialectics IV: The Dialectic Constraints Imposed by the Principles (Part III)

—As an analogy, to go beyond the narrow color dichotomy of "black" and "white" is not just to choose both "black" and "white" (as in the first meaning) but also to explore other color options (e.g., "green," "purple," "blue," etc.—and, alternatively, "shade," "line," "curve," etc.). By the same logic, to go beyond "democracy" is to transcend democracy (as in version III of the theory of "post-democracy") and to explore other possibilties of lifeforms (e.g., floating consciousness, hyper-spatial consciousness, etc., to live beyond the narrow obsession with freedom and equality).
—This dialectic character of the principles in existential dialectics has important implications for the pragmatics of existential dialectics (as will be clear shortly, in the section on the pragmatics of existential dialectics).

Notes: The examples here are solely illustrative (not exhaustive). The comparison is also relative (not absolute), nor are they mutually exclusive. As generalities, they allow exceptions.
Sources: First explicitly stated in *ALD*. Also from all other books of mine.

Table 4.8. The Syntax of Existential Dialectics V: Further Clarifications (Part I)

- **Pioneering**
  —Firstly, the total number of ontological principles is unknown, to be discovered later, as our knowledge of the world becomes more advanced.
  —Consequently, the principles as introduced in my books are not exhaustive, with new ones being added, whenever more of them are discovered in later research.
  —At least, future generations can pick up where I leave off and continue the discovery.
  —In this sense, my work should be treated as a pioneering effort for the development of a systematic, comprehensive analysis of a new general ontology for the future of knowledge.

- **Flexible**
  —Secondly, the principles are not rigidly classified, as they can be reclassified in a different way.
  —For instance, the preciseness-vagueness principle is classified under the category of "structure" but can be reclassified under the category of "method," although in so doing, it has a different meaning in the context of method.
  —The same logic applies to the same-difference principle under the category of "outcome," which can be reclassified under the category of "structure," although in so doing, once more, it has a different meaning in the context of structure.

- **Mutually Constraining**
  —Thirdly, the principles are to be understood together, not that each prinicple is to be analyzed independently of others. After all, the principles are mutually constraining, in that they work together as a whole.

(continued on next page)

Table 4.8. The Syntax of Existential Dialectics V: Further Clarifications (Part II)

- **Selectively Useful**
  —Fourthly, the principles are relevant to all subject matters, but some principles are more useful to some subject matters than others—as implied in the symmetry-asymmetry principle. This is true, even if different studies of the same kind can yield different views about the degree of relevance for each ontological principle, depending on the specific nature of a research in question, needless to say.

- **Anti-Reductionistic**
  —And fifthly, the principles constitute only two levels of analysis, this time, at the ontological and methodological levels—while other levels of analysis (from the perspectives of the mind, nature, society, and culture) are also needed, in order to understand reality in its totality (as explained in the section on "sophisticated methodological holism," so as to avoid the dual dangers of reductionism and reverse-reductionism).

Notes: The examples here are solely illustrative (not exhaustive). The comparison is also relative (not absolute), nor are they mutually exclusive. As generalities, they allow exceptions.
Sources: From my previous books like *FHC*, *FCD*, *FPHC*, *BDPD*, *BCPC*, *BNN*, *FC*, *FAE*, and so on.

Table 4.9. The Syntax of Existential Dialectics VI: The Dilemma of Specific vs. General Ontology (Part I)

• Ontology is often more complicated and imposes some seemingly insurmountable difficulties concerning what constitutes a kind of ontology which can be valid enough to be accepted by the wider intellectual community in question. An excellent example concerns what I want to call *the dilemma of ontology* in relation to the relationship between "specific ontology" and "general ontology." (M. Bunge 1999; R. Corazzon 2007)

• On the one hand, "general ontology," as Mario Bunge (1999) put it, "studies all existents." But, on the other hand, "special ontology studies one genus of thing or process—physical, chemical, biological, social, etc." (M. Bunge 1999; R. Corazzon 2007)

• Consequently, the relationship between the former and the latter is that, as an illustration, "whereas general ontology studies the concepts of space, time, and event, the ontology of the social investigates such general sociological concepts as those of social system, social structure, and social change." (M. Bunge 1999; R. Corazzon 2007)

• With this formal definition in mind, the relationship between the two forms of ontology only poses *the dilemma of ontology*, in that general ontology is possible to the extent that its general contructs must be broad enough to serve as the "lowest common denominator" for all disciplines, but this character of the lowest common denominator is not only hard to find but also its usefulness is limited. (WK 2008b)

• But specific ontology fares no better either, in that its specific constructs primarily serve a specific discipline in question, although other disciplines can appropriate them for their own purposes, but in a different context (especially, though not exclusively, when used as a metaphor from one field to another). For instance, the Kantian category of understanding under the heading of "quantity" constitutes a type of specific ontology, which is specific to the discipline of mathematics, although other disciplines can make use of the categories in their own context.

(continued on next page)

Table 4.9. The Syntax of Existential Dialectics VI: The Dilemma of Specific vs. General Ontology (Part II)

• A solution lies in my proposal of "sophisticated methodological holism," which requires all levels of analysis in any subject matter. See the tables on sophisticated methodological holism, and on reductionism and reverse-reductionism, for more details.

Source: From *Sec. 1.4* of *FPHK*

Table 4.10. The Semantics of Existential Dialectics

- **Abstract Structure vs. Specific Meanings**
  —The syntax of existential dialectics so understood in terms of ontological principles only gives us the structure of ontology in the world, in an abstract (general) sense. These principles by themselves do not tell us the specific meanings in a given context.
  —In order to grasp the specific meanings of the principles in a given context, it is necessary to study the semantics of existential dialectics. And the analysis of the ontological principles as family resemblances in the section on syntax is only a starting point (and thus overlaps a bit with the semantics of existential dialectics here).
  —With this caveat in mind, the reason that I have often gone in great lengths in my previous books on different subjects is to explain the specific meanings of the principles when applied in different contexts.

- **Specific Meanings in Specific Fields**
  —For instance, in *FPHST*, I used the first three principles (i.e., the change-constancy principle, the regression-progression principle, and the symmetry-asymmetry principle) to propose "the perspectival theory of space-time," for a better way to understand space and time—especially, though not exclusively, in relation to future post-human history (as summarized in *Table 3.6*, *Table 3.7*, *Table 3.8*, and *Table 3.9*). In so doing, I had to introduce concepts and theories specific to the field of physics and other related fields (e.g., "absolute space" and "absolute time" in "classical mechanics" and "relative space-time" in "the theory of relativity").
  —In *BNN*, I also exploited the three principles to propose the "transcendent" approach to the study of genes and memes as a new way to understand the interaction between nature and nurture. In so doing, I had to explore concepts and theories in the world of evolutionary theory (e.g., "mutation," "variation," "adaptation," "selection," and "inheritance" in Darwinian evolutionary theory) and neural biology (e.g., "chromosome," "gene," "DNA," "RNA," "protein," "neuron," "neural network," and "behavior").

Notes: The categories and examples in each are solely illustrative (not exhaustive). The comparison is also relative (not absolute), nor are they mutually exclusive. As generalities, they allow exceptions.
Sources: First explicitly stated in *ALD*. Also from all other books of mine.

Table 4.11. The Pragmatics of Existential Dialectics (Part I)

- **The Two-Way Street Connecting Theory and Meta-Theory**
  —The pragmatics of existential dialectics is not a one-way street (that is, using the ontological principles for theoretical insights in praxis) but a two-way one, that is, (a) from meta-theory to theory, and (b) from theory to meta-theory.
  —(a) On one side of the street, the ontological principles can inspire some theoretical insights in praxis, that is, in relation to some specific fields.
  —(b) On the other (opposing) side of the street, however, the study of a subject matter in the specific fields in turn reveals some more hitherto unknown ontological principles to be discovered and identified. For this reason, three new principles were added in *FC*, one in *FAE*, and two in *ALD*, on top of the original three in *BCPC*—after some research on the specific subject matters.

- **Direct and Indirect Applications**
  —*Direct*
  - The logic of existential dialectics can shed some theoretical insights on diverse phenomena in the world, and good instances are the pertinent use of the principles of existential dialectics for the theoretical insights on the freedom/unfreedom dialectics, the equality/inequality dialectics, and the wealth/poverty dialectics in my previous works.
  - My latest books like *FPHST* and *BNN* also use the principles to reveal some theoretical insights on the perspectives of space and time (as in *FPHST*) and of nature and nurture (as in *BNN*).

  —*Indirect*
  - The theoretical insights can further be used to reveal other phenomena directly from them (viz., the theoretical insights) and therefore indirectly from the principles themselves. A good instance is the use of the theoretical insights on the freedom/unfreedom and equality/inequality dialectics for the understanding of the civilization/barbarity dialectics.

(continued on next page)

Table 4.11. The Pragmatics of Existential Dialectics (Part II)

- **Direct and Indirect Applications (*cont'd*)**
  - Even in indirect applications, however, a phenomenon under study can still be directly related back to the principles themselves. In the example as cited above, the civilization/barbarity dialectics can be directly related to the principles of existential dialectics without the intermediate role of the freedom/unfreedom and equality/inequality dialectics.

- **Multiple Levels of Application**

  —The theoretical insights can be applied to different levels of analysis, even though in a given example, it may refer to one level only. For instance, in the example concerning the freedom/unfreedom dialectics, it can be used at the structural level (e.g., in relation to the theory of cyclical progression of hegemony), but it can be exploited as well for other levels (e.g., the theory of post-capitalism at the institutional level).

Notes: The categories and examples in each are solely illustrative (not exhaustive). The comparison is also relative (not absolute), nor are they mutually exclusive. As generalities, they allow exceptions.
Sources: From Ch.6 of *BCPC*. See also other books of mine.

Table 4.12. The Freedom-Unfreedom Dialectics (Part I)

- **On Having**
  - *—In Relation to the Technological*
    - (1) if freer from submission to Nature, then less free from ecological degradation (Deep and Social Ecology), even if in a hi-tech form
    - (2) if freer from technological inconvenience / backwardness, then less free from technological control and the loss of privacy
    - (3) if freer from technological (material) backwardness, then less free from the abusive (barbaric) maltreatment of the primitive Others
  - *—In Relation to the Everyday*
    - (1) if freer from abject poverty, then less free from artificial needs/discontents (Frankfurt School)
    - (2) if freer from sensual suppression, then less free from violent sublimation (Freud)
    - (3) if freer from the snobbishness of high culture, then less free from the shabbiness (leveling-off effect) of mass culture (Tocqueville)
    - (4) if freer from the inefficiency of traditional "compassionate economy," then less free from the bondage of a "ruthless [competitive] economy" (Keynes)
    - (5) if freer from anarchy in the state of nature (system fragmentation), then less free from government regulations and controls in system integration

(continued on next page)

Table 4.12. The Freedom-Unfreedom Dialectics (Part II)

- **On Belonging**
  - *—In Relation to the Good and the Just*
    - (1) if freer from disciplinary society, then less free from society of control (Foucault)
    - (2) if freer from the tyranny of one or a few, then less free from the tyranny of the majority (or sometimes, minority veto)
    - (3) if freer from elitist decision making, then less free from political gridlock/cleavage
    - (4) if freer from arbitrary (discretionary) administration, then less free from bureaucratic irrationality (Weber) and legal trickery (loopholes)

- **On Being**
  - *—In Relation to the True*
    - (1) if freer from unscientific dogmas, then less free from instrumental abyss (nihilism). Or conversely, if freer from meaninglessness, then less free from dogmas.
    - (2) if freer from the bondage of partiality/partisanship (e.g., prejudice, discrimination), then less free from the danger of impartiality and neutrality (e.g., opportunism, unrealisticness, lack of compassion, inaction)
    - (3) if freer from making generalizations, then less free from being unable to understand much of anything
  - *—In Relation to the Holy*
    - (1) if freer from collective conscience, then less free from social loneliness
    - (2) if freer from religious absoluteness, then less free from spiritual emptiness
  - *—In Relation to the Beautiful/Sublime*
    - (1) if freer from artistic non-autonomy, then less free from aesthetic disillusion (deconstruction)

(continued on next page)

Table 4.12. The Freedom-Unfreedom Dialectics (Part III)

Notes: The examples in each category are solely illustrative (not exhaustive), and the comparison is relative (not absolute), nor are they necessarily mutually exclusive. And some can be easily re-classified elsewhere. As generalities, they allow exceptions.
Sources: A reconstruction from Ch.10 of *FCD*, based on *FHC*

Table 4.13. The Equality-Inequality Dialectics (Part I)

- **On Having**
  —*In Relation to the Technological*
  (1) if more equal in treating Nature with spiritual unity, then less equal in suppressing the dominant drive to transcend it altogether
  —*In Relation to the Everyday*
  (1) if more equal in building social plurality, then less equal in leveling-off effects (e.g., the subsequent relative intolerance of high/intellectual ethos in mass culture industry)
  (2) if more equal in socioeconomic distribution beyond a certain point, then less equal in efficiency (e.g. resentment, the erosion of work ethics)
  (3) if more equal in urging an affirmative action program, then less equal in creating victim mentality (in oneself), stigma (from others), reverse discrimination (against the once privileged), and mediocracy (against the more able)

- **On Belonging**
  —*In Relation to the Good and the Just*
  (1) if more equal in banning monarchic/oligarchic exclusion, then less equal in producing "the tyranny of the majority" or of "minority veto"
  (2) if more equal in encouraging participatory decision making, then less equal in inducing political divisiveness (gridlock/cleavage in power blocs) and organizational oligarchy
  (3) if more equal in institutionalizing a decentralized bureaucracy, then less equal in falling into more territorial/turf politics (intrigues)

(continued on next page)

Table 4.13. The Equality-Inequality Dialectics (Part II)

- **On Being**
  - —In Relation to the Beautiful / Sublime
    - (1) if more equal in accepting diverse styles ("anything goes" mentality), then less equal in artistic good quality (in leveling-off effects against the best)
  - —In Relation to the True
    - (1) if more equal in tolerating multiple viewpoints (no matter how extreme), then less equal in epistemic standards
  - —In Relation to the Holy
    - (1) if more equal in celebrating any cults and sects (no matter how questionable), then less equal in spiritual depth and authenticity

Notes: The examples in each category are solely illustrative (not exhaustive), and the comparison is relative (not absolute), nor are they mutually exclusive. And some can be easily reclassified elsewhere. As generalities, they allow exceptions.

Sources: A reconstruction from Ch.10 of *FCD*, based on *FHC*

Table 4.14. The Duality of Oppression in Existential Dialectics: Oppression and Self-Oppression (Part I)

- **From the Same to the Others and Itself**
  —The Oppression by the Same against the Others
  - *By way of downgrading differences*
    –Ex: on judiciary caprice for corporate crimes (*Sec.2.2.1.2.1*)
    –Ex: on the deceptive politics of liberation (*Sec.3.5*)
    –Ex: on the humanitarian mystique (*Sec.4.4*)
    –Ex: on the fad of emotional intelligence (*Sec.5.3*)
  - *By way of accentuating differences*
    –Ex: on the legal sophistry of self-defense (*Sec.2.3*)
    –Ex: on the legal semantics of proportionality (*Sec.2.4*)
    –Ex: on the tricky politics of external threat (*Sec.3.4*)
    –Ex: on the appeal of the Far Right for democracy (*Sec.5.4*)
    –Ex: on the democratic axis of evil (*Sec.5.5*)
    –Ex: on the democratic way of brutality and revenge (*Sec.5.6*)
    –Ex: on democratic autocracy (*Sec.6.4*)

  —The Oppression by the Same against Itself
  - *By way of downgrading differences*
    –Ex: on the politics of fear (*Sec.2.2*)
    –Ex: on the trickery of compassionate conservatism (*Sec.3.2*)
    –Ex: on the deceptive politics of patriotism (*Sec.3.3*)
  - *By way of accentuating differences*
    –Ex: on the caprice of due process on domestic suspects (*Sec.2.2*)
    –Ex: on the false security/freedom dilemma (*Sec.6.5.2*)

(continued on next page)

Table 4.14. The Duality of Oppression in Existential Dialectics: Oppression and Self-Oppression (Part II)

- **From the Others to the Same and Themselves**
  - —The Oppression by the Others against the Same
    - *By way of downgrading differences*
      - –Ex: on judiciary caprice in the reverse direction (*Sec.2.2.1.2.2*)
      - –Ex: on equal pay (*Sec.6.2.1.1*)
      - –Ex: on equal representation (*Sec.6.2.1.2*)
      - –Ex: on affirmative action program (*Sec.6.3.1.1*)
      - –Ex: on same-sex marriage (*Sec.6.3.1.2*)
    - *By way of accentuating differences*
      - –Ex: on sexual harassment (*Sec.6.2.2.1*)
      - –Ex: on physical violence (*Sec.6.2.2.2*)
      - –Ex: on sexual exploitation (*Sec.6.2.2.3*)
  - —The Oppression by the Others against Themselves
    - *By way of downgrading differences*
      - –Ex: on the reverse-class mystique (*Sec.4.2*)
      - –Ex: on the reverse-black mystique (*Sec.4.3*)
      - –Ex: on self-discrimination by downgrading (*Sec.6.3.2.2*)
    - *By way of accentuating differences*
      - –Ex: on self-discrimination by accentuating (*Sec.6.3.2.1*)

Notes: The examples are solely illustrative (not exhaustive), nor are they mutually exclusive. As generalities, they allow exceptions. Also, both forms of oppression co-exist in all of the examples, so the listing of them are only meant in a relative, not absolute, sense.
Source: A summary of the sections (as cited) in Chs.2-6 of *BDPD*. See text for more info and references.

Table 4.15. The Structure of Existential Dialectics I: The Freedom/Unfreedom and Equality/Inequality Dialectics

• Each freedom and equality produces its own unfreedom and inequality, regardless of whether the pair occurs in political society (with the nation-state), in civil society (with some autonomy from the state), or elsewhere (e.g., in the private sphere of individual homes)—and regardless of whether freedom and equality are understood as "negative" or "positive."

• Oppression is dualistic, as much by the Same against the Others and itself, as by the Others against the Same and themselves.

• Both forms of oppression and self-oppression can be achieved by way of downgrading differences (between the Same and the Others) and of accentuating them.

• The relationships are relatively asymmetric between the Same and the Others and relatively symmetric within them. This is true, even when the Same can be relatively asymmetric towards itself in self-oppression, just as the Others can be likewise towards themselves.

• Symmetry and asymmetry change over time, with ever new players, new causes, and new forms.

Notes: The examples in each category are solely illustrative (not exhaustive) nor necessarily mutually exclusive, and the comparison is relative (not absolute). As generalities, they allow exceptions. "Negative" freedom is freedom "from" (e.g., freedom from poverty), whereas "positive" freedom is freedom "to" (e.g., freedom to the state of enlightenment). "Negative" equality is "procedural" equality (e.g., equality of opportunity), while "positive" equality is "substantive" equality (e.g., equality of outcome). Existential dialectics impose constraints on freedom and equality in democracy, non-democracy, and post-democracy. There is no utopia, in the end; even should there be one, dystopia would exist within it.
Sources: From *Table 1.5* of *BDPD*—and also from *FHC*, *FCD*, and *FPHC*

Table 4.16. The Structure of Existential Dialectics II: The Wealth/Poverty Dialectics

• There is no wealth without poverty, just as there is no poverty without wealth.

• The wealth/poverty dialectics occurs in the realms of having, belonging, and being, in relation to the material, relational, and spiritual.

• The wealth/poverty dialectics also expresses itself at the multiple levels of analysis in accordance to methodological holism, be they about the micro-physical, the chemical, the biological, the psychological, the organizational, the institutional, the structural, the systemic, the cultural, and the cosmological.

• The wealth/poverty dialectics is a different manifestation of existential dialectics in general, subject to the principles in its logic of ontology—just as the freedom/unfreedom and equality/inequality dialectics are likewise.

• There is no economic utopia, in the end; even should there be one, dystopia would exist within it.

Notes: The main points here are solely illustrative (not exhaustive) nor necessarily mutually exclusive, and the comparison is relative (not absolute). As generalities, they allow exceptions.
Sources: From *BCPC*. See also *FCD* and *FHC*.

Table 4.17. The Structure of Existential Dialectics III: The Civilization/Barbarity Dialectics

• There is no civilization without barbarity.

• The civilization/barbarity dialectics applies in the four civilizing processes (e.g., the rationalizing process, the pacifying process, the stewardizing process, and the subliming process).

• The civilization/barbarity dialectics is another (different) manifestation of existential dialectics in general, subject to the principles in its logic of ontology—just as the freedom/unfreedom and equality/inequality dialectics and the wealth/poverty dialectics are likewise.

• There is no utopia, in the end; even should there be one, dystopia would exist within it.

Notes: The main points here are solely illustrative (not exhaustive) nor necessarily mutually exclusive, and the comparison is relative (not absolute). As generalities, they allow exceptions.
Sources: From *BCIV*. See also *FCD*, *FHC*, and *BDPD*.

Table 4.18. The Double Sides of Virtual Organizations (Part I)

- **Psychological**
  —Ex: virtual psychosis
  —Ex: impersonality and loneliness in quaternary social relations

- **Organizational**
  —Ex: the race for power and interests
  —Ex: the world of unequal successes
  —Ex: the bureaucratic life of its own
  —Ex: lesser accountability and transparency

- **Economic**
  —Ex: the economic divides
  —Ex: the erosive impact of commercialization

- **Political**
  —Ex: the anti-authoritarian myth
  —Ex: different power struggles among groups (e.g., Conservative, Reformist, Radical)

- **Structural**
  —Ex: different localities (e.g., climates, scenery)
  —Ex: divided domains (e.g., core, peripheral, sub-peripheral)
  —Ex: substitution effect of social capital

- **Systemic**
  —Ex: uneven advances in transportation and communications, and geographical migration

- **Cultural**
  —Ex: conflicting civilizational fabrics (e.g., Confucian, Islamic, Western)
  —Ex: the bias of the Liberal Democratic agenda
  —Ex: the addiction to moral fanaticism

(continued on next page)

Table 4.18. The Double Sides of Virtual Organizations (Part II)

Notes: These categories and examples are solely illustrative (not exhaustive), and some of the items can be reclassified somewhere else. Nor are they mutually exclusive. Since they are generalities, exceptions are expected.
Source: From Ch.7 of *FCD*

Table 4.19. Beyond the World of Titans, and the Remaking of the World Order

- **Hyper-Empires**
  —Ex: The Chinese Union
  —Ex: The Indian Union

- **Meso-Empires**
  —Ex: The European Union
  —Ex: The North American Union

- **Micro-Empires**
  —Ex: The Latin American Union
  —Ex: The Middle Eastern Union

- **The Rest of the World**
  —<u>Odd Powers</u>
    - Ex: Japan
    - Ex: Russia

  —<u>The Poor Club</u>
    - Ex: The African Union

  —<u>Ambivalent Regions</u>
    - Ex: Southeast Asia
    - Ex: Oceania
    - Ex: South Asia
    - Ex: Central Asia
    - Ex: Southern/Eastern Europe
    - Ex: North Africa
    - Ex: Central America
    - Ex: Others (e.g., the Korean peninsula)

Source: A summary of Chs.2-5 (of *BWT*)

Table 4.20. The Origins of Authoritarian Liberal Democracy

- **The Geopower of Nature (Ch.4 of *ALD*)**
  —Ex: Power Character and Geographical Strategy
  —Ex: Living Space and Territorial Expansion
  —Ex: Strategic Heartland and Containment

- **The Biopsychology of the Mind (Ch.5 of *ALD*)**
  —Ex: The Bell Curve and Mass Intelligence
  —Ex: Group Analysis and Mass Knowledge
  —Ex: Groupthink and Elite (Mis)calculation

- **The Disciplinary Control of Society (Ch.6 of *ALD*)**
  —Ex: Social Organizations of Ruthlessness
  —Ex: Social Institutions of Greed
  —Ex: Social Structure of Exclusion
  —Ex: Social Systems of Violence

- **The Molding Force of Culture (Ch.7 of *ALD*)**
  —Ex: The Tradition of Conquest
  —Ex: The Rationalization of Unreason

Notes: The examples in each category are solely illustrative (not exhaustive), and they are also relative (not absolute), nor are they mutually exclusive. As generalities, they allow exceptions.
Source: A summary of Chs.4-7 of *ALD*

Table 4.21. The Theory of Post-Democracy I: The Priority of Freedom over Equality (Part I)

- **Differences**
  - —*For the aggressive Lions (the strong Elitists)*
    - •Setting up rank distinctions among unequals (e.g., between inferior humans and superior post-humans, or later among inferior post-humans and superior ones, relatively speaking)
    - •Yearning for being not only distinguished from unequals, but also the first among equals (the best of the very best)
    - •Soul-searching for a high spiritual culture (not the trashy one for the masses). Mass culture is a dirty joke for them.
  - —*For the manipulative Foxes (the weak Counter-Elitists)*
    - •Seeking a gentle hegemony by way of more communitarian concerns (for inferior humans and, later, inferior post-humans)
    - •Being more sympathetic to less formal-legalistic institutions and values

- **Similarities**
  - —*For both Lions and Foxes*
    - •Exploring different spheres of non-human consciousness in the cosmos (something vastly superior than the human one)
    - •Recognizing the democratic illusions (e.g., no freedom without unfreedom, no equality without inequality, or simply no justice without injustice, and vice versa)

(continued on next page)

Table 4.21. The Theory of Post-Democracy I: The Priority of Freedom over Equality (Part II)

Notes: The two callings and examples in each category are solely illustrative (not exhaustive), since there will be many different post-human value ideals in the distant future of post-human civilization. The comparison is also relative (not absolute) towards post-democracy, so this is not just a version of free-market democracy (nor Fascism/Nazism, as shown in the table later on democracy, non-democracy, and post-democracy). Nor are they mutually exclusive. As generalities, they allow exceptions. And the specific forms of post-human post-democratic ideals need to be further developed in future after-postmodern history, as they will be different from the ones we now know. The point here is to solely give an extremely rough picture of a small part of the world to come that we have never known.
Source: From Ch.10 of *FCD*. Refer to text for more info and references.

Table 4.22. The Theory of Post-Democracy II: The Priority of Equality over Freedom

- **Hybrid Versions of**
  —Ex: the Trans-Feminine Calling
  —Ex: the Trans-Sinitic Calling
  —Ex: the Trans-Islamic Calling
  —Ex: the Trans-Outerspace Calling

- **Qualifications**
  —These four versions of post-capitalist value ideals need not automatically be post-democratic, just as capitalism does not necessarily mean democracy. They are two different entities—though closely related.
  —But up to a certain threshold of elevating equality at the farther expense of freedom, the democratic ideals will be overcome and cease to exist.
  —The overcome will not be socialist or communist, but post-democratic with no freedom without unfreedom and no equality without inequality, subject to the constraints of existential dialectics.

Notes: The callings are solely illustrative (not exhaustive), since there will be many different post-human value ideals in the distant future of post-human lifeforms. The comparison is also relative (not absolute), nor are they mutually exclusive. As generalities, they allow exceptions. And the specific forms of post-human post-democratic ideals need to be further developed in future after-postmodern history, as they will be different from the ones we now know. The point here is to solely give an extremely rough picture of a small part of the world to come that we have never known.
Source: From Ch.10 of *FCD*. Refer to text for more info and references.

Table 4.23. The Theory of Post-Democracy III: The Transcendence of Freedom and Equality (Part I)

- **Transcending Freedom in Floating Existence**
  —*Freedom*: seeking an ultimate elimination of the body. Being without the body. The aim is to transcend freedom in the end into a metaphysical state (i.e., beyond the physique).
  —*Unfreedom*: yet facing difficult trade-offs. The sacrifice of bodily existence and its joyfulness. An eternal boredom in floating existence in dark deep space, though with alternative pleasures. There is no free lunch even in the state of transcending freedom.

- **Transcending Equality in the Rivalry of Cosmic Hegemony**
  —*Inequality*: competing to outlast other lifeforms in floating existence, or just marginalizing them for one's hegemonic expansiveness in the rest of the cosmos (and even beyond). Universalism is only for the mediocre.
  —*Equality*: accepting only those of one's rank as equal partners in the vast spacetime for cosmic supremacy. Even here, the aim is to transcend equality into a metaphysical state.

(continued on next page)

Table 4.23. The Theory of Post-Democracy III: The Transcendence of Freedom and Equality (Part II)

Notes: Do not confuse this transcendence of freedom and equality (as one version of post-democracy) with the naïve temptation to transcend the freedom/unfreedom and equality/inequality dialectics. Existential dialectics hold true for freedom and equality in all cultures and societies—past, present, or future (i.e., democracy, non-democracy, and post-democracy), regardless of whether freedom and equality are conventionally understood as "negative" or "positive."

Also, the two features and examples in each are solely illustrative (not exhaustive), since there will be many different post-human value ideals in the distant future of post-human lifeforms. The comparison is also relative (not absolute), nor are they mutually exclusive. As generalities, they allow exceptions. And the specific forms of post-human ideals even for these radically alien floating lifeforms (and others unknown to us) need to be further developed in future after-postmodern history, as they will likely be different from the ones herein illustrated. The point here is to solely give a very rough picture of a small part of the extremely alien world to come that we have never known.

Source: From Ch.10 of *FCD*. Refer to text for more info and references.

Table 4.24. Democracy, Non-Democracy, and Post-Democracy (Part I)

- **Democracy**
  - —*Theoretical Constructs*
    - •The pursuit of freedom and equality (in various degrees), regardless of whether freedom and equality can be understood as "negative" or "positive"
      - (1) more equality than freedom: The relative priority of the good over the right
      - (2) more freedom than equality: The relative priority of the right over the good
  - —*Types*
    - •Only (1): Different versions of communitarian moral universalism
    - •Only (2): Different versions of liberal moral universalism
    - •(1) or (2): Different versions of anarchic (non-nation-state) moral universalism
    - •(1) or (2): Different versions of postmodern moral localism

- **Non-Democracy**
  - —*Theoretical Constructs*
    - •The focus on (1') equality or (2') freedom, but not both, regardless of whether freedom and equality can be understood as "negative" or "positive"
  - —*Types*
    - •Only (1'): Different versions on the Far Left (e.g., Stalinism, Robespierrianism)
    - •Only (2'): Different versions on the Far Right (e.g., Nazism, absolute monarchism)

(continued on next page)

Table 4.24. Democracy, Non-Democracy, and Post-Democracy (Part II)

- **Post-Democracy**
  —*Theoretical Constructs*
  - The priority of (1'') equality over freedom, or (2'') freedom over equality, or (3'') the transcendence of freedom and equality, regardless of whether freedom and equality are "negative" or "positive." In degree, (1'') or (2'') is less than (1') or (2') but more than (1) or (2)—respectively.
  - Like democracy and non-democracy, post-democracy is also subject to the freedom/unfreedom and equality/inequality dialectics (or existential dialectics in general). Unlike them, post-democracy acknowledges the constraints of existential dialectics and no longer value freedom and equality as sacred virtues. There is no utopia, in the end; even were there one, dystopia would exist within it.

  —*Types*
  - (1''): Different versions of trans-Sinitic value ideals
  - (1''): Different versions of trans-feminine value ideals
  - (1''): Different versions of trans-Islamic value ideals
  - (1''): Different versions of trans-outerspace value ideals
  - (2''): Different versions of post-human elitist value ideals
  - (3''): Different versions of the value ideals of floating consciousness (etc.)

(continued on next page)

Table 4.24. Democracy, Non-Democracy, and Post-Democracy (Part III)

Notes: The examples are solely illustrative (not exhaustive), nor are they mutually exclusive. As generalities, they allow exceptions. "Negative" freedom is freedom "from" (e.g., freedom from poverty), whereas "positive" freedom is freedom "to" (e.g., freedom to the state of enlightenment). "Negative" equality is "procedural" equality (e.g., equality of opportunity), while "positive" equality is "substantive" equality (e.g., equality of outcome). Existential dialectics impose constraints on freedom and equality in democracy, non-democracy, and post-democracy, regardless of whether freedom and equality can be understood as "negative" or "positive" in conventional discourse. Therefore, do not confuse the transcendence of freedom and equality in (3'') with the naïve temptation to transcend existential dialectics. There is no utopia, in the end; even should there be one, it would not exist without dystopia embedded within it.
Sources: A summary, based on my previous works, especially Ch.5 of *FHC*, Chs.5-10 of *FCD*, Chs.2-4 of *FPHC*, and Chs.1 & 7 of *BDPD*. The reader should consult the books for more analysis, as this is only a summary here.

Table 4.25. Multiple Causes of the Emergence of Post-Democracy (Part I)

- **At the Micro-Physical Level**
  —Ex: intelligent life without the human physical-chemical system
  —Sources: Ch.7 of *FHC*; Chs.9-10 of *FCD*; Ch.1 of *FPHC*

- **At the Chemical Level**
  —Ex: space radiation and toxins
  —Sources: Ch.7 of *FHC*; Chs.9-10 of *FCD*

- **At the Bio-Psychological Level**
  —Ex: exo-biological evolution in deep space
  —Ex: genetic engineering of new beings
  —Ex: limits of cognitive partiality
  —Ex: illusions of emotional neutrality
  —Ex: human biological inequality
  —Ex: the rise of unfolding unconsciousness
  —Sources: Ch.2 & Chs.9-10 of *FCD*; Ch.7 of *FHC*; Ch.4 of *BCPC*; *FPHU*

- **At the Institutional Level**
  —Ex: the flawed logic of equality
  —Ex: the conflicting nature of governance
  —Sources: Ch. 5 of *FHC*; Chs. 6 & 10 of *FCD*; Ch. 3 of *FPHC*; Chs.2-5 of *BDPD*

- **At the Organizational Level**
  —Ex: e-civic alienation
  —Ex: the dark sides of formal-legalistic routines
  —Sources: Ch.3 of *FHC*; Ch.7 of *FCD*; Ch.3 of *FPHC*

- **At the Structural Level**
  —Ex: ever new forms of inequities, at home and abroad
  —Ex: the emergence of China, women, and Islam as major actors
  —Sources: Chs.5-6 of *FHC*; Chs.7, 9 & 10 of *FCD*; Chs.4-5 of *BDPD*

(continued on next page)

Table 4.25. Multiple Causes of the Emergence of Post-Democracy (Part II)

• **At the Cultural Level**
—Ex: freedom/unfreedom dialectics
—Ex: equality/inequality dialectics
—Ex: system fragmentation and integration
—Sources: Ch.5 of *FHC*; Chs. 3, 9 & 10 of *FCD*; Ch.4 of *FPHC*; Ch.1 of *BDPD*; Ch.4 of *BCPC*

• **At the Systemic Level**
—Ex: space habitats (in zero-gravity) and colonization
—Ex: ultra advanced future info systems
—Ex: qualitative demography
—Sources: Ch.7 of *FHC*; Chs.9 &10 of *FCD*

• **At the Cosmological Level**
—Ex: the colonization of multiverses
—Ex: the alteration of space-time and the creation of new matter-energy
—Ex: the expansion of floating consciousness
—Ex: the spread of hyper-spatial consciousness
—Sources: Ch.7 of *FHC*; Chs.9 &10 of *FCD*; Ch.4 of *FPHC*; *FPHST*

Notes: The examples in each category are solely illustrative (not exhaustive), and some of the items can be reclassified somewhere else. Nor are they always mutually exclusive. Since they are generalities, exceptions are expected.
Sources: Especially from *FHC*, *FCD*, *FPHC*, *BCPC*, *BDPD*, *FPHST*, and *FPHU*. See also other books and my perspectives on civilizational holism.

Table 4.26. Some Clarifications about Post-Capitalism and Post-Democracy (Part I)

• The prefix "trans-" in the first category of post-capitalism (with its four versions) refers to something "going beyond" (not "uniting" or "combining"). Ex: *Sec.10.3.3* of *FCD*; *Sec.2.4* & *Sec.4.4* of *FPHC*; *Sec.7.2* of *BCPC*

• Such terms like "post-democracy," "post-capitalism," "post-human elitist," "trans-feminine calling," and the like as used in my works are more for our current intellectual convenience than to the liking of future humans and post-humans, who will surely invent more tasteful neologisms to call their own eras, entities, and everything else, for that matter. But the didactic point here is to use the terms to foretell what the future might be like, not that its eras and entities must be called so exactly and permanently.
Ex: *Sec.11.1* of *FCD*; *Sec.7.2* of *BCPC*

• The four versions in the first category of post-capitalist value ideals need not automatically be post-democratic, just as capitalism does not necessarily mean democracy. They are two different entities—though closely related. But up to a certain threshold of elevating equality at the farther expense of freedom, the democratic ideals will be overcome and cease to exist. The same is true for the post-human elitist calling in the second category of post-capitalism in relation to post-democracy, depending on the extent to which freedom is elevated at the expense of equality.
Ex: *Sec.10.4.3.3* of *FCD*; *Table 3.9* of *FPHC*; *Table 7.6* of *BDPD*

• The comparison in each of the three realms of existence in all forms of post-capitalism is not absolute, but relative. Examples include "communal" vs. "individualistic," and the like.
Ex: Notes in *Table 10.8*, *Table 10.9*, *Table 10.10*, & *Table 10.11* of *FCD*; Chs.2-4 of *FPHC*; *Sec.7.2* of *BCPC*

(continued on next page)

Table 4.26. Some Clarifications about Post-Capitalism and Post-Democracy (Part II)

• The emergence of post-capitalism (and post-democracy, for that matter) has multiple causes (to not be reduced to one or only a few).
Ex: Ch.10 of *FCD*, Chs.2-4 of *FPHC*; *Sec.1.3* & *Sec.7.2* of *BCPC* (or *Table 1.8* & *Table 7.11*)

• The specific forms of post-capitalism (and post-democracy, for that matter) need to be further developed in future after-postmodern history, as they will be different from the ones we now know. The point here is to solely give an extremely rough sketch of a world to come that we have never known.
Ex: *Sec.10.3.3* & *Sec.10.4.3.3* of *FCD*; *Table 10.14* & *Table 10.15* of *FCD*; *Sec.7.2* of *BCPC*

• All forms of post-capitalism are not part of a "teleological law," but of "historical trends" only. The same is also true for all forms of post-democracy.
Ex: *Sec.7.1* of *FHC*; *Sec.9.5.3.2* & *Sec.10.3.4.2* of *FCD*; *Sec.7.2* of *BCPC*

• Post-capitalism is not better than capitalism in an "absolute" sense but only fits in better, on the basis of the historical contingency of culture, society, nature, and the mind in some future eras. The same is true for post-democracy in relation to democracy. The term "better" is historically relative.
Ex: *Sec.10.3.3* of *FCD*; *Sec.1.7* of *BDPD*; *Sec.1.5* of *BCPC*

(continued on next page)

Table 4.26. Some Clarifications about Post-Capitalism and Post-Democracy (Part III)

• All forms of post-capitalism and post-democracy are subject to the constraints of existential dialectics. In the process, the dialectic direction is to go beyond the conventional "either-or" dichotomies (e.g., freedom vs. unfreedom, equality vs. inequality, freedom vs. equality, individuality vs. communality, spirituality vs. materiality, formal legalism vs. informal legalism, etc.). As is true in post-civilization, to go beyond the dichotomies is to acknowledge the co-existence of both in each dichotomy, although the degree of scaling one over the over varies from case to case (e.g., the theory of post-capitalism I, the theory of post-capitalism II, the theory of post-democracy I, the theory of post-democracy II, etc.)—but is not to be extreme in largely favoring one over the other, *on average* (all things considered). There is no utopia to be had in the end; even should there be one, dystopia would exist within it.
Ex: Ch.5 of *FHC*; *Sec.10.4.4.2* of *FCD*; *Sec.1.5* of *BDPD*; *Sec.1.3* of *BCPC*; *BCIV*

• All forms of post-capitalism, however different from each other though they are, share one common feature, in that they all inspire for a higher spiritual culture. The same is also true for post-democracy.
Ex: *Sec.10.3*, *Sec.10.4* & *Sec.10.5* of *FCD*; *Chs.2-4* of *FPHC*; *Sec.7.2* of *BCPC*

• All forms of post-capitalism try to avoid the excess in capitalist consumerism by favoring more basic than artificial needs in having, but the quality and quantity of these "basic" needs will be measured by future standards, not by our current ones. Standards are historically relative.
Ex: *Sec.10.3*, *Sec.10.4* & *Sec.10.5* of *FCD*; Ch.2 of *FPHC*; *Sec.7.2* of *BCPC*

(continued on next page)

Table 4.26. Some Clarifications about Post-Capitalism and Post-Democracy (Part IV)

• All forms of post-capitalism make use of a different degree of political authority with advanced info systems in future history and strives for higher spiritual cultures (especially in the post-human age), while acknowledging the constraints of existential dialectics and no longer valuing free market (as in capitalism) and economic control (as in non-capitalism) as sacred virtues. Ex: *Sec.10.3.4.2*, *Sec.10.3*, *Sec.10.4* & *Sec.10.5* of *FCD*; Chs.2-4 of *FPHC*; *Sec.1.5* of *BDPD*; *Sec.7.2* of *BCPC*

Notes:: The main points here are solely illustrative (not exhaustive) nor necessarily mutually exclusive, and the comparison is relative (not absolute). As generalities, they allow exceptions. The sections as cited are only illustrative (not exhaustive).

Sources: From *FHC*, *FCD*, *FPHC*, and *BDPD*

Table 4.27. The Theory of Post-Capitalism I.1: By Group— Ex: Spiritual/Communal in the Trans-Feminine Calling

- **More Communal Than Individual**
  —*Sharing*: learning from others, as different ideas mutually enrich
  —*Cooperative*: encouraging a sense of shared leadership and teamwork

- **More Informal-Legalistic Than Formal-Legalistic**
  —*Specific*: listening more from the heart than from the head, to know a person as a concrete, not as an abstract, unit
  —*Affective*: thinking and acting with others on a more affective tone. Business can mix with an emotional touch.
  —*Ascriptive*: hiring (or firing) can be done on the basis of merit (or lack of it), but deep solidarity (sisterhood) is important too.
  —*Particularistic*: making decisions on the basis of cost-benefit analysis, but a given group relationship is vital

- **More Spiritual Than Secular**
  —*Long-Term Looking*: sharing for a long-term relationship (e.g., love, friendship), not just for a short-term gain
  —*Loving/Caring*: showing compassion for the sufferings of others, without quickly blaming and pre-judging
  —*Respectful*: showing acceptance about others' feelings (and thoughts)

Notes: The categories and examples are solely illustrative, since there can be different versions, and the comparison is relative (not absolute), nor are they mutually exclusive. As generalities, they allow exceptions. The specific forms of the trans-feminine version need to be further developed in future after-postmodern history, as they will be different from the ones we now know, since the prefix "trans-" here means going beyond or deconstructing the feminine values, while using them as the inspirational point at the beginning.
Source: From Ch.10 of *FCD*. Refer to text for more info and references.

Table 4.28. The Theory of Post-Capitalism I.2: By Nation-State— Ex: Spiritual/Communal in the Trans-Sinitic Calling

- **More Communal Than Individualistic**
  —*Centralized*: being more top-down in management
  —*Collective*: encouraging more group cooperation
  —*Social*: investing in trust and connection

- **More Informal-Legalistic Than Formal-Legalistic**
  —*Specific*: knowing more of those related or connected
  —*Affective*: behaving in a paternalistic, hierarchical way
  —*Ascriptive*: favoring family members and those related
  —*Particularistic*: building connection (guanxi) as imperative

- **More Spiritual Than Secular**
  —*Expansionist*: diffusing civilizational values (e.g., the superiority complex of civilizationalism)
  —*Holistic*: synthesizing things into a panoramic horizon
  —*Historical*: learning from the lessons of the ancient past
  —*Respectful*: deferential to elders and superiors

Notes: The categories and examples are solely illustrative, since there can be different versions, and the comparison is relative (not absolute), nor are they mutually exclusive. As generalities, they allow exceptions. The specific forms of the trans-Sinitic version need to be further developed in future after-postmodern history, as they will be different from the ones we now know, since the prefix "trans-" here means going beyond or deconstructing the Sinitic values, while using them as the inspirational point at the beginning.
Source: From Ch.10 of *FCD*. Refer to text for more info and references.

Table 4.29. The Theory of Post-Capitalism I.3: By Region— Ex: Spiritual/Communal in the Trans-Islamic Calling

- **More Communal Than Individualistic**
  —*Collective*: building the webs of relationships to bind individuals
  —*Sharing*: cultivating the established "wisdom" through common experience
  —*Cooperative*: stressing harmony, solidarity, and commonality

- **More Informal-Legalistic Than Formal-Legalistic**
  —*Specific*: making efforts to know well the participants (family and larger community) in matters of common concern
  —*Affective*: mixing work with language and ritual on explicit religious (Islamic) ideals, texts, stories, and examples
  —*Ascriptive*: privileging local history and custom on relationships among kinship groups
  —*Particularistic*: preferring an unbiased insider with ongoing connections to all parties

- **More Spiritual Than Secular**
  —*Historical*: learning from the lessons of the past as a source of stability and guidance
  —*Deferential*: showing respect for age, experience, status, and leadership in communal affairs
  —*Honorable*: emphasizing face, dignity, prestige, and fairness
  —*Compassionate*: giving mercy and charity ("Zahah") to others

Notes: The categories and examples are solely illustrative (not exhaustive), and the comparison is relative (not absolute), nor are they mutually exclusive. As generalities, they allow exceptions. The specific forms of the trans-Islamic version need to be further developed in future after-postmodern history, as they will be different from the ones we now know, since the prefix "trans-" here means going beyond or deconstructing the Islamic values, while using them as the inspirational point at the beginning.

Sources: From Ch.10 of *FCD*. Refer to text for more info and references, especially from the works by George Irani (2000) and C. Murphy (September 19, 2001).

Table 4.30. The Theory of Post-Capitalism I.4: By Universe— Ex: Spiritual/Communal in the Trans-Outerspace Calling

- **More Communal Than Individual**
  —*Cooperative*: requiring teamwork in small space habitats
  —*Sharing*: learning from, and enjoying being with, each other in a small group in outer space

- **More Informal-Legalistic Than Formal-Legalistic**
  —*Specific*: knowing more about each other to facilitate living and working together in space, both as fellow astronauts and space-mates
  —*Affective*: being friendly and social to each other as vital to working and living in small space quarters
  —*Ascriptive*: nurturing comaraderie among fellow astronauts as if they are family members over time
  —*Particularistic*: building work relationship with enduring memory in a space mission

- **More Spiritual Than Secular**
  —*Long-Term*: looking beyond selfish materialistic concerns in a precarious space environment with potential life or death
  —*Loving/Caring*: cultivating deep bondage for the success of a long term space mission
  —*Transcendent*: searching for life meaning in outer space

Notes: The calling and examples in each category are solely illustrative (not exhaustive), since there will be many different outer-space value ideals in the distant future of space colonization. The comparison is also relative (not absolute), nor are they mutually exclusive. As generalities, they allow exceptions. And the specific forms of trans-outer-space calling need to be further developed in future after-postmodern history, as they will be different from the ones we now know, since the prefix "trans-" here means going beyond or deconstructing the current outer-space values, while using them as the inspirational point at the beginning. The point here is to solely give an extremely rough picture of a small part of the world to come that we still do not know much about.
Source: From Ch.10 of *FCD*. Refer to text for more info and references.

Table 4.31. The Theory of Post-Capitalism II: Spiritual/Individualistic in the Post-Human Elitist Calling (Part I)

- **More Individualistic Than Communal**
  —Setting up rank distinctions among unequals (e.g., between inferior humans and superior post-humans, or later among inferior post-humans and superior ones, relatively speaking)
  —Yearning for being not only distinguished from unequals, but also the first among equals (the best of the very best)
  —Recognizing the constraints of equality/inequality dialectics (or existential dialectics in general)

- **More Spiritual Than Secular**
  —Soul-searching for a high spiritual culture (not the trashy one for the masses). Mass culture is a dirty joke for them.
  —Exploring different spheres of non-human consciousness in the cosmos (something vastly superior than the human one)
  —Recognizing the constraints of freedom/unfreedom dialectics (or existential dialectics in general)

- **Qualifications**
  —Although post-human elitist post-democracy is comparable to post-human elitist post-capitalism in some respects, the former does not necessarily imply the latter (post-human elitist post-capitalism), just as democracy does not have to entail capitalism. They are two different (though related) entities.
  —But up to a certain threshold of incorporating government intervention with advanced info systems in future civilizations for higher spiritual concerns at the expense of the free market and materialist pursuit, the capitalist ideal will be overcome.
  —The overcome will not be Fascist or feudalistic, but post-capitalist, subject to the constraints of existential dialectics.

(continued on next page)

Table 4.31. The Theory of Post-Capitalism II: Spiritual/Individualistic in the Post-Human Elitist Calling (Part II)

Notes: The calling and examples in each category are solely illustrative (not exhaustive). The comparison is also relative (not absolute), nor are they mutually exclusive. As generalities, they allow exceptions. And the specific forms of post-human elitist post-capitalism need to be further developed in future after-postmodern history, as they will be different from the ones we now know, while using them as the inspirational point at the beginning. The point here is to solely give an extremely rough picture of a small part of the world to come that we still do not know much about.
Sources: From Ch.10 of *FCD* (and also *FPHC*, *BDPD*, and *BCPC*). Refer to the text for more info and references.

Table 4.32. Capitalism, Non-Capitalism, and Post-Capitalism (Part I)

- **Capitalism**
  - —*Theoretical Constructs*
    - •Allocation of scarce resources among alternative wants largely by free market for competition (whose characteristics in its ideal form include, for instance, no barrier to entry or exit, homogeneity, perfect information, a large number of buyers/sellers, and perfect factor mobility)
    - •More formal-legalistic than informal-legalistic, more individualistic than communal, and more material (secular) than spiritual
    - •Either (1) minimal government or (2) relatively active government
  - —*Types*
    - •Only (1): Different versions of market capitalism (e.g., the U.S.)
    - •Only (2): Different versions of welfare capitalism (e.g., Sweden)

- **Non-Capitalism**
  - —*Theoretical Constructs*
    - •Allocation of scarce resources among alternative wants mainly by political authority for policies (which can be regulative, redistributive, symbolic, and participatory)
    - •More informal-legalistic than formal-legalistic
    - •Either (1') more individualistic (for the elites), often (though not always) for material (secular) concerns, or (2') more communal (for the masses), often (though not always) for spiritual concerns
  - —*Types*
    - •Only (1'): Different versions on the Right (e.g., Fascist corporate-state economy for the glory of the new Rome, medieval lord-vassal-serf economy for the power of the feudalistic order)
    - •Only (2'): Different versions on the Left (e.g., Soviet command economy for the creation of the New Socialist Man)

(continued on next page)

Table 4.32. Capitalism, Non-Capitalism, and Post-Capitalism (Part II)

- **Post-Capitalism**

—*Theoretical Constructs*

- •Allocation of scarce resources among alternative wants largely by political authority with advanced info systems in future civilizations, subject to existential dialectics. In degree of allocating by authority, post-capitalism is more than capitalism but less than non-capitalism.
- •More spiritual than secular (material)
- •Either (1'') more individualistic or (2") more communal
- •Like capitalism and non-capitalism, post-capitalism is also subject to the freedom/unfreedom and equality/inequality dialectics (or existential dialectics in general). There is no utopia, in the end; even were there one, dystopia would exist within it.
- •Unlike capitalism and non-capitalism, post-capitalism makes use of a different degree of political authority with advanced info systems in future civilizations and strives for higher-spiritual cultures (especially in the post-human age), while acknowledging the constraints of existential dialectics and no longer valuing free market (as in capitalism) and economic control (as in non-capitalism) as sacred virtues.

—*Types*

- •Only (1"): Different versions of post-human elitist value ideals
- •Only (2''): Different versions of trans-Sinitic value ideals
- •Only (2''): Different versions of trans-feminine value ideals
- •Only (2''): Different versions of trans-Islamic value ideals
- •Only (2''): Different versions of trans-outerspace value ideals

---

(continued on next page)

Table 4.32. Capitalism, Non-Capitalism, and Post-Capitalism (Part III)

Notes: The calling and examples in each category are solely illustrative (not exhaustive). The comparison is also relative (not absolute), nor are they mutually exclusive. As generalities, they allow exceptions. And the specific forms of each calling need to be further developed in future after-postmodern history, as they will be different from the ones we now know, while using them as the inspirational point at the beginning. The point here is to solely give an extremely rough picture of a small part of the world to come that we still do not know much about.
Source: From Ch.10 of *FCD*. Refer to the text for more info and references.

Table 4.33. Multiple Causes of the Emergence of Post-Capitalism (Part I)

- **At the Micro-Physical Level**
  —Ex: intelligent life without the human physical-chemical system
  —Ex: mastering of quantum mechanics, electromagnetism, and other fields for the understanding of a broad range of anomalous experiences and the application for artificial intelligence for spiritual quest
  —Sources: Ch.7 of *FHC*; Chs.9-10 of *FCD*; Ch.1 of *FPHC*

- **At the Chemical Level**
  —Ex: space radiation and toxins
  —Sources: Ch.7 of *FHC*; Chs.9-10 of *FCD*

- **At the Bio-Psychological Level**
  —Ex: exo-biological evolution in deep space
  —Ex: genetic engineering of new beings
  —Ex: limits of human cognition
  —Ex: the rise of unfolding unconsciousness
  —Sources: Ch.2 & Chs.9-10 of *FCD*; Ch.7 of *FHC*; *FPHU*

- **At the Institutional Level**
  —Ex: the flawed logic of the free market
  —Ex: the need of a post-autistic economics
  —Sources: Ch.10 of *FCD*

- **At the Organizational Level**
  —Ex: the dark sides of formal-legalistic routines
  —Sources: Ch.3 of *FHC*; Ch.7 of *FCD*; Ch.3 of *FPHC*

- **At the Structural Level**
  —Ex: ever new forms of inequities, at home and abroad
  —Ex: the emergence of China, women, and Islam as major actors
  —Sources: Chs.5-6 of *FHC*; Chs.7, 9 & 10 of *FCD*; Chs.4-5 of *BDPD*

(continued on next page)

Table 4.33. Multiple Causes of the Emergence of Post-Capitalism (Part II)

- **At the Cultural Level**
  —Ex: freedom/unfreedom dialectics
  —Ex: equality/inequality dialectics
  —Sources: Ch.5 of *FHC*; Chs.3 & 10 of *FCD*; Ch.4 of *FPHC*; Ch.1 of *BDPD*

- **At the Systemic Level**
  —Ex: space habitats (in zero-gravity) and colonization
  —Ex: ultra advanced future info systems
  —Ex: qualitative demography
  —Sources: Ch.7 of *FHC*; Chs. 9 & 10 of *FCD*

- **At the Cosmological Level**
  —Ex: the colonization of multiverses
  —Ex: the alteration of space-time and the creation of new matter-energy
  —Ex: the expansion of floating consciousness
  —Ex: the spread of hyper-spatial consciousness
  —Sources: Ch.7 of *FHC*; Chs. 9 & 10 of *FCD*; Ch.4 of *FPHC*; *FPHST*

Notes: The examples in each category are solely illustrative (not exhaustive), and some of the items can be reclassified somewhere else. Nor are they always mutually exclusive. Since they are generalities, exceptions are expected.
Sources: Especially from *FHC*, *FCD*, *FPHC*, *BCPC*, *BDPD*, *FPHST*, and *FPHU*. See also other books and my perspectives on civilizational holism.

Table 4.34. The Theoretical Debate on Civilization

- **The Progressive Theory of Civilization**
  —*Thesis*: The "civilizing" process is "good," as opposed to the "barbarizing" process as something "bad," relatively speaking.
  —*Discourse*: Especially, though not exclusively, in the Enlightenment era and a bit before. Example: Thomas Hobbes—in that the tribes in primitive societies were "savages."

- **The Romantic Theory of Barbarity**
  —*Thesis*: The "civilizing" process is "bad," as opposed to the "barbarizing" process as something "good," relatively speaking.
  —*Discourse*: Especially, though not exclusively, in the Counter-Enlightenment circle. Example: Jean-Jacques Rousseau—in that civilization "corrupts" men, and the "savages" are in fact "noble."

- **The Moderate Theory of Civilization**
  —*Thesis*: The "civilizing" process is "good," but there is a price to pay, especially in systematic (compulsive) self-control.
  —*Discourse*: Especially, though not exclusively, in some late modern and postmodern circles. Example: Norbert Elias—in that social manners become more refined in the civilizing process, but self-control also becomes more systematic.

- **The Theory of Post-Civilization**
  —*Thesis*: The civilizing process is as evil and good as barbarity, and each cannot exist without the other, to be eventually superseded by post-civilization unto the post-human age.
  —*Discourse*: Proposed by Peter Baofu. See the rest of *BCIV* for more analysis.

Source: From *BCIV* on the theoretical debate

Table 4.35. No Freedom Without Unfreedom in the Civilizing Processes (Part I)

- **The Rationalizing Process (at the Level of Culture)**
  —if freer from the dominance of unreason (as in barbarism) in the civilizing process, then less free from the rationalizing process (be it in the form of the principle of either transcendence or immanence)
  —if freer from the principle of immanence in the rationalizing process, then less free from the inclination to commit terror in the name of reason and the relative underdevelopment of non-reason (e.g., in relation to yoga and meditation)
  —if freer from the principle of transcendence in the rationalizing process, then less free from the relative underdevelopment of reason (e.g., in relation to systematic methodology) and the occurrence of oppression in the name of non-reason

- **The Pacifying Process (at the Level of Society)**
  —if freer from the dominance of pillage (as in savagery) in the civilizing process, then less free from the pacifying process (be it in the form of external control or self-control)
  —if freer from self-control in the pacifying process, then less free from the temptation of expansionist oppression and rebellious mindset in external control
  —if freer from external control in the pacifying process, then less free from the gruesome psychological self-torture and conformism in self-control

- **The Stewardizing Process (at the Level of Nature)**
  —if freer from the dominance of nature (as in the state of nature) in the civilizing process, then less free from the stewardizing process (be it in the form of the stewardship of creation or the covenant with nature)
  —if freer from the stewardship of creation in the stewardizing process, then less free from material underdevelopment, relatively speaking, and spiritual exclusion in the covenant with nature
  —if freer from the covenant with nature in the stewardizing process, then less free from ecological degradation and spiritual disconnection from nature in the stewardship of creation

(continued on next page)

Table 4.35. No Freedom Without Unfreedom in the Civilizing Processes (Part II)

- **The Subliming Process (at the Level of the Mind)**
  —if freer from the dominance of spontaneity (as in the wild state of the mind) in the civilizing process, then less free from the subliming process, be it in the form of (cyclical-centric) self-refinement or (linear-centric) self-discipline
  —if freer from (cyclical-centric) self-refinement in the subliming process, then less free from the (linear-centric) self-regimen (as a form of neurosis)
  —if freer from (linear-centric) self-discipline in the subliming process, then less free from the (cyclical-centric) self-torture (equally as a form of neurosis)

Notes: The examples in each category are solely illustrative (not exhaustive), and the comparison is relative (not absolute), nor are they necessarily mutually exclusive. And some can be easily re-classified elsewhere. As generalities, they allow exceptions.
Sources: From *BCIV*. See also *FHC*, *FCD*, *FPHC*, *BDPD*, and *BCPC*.

Table 4.36. No Equality Without Inequality in the Civilizing Processes (Part I)

- **The Rationalizing Process (at the Level of Culture)**
  —if more equal for the role of rationalization in the rationalizing process (of civilizational making), then less equal for that of mythicization (as in barbarism)
  —if more equal for the principle of transcendence in (linear-centric) rationalizing process, then less equal for the principle of immanence
  —if more equal for the principle of immanence in (cyclical-centric) rationalizing process, then less equal for the principle of transcendence

- **The Pacifying Process (at the Level of Society)**
  —if more equal for pacification in civilizational making, then less equal for the institution of pillaging and others (as in savagery)
  —if more equal for external control, relatively speaking, in pacifying process, then less equal for self-control
  —if more equal for self-control, relatively speaking, in pacifying process, then less equal for external-control

- **The Stewardizing Process (at the Level of Nature)**
  —if more equal for stewardship in the stewardizing process (of civilizational making), then less equal for reverent (submissive) existence (as in barbarism)
  —if more equal for the stewardship of creation in (linear- centric) stewardizing process, then less equal for the (cyclical-centric) covenant with nature for harmonious co-existence
  —if more equal for the (cyclical-centric) covenant with nature in the stewardizing process, then less equal for the (linear-centric) stewardship of nature for domination

(continued on next page)

Table 4.36. No Equality Without Inequality in the Civilizing Processes (Part II)

- **The Subliming Process (at the Level of the Mind)**
  —if more equal for the role of reason in the subliming process, then less equal for that of unreason (as in the natural state of wildness)
  —if more equal for the primacy of reason in (linear-centric) subliming process, then less equal for other faculties (e.g., intuition, existential feelings, and analogous thinking) in cyclical-centric one
  —if more equal for the exercise of other faculties (e.g., intuition, existential feelings, and analogous thinking) in cyclical-centric subliming process, then less equal for the role of reason in linear-centric counterpart

Notes: The examples in each category are solely illustrative (not exhaustive), and the comparison is relative (not absolute), nor are they mutually exclusive. And some can be easily reclassified else-where. As generalities, they allow exceptions.
Sources: From *BCIV*. See also *FHC*, *FCD*, *FPHC*, *BDPD*, and *BCPC*.

Table 4.37. Five Theses on Post-Civilization

• Post-civilization no longer treats civilization as good and barbarity as evil (relatively speaking), nor does it nostalgically regard barbarity as good and civilization as evil (relatively speaking again). Civilization is as evil and good as barbarity.

• Post-civilization also no longer accepts the dichotomy between civilization and barbarity. Civilization cannot exist without barbarity. It is no longer necessary to preserve civilization, any more than it is imperative to destroy barbarity. To go beyond civilization and barbarity is to acknowledge the co-existence of both, although the degree of scaling one over the over varies from case to case—but is not to be extreme in largely favoring one over the other, *on average* (subject to the constraints of existential dialectics).

• Post-civilization is thus subject to the constraints of existential dialectics. There is no freedom without unfreedom, and no equality without inequality, for instance. There will be no utopia; even should there be one, there would be dystopia embedded within it.

• Post-civilization will eventually replace civilization (as a form of life settlement), to be dominated by post-capitalist and post-democratic lifeforms here on earth and in deep space (besides other alien lifeforms that we have never known), unto the post-human age in multiverses. Those few post-humans who keep civilization will live in a "post-human civilization," while the rest (the majority), who choose post-civilization, will evolve towards the state of "post-human post-civilization." One therefore should not confuse "post-human civilization" with "post-human post-civilization," as the two are not the same.

• Post-civilization will confront psychosis as a primary problem in the culture of virtuality unto the post-human age, just as civilization has neurosis as a primary one of its own (although both neurosis and psychosis are major problems in both).

Notes: The comparison in each category is relative (not absolute), nor are they necessarily mutually exclusive. And some can be easily re-classified elsewhere. As generalities, they allow exceptions.
Sources: From *BCIV*. See also *FHC*, *FCD*, *FPHC*, *BDPD*, and *BCPC*.

Table 4.38. Barbarity, Civilization, and Post-Civilization

- **The Rationalizing Process (at the Level of Culture)**
  —*Barbarity*
    - More mythicizing than rationalizing, relatively speaking

  —*Civilization*
    - More rationalizing than mythicizing, relatively speaking

  —*Post-Civilization*
    - Beyond the dichotomy, subject to existential dialectics

- **The Pacifying Process (at the Level of Society)**
  —*Barbarity*
    - More pillaging than pacifying, relatively speaking

  —*Civilization*
    - More pacifying than pillaging, relatively speaking

  —*Post-Civilization*
    - Beyond the dichotomy, subject to existential dialectics

- **The Stewardizing Process (at the Level of Nature)**
  —*Barbarity*
    - More revering than stewardizing, relatively speaking

  —*Civilization*
    - More stewardizing than revering, relatively speaking

  —*Post-Civilization*
    - Beyond the dichotomy, subject to existential dialectics

- **The Subliming Process (at the Level of the Mind)**
  —*Barbarity*
    - More impulsing than subliming, relatively speaking

  —*Civilization*
    - More subliming than impulsing, relatively speaking

  —*Post-Civilization*
    - Beyond the dichotomy, subject to existential dialectics

Notes: The comparison in each category is relative (not absolute), nor are they necessarily mutually exclusive. And some can be easily re-classified elsewhere. As generalities, they allow exceptions.
Sources: From *BCIV*. See also *FHC*, *FCD*, *FPHC*, *BDPD*, and *BCPC*.

Table 4.39. Types of Super Civilization in the Cosmos (Part I)

- **Type I**
  —a civilization which gains control of and uses the total energy output "falling on its planet from its sun for interstellar communication" (or, in general, space colonization). For N. Kardashev, who proposed the first three types, human civilization is currently Type Zero (Type O), which is below even Type I, since its present energy consumption for all purposes, let alone for interstellar communication, is still 10,000 times less.

- **Type II**
  —a civilization which gains control of and uses directly the total energy output of its sun for interstellar communication (or, in general, space colonization).

- **Type III**
  —a civilization which gains control of and uses the total energy output of its galaxy for interstellar communication (or, in general, space colonization).

- **Type IV**
  —a civilization which gains control of and uses the total energy output of its cluster of galaxies for interstellar communication (or, in general, space colonization).

- **Type V**
  —a civilization which gains control of and uses the total energy output of its supercluster of galaxies for interstellar communica-tion (or, in general, space colonization).

(continued on next page)

Table 4.39. Types of Super Civilization in the Cosmos (Part II)

- **Type…n**
  —So continues the series in what I call the cyclical progression of hegemony in the cosmos and beyond.

Notes: The Russian astrophysicist Nikolai Kardashev proposed the first three types of super civilization in terms of total energy out-put for interstellar communication. (CSM 1979) I extend his argument further to propose Type IV, Type V, Type VI, and Type…n, in the context of my claim about the cyclical progression of he-gemony in the cosmos and beyond.
Sources: From *Table 9.4* of *FCD.* See *FHC*, *FCD*, and *FPHC* for more info.

Table 4.40. The Civilizational Project from Pre-Modernity to After-Postmodernity (Part I)

	Pre-Modern	*Modern*	*Postmodern*	*After-Postmodern*
Main narratives	•Sacralness •Courtliness •Vitalism •Animism	•Freedom •Equality •Fraternity	•Multiplicity •Hybridization	•Naked contingency •Cyclical progression of hegemony
Main institutions	•Monarchy •Aristocracy •Feudalism •Holy order •Primitivism	•Capitalism •Liberalism •Socialism •Nazism •Fascism	•Capitalism •Liberalism •Postmodern politics of difference	•Post-Capitalism •Post-Democracy •Others
Main techno-logical and economic revolutions	•Agricultural	•Service •Industrial	•Informational	•Biological •Material •Energy •Space •Others

(continued on next page)

Table 4.40. The Civilizational Project from Pre-Modernity to After-Postmodernity (Part II)

	Pre-Modern	*Modern*	*Postmodern*	*After-Postmodern*
Main agents	•Males •Upper strata •Mini-states	•Males •Upper strata •Whites •Empires	•Males •Upper strata •Whites •Others •Supra-states •IO's	•Post-humans •Humans •Others
Main impacts	•Local	•Inter-national	•Global	•Outer-space •Multiverse
Main outcomes	•Towards moderntiy •Rise of linear- & cyclical-centric civiliza-tions	•Towards post-modernity •Dominance of linear-centric civilization	•Towards after-post-moderntiy •Linear-centric civiliza-tion in crisis	•Towards human (& maybe post-human) extinction •Rise of post-civiliza-tion, especially in post-human forms of space-time

Notes: The examples in each category are solely illustrative (not exhaustive) nor necessarily mutually exclusive, and the comparison is relative (not absolute). As generalities, they allow exceptions.

Sources: From *Table 10.16* of *FCD*—and also from *BCIV* on post-civilization (and *FPHST*)

Table 4.41. Civilizational Holism
(Part I)

- **At the Micro-Physical Theoretical Level**
  —Ex: Mastering of quantum mechanics, electromagnetism, and other fields for the understanding of a broad range of anomalous experiences and theapplication for artificial intelligence (*Sec.1.4.1* of *FPHC*)

- **At the Chemical Theoretical Level**
  —Ex: Unprecedented expansion of (and violence to) the mind through ever new forms of drugs (and virtual technologies, for that matter) (Ch.9 of *FCD*)

- **At the Biological Theoretical Level**
  —Ex: Humans are not biologically equal, on the basis of race, gender, ethnicity, age, and whatnot. (*Sec.2.6* & Ch.10 of *FCD*; *BNN*) And post-humans will experience the same fate, in an even more amazing way.

- **At the Psychological Theoretical Level**
  —Ex: Human cognitive impartiality and emotional neutrality are quite limited. (*Secs.2.4-2.5* of *FCD*)
  —Ex: Rise of Floating Consciousness (Ch.10 of *FCD*; Chs.1 & 4 of *FPHC*) and Unfolding Unconsciousness (*FPHU*)

- **At the Organizational Theoretical Level**
  —Ex: Administrative colonization of deep space, with less legal-formalism in some corners. (Chs.9-10 of *FCD*)

- **At the Institutional Theoretical Level**
  —Ex: Both capitalism and democracy will not last, to be superseded by different versions of post-capitalism and post-democracy in after-postmodernity. (Ch.10 of *FCD*)

(continued on next page)

Table 4.41. Civilizational Holism
(Part II)

- **At the Structural Theoretical Level**
  —Ex: Social stratification reappears in ever new forms, also with new causes and new players in the cyclical progression of hegemony. (Chs.8-10 of *FCD*)
  —Ex: The world of hyper-empires, and the union of the unions (*BWT*)

- **At the Systemic Theoretical Level**
  —Ex: Outerspace expansion: local → regional → global → solar → galactic → clustery → multiversal (Ch.9 of *FCD*)
  —Ex: Demographic transition: human extinction, and the rise of post-humans (e.g., cyborgs, thinking machines, thinking robots, genetically altered superior beings, floating consciousness, hyper-spatial consciousness) (Ch.4 of *FPHC*; Ch.10 of *FCD*; & Ch.7 of *FHC*)
  —Ex: New technological forces in material sciences, electronic and communication sciences, energy sciences, biosciences, manufacturing and engineering sciences, and space sciences (Ch.10 of *FCD* & Ch.7 of *FHC*)
  —Ex: Systematic dominance towards nature for space colonization (Chs.9-10 of *FCD*; Chs.2 & 7 of *FHC*)

- **At the Cultural Theoretical Level**
  —Ex: The post-human transcendence of freedom and equality (Ch.10 of *FCD*)
  —Ex: Methodological Holism (Ch.1 of *FCD*; Ch.1 of *FPHC*; *Sec.2.1* & *Sec.2.5* of *BCPC*)
  —Ex: The Evolution from Barbarity to Post-Civilization (*BCIV*)

- **At the Cosmological Theoretical Level**
  —Ex: Mastering of dark matter and dark energy, and the exploration of multiverses (Ch.4 of *FPHC*; Ch.10 of *FCD*; & Ch.7 of *FHC*)
  —Ex: Alternation of space-time (*FPHST*)
  —Ex: The emergence of hyper-spatial consciousness (*FPHC*)

(continued on next page)

Table 4.41. Civilizational Holism (Part III)

- **At Other Levels**
  —Ex: Historical: pre-modernity → modernity → postmodernity → after-postmodernity (human distinction, and the rise of post-humans, including floating consciousness, hyper-spatial consciousness, and unfolding unconsciousness) (Ch.7 of *FHC*; Ch.10 of *FCD*; *FPHC*; *FPHU*)

Notes: These examples are solely illustrative (not exhaustive), and some of the items can be reclassified somewhere else. Nor are they always mutually exclusive. Since they are generalities, exceptions are expected. And the comparison is relative, not absolute.
Sources: From *Table 5.1* of *FPHC*—with details from *FHC*, *FCD*, and the rest of my books. Not every aspect in each category as discussed in all my books are presented here, since there are too many issues. For more info, also consult the table on theories on civilizational holism and, of course, the books themselves.

Table 4.42. Theories on Civilizational Holism (Part I)

I. Theories in Relation to Nature

—At the Macro-Physical (Cosmological) Theoretical Level

- • 39. Theory of Hyper-Spatial Consciousness (Peter Baofu) (Ch.4 of *FPHC*; *FPHG*)
- (• 37). Selective Theory of Geometry (Peter Baofu) (*FPHG*)
- (• 36). Perspectival Theory of Space-Time (Peter Baofu) (*FPHST*)
- (• 35). Dialectic Theory of Complexity (Peter Baofu) (*FC*)
- (• 8). Theory of Floating Consciousness (Peter Baofu) (Ch.10 of *FCD*; Chs.1 & 4 of *FPHC*)
- • 38. Theory of the Geopower of Nature (Peter Baofu) (Ch.4 of *ALD*)

—At the Micro-Physical Theoretical Leve

- • 37. Selective Theory of Geometry (Peter Baofu) (*FPHG*)
- • 36. Perspectival Theory of Space-Time (Peter Baofu) (*FPHST*)
- • 35. Dialectic Theory of Complexity (Peter Baofu) (*FC*)

(continued on next page)

Table 4.42. Theories on Civilizational Holism (Part II)

II. Theories in Relation to Culture

—*At the Cultural Theoretical Level*

- 34. Dualistic Theory of Mass Culture (Peter Baofu)
  (Ch.2 of *FHC*)
- 33. Comparative Theory of Religion (Peter Baofu)
  (Ch.3 of *FHC*; Ch.9 of *FCD*; Ch.1 of *FPHK*)
- 32. Theory of Post-Civilization (Peter Baofu)
  (*BCIV*)
- 31. Theory of the Trinity of Modernity to Its After-Postmodern Counterpart (Peter Baofu)
  (*FHC*; Ch.10 of *FCD*)
- 30. Transformative Theory of Aesthetic Experience (Peter Baofu)
  (*FAE*)

(• 26). Theory of Post-Capitalism (Peter Baofu)
  (Ch.10 of *FCD*; Chs.2 & 4 of *FPHC*; *BCPC*)

(• 25). Theory of Post-Democracy (Peter Baofu)
  (Ch.10 of *FCD*; Chs.3 & 4 of *FPHC*; *BDPD*)

(• 4). Theory of Existential Dialectics,
  or the Holistic Theory of Knowledge (Peter Baofu)
  (*FHC*; *FCD*; *FPHC*; *BDPD*; *FC*; *FAE*; *ALD; FIA; FPHK*; etc,)

(• 3). Contrastive Theory of Rationality (Peter Baofu)
  (*FPHML*)

(• 2). Theory of Methodological Holism (Peter Baofu)
  (Ch.1 of *FCD*; Ch.1of *FPHC*; *Sec.2.1* & *Sec.2.5* of *BCPC*;
  FC; *FPHK*; etc.)

(continued on next page)

Table 4.42. Theories on Civilizational Holism (Part III)

III. Theories in Relation to Society

—*At the Organizational Theoretical Level*

- 29. Theory of E-Civic Alienation (Peter Baofu) (Ch.7 of *FCD*)
- 28. Combinational Theory of Organization (Peter Baofu) (*FPHO*; Ch.6 of *ALD*)

—*At the Institutional Theoretical Level*

- 27. Reconstruction Theory of Law (Peter Baofu) (*FPHLAW*)
- 26. Theory of Post-Capitalism (Peter Baofu) (Ch.10 of *FCD*; Chs.2 & 4 of *FPHC*; *BCPC*)
- 25. Theory of Post-Democracy (Peter Baofu) (Ch.10 of *FCD*; Chs.3 & 4 of *FPHC*; *BDPD*)
- 24. Dynamic Theory of Comparative Political Systems (Peter Baofu) (*ALD*)

—*At the Systemic Theoretical Level*

- 23. Contingent Theory of Urban Planning (Peter Baofu) (*FPHUP*)
- 22. Totalistic Theory of Communication (Peter Baofu) (*FPHMM*; *FCD*; *FHC*)
- 21. Ambivalent Theory of Technology (Peter Baofu) (*FPHE*; *FCD*; *FHC*)
- 20. Multifaceted Theory of War and Peace (Peter Baofu) (Ch.9 of *FCD*; Ch.1 of *FPHK*)
- 19. Theory of Post-Humanity (Peter Baofu) (Ch.7 of *FHC*; Chs.3, & 10 of *FCD*; Chs.1, 3 & 4 of *FPHC*; and other books of mine)
- 18. Theory of the Cyclical Progression of System Integration and Fragmentation (Peter Baofu) (Chs.9-10 of *FCD*)
- 17. Synthetic Theory of Information Architecture (Peter Baofu) (*FIA*)

(continued on next page)

Table 4.42. Theories on Civilizational Holism (Part IV)

III. Theories in Relation to Society (*cont'd*)

—*At the Structural Theoretical Level*

- 16. Theory of the Cyclical Progression of Hegemony (Peter Baofu) (Chs.9-10 of *FCD*; Chs.1, 3 & 4 of *FPHC*; *BDPD*)
- 15. Theory of the Cyclical Progression of Empire-Building (Peter Baofu) (*BWT*)

IV. Theories in Relation to the Mind

—*At the Biological Theoretical Level*

- 14. Theory of Contrastive Advantages (Peter Baofu) (*Sec.2.6* & Ch.10 of *FCD; BNN*)
- (• 8). Theory of Floating Consciousness (Peter Baofu) (Ch.10 of *FCD*; Chs.1 & 4 of *FPHC*)

—*At the Psychological Theoretical Level*

- 13. Theory of Virtual Sexuality (Peter Baofu) (*FPHS*)
- 12. Expansive-Contractive Theory of Martial Arts (Peter Baofu) (*FPHMA*)
- 11. Multilogical Theory of Learning (Peter Baofu) (*FPHL*)
- 10. Comprehensive Theory of Creative Thinking (Peter Baofu) (*FPHCT*)
- 9. Theory of Unfolding Unconsciousness—also known as the Unfolding Theory of Anomalous Experience (Peter Baofu) (*FPHU*)
- 8. Theory of Floating Consciousness (Peter Baofu) (Ch.10 of *FCD*; Chs.1 & 4 of *FPHC*)
- 7. Theory of Cognitive Partiality (Peter Baofu) (*Sec.2.4* of *FCD*; *Sec.4.5.1.1* of *BCPC*)
- 6. Theory of Emotional Non-Neutrality (Peter Baofu) (*Sec.2.5* of *FCD*; *Sec.4.5.2* of of *BCPC*)
- 5. Theory of Behavioral Alteration (Peter Baofu) (*Sec.4.5.3* of *BCPC*)

(continued on next page)

Table 4.42. Theories on Civilizational Holism (Part V)

V. Meta-Theories (in Relation to Theories)

—*At the Ontological Meta-Theoretical Level*

- 4. Theory of Existential Dialectics, or the Holistic Theory of Knowledge (Peter Baofu) (*FHC*; *FCD*; *FPHC*; *BDPD*; *FC*; *FAE*; *ALD; FIA; FPHK*; etc,)
- 3. Contrastive Theory of Rationality (Peter Baofu) (*FPHML*)

—*At the Methodological Meta-Theoretical Level*

- 2. Theory of Methodological Holism (Peter Baofu) (Ch.1 of *FCD*; Ch.1of *FPHC*; *Sec.2.1* & *Sec.2.5* of *BCPC*; *FC*; *FPHK*; etc.)

VI. Theories in Relation to the Rest

—*At Other Levels (Historical)*

- 1. Theory of the Evolution from Pre-Modernity to After-Postmodernity (Peter Baofu) (*FHC*; Ch.9-10 of *FCD*; *FPHC*)

Notes: All these theories are my constructions, as some of the main contributions of my grant project on civilization and its future. These examples are solely illustrative (not exhaustive), and some of the items can be reclassified somewhere else. Nor are they always mutually exclusive. Since they are generalities, exceptions are expected.

Sources: From my previous books

Bibliography

American Heritage Dictionary (AHD). 2009. "Property." <http://www.bartleby. <com/cgi-bin/texis/webinator/sitesearch?FILTER=col61&query=property&x =0&y=0>.

Amnesty International (AI). 2002. "The International Criminal Court—A Historic Development in the Fight for Justice" (April). <http://www.amnesty.org/ en/library/info/IOR40/008/2002>.

Anderson, R. Lanier. 1994. "Nietzsche's Will to Power as a Doctrine of the Unity of Science." *Studies in History and Philosophy of Science*, 25 (5): 738.

Aristotle. 2009. *The Politics*. Ernest Barker. R.F. Stalley, intro. Oxford, England: Oxford University Press.

Baofu, Peter. 2010. *The Future of Post-Human Sexuality: A Preface to a New Theory of the Body and Spirit of Love Makers*. Cambridge, England: Cambridge Scholars Publishing.

_____,2009. *The Future of Post-Human Martial Arts: A Preface to a New Theory of the Body and Spirit of Warriors*. Cambridge, England: Cambridge Scholars Publishing.

_____.2009a. *The Future of Post-Human Organization: A Preface to a New Theory of Communication, Decision-Making, and Leadership*. Cambridge, England: Cambridge Scholars Publishing.

_____.2009b. *The Future of Post-Human Language: A Preface to a New Theory of Structure, Context, and Learning*. Cambridge, England: Cambridge Scholars Publishing.

_____.2009c. *The Future of Post-Human Urban Planning: A Preface to a New Theory of Density, Void, and Sustainability*. Cambridge, England: Cambridge Scholars Publishing.

_____.2009d. *The Future of Post-Human Geometry: A Preface to a New Theory of Infinity, Symmetry, and Dimensionality*. Cambridge, England: Cambridge Scholars Publishing.

_____.2009e. *The Future of Post-Human Creative Thinking: A Preface to a New Theory of Invention and Innovation*. Cambridge, England: Cambridge Scholars Publishing.

_____.2009f. *The Future of Post-Human Mass Media: A Preface to a New Theory of Communication*. Cambridge, England: Cambridge Scholars Publishing.

_____.2009g. *The Future of Post-Human Engineering: A Preface to a New Theory of Technology*. Cambridge, England: Cambridge Scholars Publishing.

_____.2008. *The Future of Post-Human Mathematical Logic: A Preface to a New Theory of Rationality*. Cambridge, England: Cambridge Scholars Publishing.

_____.2008a. *The Future of Post-Human Knowledge: A Preface to a New Theory of Methodology and Ontology*. Oxford, United Kingdom: Chandos Publishing (Oxford) Ltd.

_____.2008b. *The Future of Post-Human Unconsciousness: A Preface to a New Theory of Anomalous Experience*. Cambridge, England: Cambridge Scholars Publishing.

_____.2008c. *The Future of Information Architecture: Conceiving a New Way to Understand Taxonomy, Network, and Intelligence*. Oxford, United Kingdom: Chandos Publishing (Oxford) Ltd.

_____.2007. *The Rise of Authoritarian Liberal Democracy: A Preface to a New Theory of Comparative Political Systems*. Cambridge, England: Cambridge Scholars Publishing.

_____.2007a. *The Future of Aesthetic Experience: Conceiving a Better Way to Beauty, Ugliness, and the Rest*. Cambridge, England: Cambridge Scholars Publishing.

_____.2007b. *The Future of Complexity: Conceiving a Better Way to Understand Order and Chaos*. London, United Kingdom: World Scientific Publishing Co.

_____.2007c. *Beyond the World of Titans, and the Remaking of World Order: A Preface to a New Logic of Empire-Building*. Cambridge, England: Cambridge Scholars Publishing.

_____.2006. *Beyond Nature and Nurture: Conceiving a Better Way to Understand Genes and Memes*. Cambridge, England: Cambridge Scholars Publishing.

_____.2006a. *The Future of Post-Human Space-Time: Conceiving a Better Way to Understand Space and Time*. New York: Peter Lang Publishing, Inc.

_____.2006b. *Beyond Civilization to Post-Civilization: Conceiving a Better Model of Life Settlement to Supersede Civilization*. New York: Peter Lang Publishing, Inc.

_____.2005. *Beyond Capitalism to Post-Capitalism: Conceiving a Better Model of Wealth Acquisition to Supersede Capitalism*. New York: The Edwin Mellen Press.

_____.2004. *The Future of Post-Human Consciousness*. New York: The Edwin Mellen Press.

_____.2004a. *Beyond Democracy to Post-Democracy: Conceiving a Better Model of Governance to Supersede Democracy*. Volume 1. New York: The Edwin Mellen Press.

_____.2004b. *Beyond Democracy to Post-Democracy: Conceiving a Better Model of Governance to Supersede Democracy*. Volume 2. New York: The Edwin Mellen Press.

_____.2002. *The Future of Capitalism and Democracy*. Maryland: The University Press of America.

_____.2000. *The Future of Human Civilization*. Volume 1. New York: The Edwin Mellen Press.

_____.2000a. *The Future of Human Civilization*. Volume 2. New York: The Edwin Mellen Press.

Barash, David. 2002. "Evolution, Males, and Violence" (May 24). *The Chronicle of Higher Education*. <http://www.physics.ohio-state.edu/~wilkins/writing/Assign/so/male-violence.html>.

_____. & Judith Eve Lipton. 2002a. *Gender Gap: The Biology of Male-Female Differences*. New Brunswick, NJ: Transaction Publishers.

Barrow, John D. 1998. *Impossibility: The Limits of Science and the Science of Limits*. Oxford: Oxford University Press.

Bastiat, Frédéric. 1944. *The Law*. Los Angeles, CA: Pamphleteers.

BBC News (BBC). 2008. "Viacom Will Sue YouTube for $1bn." <http://news.bbc.co.uk/1/hi/business/6446193.stm>.

_____.2008a. "YouTube Law Fight 'Threatens Net.'" <http://news.bbc.co.uk/1/hi/technology/7420955.stm>.

_____.2009b. "Google Must Divulge YouTube Log." <http://news.bbc.co.uk/1/hi/technology/7488009.stm>.

Bendix, Reinhard. 1977. *Max Weber: An Intellectual Portrait*. California: University of California Press. <http://books.google.com/books?visbn=0520031946&id=63sC9uaYqQsC&pg=PA1&lpg=PA1&sig=g-kn8gtBIRvG-ss0I_-BmrBz9YE>.

Bergkamp, Lucas. 2001. *Liability and Environment: Private and Public Law Aspects of Civil Liability for Environmental Harm in an International Context*. New York: Martinus Nijhoff Publishers.

Berkowitz, Peter. 1990. "On the Laws Governing Free Spirits and Philosophers of the Future: A Response to Nonet's 'What is Positive Law?" *Yale Law Journal*, 701.

Biletzki, Anat; & Anat Matar. 2006. "Ludwig Wittgenstein" (Nov. 17). *Stanford Encyclopedia of Philosophy*. <http://plato.stanford.edu/entries/wittgenstein/>.

Bolton, John. 2002. "International Criminal Court: Letter to UN Secretary General Kofi Annan" (May). U.S. Department of State. <http://www.state.gov/>.

Brett, D. Schaefer. 2001. "Overturning Clinton's Midnight Action on the International Criminal Court." The Heritage Foundation. <http://www.heritage.org/Research/InternationalOrganizations/EM708.cfm>.

Brobjer, Thomas H. 1997. "Nietzsche's Reading and Private Library, 1885-1889." *Journal of the History of Ideas*, 58 (4): 663-693.

Bunge, Mario. 1999. *Dictionary of philosophy*. Amherst, MA: Prometheus Books.

BusinessDictionary.com (BD). 2009. "Property Definition." <http://www.businessdictionary.com/definition/property.html>.

Catholic Encyclopedia (CE). 2009. "Moral Aspect of Divine Law" (September 17). <http://www.newadvent.org/cathen/09071a.htm>.

Chase, Scott. 1993. "Tachyons" (March). *Physics FAQ*. <http://math.ucr.edu/home/baez/physics/ParticleAndNuclear/tachyons.html>.

CNNMoney.com (CNN). 2008. "Mediaset Files EUR500 Million Suit Vs Google's YouTube." <http://money.cnn.com/news/newsfeeds/articles/djf500/200807301025DOWJONESDJONLINE000654_FORTUNE5.htm>.

Coase, Ronald H. 1960. "The Problem of Social Cost." *Journal of Law and Economics*, 3: 1–44. <http://www.sfu.ca/~allen/CoaseJLE1960.pdf>.

Corazzon, Raul. 2007. "Definitions of Ontology: From Nicolai Hartmann to the Present Time." <http://www.formalontology.it/section_4_two.htm>.

Corbett, Dan. 2008. "Introduction to String Theory" (November 23). *ThinkQuest*. <http://library.thinkquest.org/27930/stringtheory1.htm>.

Cotterrell, Roger. 1999. *Emile Durkheim: Law in A Moral Domain*. Stanford, CA: Stanford University Press.

Daily Telegraph (DT). 2008. "Premier League to Take Action against YouTube." <http://www.telegraph.co.uk/sport/main.jhtml?xml=/sport/2007/05/05/ufnrup05.xml>.

Derrida, Jacques. 1984. *The Ear of the Other: Otobiography, Transference, Translation*. Claude Levesque and Christie McDonald, eds. Peggy Kamuf, tr. NY: Schocker Books.

Devichand, Mukul. 2008. "Is English Law Related to Muslim Law?" *BBC News*. <http://news.bbc.co.uk/1/hi/magazine/7631388.stm>.

Elliott, Mark. 1999. "The Ultra Vires Doctrine in a Constitutional Setting: Still the Central Principle of Administrative Law." *Cambridge Law Journal*, 58: 129.

Encyclopedia Britannica (EB). 1994. "Modernization and Industrialization." Chicago: The University of Chicago Press.

Engelhardt, Tom. 2009. "Biking Out of Iraq: On Troops That Don't Depart, Experts Who Never Leave the Scene, an Air Force That Suddenly Wasn't There, and a War That No Longer Needs a Justification" (Thursday, August 13). <http://www.commondreams.org/view/2009/08/13-9>.

Everett, Hugh. 1957. "'Relative State' Formulation of Quantum Mechanics" (July). *Reviews of Modern Physics*, vol. 29, no.3. <http://www.univer.omsk.su/omsk/Sci/Everett/paper1957.html>.

Firehammer, Reginald. 2005. "Basic Principles of Ontology" (January 05). <http://usabig.com/autonomist/philosophy/ontology2.html>.

Fried, Charles. 1981. *Contract as Promise: A Theory of Contractual Obligation*. Cambridge, MA: Harvard University Press.

Friedman, Lawrence Meir. 2005. *A History of American Law*. New York: Simon and Schuster.

Fuller, Buckminster. 1938. *Nine Chains to the Moon*. Philadelphia: J. B. Lippincott Company.

Garner, Bryan A. 2001. *A Dictionary of Modern Legal Usage*. England: Oxford University Press.

Gott, J. Richard. 2002. *Time Travel in Einstein's Universe*. Boston : Houghton Mifflin.

Gray, John. 2009. "Public Nuisance: A Historical Perspective." *NuisanceLaw.Com*. <http://www.nuisancelaw.com/learn/historical>.

Greig, D. W. 1976. *International Law*. London, England: Butterworths.

Guth, Alan. 1997. *The Inflationary Universe: The Quest for a New Theory Of Cosmic Origins*. New York: Helix Books.

Harris, Anthony; Stephen Thomas; Gene Fisher; & David Hirsch. 2002. "Murder and Medicine: The Lethality of Criminal Assault 1960-1999." (May). *Homicide Studies*, 6 (2): 128–166. <http://hsx.sagepub.com/cgi/content/abstract/6/2/128>.

Hawkins, Bryan. 2006. "The Glucksberg Renaissance: Substantive Due Process since Lawrence v. Texas." *Michigan Law Review*, 105. <http://students.law.umich.edu/mlr/archive/105/2/hawkins.pdf>.

Hodgson, Geoffrey M. 2004. "Social Darwinism in Anglophone Academic Journals: A Contribution to the History of the Term." *Journal of Historical Sociology*, 17(4): 428–63.

Hopkins, Jim. 2006. "Surprise! There's a third YouTube co-founder." *USA Today*. <http://www.usatoday.com/tech/news/2006-10-11-youtube-karim_x.htm>.

Horn, Anette. 2005. "Nietzsche's Interpretation of His Sources on Darwinism: Idioplasma, Micells and Military troops." *South African Journal of Philosophy*, 24 (4): 260-272.

Hughes, Graham. 1996. *Common Law Systems. Fundamentals of American Law*. Alan B. Morrison. England: Oxford University Press.

Hume, David. 2003. *A Treatise of Human Nature*. New York: Dover.

International Criminal Court, the (ICC), 2007. "Situations and Cases." <http://www.icc-cpi.int/cases.html>.

Jakoby, Stanford M. 2005. "Economic Ideas and the Labour Market." *Comparative Labor Law and Policy Journal*, 25 (1): 43–78. <http://www.law.uiuc.edu/publications/cll&pj/archive/vol_25/issue_1/Jacoby Article25-1.pdf>.

Jary, David; & Julia Jary. 1995. *Collins Dictionary of Sociology*. New York:

HarperCollins.

Josephy, Alvin, Jr. ed. 1965. *The American Heritage History of The Great West.* New York: Simon and Shuster.

Kaku, Michio. 1994. *Hyperspace: A Scientific Odyssey Through Parallel Universes, Time Warps, and The Tenth Dimension.* Illustrations by Robert O'Keefe. Oxford: Oxford University Press.

Kangas, Steve. 2008. "Ronald Coase and the Coase Theorem" (December 28). <http://www.huppi.com/kangaroo/L-chicoase.htm>.

Kant, Immanuel. 1961. *Observations on the Feeling of the Beautiful and Sublime.* John T. Goldthwait, tr. CA: University of California Press.

_____.1953. *Groundwork of the Metaphysics of Morals.* H.J. Paton, tr. New York: Harper Press.

Kazantzakis, Nikos. 1909. *Friedrich Nietzsche and the Philosophy of Law and Polity.* Athens: Editions Kazantzakis.

Kiernan, Victor. 1982. *European Empires from Conquest to Collapse, 1815-1960.* Leicester, England: Leicester University Press.

Kohn, Livia. 2000. *Daoism Handbook (Handbook of Oriental Studies–Part 4: China, 14).* Boston, MA: Brill Academic Publishers.

Lamar, Howard R.. 1977. *The Reader's Encyclopedia of the American West.* NY: Harper & Row.

Linarelli, John. 2004. "Nietzsche in Law's Cathedral: Beyond Reason and Postmodernism." *Catholic University Law Review,* 53: 413–457. <http://papers.ssrn.com/sol3/papers.cfm?abstract_id=421040>.

Lloyd, Sharon; & Susanne Sreedhar. 2008. "Hobbes's Moral and Political Philosophy" (August 23). *Stanford Encyclopedia of Philosophy.* <http://plato.stanford.edu/entries/hobbes-moral/#StaNat>.

Locke, John. 1986. *The Second Treatise on Civil Government.* Buffalo, New York: Prometheus Books.

MacIntyre, Alasdair. 1981. *After Virtue: A Study in Moral Philosophy.* Notre Dame, IN: University of Notre Dame Press.

Magstadt, Thomas, & Peter M.Schotten. 1998. *Nations and Governments: Comparative Politics in Regional Perspective.* NY: St. Martin's Press.

Makdisi, John. 2005. *Islamic Property Law: Cases and Materials for Comparative Analysis with the Common Law.* Durham, NC: Carolina Academic Press.

_____.1999. "The Islamic Origins of the Common Law." *North Carolina Law Review,* 77 (5): 1635–1739.

Marsden, Rhodri. 2009. "Why Did My YouTube Account Get Closed Down?" *The Independent.* <http://www.independent.co.uk/life-style/gadgets-and-tech/features/rhodri-marsden-why-did-my-youtube-account-get-closed-down-1770618.html>.

Marx, Karl & Frederick Engels. 1948. *The Communist manifesto*. New York: New York Labor News.

Matteson, Michael; Robert Konopaske; & John Ivancevich. 2005. *Organizational Behavior and Management.* New York: McGraw-Hill Irwin.

Maugh, Thomas. 2002. "WHO: 1.6 million Die in Violence Annually" (Oct. 04). *Los Angeles Times*. <http://online.sfsu.edu/~rone/Buddhism/FivePrecepts/AnnualViolence.html>.

McCormick, John. 2004. *Comparative Politics in Transition.* CA: Wadsworth/Thomas Learning.

Merriam-Webster's Collegiate Dictionary Online (MWD). 2009. "Law" (August 28). <http://www.merriam-webster.com/dictionary/law>.

_____.2009a. "Lie" (August 28). <http://www.merriam-webster.com/dictionary/lie>.

_____. 2007. "Agency" (March 20). <http://www.m-w.com/dictionary/agency>.

McAleer, Neil. 1987. *The Mind-Boggling Universe.* New York: Doubleday & Co.

Mommsen, Wolfgang, 1992. *The Political and Social Theory of Max Weber: Collected Essays*. Chicago, IL: University of Chicago Press.

Moore, George Edward. 1903. *Principia Ethica.* Cambridge: Cambridge University Press. <http://fair-use.org/g-e-moore/principia-ethica>.

Moore, Gregory. 2002. *Nietzsche, Biology, Metaphor.* New York: Cambridge University Press.

Müller-Lauter, Wolfgang. 1999. "The Organism as Inner Struggle: Wilhelm Roux's Influence on Nietzsche." *Nietzsche: His Philosophy of Contradictions and the Contradictions of His Philosophy*. David J. Parent, tr. Chicago, IL: The University of Illinois Press.

Nietzsche, Friedrich. 1974. *The Gay Science*. Walter Kaufmann, tr. New York: Random House.

_____. 1969. "On the Genealogy of Morals." *The Birth of Tragedy and the Genealogy of Morals*. W. Kaufmann, et al., trs. NY: Vintage Books.

Nova Online (NO). 2000. "Time Can Vary." <http://www.pbs.org/wgbh/nova/time/thinktime.html>.

Oppy, Graham. 2005. "Property." *The Shorter Routledge Encyclopedia of Philosophy*. Edward Craig, ed. New York: Routledge.

Parrillo, V. 1985. *Contemporary Social Problems*. New York: John Wiley & Sons.

Raman, Shankar. 1997. Lectures on Literary Theory. Cambridge, MA: MIT (spring).

Rand, Ayn. 1957. *Atlas Shrugged.* New York, Random House.

Redfem, Alan. 2004. "Regulation of International Arbitration." *Law and Practice of International Commercial Arbitration*. London: Sweet & Maxwell.

Ritzer, George. 2004. *Enchanting a Disenchanted World: Revolutionizing the*

Means of Consumption. Thousand Oaks, CA: Pine Forge Press.

Ross, Ellen; & Rayna Rapp. 1981. "Sex and Society: A Research Note from Social History and Anthropology" (January). *Comparative Studies in Society and History*, 23 (1): 51-72. <http://www.jstor.org/pss/178382>.

Rousseau, Jean-Jacques. 1984. *A Discourse on Inequality*. Maurice Cranston, intro. New York, NY: Penguin Books.

Salmond, John William. 1907. *Jurisprudence, or, The Theory of the Law*. London, England: Stevens and Haynes.

San Francisco Chronicle (SFC). 2008. "Woman Can Sue Over YouTube Clip De-posting." <http://www.sfgate.com/cgi-bin/article.cgi?f=/c/a/2008/08/20/MNU412FKRL.DTL>.

Sashkin, Marshall. 2002. *Leadership That Matters*. San Francisco, CA: Berrett-Koehler Publishers.

Savigny, Friedrich Carl von. 1831. *On the Vocation of Our Age for Legislation and Jurisprudence*. Abraham A. Hayward, tr.

Schopenhauer, Arthur. 1965. *On the Basis of Morality*. E. F. J. Payne, tr. Indianapolis, IN: Bobbs-Merrill.

Schrems, John. 2004. *Understanding Principles of Politics and the State*, Portage, MI: PageFree Publishing.

Searle, John R. 1995. *The Construction of Social Reality*, New York: Free Press.

_____1964. "How to Derive 'Ought' From 'Is.'" *Philosophical Review*, 73: 43-58.

Shlain, Leonard. 1991. *Art and Physics: Parallel Visions in Space,Time, and Light*. New York: William Morrow and Co., Inc.

Small, Robin. 2001. *Nietzsche in Context*. Burlington: Ashgate.

Smith, Adam. 1977. *The Wealth of Nations*. William Letwin, intro. New York: Dutton.

Sullivan, Arthur; & Steven M. Sheffrin. 2003. *Economics: Principles in Action*. Upper Saddle River, NJ: Pearson Prentice Hall.

United Nations, the (UN). 2009. "Rome Statute of the International Criminal Court." United Nations Treaty Collection. <http://treaties.un.org/Pages/ViewDetails.aspx?src=TREATY&mtdsg_no=XVIII-10&chapter=18&lang=en>.

_____.2002. "The International Criminal Court" (December). Department of Public Information. <http://www.un.org/News/facts/iccfact.htm>.

U.S. Department of State (USDS). 2003. "Frequently Asked Questions About the U.S. Government's Policy Regarding the International Criminal Court (ICC)" (July). <http://www.state.gov/>.

Utley, Robert, ed. 2003. *The Story of The West*. New York: DK Publishing.

Van Norden, Bryan; & Philip Ivanhoe. 2005. *Readings in Classical Chinese Philosophy*. Indianapolis, Indiana: Hackett Publishing Company.

Weber, Max. 1978. *Economy and Society: An Outline of Interpretative Sociology.* Guenther Roth and Claus Wittich. Berkeley, eds. Los Angeles, CA: University of California Press.

_____.1930. *The Protestant Ethic and the Spirit of Capitalism.* Talcott Parsons, tr. New York: Scribner.

Weber, Tim. 2009. "BBC Strikes Google-YouTube deal." *BBC.* <http://news.bbc.co.uk/1/hi/business/6411017.stm>.

Wehberg, Hans. 1959. "Pacta Sunt Servanda." *The American Journal of International Law*, vol. 53, no. 4 (Oct.): 775.

White, G. Edward. 2000. *The Constitution and the New Deal.* Cambridge, MA: Harvard University Press. .

_____.2003. *Tort Law in America: An Intellectual History.* New York: Oxford University Press.

White, Richard. 1991. *A New History of the American West.* Oklahoma: University of Oklahoma Press.

Whitlock, Greg. 1996. "Roger Boscovich, Benedict de Spinoza and Friedrich Nietzsche: The Untold Story." *Nietzsche Studien*, 25: 200-220.

Wikipedia (WK). 2009. "Law" (August 28). <http://en.wikipedia.org/wiki/Law>.

_____.2009a. "Public Law" (August 28). <http://en.wikipedia.org/wiki/Public_law>.

_____.2009b. "Criminal Law" (August 28). <http://en.wikipedia.org/wiki/Criminal_law>.

_____.2009c. "Property Law" (August 28). <http://en.wikipedia.org/wiki/Property_law>.

_____.2009d. "Trust Law" (August 29). <http://en.wikipedia.org/wiki/Trust_law>.

_____.2009e. "Contract Law" (August 29). <http://en.wikipedia.org/wiki/Contract_law>.

_____.2009f. "Tort Law" (August 29). <http://en.wikipedia.org/wiki/Tort_law>.

_____.2009g. "Jurisprudence" (August 29). <http://en.wikipedia.org/wiki/Jurisprudence>.

_____.2009h. "Analytic Jurisprudence" (August 29). <http://en.wikipedia.org/wiki/Analytic_jurisprudence>.

_____.2009i. "Normative Jurisprudence" (August 29). <http://en.wikipedia.org/wiki/Normative_jurisprudence>.

_____.2009j. "Groundwork of the Metaphysic of Morals " (August 29). <http://en.wikipedia.org/wiki/Groundwork_of_the_Metaphysic_of_Morals>.

_____.2009k. "David Hume" (August 29). <http://en.wikipedia.org/wiki/David_Hume>.

_____.2009l. "Averroes" (August 29). <http://en.wikipedia.org/wiki/Averroes>.

_____.2009m. “Early Islamic Philosophy” (August 29). <http://en.wikipedia.org/wiki/Early_Islamic_philosophy>.

_____.2009n. “Sources of Islamic Law” (August 29). <http://en.wikipedia.org/wiki/Sources_of_Islamic_law>.

_____.2009o. “Sturges v. Bridgman” (August 30). <http://en.wikipedia.org/wiki/Sturges_v_Bridgman>.

_____.2009p. “German_Historical_School” (August 30). <http://en.wikipedia.org/wiki/German_Historical_School>.

_____.2009q. “Immanuel Kant” (August 30). <http://en.wikipedia.org/wiki /Immanuel_Kant>.

_____.2009r. “Signmund Freud” (August 30). <http://en.wikipedia.org/wiki/Sigmund_Freud>.

_____.2009s. “Murder” (August 31). <http://en.wikipedia.org/wiki/Murder>.

_____.2009t. “Strict Liability (Criminal)” (August 31). <http://en.wikipedia.org/wiki/Strict_liability_(criminal)>.

_____.2009u “Strict Liability” (August 31). <http://en.wikipedia.org/ wiki/Strict_liability>.

_____.2009v “Those Who Would Give Up Essential Liberty” (August 31). <http: //en.wikipedia.org/wiki/Those_who_would_give_up_Essential_Liberty>.

_____.2009w “Law of the Jungle” (August 31). <http://en.wikipedia.org/wiki/Law_of_the_jungle>.

_____.2009x “Social Darwinism” (August 31). <http://en.wikipedia.org/wiki/Social_Darwinism>.

_____.2009y “Herbert Spencer” (August 31). <http://en.wikipedia.org/wiki/Herbert_Spencer>.

_____.2009z “American Old West” (August 31). <http://en.wikipedia.org/wiki/Wild_West>.

_____.2009aa “Manifest Destiny” (August 31). <http://en.wikipedia.org/wiki/Manifest_Destiny>.

_____.2009bb “Natural Law” (September 01). <http://en.wikipedia.org/wiki/Natural_laws>.

_____.2009cc “Lao Tze” (September 01). <http://en.wikipedia.org/wiki/Lao_Tze>.

_____.2009dd “Tao” (September 01). <http://en.wikipedia.org/wiki/Tao>.

_____.2009ee. “Patent.” (October 07). <http://en.wikipedia.org/wiki/Patent>.

_____.2009ff. “International Public Law.” (September 01). <http://en.wikipedia.org/wiki/International_public_law>.

_____.2009gg. “International Criminal Court.” (September 01). <http://en.wikipedia.org/wiki/International_criminal_court >.

_____.2009hh. "Category: People Convicted of Crimes against Humanity by Nationality" (September 01). <http://en.wikipedia.org/wiki/Category: People_ convicted_of_crimes_against_humanity_by_nationality>.

_____.2009ii. "Category: Argentine People Convicted of Crimes against Humanity by Nationality" (September 05). <http://en.wikipedia.org/wiki/Category: Argentine_people_ convicted_of_crimes_against_humanity_by_nationality>.

_____.2009jj. "Category: Austrian People Convicted of Crimes against Humanity by Nationality" (September 05). <http://en.wikipedia.org/wiki/Category: Austrian_people_ convicted_of_crimes_against_humanity_by_nationality>.

_____.2009kk. "Category: Bosnia and Herzegovina People Convicted of Crimes against Humanity by Nationality" (September 05). <http://en.wikipedia.org/wiki/Category: Bosnia_and_Herzegovina_people_ convicted_of_crimes_against_humanity_by_nationality>.

_____.2009ll. "Category: Chilean People Convicted of Crimes against Humanity by Nationality" (September 05). <http://en.wikipedia.org/wiki/Category: Chilean_people_ convicted_of_crimes_against_humanity_by_nationality>.

_____.2009mm. "Category: Croatian People Convicted of Crimes against Humanity by Nationality" (September 05). <http://en.wikipedia.org/wiki/ Category: Croatian_people_convicted_of_crimes_against_humanity_by_ nationality>.

_____.2009nn. "Category: Ethiopian People Convicted of Crimes against Humanity by Nationality" (September 05). <http://en.wikipedia.org/wiki/ Category: Ethiopian_people_convicted_of_crimes_against_humanity_by_ nationality>.

_____.2009oo. "Category: French People Convicted of Crimes against Humanity by Nationality" (September 05). <http://en.wikipedia.org/wiki/Category: French_people_ convicted_of_crimes_against_humanity_by_nationality>.

_____.2009pp. "Category: German People Convicted of Crimes against Humanity by Nationality" (September 05). <http://en.wikipedia.org/wiki/Category: German_people_ convicted_of_crimes_against_humanity_by_nationality>.

_____.2009qq. "Category: Haitian People Convicted of Crimes against Humanity by Nationality" (September 05). <http://en.wikipedia.org/wiki/Category: Haitian_people_ convicted_of_crimes_against_humanity_by_nationality>.

_____.2009rr. "Category: Iraqi People Convicted of Crimes against Humanity by Nationality" (September 05). <http://en.wikipedia.org/wiki/Category: Iraqi_people_ convicted_of_crimes_against_humanity_by_nationality>.

_____.2009ss. "Category: Japanese People Convicted of Crimes against Humanity by Nationality" (September 05). <http://en.wikipedia.org/wiki/Category: Japanese_people_ convicted_of_crimes_against_humanity_by_nationality>.

_____.2009tt. "Category: Kosovar People Convicted of Crimes against Humanity by Nationality" (September 05). <http://en.wikipedia.org/wiki/Category:

Kosovar_people_ convicted_of_crimes_against_humanity_by_nationality>.

_____.2009uu. “Category: Rwandan People Convicted of Crimes against Humanity by Nationality” (September 05). <http://en.wikipedia.org/wiki/Category: Rwandan_people_convicted_of_crimes_against_humanity_by_nationality>.

_____.2009ww. “Category: Serbian People Convicted of Crimes against Humanity by Nationality” (September 05). <http://en.wikipedia.org/wiki/Category: Serbian_people_ convicted_of_crimes_against_humanity_by_nationality>.

_____.2009xx. “Category: Sierra Leonean People Convicted of Crimes against Humanity by Nationality” (September 05). <http://en.wikipedia.org/wiki/Category: Sierra_Leonean_people_convicted_of_crimes_against_humanity_by_nationality>.

_____.2009yy. “Category: South African People Convicted of Crimes against Humanity by Nationality” (September 05). <http://en.wikipedia.org/wiki/Category: South_African_people_ convicted_of_crimes_against_humanity_by_nationality>.

_____.2009zz. “Constitutional Law” (September 16). <http://en.wikipedia.org/wiki/Constitutional_law>.

_____.2009aaa. “Balance of Power (Federalism)” (September 16). <http://en.wikipedia.org/wiki/Balance_of_power_(federalism)>.

_____.2009bbb. “Balance of Power (Parliament)” (September 16). <http://en.wikipedia.org/wiki/Balance_of_power_(parliament)>.

_____.2009bcc. “Divine Law” (September 17). <http://en.wikipedia.org/wiki/Divine_law>.

_____.2009ddd. “Divine Command Theory” (September 17). <http://en.wikipedia.org/wiki/Divine_command_theory>.

_____.2009eee. “Equity (Law)” (September 18). <http://en.wikipedia.org/wiki/Equity_(law)>.

_____.2009fff. “Common Law” (September 18). <http://en.wikipedia.org/wiki/Common_law>.

_____.2009ggg. “Jus Inter Gentes” (September 20). <http://en.wikipedia.org/wiki/Jus_inter_gentes>.

_____.2009hhh. “Monism and Dualism in International Law” (September 20). <http://en.wikipedia.org/ wiki/Monism_and_dualism_in_international_law>.

_____.2009iii. “Analytical Jurisprudence” (September 20). <http://en.wikipedia.org/wiki/Analytic_jurisprudence>.

_____.2009jjj. “Naturalistic Fallacy” (September 21). <http://en.wikipedia.org/wiki/Naturalistic_fallacy>.

_____.2009kkk. “Is-Ought Problem” (September 21). <http://en.wikipedia.org/wiki/Is-ought_problem>.

_____.2009lll. "Logical Positivism" (September 23). <http://en.wikipedia.org/wiki/Logical_positivism>.

_____.2009mmm. "Tort" (September 23). <http://en.wikipedia.org/wiki/Tort>.

_____.2009nnn. "Negligence" (September 23). <http://en.wikipedia.org/wiki/Negligence>.

_____.2009ooo. "Will to Power" (September 24). <http://en.wikipedia.org/wiki/Will_to_power>.

_____.2009ppp. "Property Law" (September 25). <http://en.wikipedia.org/wiki/Property>.

_____.2009qqq. "Property" (September 25). <http://en.wikipedia.org/wiki/Property_law>.

_____.2009rrr. "Personal Rights" (September 25). <http://en.wikipedia.org/wiki/Personal_rights>.

_____.2009sss. "Copyright infringement" (September 25). <http://en.wikipedia.org/ wiki/Copyright_infringement>.

_____.2009ttt. "Criticism of YouTube" (September 25). <http://en.wikipedia.org/wiki/Criticism_of_YouTube>.

_____.2009uuu. "YouTube" (September 25). <http://en.wikipedia.org/wiki/You Tube>.

_____.2009vvv. "Jean-Jacques Rousseau" (September 26). <http://en.wikipedia.org/wiki/Jean_Jacques_Rousseau>.

_____.2009www. "Sociology of Law" (September 26). <http://en.wikipedia.org/wiki/Sociology_of_law>.

_____.2009xxx. "Max Weber" (September 26). <http://en.wikipedia.org/ wiki/Max_Weber>.

_____.2009yyy. "Emile Durkheim" (September 26). <http://en.wikipedia.org/wiki/Emile_Durkheim>.

_____.2009zzz. "Pierre Bourdieu" (September 26). <http://en.wikipedia.org/wiki/Pierre_Bourdieu>.

_____.2009aaaa. "Contract" (September 27). <http://en.wikipedia.org/wiki/Contract>.

_____.2009bbbb. "Critical Legal Studies" (September 28). <http://en.wikipedia.org/wiki/Critical_legal_studies>.

_____.2009cccc. "Administrative Law" (September 28). <http://en.wikipedia.org/wiki/Administrative_law>.

_____.2009dddd. "Administrative Court" (September 28). <http://en.wikipedia.org/wiki/Administrative_court>.

_____.2009eeee. "United States Administrative Court" (September 28). <http://en.wikipedia. org/wiki/United_States_Administrative_court>.

_____.2009ffff. “Due Process” (September 28). <http://en.wikipedia.org/wiki/Due_process>.

_____.2009gggg. “Ultra Vires” (September 28). <http://en.wikipedia.org/wiki/Ultra_vires>.

_____.2008. “Posthumanism” (October 20). <http://en.wikipedia.org/wiki/Posthumanism>.

_____.2008a. “Transhumanism” (October 20). <http://en.wikipedia.org/wiki/Transhumanism>.

_____.2008b. “Lowest Common Denominator” (March 26). <http://en.wikipedia.org/ wiki/Least_common_denominator>.

_____.2008c. “Infinity” (November 11). <http://en.wikipedia.org/wiki/Infinity>.

_____.2008d. “Transfinite Number” (November 10). <http://en.wikipedia.org/wiki/Transfinite_ number>.

_____.2008e. “Quantum Mechanics” (November 26). <http://en.wikipedia.org/wiki/Quantum_mechanics>.

_____.2008f. “Copenhagen Interpretation” (November 26). <http://en.wikipedia.org/wiki/Copenhagen_interpretation >.

_____.2008g. “Many Worlds Interpretation” (November 26). <http://en.wikipedia.org/wiki/Many_Worlds_Interpretation>.

_____.2008h. “Hyperspace (Science Fiction)” (November 23). <http://en.wikipedia.org/wiki/Hyperspace_(science_fiction)>.

_____.2008i. “Time Travel” (November 26). <http://en.wikipedia.org/wiki/Time_travel#Time_dilation>.

_____.2008j. “Wormhole” (November 25). <http://en.wikipedia.org/wiki/Wormhole>.

_____.2007. “Linguistics” (March 04). <http://en.wikipedia.org/wiki/Linguistics>.

Wikiversity (WKV). 2008. “Why 10 Dimensions” (November 23). <ttp://en.wikiversity.org/wiki/Why_10_dimensions>

Williams, Glanville. 1951. “The Aims of the Law of Tort.” *Current Legal Problems,* 137.

Williams, Linda L. 1996. “Will to Power in Nietzsche's Published Works and the Nachlass.” *Journal of the History of Ideas*, 57 (3): 450.

Wilmhurst, Elizabeth. 1999. “Jurisdiction of the Court.” *The International Criminal Court: The Making of the Rome Statute*. Roy S Lee, ed. The Hague: Kluwer Law International. <http://www2.icc-cpi.int/Menus/ICC/>.

Wittgenstein, Ludwig.1953. *Philosophical Investigations*. G. E. M. Anscombe and R. Rhees, eds. G.E.M. Anscombe, tr. Oxford: Blackwell.

WordNet (WN). 2009. “Property.” <http://wordnet.princeton.edu/perl/webwn?s=property&sub=Search+WordNet&o2=&o0=1&o7=&o5=&o1=1&o6=&o4=&o3=&h=>.

Yeo, Tiong Min. 2006. "A Note on Some Differences in English Law, New York Law, and Singapore Law." <http://www.singaporelaw.sg/content/SomeDifferences.html>.

YoutTube (YT). 2008. "What Is YouTube's Video Identification tool?" <http://www.google.com/support/youtube/bin/answer.py?answer=83766&hl=en-uk>.

Zaheer, Khalid. 2004. "Why Is Riba Al-Fadl Unacceptable?" *Monthly Renaissance*, 14 (9). <http://www.renaissance.com.pk/Septrefl2y4.html>.

INDEX

•A•

academic works vs. common law, 177
    see also Common law
actus reus, 124
    see also Criminal law
Adams, R. M., 169
adjudication
    and administrative law, 251-252, 265
    see also Administrative law
administrative decisions, 250-251, 265
    see also Administrative law
administrative law, 6, 61, 185
    and cultural traditions, 185, 250-259, 261
    see also Law
administrative power, 251-253, 265
    see also Administrative law
administrative principles, 253-258, 265
    see also Administrative law
Afghanistan
    and war crimes by major powers, 151
after-postmodernism
    see After-Postmodernity
after-postmodernity,
    and existential dialectics
        (1) freedom/unfreedom and equality/inequality dialectics, 40-41, 340-344, 347, 380-383
        (2) wealth/poverty dialectics, 36-37, 46, 348
        (3) civilization/barbarity dialectics, 40-41, 349
        (4) oppression/self-oppression, 45-46, 345-346
    and civilizational holism
        (1) structure, 390-392
        (2) theories, 393-397
    and post-human civilization vs. post-human post-civilization, 384
    and super civilizations, 386-387
    and the five theses of post-civilization, 384-385
    and the theoretical debate on civilization, 379-383, 385
    and my unified theory of everything, 20
    barbarity, and post-civilization, 385
    Cophenhagen interpretation vs. Everett's interpretation, 70-71
    from pre-modernity to after-postmodernity in civilization
        (1) the trinity of pre-modernity, 41, 45, 109, 388-389
        (2) the trinity of modernity, 41, 45, 109-110, 388-389

(3) the trinity of post-modernity, 41, 45, 111, 388-389
(4) the trinity of after-postmodernity, 41, 45, 112, 388-389
in regard to different kinds of consciousness
(1) floating consciousness, 43, 97-98
(2) hyper-spatial consciousness, 43-44, 72-78, 96
(3) unfolding unconsciousness, 43, 99-100
in relation to different causes of post-capitalism, 377-378
in relation to different causes of post-democracy, 36, 362-364
in relation to different versions of post-capitalism, 36-37, 368-373
in relation to different versions of post-democracy,36, 354-358
in relation to the distinctions between capitalism, non-capitalism, and post-capitalism, 374-376
in relation to the distinctions between democracy, non-democracy, and post-democracy, 359-361
in relation to the distinctions between post-democracy, and post-capitalism, 364-367
in the context of different versions of post-humanity, 37-39, 42-43, 72-78, 96-100, 104-107, 301-302
in the context of post-humanism, posthuman-ism, and trans-humanism, 38-39, 104
in the context of the distinction among finity, transfinity, and infinity, 67-68
in the context of the micro-world, 66
in the context of the reasons for the alteration of space-time, 65
in the context of the theoretical debate on space-time, 63-64
in the context of the theoretical speculations of the cosmos
(1) different versions of multiverses, 69
(2) "many worlds" vs. "multiverse," 70-71
in the context of time travel,
(1) into the future, 74-75
(2) into the past, 76-78
see also Consciousness, holistic organization of an inquiry, methodological holism, nature-nurture debate, post-civilization
after-postmodernization
see After-Postmodernity
agency
see Existential dialectics
agents
see Civilization, civilizational project
aggression
and the Mosaic law, 164-170
agricultural law, 250-251
America
see United States, the
American wild west, 135-137
analytical jurisprudence
see Jurisprudence

anti-authoritarianism,
and Taoism, 139-145
see also Law
appeal
vs. judicial review, 254
see also Administrative law
Aquinas, Thomas, 12, 164, 169
Aristotle, 3
authoritarian liberal democracy
see Democracy, empires, post-democracy
autonomy in Kantian ethics, 118
see also Law of reason
Austin, John, 198
Averroes, 14

•B•

balance of power
and constitutional law, 157-163, 183, 185
see also Law
Baofu, Peter,
and the debate on law, 18-19
and the theories on civilizational holism, 393-397
Barash, David, 128-130
barbarity
see Civilization
Barrow, J., 66
Bastiar, Frederic, 221
Baumler, Alfred, 211
beautiful, the
and existential dialectics
(1) freedom/unfreedom and equality/inequality dialectics, 40-41, 340-344, 347, 380-
from pre-modernity to after-postmodernity in civilization
(1) the trinity of pre-modernity, 41, 45, 109, 388-389
(2) the trinity of modernity, 41, 45, 109-110, 388-389
(3) the trinity of post-modernity, 41, 45, 111, 388-389
(4) the trinity of after-postmodernity, 41, 45, 112, 388-389
see also Holistic organization of an enquiry
Becker, Gary, 17
behavior
see Consciousness, holistic organization of an enquiry
being
see Consciousness
belonging
see Consciousness
Bentham, Jeremy, 196
Bill of Rights, the, 6
biological, the
see Holistic organization of an inquiry
biology
and criminal law, 128-130
see also Criminal law
black hole
see Multiverse
Bohr, Niels, 70-71
Boscovich, Roger Joseph, 209-210, 262
Bourdieu, Pierre, 233-234
British empire, and common law, 173-183
see also Law
bureaucracy
in modern times, 229-231

•C•

Cantor, Georg, 68
Capitalism
    see After-postmodernity, post-capitalism, post-democracy
capitalist modernity
    see Modernity, post-capitalism
capitalist postmodernity
    see Postmodernity, post-capitalism
care, 9-10, 185
    and tort law, 201-208
    see also Tort law
Carnegie, Andrew, 134
categorical imperative, 13-14, 116-123, 183
    see also *Law*
Catholic tradition
    and the divine law, 164-170
centers of force, 209
charismatic domination
    in modern times, 229-231
chemical, the
    see Holistic organization of an inquiry
civil law vs. common law, 174, 186
    see also Common law
civilization
    and existential dialectics
        (1) freedom/unfreedom and equality/inequality dialectics, 40-41, 340-344, 347, 380-383
        (2) wealth/poverty dialectics, 36-37, 46, 348
        (3) civilization/barbarity dialectics, 40-41, 349
        (4) oppression/self-oppression, 45-46, 345-346
    and civilizational holism
        (1) structure, 390-392
        (2) theories, 393-397
    and post-human civilization vs. post-human post-civilization, 384
    and super civilizations, 386-387
    and the five theses of post-civilization, 384-385
    and the theoretical debate on civilization, 379-383, 385
    and my unified theory of everything, 20
    barbarity, and post-civilization, 385
    Cophenhagen interpretation vs. Everett's interpretation, 70-71
    from pre-modernity to after-postmodernity in civilization
        (1) the trinity of pre-modernity, 41, 45, 109, 388-389
        (2) the trinity of modernity, 41, 45, 109-110, 388-389
        (3) the trinity of post-modernity, 41, 45, 111, 388-389
        (4) the trinity of after-postmodernity, 41, 45, 112, 388-389
    in regard to
        (1) having, 84-85, 340, 343
        (2) belonging, 84, 86, 341, 343
        (3) being, 84, 87-88, 341, 344
    in regard to different kinds of consciousness
        (1) floating consciousness, 43, 97-98
        (2) hyper-spatial

consciousness, 43-44, 72-78, 96
(3) unfolding unconsciousness, 43, 99-100
in relation to different causes of post-capitalism, 377-378
in relation to different causes of post-democracy, 36, 362-364
in relation to different versions of post-capitalism, 36-37, 368-373
in relation to different versions of post-democracy,36, 354-358
in relation to the distinctions between capitalism, non-capitalism, and post-capitalism, 374-376
in relation to the distinctions between democracy, non-democracy, and post-democracy, 359-361
in relation to the distinctions between post-democracy, and post-capitalism, 364-367
in the context of different versions of post-humanity, 37-39, 42-43, 72-78, 96-100, 104-107, 301-302
in the context of post-humanism, posthuman-ism, and trans-humanism, 38-39, 104
in the context of the distinction among finity, transfinity, and infinity, 67-68
in the context of the micro-world, 66
in the context of the reasons for the alteration of space-time, 65
in the context of the theoretical debate on space-time, 63-64
in the context of the theoretical speculations of the cosmos
(1) different versions of multiverses, 69
(2) "many worlds" vs. "multiverse," 70-71
in the context of time travel,
(1) into the future, 74-75
(2) into the past, 76-78
see also Consciousness, holistic organization of an inquiry, methodological holism, nature-nurture debate, post-civilization
civilization holism
and
(1) structure, 390-392
(2) theories, 393-397
see also Civilization, methdological holism
civilizing process
see Civilization, existential dialectics, holistic organization of an inquiry
civilizational project, 388-389
see also Civilization, existential dialectics
Coase, Ronald, 16-17, 205-206
cognition
see Consciousness
cognitive partiality
and civilizational holism
(1) structure, 390-392
(2) theories, 393-397
see also Consciousness
common law
and its main characteristics, 173-183, 189
and the British empire, 173-183

and unwritten law of the land, 158
see also Law
common mistake, 243
communist theory of property, 222, 263
compromise fallacy, the
see Existential dialectics, methodolgocial holism
conception
see Existential Dialectics
conflict of laws, 5
see also Law
consciousness
after authoritarian liberal democracy, 36, 353
and different empires, 36, 352
and existential dialectics
(1) freedom/unfreedom and equality/inequality dialectics, 40-41, 340-344, 347, 380-383
(2) wealth/poverty dialectics, 36-37, 46, 348
(3) civilization/barbarity dialectics, 40-41, 349
(4) oppression/self-oppression, 45-46, 345-346
and civilizational holism
(1) structure, 390-392
(2) theories, 393-397
and post-human civilization vs. post-human post-civilization, 384
and super civilizations, 386-387
and the five theses of post-civilization, 384-385
and the theoretical debate on civilization, 379-383, 385
and my unified theory of everything, 20
barbarity, and post-civilization, 385
Cophenhagen interpretation vs. Everett's interpretation, 70-71
from pre-modernity to after-postmodernity in civilization
(1) the trinity of pre-modernity, 41, 45, 109, 388-389
(2) the trinity of modernity, 41, 45, 109-110, 388-389
(3) the trinity of post-modernity, 41, 45, 111, 388-389
(4) the trinity of after-postmodernity, 41, 45, 112, 388-389
in different mental faculties
(1) cognition, 89, 91-92
(2) emotion, 90, 91, 93
(3) behavior, 90, 91, 93
in different mental states
(1) consciousness, 79-90, 92-93, 96-98
(2) subconsciousness, 89-90, 92-93
(3) unconsciousness, 89-93, 99-100
in regard to
(1) having, 84-85, 340, 343
(2) belonging, 84, 86, 341, 343
(3) being, 84, 87-88, 341, 344
in regard to different kinds of consciousness
(1) floating consciousness, 43, 97-98
(2) hyper-spatial consciousness, 43-44,

72-78, 96
(3) unfolding unconsciousness, 43, 99-100
in relation to
(1) its conceptual dimensions, 79
(2) its theoretical levels, 80-82
(3) its thematic issues, 83
in relation to creative thinking, 43-44, 101-103
in relation to the body, brain, mind, and spirit, 41-42, 53
in relation to the martial body, 42, 105-106
in relation to the sexual body, 42, 107
in the context of different versions of post-humanity, 37-39, 42-43, 72-78, 96-100, 104-107, 301-302
in the context of post-humanism, posthuman-ism, and trans-humanism, 38-39, 104
see also Existential dialectics, methodological holism
consequentialism vs. Kantian ethics, 116-123
see also Law of reason
consideration
and contract law, 239-240, 264
see also Contract law
constitutional law, 6, 61
and the balance of power, 157-163, 183, 185
vs. unwritten law of the land, 158
see also Law
contingency
and the perspectives
(1) the mind
(a) analytical Jurisprudence, and Hume's "is-ought" problem, 194-200, 261
(b) tort law and its controversy, 201-208, 261
(2) nature
(a) the will to power in nature, and the law, 209-217, 261
(3) society
(a) property law, and copyright violation, 217-229, 261
(b) sociological analysis, and the law, 229-236, 261
(4) culture
(a) contract law, and the tradition of promise, 237-250, 261
(b) administrative law from different traditions, 250-259, 261
and the theoretical debate on law, 16-18
contract law, 8-9, 61, 185
and the culture of promise, 237-249, 261, 264
see also Law
control
and the law, 233-234
convention
and unwritten law of the land, 158
see also Law
copyright violation
and property law, 217-228, 261
cosmic hegemony

see Post-democracy
cosmological the
see Holistic organization of an inquiry
cosmology
in the context of the distinction among finity, transfinity, and infinity, 67-68
in the context of the micro-world, 66
in the context of the reasons for the alteration of space-time, 65
in the context of the theoretical debate on space-time, 63-64
in the context of the theoretical speculations of the cosmos
(1) different versions of multiverses, 69
(2) "many worlds" vs. "multiverse," 70-71
in the context of time travel,
(1) into the future, 74-75
(2) into the past, 76-78
see also Multiverse
cosmos
see Holistic organization of an inquiry
counter-elitists
see Post-capitalism, post-emocoracy
countervailing forces
see After-Postmodernity
creative techniques
see Consciousness
creative thinking
see Consciousness
creative trait
see Consciousness
crimes
and the power politics of the prosecution of crimes against humanity, 151-155
in Iraq by major powers, 3-4
crimes against humanity
see Crimes
crime of humanity
see Crimes
crimiinal law, 7, 61
and the maleness of violence, 123-132, 183, 185
see also Law
critical legal studies, 12, 247
see also Jurisprudence
cultural
and the theoretical debate on law, 17-18
cultural, the
see Holistic organization of an inquiry
culture
see Civilization, holistic organization of an inquiry,
culture, and the law
in relation to the contingency
(1) two case studies
(a) contract law, and the tradition of promise, 237-250, 251
(b) administrative law from different traditions, 250-259, 251
in relation to necessity
(1) two case studies
(a) divine law, morality, and legal sanctions, 163-172, 183, 251
(b) common law, and the cultural legacy of the British empire, 173-182, 183, 251
see also Law
culture, common law, and the Britisih empire, 173-182
see also Law

custom
and unwritten law of the land, 158
see also Law
customs and convention theory of property, 220-221, 263
cyborgs
in the context of different versions of post-humanity, 37-39, 42-43, 72-78, 96-100, 104-107, 301-302
in the context of post-humanism, posthuman-ism, and trans-humanism, 38-39, 104
see also After-postmodernity, post-capitalism, post-civilization, post-democracy, post-humans, multiverse
cyclical progression
and civilizational holism
(1) structure, 390-392
(2) theories, 393-397
of empire-building, 37
of hegemony, 37
of system integration and fragmentation, 39
see also Civilization, existential dialectics, methodological holsim, post-civilization

•D•

dark energy
see Multiverse
dark matter
see Multiverse
Darwin, Charles, 134-135
Darwinian evolution
see Nature-nurture debate
Darwinism,
and the survival of the fittest, 134-136, 183
vs. the will to power, 209-213
see also Law of the jungle
decentralization
and constitutional law, 158-160
see also Constitutional law
degrees of truth
and principles as short cuts, 28-29, 327-328
see also Existential dialectics
democracy
after authoritarian liberal democracy, 36, 353
and different empires, 36, 352
see also Post-democracy
demographics of violence, 127-128
see also Criminal law
Derrida, Jacques, 16, 214-215
deterrence in criminal law, 128, 185
see also Criminal law
dialectics
see Existential dialectics
dignity
vs. egosim, 232-233
discrimination and the will to power, 214-215
distress
and tort law, 204-205
divine command theory
and the Mosaic law, 164-170, 187-188
divine law, 163-172, 183, 187-188
and the naturalistic fallacy, 196-197
see also Law
divorce
and the Mosaic law, 164-170
domination and legal rationalism
in modern times, 229-231

dualism
and international law, 148, 184, 186
see also International law
due process
and administrative law, 185, 254-256, 265
Dumont, Leon, 209-210, 262
duress
and contract law, 244, 264
see also Contract law
Durkheim, Emile, 231-232

•E•

economic, the
see Institutional
economic revolutions
see Civilizational project
effective approach to interpretation
and international law, 148, 184
see also International law
efficient breach theory of contract, 246-247
egoism
vs. human dignity, 232-233
Einstein, Albert, 63, 72-78
emotion
see Consciousness
emotional non-neutrality
see Consciousness
empires,
see also Authoritarian liberal democracy, democracy, post-democracy
energy
see Multiverse
enumerated due process
see Due process
enforcement problem
and administrative law, 251, 265
and international law, 149
see also International law
Engelhardt, Tom, 3, 154
epistemic absolutism
see Methodological holism
epistemic emergencism
see Methodological holism
epistemic historicism
see Methodological holism
epistemic non-subjectivism
see Methodological holism
epistemic objectivism
see Methodological holism
epistemic reductionism
see Methodological holism
epistemic relativism
see Methodological holism
epistemic subjectivism
see Methodological holism
epistemology
see Existential dialectics, methodologicalholism
equality
see Authoritarian liberal democracy, democracy, empires, existential dialectics, post-capitalism, post-democracy
equality and the will to power, 211-215
equity vs. common law, 174-175, 185
see also Common law
estoppel
and contract law, 239-240, 264
Everett, Hugh, 70-71
everyday, the
and existential dialectics
(1) freedom/unfreedom and equality/inequality dialectics, 40-41, 340-344, 347, 380-383

(2) wealth/poverty dialectics, 36-37, 46, 348
(3) civilization/barbarity dialectics, 40-41, 349
(4) oppression/self-oppression, 45-46, 345-346
from pre-modernity to after-postmodernity in civilization
(1) the trinity of pre-modernity, 41, 45, 109, 388-389
(2) the trinity of modernity, 41, 45, 109-110, 388-389
(3) the trinity of post-modernity, 41, 45, 111, 388-389
(4) the trinity of after-postmodernity, 41, 45, 112, 388-389
see also Holistic organization of an enquiry
evolution
see Nature-nurture debate, sexuality
evolutionary biology
and criminal law, 128-130
see also Criminal law
existential dialectics
and
(1) freedom/unfreedom and equality/inequality dialectics, 40-41, 340-344, 347, 380-383
(2) wealth/poverty dialectics, 36-37, 46, 348
(3) civilization/barbarity dialectics, 40-41, 349
(4) oppression/self-oppression, 45-46, 345-346
and civilizational holism
(1) structure, 390-392
(2) theories, 393-397
and post-human civilization vs. post-human post-civilization, 384
and super civilizations, 386-387
and the five theses of post-civilization, 384-385
and the theoretical debate on civilization, 379-383, 385
and my unified theory of everything, 20
barbarity, and post-civilization, 385
Cophenhagen interpretation vs. Everett's interpretation, 70-71
from pre-modernity to after-postmodernity in civilization
(1) the trinity of pre-modernity, 41, 45, 109, 388-389
(2) the trinity of modernity, 41, 45, 109-110, 388-389
(3) the trinity of post-modernity, 41, 45, 111, 388-389
(4) the trinity of after-postmodernity, 41, 45, 112, 388-389
in regard to its conception and basic concepts, 21-22, 311-312
and the ontic dispute, 22-23
definitions of method, structure, process, agency, and outcome, 23
in regard to its pragmatics
(1) theory and meta-theory, 34-35, 338

(2) theoretical application
(a) society, 35-39
(b) culture, 39-41
(c) the mind, 41-44
(d) nature, 44
(e) the rest, 44-46
(3) direct/indirect application, 46-47, 338-339
(4) multiple levels of application, 47, 339
in regard to its semantics (or ontosemantics), 32-33, 337
in regard to its syntax (ontomethodology and ontologic)
(1) method
(a) formalness-informalness principle, 121, 155, 170, 235, 271-272, 312, 314
(b) absoluteness-relativeness principle, 19, 121, 130, 137, 143, 155, 161, 170, 180, 198, 206-207, 215, 228, 235, 247-248, 257, 270, 278-280, 312, 316
(c) partialtiy-totality principle, 137, 271-272, 308, 312, 315
(d) predictability-unpredictability principle, 19, 121, 131, 137, 143, 155-156, 161, 170, 180, 198, 207, 215, 228, 235, 248, 257-258, 270, 281-283, 312, 315
(e) explicability-inexpicability principle, 19, 121-122, 131, 137, 143, 156, 161, 170-171, 180, 198-199, 207, 215, 228, 235, 248, 258, 270, 283-285, 312, 314
(2) structure
(a) finiteness-transfiniteness principle, 122, 272, 312, 317
(b) preciseness-vagueness principle, 19, 122, 131, 137-138, 143, 156, 161-162, 171, 180, 199, 207, 215-216, 227, 235, 248, 258, 270, 286-288, 312, 318
(c) simpleness-complicated principle, 19, 122, 131, 138, 143, 156, 162, 171, 180, 199, 207, 216, 228, 235, 248, 258, 270, 288-290, 312, 318
(d) openness-hiddenness principle, 19, 122, 131, 138, 144, 156, 162, 171, 180, 199, 207, 216, 228, 235, 248, 258, 270, 290-292, 312, 319
(e) denseness-emptiness principle, 122, 131, 138, 144, 156, 162, 171,

180-181, 199, 207-208, 216, 228, 235, 248-249, 272-274, 312, 319
(3) process
(a) change-constancy principle, 144, 156, 171, 274, 312, 321
(b) order-chaos principle, 138, 274, 312, 321
(c) slowness-quickness principle, 181, 312, 320
(d) expansion-contraction principle, 122, 131, 138, 144, 157, 162, 171, 181, 199-200, 216, 228, 235, 249, 258, 274-276, 312, 320
(4) agency
(a) theory-praxis principle, 144, 172, 200, 216, 228, 258, 276, 312, 322
(b) convention-novelty principle, 122, 131-132, 138, 144, 162, 172, 181, 200, 208, 216, 228, 235, 249, 258-259, 276-278, 312, 325
(c) evolution-transformation principle, 19, 122-123, 132, 138, 144, 157, 162-163, 172, 181, 200, 208, 216, 228, 235, 249, 259, 270, 292-294, 312, 324
(d) symmetry-asymmetry principle, 19, 123, 132, 138, 144-145, 157, 163, 172, 181, 200, 208, 217, 228, 235, 249, 259, 270-271, 294-297, 312, 323
(e) softness-hardness principle, 123, 132, 139, 172, 200, 235, 249, 278, 312, 322
(5) outcome
(a) regression-progression principle, 19, 132, 139, 145, 157, 163, 172, 181, 200, 208, 217, 228, 235, 249, 259, 270, 297-298, 312, 326
(b) same-difference principle, 119, 123, 132, 139, 145, 157, 163, 172, 181-182, 200, 208, 217, 229-330, 235, 249-250, 259, 270, 299-301, 312, 326
in regard to ontological princples
(1) selection criteria, 24-25
(2) the qualifications on classification
(a) as a pioneering work, 25, 333
(b) as flexible, 25, 333
(c) as mutually constraining, 25, 333
(d) selectively useful, 25, 334
(e) anti-reductionistic 25, 334

(3) ontomethodology, 26
(4) ontologic, and history of creating new principles, 26-28
(5) as short cuts, 28-29, 327-328
(6) as family resemblances, 29-30, 329
(7) dialectic constraints imposed by ontological principles, 30-32, 330-332
(8) specific vs. general ontology, 335-336
in the context of methodological holism
(1) not against methodological individualism, 48, 304
(2) critical to systems approach, 20, 48, 307
(3) for a unified theory of everything, 20, 48, 307
(4) ontological constraints, 48-49
(5) against reductionism, 49-51, 308-310
(a) and the foundation fallacy, 49, 308
(6) against reverse-reductionism, 51-52, 310
(a) and the compromise fallacy, 51, 310
(b) and the pluralist fallacy, 51-52, 310
(7) holistic organization of an nquiry, 52-54
(a) the mind, brain, body, and spirit, 53
(b) classification of the mind, nature, society, and culture, 53-54
(8) three clarifications, 54-55
(9) distinctive usefulness, 55
(10) some clarifications, 56-60
(11) more elaborations in table, 304-307
in the context of the theoretical debate on law
(1)the necessity argument, 13-16, 115-189
(2) the contingency argument, 16-18, 193-265
(3) the reconstruction argument, 18-19, 271-303
see also After-postmodernity, methodological holism, post-capitalism, post-democracy
expansion of power, 209, 262
Eysenck, Hans, 94

•F•

fair use, and copyright violation, 223-224, 263
see also Property law
fairness
and administrative law, 256-257, 265
see also Administrative law
family resemblance
and the syntax of existential dialectics, 29-30, 329
see also Existential dialectics, methodological holism
Fauconnet, Paul, 232

federalism
and constitutional law, 158-160
see also Constitutional law
finity
see Multiverse
Firehammer, Reginald, 22
floating consciousness
see Consciousness
floating existence
see Consciousness
formal rulemaking
and administrative law, 252-253
formality
and contract law, 241-242, 264
see also Contract law
foundation fallacy, the
see Methodolgocial holism
Franklin, Benjamin, 127
free-spirited after-postmodernity
see After-postmodernity
free-spirited modernity
see Modernity
free-spirited postmodernity
see Postmodernity
freedom
see Authoritarian liberal democracy, democracy, empires, existential dialectics, post-democracy
freedom and the moral law, 119
practical vs. transcendental, 119
Fried, Charles, 246
Friedman, Milton, 17
Fuller, R. Buckminster, 142
fusion of power
and constitutional law, 157-163, 185
see also Law

•G•

Galton, Francis, 134-135
genetic approach
see Nature-nurture debate
genetically altered superior beings
in the context of different versions of post-humanity, 37-39, 42-43, 72-78, 96-100, 104-107, 301-302
in the context of post-humanism, posthuman-ism, and trans-humanism, 38-39, 104
see also After-postmodernity, post-capitalism, post-civilization, post-democracy, post-humans, multiverse
genocide
see Crimes
German Historical School of Law, 17-18
Golden Rule vs. moral imperative, 13-14
Goldthwait, John, 120-121
good, the
and existential dialectics
(1) freedom/unfreedom and equality/inequality dialectics, 40-41, 340-344, 347, 380-383
(2) wealth/poverty dialectics, 36-37, 46, 348
(3) civilization/barbarity dialectics, 40-41, 349
(4) oppression/self-oppression, 45-46, 345-346
from pre-modernity to after-postmodernity in civilization
(1) the trinity of

pre-modernity, 41, 45, 109, 388-389
(2) the trinity of modernity, 41, 45, 109-110, 388-389
(3) the trinity of post-modernity, 41, 45, 111, 388-389
(4) the trinity of after-postmodernity, 41, 45, 112, 388-389
see also Existential dialectics, holistic organization of an enquiry, methodological holism,
Gould, Stephen Jay, 94
guilty act in criminal law
see *Actus Reus*
guilty mind in criminal law
see *Mens Rea*
Guth, Alan, 69

•H•

Habermas, Jurgen, 233
Haeckel, Ernst, 209
Hart, H. L. A., 11, 194
having
see Consciousness
Hawking, Stephen, 69
hegemonic after-postmodernity
see After-postmodernity
hegemonic modernity
see Modernity
hegemonic postmodernity
see Postmodernity
hegemonic pre-modernity
see Pre-modernity
hegemony
see Cyclical progression
Heisenberg, Werner, 70
historical
and civilizational holism
(1) structure, 390-392
(2) theories, 393-397
see also Holistic organization of inquiry
historicism
see Methodological holism
holism
see Existential dialectics, methodological holism
holistic organization of an inquiry,
and civilizational holism
(1) structure, 390-392
(2) theories, 393-397
and post-human civilization vs. post-human post-civilization, 384
and super civilizations, 386-387
and the five theses of post-civilization, 384-385
and the theoretical debate on civilization, 379-383, 385
and my unified theory of everything, 20
barbarity, and post-civilization, 385
Cophenhagen interpretation vs. Everett's interpretation, 70-71
from pre-modernity to after-postmodernity in civilization
(1) the trinity of pre-modernity, 41, 45, 109, 388-389
(2) the trinity of modernity, 41, 45, 109-110, 388-389
(3) the trinity of post-modernity, 41, 45, 111, 388-389
(4) the trinity of after-postmodernity, 41,

45, 112, 388-389
in regard to
(1) having, 84-85, 340, 343
(2) belonging, 84, 86, 341, 343
(3) being, 84, 87-88, 341, 344
in regard to different kinds of consciousness
(1) floating consciousness, 43, 97-98
(2) hyper-spatial consciousness, 43-44, 72-78, 96
(3) unfolding unconsciousness, 43, 99-100
in relation to different causes of post-capitalism, 377-378
in relation to different causes of post-democracy, 36, 362-364
in relation to different versions of post-capitalism, 36-37, 368-373
in relation to different versions of post-democracy,36, 354-358
in relation to the distinctions between capitalism, non-capitalism, and post-capitalism, 374-376
in relation to the distinctions between democracy, non-democracy, and post-democracy, 359-361
in relation to the distinctions between post-democracy, and post-capitalism, 364-367
in the context of different versions of post-humanity, 37-39, 42-43, 72-78, 96-100, 104-107, 301-302
in the context of post-humanism, posthuman-ism, and trans-humanism, 38-39, 104
in the context of the distinction among finity, transfinity, and infinity, 67-68
in the context of the micro-world, 66
in the context of the reasons for the alteration of space-time, 65
in the context of the theoretical debate on space-time, 63-64
in the context of the theoretical speculations of the cosmos
(1) different versions of multiverses, 69
(2) "many worlds" vs. "multiverse," 70-71
in the context of time travel,
(1) into the future, 74-75
(2) into the past, 76-78
see also Consciousness, methodological holism
holy, the
and existential dialectics
(1) freedom/unfreedom and equality/inequality dialectics, 40-41, 340-344, 347, 380-383
from pre-modernity to after-postmodernity in civilization
(1) the trinity of pre-modernity, 41, 45, 109, 388-389
(2) the trinity of modernity, 41, 45, 109-110, 388-389
(3) the trinity of post-modernity, 41, 45, 111, 388-389

(4) the trinity of after-postmodernity, 41, 45, 112, 388-389
see also Holistic organization of an enquiry
Hugo, Gustav, 17-18
human dignity
vs. egosim, 232-233
humanoids
in the context of different versions of post-humanity, 37-39, 42-43, 72-78, 96-100, 104-107, 301-302
in the context of post-humanism, posthuman-ism, and trans-humanism, 38-39, 104
see also After-postmodernity, post-capitalism, post-civilization, post-democracy, post-humans, multiverse
Hume, David, 11, 14, 120, 194-200, 221, 261, 269
humility
see Taoism
Huvelin, Paul, 232
Hybrid rulemaking
and administrative law, 252-253
hyper-martial body, 42, 105-106
hyper-sexual body, 42, 107
hyper-spatial consciousness
see Consciousness
hypothetical imperative, 13-14, 116-123, 183

•I•

idealism
see Methodological holism
illegality
and contract law, 245, 264
see also Contract law
impacts
see Civilizational project
impulsing
see Civilization, post-civilization
incapacitation in criminal law, 128, 185
see also Criminal law
incapacity
and contract law, 244-245, 264
see also Contract law
incompleteness
and contract law, 245-246, 264
see also Contract law
inconsistency
and the Mosaic law, 164-170, 187-188
see also Divine law
independent use, and copyright violation, 223-224, 263
Indian question, the, 135-136
see also Social Darwinism
inequality
see Equality
infinity
see Multiverse
informal rulemaking
and administrative law, 252-253
injury
and tort law, 9-10
see also Tort law
institutional, the
see Holistic organization of an inquiry
institutional facts, and promise, 197-198
institutions
see Civilizational project
intellectual property

see Property
intelligence life
in the context of different versions of post-humanity, 37-39, 42-43, 72-78, 96-100, 104-107, 301-302
in the context of post-humanism, posthuman-ism, and trans-humanism, 38-39, 104
see also After-postmodernity, post-capitalism, post-civilization, post-democracy, post-humans, multiverse
intentionalitiy
and criminal law, 123-132
and property law, 240-241
and tort law, 9-10, 201-206
International Court of Justice, 149-150
see also International law
International Criminal Court, 145-157, 183
see also Law
international custom, 146-147, 184
see also International law
international law
see Law
international public law, 145-157, 183
and enforcement, 149, 184
and interpretation, 147-148, 184
and its travesty, 149-155
scope of, 146, 184
sources of, 146-147, 184
see also Law
international treatises, 146-147, 184
see also International law
interpretation
and international public law, 147-155
and property law, 224-225
see also International public law
Iraq
and war cimes by major powers, 3-4, 151
is-ought problem, 194-200, 269
Islam and law, 14-15
Islamic law vs. common law, 174, 186
see also Common law
Israel, and the abuses of the Mosaic law, 164-170

•J•

Jackson, Andrew, 136
judicial decisions and teachings
and international law, 146-147, 184
see also International law
judicial review
vs. appeal, 254
jurisprudence
and analytical jurisprudence vs. legal formalism, 11
and Hume's "Is-Ought" problem, 194-200
and Kantian ethics, 120-121
and law, 10-12
and Taoism, 141-142
and the will to power, 211-215
and types
(1) analytical, 11, 62, 194-200
(2) normative, 11-12, 62
just, the
and existential dialectics
(1) freedom/unfreedom and equality/inequality

dialectics, 40-41, 340-344, 347, 380-383
(2) wealth/poverty dialectics, 36-37, 46, 348
(3) civilization/barbarity dialectics, 40-41, 349
(4) oppression/self-oppression, 45-46, 345-346
from pre-modernity to after-postmodernity in civilization
(1) the trinity of pre-modernity, 41, 45, 109, 388-389
(2) the trinity of modernity, 41, 45, 109-110, 388-389
(3) the trinity of post-modernity, 41, 45, 111, 388-389
(4) the trinity of after-postmodernity, 41, 45, 112, 388-389
see also Holistic organization of an enquiry, law

justice
to be transcended, 19, 56, 270, 302-303
to co-exist with injustice, 18-19, 56, 270, 302-303

justice, and international public law, 149-155

•K•

Kangas, Steve, 17
Kant, Immanuel, 13-14, 116-121
Kardashev, Nikolai, 387
Kelsen, Hans, 198
Kiernan, Victor, 193
Kipling, Rudyard, 133-134

•L•

labor theory of property, 220-221, 263
Lao, Zi, 139
law
and clarifications on the book,
(1) in conversation with previous books, 57-59
(2) case studies/examples, 59
(3) detailed analysis vs. overall synthesis, 59-60
(4) use of neologisms,60
and its differrent types
(1) public law and private law, 4-10, 61
(2) international law and national law, 5
and meta-theory,
in relation to my unified theory of everything, 20
and the need to go beyond justice, 303
and the theoretical debate
(1) the necessity argument, 13-16, 115-189
(2) the contingency argument, 16-18, 193-265
(3) the reconstruction argument, 18-19
(a) absoluteness-relativeness principle, 19, 121, 130, 137, 143, 155, 161, 170, 180, 198, 206-207, 215, 228, 235, 247-248, 257, 270, 278-280, 312, 316
(b) predictability-unpredictability

principle, 19, 121, 131, 137, 143, 155-156, 161, 170, 180, 198, 207, 215, 228, 235, 248, 257-258, 270, 281-283, 312, 315
(c) explicability-inexpicability principle, 19, 121-122, 131, 137, 143, 156, 161, 170-171, 180, 198-199, 207, 215, 228, 235, 248, 258, 270, 283-285, 312, 314
(d) simpleness-complicated principle, 122, 131, 138, 144, 156, 162, 171, 180-181, 199, 207-208, 216, 228, 235, 248-249, 272-274, 312, 319
(e) openness-hiddenness principle, 19, 122, 131, 138, 144, 156, 162, 171, 180, 199, 207, 216, 228, 235, 248, 258, 270, 290-292, 312, 319
(f) denseness-emptiness principle, 122, 131, 138, 144, 156, 162, 171, 180-181, 199, 207-208, 216, 228, 235, 248-249, 272-274, 312, 319
(g) convention-novelty principle, 122, 131-132, 138, 144, 162, 172, 181, 200, 208, 216, 228, 235, 249, 258-259, 276-278, 312, 325
(h) symmetry-asymmetry principle, 19, 123, 132, 138, 144-145, 157, 163, 172, 181, 200, 208, 217, 228, 235, 249, 259, 270-271, 294-297, 312, 323
(i) post-human reconstruction, 19, 56, 270, 301-303
(j) and other principles, 270-278
in relation to the contingency
(1) the mind
(a) analytical Jurisprudence, and Hume's "is-ought" problem, 194-200, 261
(b) tort law and its controversy, 201-208, 261
(2) nature
(a) the will to power in nature, and the law, 209-217, 261
(3) society
(a) property law, and copyright violation, 217-229, 261
(b) sociological analysis, and the law, 229-236, 261
(4) culture
(a) contract law, and the tradition of promise, 237-250, 261
(b) administrative law

from different traditions, 250-259, 261
in relation to necessity
(1) the mind
(a) the law of reason, and the categorical imperative, 116-123, 183
(b) criminal law, and the maleness of violence, 123-132, 183
(2) nature
(a) the laws of the jungle in nature, and social Darwinism, 133-139, 183
(b) natural law, and Taoist anti-authoritarianism, 139-145, 183
(3) society
(a) international public law, and the international criminal court, 145-157, 183
(b) constitutional law and the balance of power, 157-163, 183
(4) culture
(a) divine law, morality, and legal sanctions, 163-172, 183
(b) common law, and the cultural legacy of the British empire, 173-182, 183
in relation to theory and meta-theory, 20
in the context of different versions of post-humanity, 37-39, 42-43, 72-78, 96-100, 104-107, 301-302
in the context of post-humanism, posthuman-ism, and trans-humanism, 38-39, 104
see also Consciousness, existential dialectics, methodological holism
law of the jungle, 133-139, 183
see also Law
law of reason, 116-123, 183
see also Law
legal domination
in modern times, 229-231
legal formalism vs. analytical jurisprudence, 11
legal formalism vs. legal positivism, 194-195
legal interpretation
see Interpretation
legal positivism vs. legal formalism, 194-195
legal rationalism, 185
and bureaucracy, 230-231
and leadership, 229-230
legal realism, 247
legal sanctions and the divine law, 163-172, 183
see also Law
legal treatises vs. common law, 177
see also Common law
legislating
and administrative law, 251-252, 265
Lenz, Stephanie, 226
level of analysis
see Existential dialectics, methodological holism
liability, 125-126
see also Criminal law
libertarian theory of property, 222, 263
licentious desires
and the Mosaic law, 164-170,

187-188
Linde, Andre, 69
Lipton, Judith Eve, 128
Locke, John, 221
Lorenz, Konrad, 94
Luhmann, Niklas, 233

•M•

MacIntyre, Alasdair, 197-198
Magna Carta, 6
maleness of violence, 123-132, 183
 see also Law
Malthus, Thomas, 134-135
manifest destiny, 134-136
 see also Law of the jungle
many worlds
 Cophenhagen interpretation vs. Everett's interpretation, 70-71
 see also Multiverse
Marx, Karl, 222-223
matter
 see Multiverse
Mauss, Marcel, 232
mens rea, 124-125
 see also Criminal law
mechanical solidarity
 see Solidarity
metaphysics
 see Existential dialectics
meta-theory
 see Existential dialectics, methodological holism
method
 see Existential dialectics, methodological holism
methodological holism
 and civilizational holism
  (1) structure, 390-392
  (2) theories, 393-397
 and its essential features
  (1) not against methodological individualism, 48, 304
  (2) critical to systems approach, 20, 48, 307
  (3) for a unified theory of everything, 20, 48, 307
  (4) ontological constraints, 48-49
  (5) against reductionism, 49-51, 308-310
   (a) and the foundation fallacy, 49, 308
  (6) against reverse-reductionism, 51-52, 310
   (a) and the compromise fallacy, 51, 310
   (b) and the pluralist fallacy, 51-52, 310
  (7) holistic organization of an nquiry, 52-54
   (a) the mind, brain, body, and spirit, 53
   (b) classification of the mind, nature, society, and culture, 53-54
  (8) three clarifications, 54-55
  (9) distinctive usefulness, 55
  (10) some clarifications, 56-60
  (11) more elaborations in table, 304-307
 see also Existential dialectics, holistic organization of an inquiry, methodological indvidualism
methodological individualism

see Existential dialectics, methodological holism
micro-physical
see Holistic organization of an inquiry
mind, the
see Consciousness, holistic organization of inquiry,
mind, the, and the law
in relation to the contingency
(1) two case studies
(a) analytical Jurisprudence, and Hume's "is-ought" problem, 194-200, 261
(b) tort law and its controversy, 201-208, 261
in relation to necessity
(1) two case studies
(a) the law of reason, and the categorical imperative, 116-123, 183, 261
(b) criminal law, and the maleness of violence, 123-132, 183, 261
see also Law
misrepresentation
and contract law, 242-243, 264
see also Contract law
mistake
and contract law, 243, 264
see also Contract law
moderate
see Civilization, post-civilization
moderation
see Taoism
modernism
see Modernity
modernity
see After-postmodernity
modernization
see Modernity
monism
and international law, 148, 186
see also International law
Moore, G. E., 195-196
moral
and the theoretical debate on law, 13-14
morality and the divine law, 163-172, 183
see also Law
Mosaic law, 164-170, 187-188
multiverse
and civilizational holism
(1) structure, 390-392
(2) theories, 393-397
and post-human civilization vs. post-human post-civilization, 384
and super civilizations, 386-387
and the five theses of post-civilization, 384-385
and the theoretical debate on civilization, 379-383, 385
and my unified theory of everything, 20
barbarity, and post-civilization, 385
Cophenhagen interpretation vs. Everett's interpretation, 70-71
from pre-modernity to after-postmodernity in civilization
(1) the trinity of pre-modernity, 41, 45, 109, 388-389
(2) the trinity of modernity, 41, 45, 109-110, 388-389
(3) the trinity of

post-modernity, 41, 45, 111, 388-389
(4) the trinity of after-postmodernity, 41, 45, 112, 388-389
in regard to different kinds of consciousness
(1) floating consciousness, 43, 97-98
(2) hyper-spatial consciousness, 43-44, 72-78, 96
(3) unfolding unconsciousness, 43, 99-100
in relation to different causes of post-capitalism, 377-378
in relation to different causes of post-democracy, 36, 362-364
in relation to different versions of post-capitalism, 36-37, 368-373
in relation to different versions of post-democracy,36, 354-358
in relation to the distinctions between capitalism, non-capitalism, and post-capitalism, 374-376
in relation to the distinctions between democracy, non-democracy, and post-democracy, 359-361
in relation to the distinctions between post-democracy, and post-capitalism, 364-367
in the context of different versions of post-humanity, 37-39, 42-43, 72-78, 96-100, 104-107, 301-302
in the context of post-humanism, posthuman-ism, and trans-humanism, 38-39, 104
in the context of the distinction among finity, transfinity, and infinity, 67-68
in the context of the micro-world, 66
in the context of the reasons for the alteration of space-time, 65
in the context of the theoretical debate on space-time, 63-64
in the context of the theoretical speculations of the cosmos
(1) different versions of multiverses, 69
(2) "many worlds" vs. "multiverse," 70-71
in the context of time travel,
(1) into the future, 74-75
(2) into the past, 76-78
see also After-postmodernity, existential dialectics, post-civilization, post-humans
Murray, C., 95
mutual mistake, 243
mythicizing
see Civilization, post-civilization

•N•

Napoleonic code, 8
narratives
see Civilizational project
national law
see Law
natural
and laws of the jungle,

133-139, 183
and Taoism, 139-145, 183
and the theoretical debate on law, 15-16
natural law, 15-16
and Taoism, 139-145, 183
and unjust law, 115
see also Law
natural selection
see Nature-nurture debate
naturalistic fallacy, 196-197
nature
see Consciousness, holistic organization of inquiry,
nature, and the law
in relation to the contingency
(2) a case study
(a) the will to power in nature, and the law, 209-217, 261
in relation to necessity
(1) two case studies
(a) the laws of the jungle in nature, and social Darwinism, 133-139, 183, 261
(b) natural law, and Taoist anti-authoritarianism, 139-145, 183, 261
see also Law
nature-nurture debate, 94-95
and contrastive advantages, 95
see also Consciousness
Nazism and the will to power, 16, 214
necessity
and the perspectives
(1) the mind
(a) the law of reason, and the categorical imperative, 116-123, 183
(b) criminal law, and the maleness of violence, 123-132, 183
(2) nature
(a) the laws of the jungle in nature, and social Darwinism, 133-139, 183
(b) natural law, and Taoist anti-authoritarianism, 139-145, 183
(3) society
(a) international public law, and the international criminal court, 145-157, 183
(b) constitutional law and the balance of power, 157-163, 183
(4) culture
(a) divine law, morality, and legal sanctions, 163-172, 183
(b) common law, and the cultural legacy of the British empire, 173-182, 183
and the theoretical debate on law, 13-16
negligence
in criminal law, 125, 185
in tort law, 185, 203-205
see also Criminal law
neo-Darwinian evolution,
see Nature-nurture debate
Newton, Isaac, 63
Nietzsche, Friedrich, 15-16, 208-217, 262
noble morality and the law, 211-214, 262
non-capitalism

see After-postmodernity, post-capitalism
non-democracy
see After-postmodernity, post-capitalism
normative jurisprudence
see Jurisprudence
norms
and unwritten law of the land, 158
see also Law
nuisance
and transaction costs, 16-17, 185
nurture
see nature-nurture debate

•O•

obligation
and the culture of promise, 237-238
see also Contract law
Ockham, William of, 168
ontic dispute
see Existential dialectics
ontics
see Existential dialectics
ontologic
see Existential dialectics
ontomethodology
see Existential dialectics
ontopragmatics
see Existential dialectics
ontosemantics
see Existential dialectics
ontology
see Existential dialectics, methodological holism
ontomethodology
see Existential dialectics, methodological holism
ontopragmatics
see Existential dialectics
ontosemantics
see Existential dialectics
oppression
and existential dialectics
(1) freedom/unfreedom and equality/inequality dialectics, 40-41, 340-344, 347, 380-383
(2) wealth/poverty dialectics, 36-37, 46, 348
(3) civilization/barbarity dialectics, 40-41, 349
(4) oppression/self-oppression, 45-46, 345-346
and civilizational holism
(1) structure, 390-392
(2) theories, 393-397
and post-human civilization vs. post-human post-civilization, 384
and super civilizations, 386-387
and the five theses of post-civilization, 384-385
and the theoretical debate on civilization, 379-383, 385
and my unified theory of everything, 20
barbarity, and post-civilization, 385
see also Existential dialectics
organic solidarity
see Solidarity
organization
and legal rationalism in modern times, 229-231
organizational, the
see Holistic organization of an inquiry

originalists
and admnistrative law, 253-257
ought-is problem, 194-200
outcome
see Civilizational project, existential dialectics

•P•

pacifying process
see Civilization
parallel universe
see Multiverse
parlimentary procedures
and constitutional law, 159-160
see also Law
Parsons, Talcott, 233
penal law
see Criminal Law
personal property
see Property
physical
see Cosmological, micro-physical
pillaging
see Civilization
pluralist fallacy
see Methodological holism
political, the
see Institutional
polygamy
and the Mosaic law, 164-170
possession theory of property, 185, 220, 263
post-capitalism
and existential dialectics
(1) freedom/unfreedom and equality/inequality dialectics, 40-41, 340-344, 347, 380-383
(2) wealth/poverty dialectics, 36-37, 46, 348
(3) civilization/barbarity dialectics, 40-41, 349
(4) oppression/self-oppression, 45-46, 345-346
and civilizational holism
(1) structure, 390-392
(2) theories, 393-397
and post-human civilization vs. post-human post-civilization, 384
and super civilizations, 386-387
and the five theses of post-civilization, 384-385
and the theoretical debate on civilization, 379-383, 385
and my unified theory of everything, 20
barbarity, and post-civilization, 385
Cophenhagen interpretation vs. Everett's interpretation, 70-71
from pre-modernity to after-postmodernity in civilization
(1) the trinity of pre-modernity, 41, 45, 109, 388-389
(2) the trinity of modernity, 41, 45, 109-110, 388-389
(3) the trinity of post-modernity, 41, 45, 111, 388-389
(4) the trinity of after-postmodernity, 41, 45, 112, 388-389
in regard to
(1) having, 84-85, 340, 343
(2) belonging, 84, 86, 341, 343

(3) being, 84, 87-88, 341, 344
in regard to different kinds of consciousness
(1) floating consciousness, 43, 97-98
(2) hyper-spatial consciousness, 43-44, 72-78, 96
(3) unfolding unconsciousness, 43, 99-100
in relation to different causes of post-capitalism, 377-378
in relation to different causes of post-democracy, 36, 362-364
in relation to different versions of post-capitalism, 36-37, 368-373
in relation to different versions of post-democracy,36, 354-358
in relation to the distinctions between capitalism, non-capitalism, and post-capitalism, 374-376
in relation to the distinctions between democracy, non-democracy, and post-democracy, 359-361
in relation to the distinctions between post-democracy, and post-capitalism, 364-367
in the context of different versions of post-humanity, 37-39, 42-43, 72-78, 96-100, 104-107, 301-302
in the context of post-humanism, posthuman-ism, and trans-humanism, 38-39, 104
in the context of the distinction among finity, transfinity, and infinity, 67-68
in the context of the micro-world, 66
in the context of the reasons for the alteration of space-time, 65
in the context of the theoretical debate on space-time, 63-64
in the context of the theoretical speculations of the cosmos
(1) different versions of multiverses, 69
(2) "many worlds" vs. "multiverse," 70-71
in the context of time travel,
(1) into the future, 74-75
(2) into the past, 76-78
see also After-postmodernity, consciousnesss, existential dialectics, methodological holism, post-democracy
post-capitalist after-postmodernity
see After-postmodernity, post-capitalism
post-civilization
see Civilization
post-democracy
after authoritarian liberal democracy, 36, 353
and different empires, 36, 352
and its different versions, 36, 354-358
in relation to the distinctions between democracy, non-democracy, and post-democracy, 359-361
in relation to the distinctions between post-democracy, and post-capitalism,

364-367
see also After-postmodernity, consciousnesss, existential dialectics, methodological holism, post-capitalism
post-human civilization
not to confuse post-human civilization with post-human post-civilization, 384
see also Civilization, post-civilization
post-human elitist calling, 360, 372-373, 375
see also After-postmodernity, consciousnesss, existential dialectics, methodological holism, post-capitalism
post-human post-civilization
and the five theses of post-civilization, 384-385
see also Civilization, post-civilization, post-humans
post-humanism
to not confuse with posthuman-ism, and trans-humanism, 38-39, 104
see also After-postmodernity
post-humanity
see Post-humans
post-humans
see After-postmodernity
post-modernism
see Post-modernity
post-modernity
see After-postmodernity
post-modernization
see Post-modernity
posthuman-ism
to not confuse with post-humanism, and trans-humanism, 38-39, 104
see also After-postmodernity
power and constitutional law, 158-163
see also Constitutional law
practical freedom and the moral law, 119
see also Law
pragmatics
see Existential dialectics, language
pre-capitalist pre-modernity
see Pre-modernity
pre-consciousness
see Consciousness,
pre-free-spirited pre-modernity
see Pre-modernity
pre-modernism
see Pre-modernity
pre-modernity
see After-postmodernity
pre-modernization
see Pre-modernity
preciseness
and common law, 178
principles of law
and international law, 146-147, 184-185
see also International law
private law
see Law
private property
see Property
procedural due process
see Due process
process
see Existential dialectics, methodological holism
progression
see Existential dialectics, knowledge
progressive

see Civilization
promise
  and contract law, 237-250, 261
  see also Law
property law, 7-8, 61, 185
  and copyright violation, 217-229, 261, 263
  see also Law
prosecution and power politics
  in regard to crimes against humanity, 151-155
  in regard to crimes against Iraq by major powers, 3-4
  see also International public law
prostitution
  and property rights, 219-220
  see also Property law
psychological, the
  see Holistic organization of an inquiry
psychosis
  and the five theses of post-civilization, 384-385
  and virtual organizations, 350-351
  see also Civilization, post-civilization
public law
  see Law
public property
  see Property

•Q•

quantum decoherence, 70-71
  see also Multiverse
quantum mechanics
  and consciousness, 80
  and unconsciousness, 100
  Cophenhagen interpretation vs. Everett's interpretation, 70-71
  see also Multiverse
Qur'an
  see Islam

•R•

Rand, Ayn, 221
rank distinction
  see Post-capitalism, post-civilization post-democracy
Rapp, Rayna, 130
rational autonomy in Kantian ethics, 118
  see also Law of reason
rationalizing process
  see Civilization
Raz, Joseph, 198
reconstruction
  and the theoretical debate on law, 18-19
recklessness in criminal law, 125
  see also Criminal law
reductionism
  see Methodological holism,
regression
  see Existential dialectics
regulatory law
  and common law, 173-175
rehabilitation in criminal law, 128, 185
  see also Criminal law
relativism
  see Existential dialectics, methodological holism
reliability
  and common law, 178
religious
  and the theoretical debate on

law, 14-15
restitution
and restitutive law in modern times, 185, 231-232
in criminal law, 127-128, 185
see also Criminal law
retribution in criminal law, 127
see also Criminal law
revering
see Civilization
reverse-reductionism
see Methodological holism
rights
of the individual
and constitutional law, 159
to use property, 218-219, 263
see also Law
robots
in the context of different versions of post-humanity, 37-39, 42-43, 72-78, 96-100, 104-107, 301-302
in the context of post-humanism, posthuman-ism, and trans-humanism, 38-39, 104
see also After-postmodernity, post-capitalism, post-civilization, post-democracy, post-humans, multiverse
Roph, William, 210, 262
romantic
see Civilization, post-civilization
Ross, Ellen, 130
Rousseau, Jean-Jacques, 220
Roux, Wilhelm, 209-210, 262
rulemaking
and administrative law, 252-253, 265
see also Administrative law

•S•

sale doctrine, and copyright violation, 224, 263
Schopenhauer, Arthur, 14, 120, 209, 262
Scotus, Duns, 168
Searle, John, 197, 246
selection
see Nature-nurture debate
self-oppression
see Oppression
Selznick, Philip, 233
semantics
see Existential Dialectics, language
severance
and contract law, 245-246, 264
Shakespeare, William, 60
Siegel, Warren, 69
simplicity
see Taoism
slavery
and property rights, 219-220
and the Mosaic law, 164-170, 187-188
see also Divine law, property law
Smith, Adam, 221
social
see Post-capitalism
social control, 233-234
social Darwinism, 134-136, 183
see also Law of the jungle
social hierarchy
see Structural
social institutional
see Institutional
social organizational
see Organizational
social structure
see Structural
social systems

see Systemic
socialist law vs. common law, 174, 186
see also Common law
socialist theory of property, 222, 263
see also Property law
societal
and the theoretical debate on law, 16-17
society
see Holistic organization of inquiry
society, and the law
in relation to the contingency
(1) two case studies
(a) property law, and copyright violation, 217-229, 261
(b) sociological analysis, and the law, 229-236, 261
in relation to necessity
(1) two case studies
(a) international public law, and the international criminal court, 145-157, 183, 261
(b) constitutional law and the balance of power, 157-163, 183, 261
sociological analysis, and the law, 229-236, 261
solidarity
and restitutive law, 231-232
see also Existential dialectics
space
see Multiverse
space-time
see Multiverse
Spencer, Herbert, 134
statutory law
and common law, 173-175
and unwritten law of the land, 158
see also Law
stewardizing process
see Civilization
strict liability
see Liability
structural, the
see Holistic organization of an inquiry
struggle
for existence at the cellular level, 209, 262
of parts in the organism, 209, 262
subconsciousness
see Consciousness
subjective approach to interpretation
and international law, 148, 184
see also International law
subjectivism
see Methodological holism
sublime, the
see Beautiful
subliming process
see Civilization
substantive due process
see Due process
super-civilizations,
see also Civilization, post-civilization
survival of the fittest, 134-136
see also Law of the jungle
symbolic violence, 233-234
syntax
see Existential Dialectics, language
systemic, the
see Holistic organization of an inquiry, methodological holism

•T•

Tao
see Taoism
Taoism
and nature, 139-145, 183
see also Law
technological, the
and existential dialectics
(1) freedom/unfreedom and equality/inequality dialectics, 40-41, 340-344, 347, 380-383
from pre-modernity to after-postmodernity in civilization
(1) the trinity of pre-modernity, 41, 45, 109, 388-389
(2) the trinity of modernity, 41, 45, 109-110, 388-389
(3) the trinity of post-modernity, 41, 45, 111, 388-389
(4) the trinity of after-postmodernity, 41, 45, 112, 388-389
in the context of the micro-world,
see also Holistic organization of an inquiry, methodological holism
technological reductionism
see also Methodological holism
technological revolutions
see Civilizational project
textual approach to interpretation
and international law, 148, 184
see also International law
theory
and civilizational holism
(1) structure, 390-392
(2) theories, 393-397
and meta-theory,
see also Existential dialectics, methodological holism
theory of relativity
see Multiverse
thinking machines
in the context of different versions of post-humanity, 37-39, 42-43, 72-78, 96-100, 104-107, 301-302
in the context of post-humanism, posthuman-ism, and trans-humanism, 38-39, 104
see also After-postmodernity, post-capitalism, post-civilization, post-democracy, post-humans, multiverse
thinking robots
see Robots
third parties
and contract law, 241, 264
see also Contract law
time
see Multiverse
time travel
see Multiverse
titans
see Empires
tort law, 9-10, 61, 185
and the mind, 201-209
(1) intentional cases, 201-203, 261
(2) unintentional cases 203-205, 261
see also Law
traditional rationalism
in modern times, 229-231
trail of tears, 135-136
see also Law of the jungle

trans-feminine calling, 360, 368, 375
see also Post-capitalism, post-democracy
trans-humanism
to not confuse with posthuman-ism, and post-humanism, 38-39, 104
see also After-postmodernity
trans-Islamic calling, 360, 370, 375
see also Post-capitalism, post-democracy
trans-outerspace calling, 360, 371, 375
see also Post-capitalism, post-democracy
trans-Sinitic calling, 360, 369, 375
see also Post-capitalism, post-democracy
transaction costs, 16-17
transcendental freedom and the moral law, 119
see also Law
transcendent
and existential dialectics, 30-32, 330-332
see also Existential dialectics, methodological holism, post-capitalism, post-democracy
transfinity
see Multiverse
travesty of justice,
and international public law, 149-155
trinity
see After-postmodernity, modernity, postmodernity, pre-modernity
trivial use, and copyright violation, 223-224, 263
true, the
and existential dialectics
(1) freedom/unfreedom and equality/inequality dialectics, 40-41, 340-344, 347, 380-383
from pre-modernity to after-postmodernity in civilization
(1) the trinity of pre-modernity, 41, 45, 109, 388-389
(2) the trinity of modernity, 41, 45, 109-110, 388-389
(3) the trinity of post-modernity, 41, 45, 111, 388-389
(4) the trinity of after-postmodernity, 41, 45, 112, 388-389
see also Holistic organization of an enquiry, methodological holism
trust law, 8, 61, 185
see also Law
truth
based on faith vs. philosophy, 14-15

•U•

ultra vires
and administrative law, 185, 254-256, 265
uncertainty
and contract law, 245-246, 264
unconsciousness
see Consciousness
undue influence
and contract law, 244, 264
see also Contract law
unenumerated due process
see Due process

unfolding unconsciousness
see Consciousness
unfreedom
see Freedom
United Nations Security Council
and international law, 151
see also International law
unified theory of everything
see Existential dialectics
unilateral mistake, 243
unintentional
see Intentionality
unitary state
and constitutional law, 158-160
see also Constitutional law
United States, the
war crimes against Iraq, 3-4, 150-154
universe
see Multiverse
univeral law in Kantian ethics, 117-118
see also Law of reason
unjust law, 115
unwritten law of the land
see Constitutional law
utilitarianism vs. Kantian ethics, 116-123
see also Law of reason

•V•

Viacom, 225-226
violence and maleness, 123-132
see also Law
virtual organizations, 350-351
virtual psychosis,
and virtual organizations, 350-351
see also Civilization, post-civilization
virtual recall, 42
virtual sex, 42
virtual sexuality, 42
virtue jursisprudence, 12
see also Jurisprudence
von Burg, Sylvan, xvii
von Helmholtz, Hermann, 209
von Naheli, Karl Wilhelm, 210, 262
von Savigny, Friedrich Carl, 17-18

•W•

war crimes
see Crimes
wealth
see Consciousness, existental dialectics, methodological holism, post-capitalism
Weber, Max, 230-231
will to live, 209, 262
will to power, 15-16, 209-217, 261-262
Wittgenstein, Ludwig, 29-30, 329
women, and the maleness of violence, 123-132, 183

•X•

X and neologisms, 60
X and Y in dialectic constraints, 31-32, 330-332

•Y•

Y and X in dialectic constraints, 31-32, 330-332
YouTube, 225-226